Building Your Own House

Building Your Own House

From Foundations to Framing

by Robert Roskind

the
**Owner
Builder
Center**

Ten Speed Press
BERKELEY, CALIFORNIA

🔟

TEN SPEED PRESS
P O Box 7123
Berkeley, California 94707

Library of Congress Catalog Number: 83-40029
ISBN: 0-89815-110-4

Book Design by Hal Hershey
Cover Design by Brenton Beck
Illustrations by Valerie Sharpe
Plans by Mark Robert Thomas and Kathleen Rousseau
Drawings on pages 13 and 54 by Jon Larson

Printed in the United States of America

4 5 — 90 89 88 87

To Julia
And to the Light that
shines within us all.

Contents

Acknowledgements

I COULD NEVER really name all the people that in some way had something to do with this book. Students, owner builders, teachers, staff of the Owner Builder Center—the list goes on. It only serves to remind me how connected we all are and that nothing occurs separate from anything else. There are a few I would like to thank, however.

Thanks to:

Valerie Sharp for taking my scraps of paper and turning them into beautiful diagrams.

Tom Cuthbertson whose support and editing assistance helped keep me sane.

Jon Larson for the friendly illustrations.

Kathy Rousseau and Mark Robert Thomas for all the plan diagrams.

Hal Hershey, the book designer, who smiled no matter what (and meant it).

George and Phil, of Ten Speed Press, for all the patience as I fell farther and farther behind my deadline.

Maria Hirano, my editor, for her refinement of my mess.

Kal Stein and Jim Phoenix for the articles in the Introduction.

Brent Beck for another creative cover.

And Blair Abee for being my partner through so many beginnings and endings.

ROBERT ROSKIND
March, 1984

Introduction

OVER SEVEN YEARS AGO I began teaching people how to build their own homes. Four years ago I co-founded The Owner Builder Center in Berkeley, California. The country's largest owner builder school, it now does almost a million-dollar-a-year business in teaching people to do-it-themselves. In the beginning, I had some real reservations about teaching, and thereby encouraging, people to undertake a project as demanding as building their own home. Should people be encouraged? Was it a sane goal to attempt? Would graduates return in failure scolding us for ever having encouraged them? Although these questions haunted me, until we tried it, there was no way to know.

Since that time, hundreds of our graduates have built their own homes. Many of these people literally never held a tool before taking our courses. Instead of abuse from frustrated failures, we received praise from successful novices. My reservations placated, I have thrown myself into this work. I now know that people with little or no previous experience can successfully complete a major building or remodeling project.

Figure I-1. One story passive solar home. 1470 square feet, 3 bedrooms, 2 baths. Designer: David Norton, Habitat Construction, Nevada City, California.

Figure I-2. Victorian ranch house—a challenging project for a novice builder. 2670 square feet, 3 bedrooms, 3 baths. Designer: Richard Drace, Homestead Design, Nevada City, California.

Even with these successes, we have never tried to paint a rosy picture of the tasks involved. That would be irresponsible and do much harm. In all our courses and in this book, it has been our attempt to tell you of the frustrations as well as the joys; the ants as well as the picnic. The decision to build, contract or remodel your own home is a major one and should be well thought out. It ranks up there with moving, changing jobs, marriage and major investments. Unfortunately, many novice builders do not realize this until it is too late. Building a house for a novice cannot easily be compared to building a house with a team of 30 to 40 professional tradespeople (plumbers, electricians, framers, etc.).

Owner-built homes usually take from 1 to 3 years to complete. They require a stable marriage or partner relationship of the owner builder. An attitude of mutual support and understanding of the people involved is critical.

If you are planning to build, contract or remodel your own home, there are many factors that need to be wisely planned for the whole project to be a success. Buying land or a lot; choosing the site; planning water and waste systems, a source of power, and a driveway, road and bridge; obtaining permits; being aware of codes and inspections; getting insurance and financing; and determining whether you have what it takes to build your own house are all factors to consider before getting started. Since these issues have been dealt with in our book *Before You Build* (Ten Speed Press, 1981), they will not be covered in this book. Be sure you have given

ample thought to these factors before you begin to build.

There are three other areas, however, that are very important which novice builders can easily overlook. These are timing, design and estimating. They are the "soft" areas as opposed to the "hard" areas, such as building your foundation or roof. The rest of this book is about the "hard" areas, so let's look at these "soft" areas before beginning.

Timing

For years many banks have been reluctant to lend owner builders construction money. The reasons are several. The most obvious is that they have no way of evaluating the quality of the house you are going to build with their money.

Many bankers will also tell you that the rate of divorce is great with owner builders and this can endanger the entire project (and their money). For the most part I would have to agree with this statement. In Ken Kern's recent book *The Work Book: The Politics of Building Your Own Home* (Owner Builder Publications), he describes many case histories that have ended in broken partnerships. Fortunately, few of our graduates' marriages have ended in divorce. This is not, however, because they are more emotionally stable than others, but because we have always taken great pains to impress upon our students not to begin a project of this size unless the partnership is working well. The project can serve as a wedge if there are any cracks in the relationship.

Some partners enter this type of project with a "This is your project and don't expect me to help very much" attitude. One partner really wants to do it and the other is somewhat reluctant. Be careful of beginning the project in this case. Building or remodeling your own home is too large a project for it not to be continually spilling over into the entire family's life. I am not saying that one person cannot handle most of the responsibilities and take the lead. But that person will need the understanding and total support of a family who understands there will be sacrifices for them no matter what the preconstruction promises.

All this relates to timing. When, if ever, is the best time of your life to start such a project? If there are major demands in your life already (family, job, personal, financial, etc.), it may be best to put this off until they are handled. There may be no major stress areas in your life and you think it is time to begin, but maybe you are already operating at maximum efficiency. Add one thing and the whole house of cards falls. Be sure you have made enough extra room in your life for this type of project and that this is what you really want to do.

I remember a man in one of my earlier classes in Raleigh, North Carolina. For seven years he had hung wallpaper to save enough money to build a house for himself and his family. He was now ready to start. He was one of my most eager students, asking lots of questions and taking lots of notes. A year later, I passed him on a street in Chapel Hill, North Carolina, and asked him how his house was going. Much to my surprise, he told me he had decided not to build but to enter veterinarian school instead. His explanation made perfect sense. He had needed a challenge in his life (wallpapering only has so many challenges) and had decided to build his own house. After taking the class, he realized that he could build a house without great difficulty. He was then able to consider a greater challenge that he had been fearful of attempting: changing his profession and becoming a vet. His timing was perfect for becoming a vet, but not for building his own house. Ask yourself if this is absolutely what you are ready to do. What else could you accomplish with the same time, energy and money? Be honest with yourself.

Remember, we live in a society that is so rushed it has forgotten where it is going and why. A number of forces will come to bear on your decision, when to begin your home. You will think, the prices are going up, all the land is running out, if not now, then when, etc., etc. Stay evenly paced and know that when the time is right, you will know it. Wait for that knowing before beginning.

Design

Design is by far the most important single process of the entire project. Along with good workmanship and sound engineering, design is a keynote in the building of a successful house.

Figure 1-3. Two-story passive solar home. 1558 square feet, 3 bedrooms, 2½ baths. Designer: Lee Aaron Ward, Solar Solutions, Napa, California.

If it is designed poorly to begin with, no amount of expert craftsmanship can correct the mistakes that are written into the design. Before you ever start to build, consider this point well. A successful design is one that is the most supportive of the lives of you and your family, a place that feels like a loving home, a basis from which to grow and confidently confront the rest of the world. This is the basic function of a home. The farther away from that concept you get, the less successful your house will be. Most homes in America are usually built with one concept in mind—profit. If they are designed by an architect, they are often built to satisfy his artistic whim, a piece of sculpture to be placed in the woods, rather than a home for a family to live in. Frank Lloyd Wright once said that he could design a house that could cause a couple to have a divorce; to a certain extent that has been done in most modern American homes.

Let the design reflect you. Let this be your home. Imagine your ideal dwelling, just as you want it, and then build it. Unless your fantasy has always been a certain style home, let your mind run free, and find the house that is you. Be aware of your abilities, but do not be afraid to extend yourself. The object is not to extend your capabilities beyond yourself, but yourself beyond your capabilities. This is growth, this is moving one step further than where you are. Anything less is complacency or fear. Originality and character can be incorporated in any design, and still have that design remain simple.

Design must be seen as a dynamic, not static, process. It is not something that is drawn up in the beginning and then rigidly held to till the end. It is a process of becoming, a growth process. In the beginning, when you are working on design, do not accept your first draft. It is the one that comes at the beginning of your thought processes, and as you get deeper and deeper into them your design changes, as more and better ways become clear. After much thought and revision, form in your mind and on paper the design you plan to begin with. I say begin with because it is your basic plan, but should always remain open to change. As your construction begins, you will learn things about your house that you had no way of knowing about beforehand. This is one of the great advantages of the designer being the builder as well. The design needs to be flexible enough to incorporate this new information. By moving a window two feet on a wall, you get a better view of a rock formation you had not noticed before; by removing a wall, an upstairs storage room becomes a sleeping loft; by moving the stairs, you free more usable space. Ideas will flood you when you actually start to build and spend many hours of the day working and thinking about the house. Any good design should allow for changes to be incorporated. Always be looking to see how the design can be improved upon.

Design your home from the inside out. It is a good idea to spend time in other people's homes to get an idea of how the structure feels to live in. When you are designing, imagine

Figure I-4. "The Carlyle," a three-level home with 10-foot ceilings in the main living area. 1856 square feet, 3 bedrooms, 2½ baths. Designer: Cazwell, Inc., Chapel Hill, North Carolina.

Figure I-5. Passive solar contemporary design with integrated solar greenhouse. 1400 square feet, 2 bedrooms, 2 baths. Designer: Mike Funderberh, Raleigh, North Carolina.

your inner living spaces and how you want them to be. Then tie all these parts into an integral whole with a pleasing exterior design. I am not suggesting that you ignore completely the aesthetic value of the exterior design, but only that you remember the primary function of the house is to live in, not to look at. Imagine in your mind each room. What kind of a feeling do you want in the room, where and how high do you want the windows placed, which rooms do you want adjacent to each other, which separate, what type of dividers and entrances between these rooms, what type of relationship and access to the outside, how high do you want the ceilings, etc. Do this for each room and the house as a whole. Once you have designed the entire house, live in it awhile in your mind. Work, play, entertain, cook and relax in that house; imagine all its functions. Then in your mind, go outside and see it on your site, and if all this pleases you, you have a good design to start with.

Design your total environment, not just the house. Remember that your living space extends past the walls of your house onto your land outside and the design should incorporate this concept. The relationship between your indoor and outdoor environment is a very sensitive one and should be developed with care and consideration. This should be done from the very beginning by blending your site with the land. This can often be a rather difficult task. It is possible to establish a union between your house and your land in such a way that the house seems to blend with the lot, almost grow from it, rather than having been imposed on it. Your land will

probably never be more beautiful than before you touch it; treat the land as gently and harmoniously as possible. The type of land, the terrain, the height of the surrounding trees and hills should all affect the design. Perhaps you might sit on your site for a few days and try to imagine your house growing up from the ground. Try to make the lines of the house merge with the lines of your land. If it is a very steep lot with high trees, the lines might need to be more vertical. If it is a slightly sloping or level lot, horizontal lines might be better.

Use your porches, verandas, entranceways, doors and windows as transitions between the indoors and the outdoors. Windows and especially doors opening to the outside or to a porch tend to bring the outdoors into your house and connect the two. Consider this as you design each room and the house as a whole. Porches are very inexpensive to build per square foot and serve as a very beautiful and usable living space, especially an open covered porch. Having an outdoor entrance into every living or sleeping area is also a good fire safety technique, which is of more importance in wooden structures that have fireplaces or are heated by wood, or are far away from the closest fire station.

Consider well the size of the rooms and size of the entire house in your design. Thoreau once said that people are rich in proportion to what they can do without. Something to consider when you are pondering what size your house should be. There are really few guidelines I can offer here, for only you can determine what size house and rooms you need. I can only suggest that you consider it well. The larger

Figure I-6. "The Bedford," a three-level home. 1875 square feet, 3 bedrooms, 2 baths. Designer: Cazwell, Inc., Chapel Hill, North Carolina.

the house, the greater the time and expense, both in construction and in upkeep. Yet, you still need enough space for all your indoor activities and so that you won't feel closed in. Everyone living in the house will need to have enough of their own private space in order to live together compatibly.

Often it is not how much space you have, but rather how the space is put together that is important. The total design and placement of rooms has a large effect on the volume of space enclosed. A well-designed 750-square-foot house can often feel larger than one twice that size which is poorly designed. Some people like all rooms opening to a large central living area, tying the whole house and the activities within together at all times. Others like the house more spread out and the rooms far away from each other, offering greater privacy and isolation of activities. Consider all these ideas well and take into account any additions or changes in the size or needs of the family. Children can wear thin during a long winter, and it is often a good idea to give them a playroom of their own at the far end of the house or build a separate playhouse for them.

You might want to design your house so that it can be built in stages or added on to as the need arises or as you acquire more time and money. Building a series of buildings, all tied together by walkways or courtyards, is another alternative. This further separates the activities and affords greater privacy and quiet. It also enables you to finish the most important structures first and move into them as you work on the others. Your work will improve with each building and

you can work out some of your mistakes on the smaller buildings before you begin with the main structures. The buildings can be joined in a whole indoor-outdoor living environment and afford much privacy and space. Just building your workshop or guest house or bedroom some distance from the main house can make a big difference.

The height of your ceilings and the number, size and placement of your windows and doors have a lot to do with your feeling of space. A relatively small room with the right number and location of windows and perhaps a skylight can seem much bigger than it actually is. Lofts are also effective where you want high or cathedral ceilings, yet want to use part of that space for a living area. Be careful of very large rooms with cathedral ceilings. They are often very hard to heat and they give some people the feeling of being so lost in the room's volume that it becomes hard to relax and feel intimate in the room. Again, it will be up to your personal tastes as to what feels right for you. There is a very subtle balance that needs to be achieved: large enough to feel spacious and unconfining, yet small enough to feel warm and comfortable.

A free-flowing, "open plan" type house is much healthier to live in than a series of boxes within a large box. Most houses built in this country are a series of tightly-enclosed small boxes arranged in a very orderly, linear fashion within another very orderly, linear box, grouped with other boxes in a very orderly manner on a very linear street. This is one reason we are all so crazy. The only person who ever thought that this was a "natural" way for man to live was probably the contractor, who makes more money by keeping costs down, since houses go up quickly in this manner. With labor costs being what they are, it would be hard to hire someone to build almost anything other than boxes, but sloping ceilings and off-square rooms are not out of the question. It is often not a matter of finances, but rather consciousness, that determines the design. A house whose living and activity spaces flow into one another with entranceways and movable panels rather than fixed walls and small doorways not only gives the occupant more of a sense of space, but makes the house more adaptable to the changes that future needs might demand. Allowing the house and its activities to flow together, rather than having distinct separation and divisions, will add continuity and order to your life in general.

Build with respect for the land. Perhaps for millions of years your land has been untouched by humans and it is beautiful and pure. For 30 to 60 years you will live on your land, so consider well what kind of impact your brief stay will have on that land. It is not really "your land," for we can never really own that land. We only have the privilege to use it as we will for a period of time. Before us and after us will come many other caretakers. It is possible for one man in his lifetime to destroy the aesthetic quality and usability of a piece of land for many generations to come. We are seeing this done all around us and for many of us, it is one of the many reasons we want to retreat into the shelter of our own home. Treat your land with love and respect, and appreciate the gift it is giving to you, with its beauty, its quiet, and its love. Design

and build with this in mind, and your land will reward you a hundredfold. Try to use as few non-decomposing materials as possible, plastic, fiberglass, asbestos, etc. Use instead materials that are only recently from the earth, and ready to return in a natural manner, such as wood, stone, etc. These items are usually much cheaper than manufactured items and have much more warmth and character than the mass-produced "dead" materials. If you have access to any used materials, make use of them. They are usually cheaper and often of higher quality than new materials, especially wood, since the wood will be drier than new green stock. But more important than this, in the recycling of used materials you will be helping the earth and all the people on it by not wasting more of our resources.

Let the function of your house determine its form. Be clear of your intent in building. Decide in which way exactly you want this house to serve you, and then design it and build it to do that for you. This is one of the hardest things to do sometimes—to determine how you want the house to function for you. Often our expectations and our fantasies overpower what it is that we really want. Often we follow a fantasy, whether it is in a design of a house or another situation in our life, only to discover the fantasy did not give the rewards we had hoped for and what we really wanted was something quite different. So try to determine what it is exactly that you want this house to do. If you want it to impress your friends and neighbors, build it that way. Maybe you want it to provide a warm, loving center for your family, one that will aid in

Figure I-7. Two-story passive solar home. 1680 square feet, 2 bedrooms, 1½ baths. Designer: David Wright, SEA group, Nevada City, California.

their communication and closeness, or perhaps just a small private place for you, or perhaps you and a mate. Maybe you want something that you can change over the years as you and your lifestyle change. Whatever that thing is for you, make it clear to yourself and then design and build with that intent in mind. Some may say that this plan is not always practical, efficient or functional—that people must use their intellects and build according to what their minds say is best, disregarding things of the heart and emotional centers. I think what is missing here is what is practical; what is most efficient for life on this planet, both for the individual and the species as a whole, is whatever aids a person to becoming a happy, secure, loving individual. *The most practical home for you is the one that feels most like you, the one that brings you the most peace of mind.* This is the ultimate criterion for what is reasonable and practical. If it feels right to you and it does not get in the way of someone else pursuing what feels right to them, *do it.* And if that thing is for you a house shaped like a bear wearing a petticoat and sitting full lotus on top of a replica of Charles de Gaulle's nose, then build it. *And* accept the responsibility for what that entails, both in building it and reselling it. This same idea applies not only to the house as a whole, but to each individual space or room also. Again, determine what you want that room to do for you. Do you want it to be open and expansive, with lots of space to serve the more social, extroverted areas of your nature, or do you want it warm and intimate, more like a cosy cave to serve the more private, introverted parts of your nature? If it is a child's room, let it serve the child, at the age he is now, with adaptability as he grows. Determine its function, then determine its form.

Try to be realistic as to how much time, energy and money your particular design will take and see if there are some acceptable changes you could make if you feel the design is beyond your capacity. Needless to say, but here I am saying it, the more complex the design, the longer and harder it will be to build. Often a house can be pleasing and have character without being very complex. If you do decide to utilize a complex design, be aware of the extra time and energy required. The materials used to do custom work often take much longer to assemble than prefab components. They are usually individual boards and stones, rather than large preassembled products. They cost much less, but take more time. In this case, I feel it is definitely worth the extra time to be able to use "live" materials. It can make a difference in your life for as long as you live in your house.

Design the house so that the rooms have a relationship to each other that is determined by the activity in that room and the rooms close to it. Once you have determined what the function of a room is, locate it in the house in such a way that the activities in the rooms adjacent to it will not conflict, and if possible, design it so that adjacent activities will support each other. You might not want to locate your study next to the children's play area, but rather next to the courtyard or greenhouse which might be pleasing to you.

Figure I-8. Two-story passive solar design. 2200 square feet, 2 bedrooms, 3 baths. Designer: Richard Drace, Homestead Design, Grass Valley, California.

Figure I-9. One-and-a-half-story passive solar home with an integrated solar greenhouse. 1728 square feet, 3 bedrooms, 2 baths. Designer: Shannon T. St. John, Horizon Design, Anchorage, Alaska.

Estimating

The home which actually costs less than its estimate is so rare that it ascends into the realm of miracles. Houses go over their estimated costs so often, that doing so falls into the category of the inevitable. The consequences of housebuilding costs exceeding their planned amounts can be ruinous, and homeowners may face an additional several hundred dollars a month in loan or mortgage payments. Such a long-term burden can put an unhappy dent in your ability to realize other fantasies like vacations, a new car or boat, and travel, for twenty years or more. Before you take this risk, consider some things which may put you ahead in the art of estimating.

In estimating housebuilding costs, our fallibility usually falls in two areas. First, we try to incorporate more features in our designs than we can really afford. Second, adequate account is not made for unknowns in the job; the hidden costs.

For those of us that feel we are putting up the only house we will ever get to build, and one we may live in for many years, our desires to have everything we want will tempt us with peculiar potency. Cutting back on features we have dreamed of for years may appall us. Changes along the way that seem small may add up to a large increase in price. The tendency is to choose designs which are larger, more complex or more expensive than that which can actually be afforded.

It pays to remember the scale of your investment. In planning a house, we make decisions involving thousands or ten-thousands of dollars. Most of us lack familiarity with spending these amounts, and our perspectives can be lost and regained too late. Give yourself a healthy margin of estimating. Allow some decisions to be made later in the process; as construction moves along, final costs become more predictable. Then may be the time to decide on an extra wing, the types of furnishings and fixtures you will put in, or how the garage will be. Always try to remain conscious of how much money you can afford to spend and of how much house that money will buy.

Now, about those aspects of the art of estimation which make it tricky even for a pro. (The contracting business casualty rate is one of the highest, and it is poor estimating which often boots otherwise competent people out the door.) It must be said that very accurate estimates can be made on conventional or tract homes. Most of these homes are designed to use prefabricated components such as plywood, paneling, sheetrock and cabinets. These go up with a predictable speed and energy input. Also, since similar houses go up regularly, there are relatively few unknowns. Work can progress smoothly and costs may be calculated based upon square footage. Any knowledgeable person in the housebuilding industry in your area should be able to give you a reliable cost factor to multiply by square footage.

CUSTOM BUILDING, on the other hand, challenges any

Figure I-10. Passive solar two-story house. 1745 square feet, 3 bedrooms, 2 baths. Designer: Curt Burbick, Berkeley, California.

estimator. Many builders will operate only on a cost-plus basis. Any custom house is unique, a prototype. One like it has never been built before and the problems are unknown. These houses are very labor-intensive, which is also very expensive. I am not recommending that you forget custom building, for to my mind custom homes often possess more life and character than conventional ones. However, be aware of their added costs!

NON-HOUSE EXPENSES such as wells, roads, septic systems, water storage and filtering systems, and getting power to the land often overtip the cost of construction even when the basic estimate of the structure itself remains sound. Remember that there are often legal fees required, and custom building may necessitate costly structural engineering fees, as well.

INFLATION often leads to underestimation. Housebuilding costs for materials and labor may rise 5 to 10% just in the 6 months between the drawings and calculation of the estimate at the start of the work. Similar increases can occur during the construction period. Building materials can jump 10 to 30% overnight. This summer I saw cedar shakes go from $63 to $80 a square in a month, a 26% increase. Allow margins for these raises.

SITE AND LOCATION of a house can bear strongly on its cost. Costs rise with difficult or inaccessible sites. Foundations may need to be more complex on steep slopes, and construction is generally more difficult. Locations remote from hardware and building supply stores make the job more time consuming for the contractor, carpenters, and other workmen, and add to costs. Delays and added expense in the delivery of materials can frequently occur in remote areas. Also, power, roads and water in such instances can become prohibitively expensive.

INEFFECTIVE ORGANIZATION can be costly. The entire project requires a considerable amount of coordination between people, and a proper progression of processes. Poor organization results in less production. If contractors and workmen slip even 10 to 20% from maximum efficiency, it is liable to mean wasting thousands of your dollars. Try to insure that all the people involved work together well and are interested in providing maximum productivity for minimum time and effort.

Remember, housebuilding is a many-faceted undertaking. Estimating costs is a key process and can be a difficult one. You have a good headstart if you avoid some of the pitfalls I've been discussing. Watch for sudden or hidden costs. Remember there is a tendency in each of us at times to be somewhat too optimistic. We estimate on the low side, in an effort to convince ourselves that our dream house can be all that we want it to be. If you are doing that, remind yourself to take care and be cautious with your dollars. A successful project is one where you get the house that you really want, built for the price you can afford, built at a time when you are ready for the project!

Except for Figures I-4 and I-6, the drawings in this section are from *The Owner Builder Plan Book,* available from the Owner Builder Center, Berkeley, California.

1 Before You Build

IF YOU HAVE DONE all the preliminaries: if you have purchased the land and chosen a site; if you have made decisions on your water and waste systems and source of power; planned a driveway, access road and bridges; if you have dealt with permits, codes and inspections; and if you are sure about timing, design and estimating, you are ready to begin, well almost. In this chapter we will be providing additional information you will need before you build, such as when to hire or contract, insurance, purchasing, tips on lumber, work habits and attitudes, and how to use this book. Chapters 2, 3, and 5 are devoted to describing the different types of construction (2), tools (3) and types of foundations (5).

Included at the end of this chapter is a construction schedule showing the 60 steps necessary to build a house. The first 14 steps are in *Before You Build* (Ten Speed Press, 1981). Steps 15 through 33 are contained in this volume and Steps 34 to 60 are in the sequel to this volume.

In addition, there is a set of safety rules at the back which we have found essential to insure the safety of novice builders at the Center. At times they may seem excessive, but better 20% more cautious than 1% too lax. Both of these pages can be copied and placed at the work site for your convenience and safety.

When to Hire or Contract

You probably have chosen to build for a variety of reasons: you wanted to save money, you wanted to know what went into the construction of your home, you wanted to enjoy the feeling of accomplishment at having mastered the necessary skills. You may, however, want or need to hire professional contractors to help you with certain phases of construction. Though this can save time and money, hiring from a position of ignorance can present problems. Learn as much as you can about the building process, especially the phases for which you hire, so that you know what the job is worth and have a basis on which to judge the work done for you.

In order to decide when to hire a contractor, you will want to evaluate your own areas of expertise and where you lack confidence. Often, much of the anxiety of the entire project is directed toward a particular area, such as the foundation work or the electrical and plumbing systems. Sheetrock taping, tile work, cabinetry and finishing work are areas where you may feel you need the expertise of a professional. These are all areas of work that you can master if you have the time to educate yourself. What you need to do is sit down and plan the project, this time from the point of view of the actual knowledge and skills required to complete the job. Figure out where you need help and consult a professional.

You will want to begin this evaluation process at the design stage. You may wish to hire a designer or architect to help you shape your ideas into a workable plan. Perhaps you have drawn up a complete set of plans or know of a home you would like to duplicate. In this case, you may only need a draftsman. There is no law that says you cannot draft the plans yourself, but you may want someone with a designer's eye to check over your plans to see that you have not missed some basic flaw in the structure or a subtle problem, such as traffic flow. Money can be saved by getting advice from a professional at this stage.

The next step is to decide how much of the work you want to do yourself. For those owner builders who plan to use contractors for much of the work, there will be a fee, but contractors usually will not sign the plans. You will not be safeguarded the way you would be if you hired them to handle the entire job. Many contractors can be hired on a consulting basis. If you feel that you will need expertise at some point, try to figure out when: before you begin a particular phase, or after you have reached a point beyond which you can not proceed. Remember, many contractors will not want to finish work you have begun. They cannot be responsible for problems that arise from your mistakes, and it is difficult to troubleshoot when they don't really know what went into the work.

If you plan to hire a contractor to do a particular phase of the work, look around; talk to as many contractors as you can. There is a difference between a licensed professional and one that is unlicensed. A professional who is licensed can sign a legal contract and be taken to court if problems arise. One that is unlicensed is essentially your employee, and your only recourse is to fire them. The unlicensed tradesperson may be cheaper and just as skilled, knowledgeable and experienced, but you will have to cover them with workman's compensation insurance. Licensed people carry their own workman's compensation and build the cost into the bid. It all depends on your own willingness to carry the brunt of the responsibility.

Hiring a professional can be a learning experience in itself. Some contractors will be willing for you to work along with them as an assistant. Many, however, prefer to work completely on their own. The relationship between you and them can become confused if you hire them and yet you are their assistant. Who is the boss?

You may prefer to hire small contractors, even if they are not well known. A big contractor may have several projects underway at one time and their attention may be split. They may not be on your job all the time or even every day. Smaller contractors have less overhead, making the job cheaper. On the other hand, larger contractors are able to purchase materials at a better price because they are buying in greater bulk. You have to ask questions.

When you approach a contractor, make a list, not only of the tasks you want performed, but also of your fears and concerns about the job. Spell everything out, from when you expect the job to be completed to who will do the cleanup. Deal with as many of the details as you can. It is the gray area that will give rise to problems down the road.

There are a couple of other alternatives. You can hire individuals who hold down construction jobs to work for you on weekends or evenings. You can hire an unlicensed person who works for a licensed contractor. You could actually get the same worker you would get if you hired the contractor and probably for less money. You can go around to construction sites and watch the workers. If you see one particular person who seems to be working extra hard and/or well, you may be able to hire them during their off-hours. Problems that can arise here are that they may not be able to give you as much time as you need when you need it, or that they will suddenly be asked to work overtime for their main employer and you would be left out in the cold. If you really know what you are doing, you may just need to hire a go-fer, someone to hand you planks and nails.

As for inspecting the quality of your work, some people rely on the official inspectors. Be careful about this. Inspectors inspect for health and safety, not for quality. They may not be as regular about coming around to your job site as you might expect or need. If you are doing your own work and feel the need for someone to check what you have done, you can hire a contractor on a consulting basis. Don't take chances if you are in doubt, but don't think that you can't do it yourself. You are not alone out there. There are people who can and will help you.

Insurance[1]

It is easy for owner builders, being a bolder element of the population to begin with, to overlook the need for certain types of insurance while building. DON'T! Construction, by nature, is a dangerous trade. Building or contracting your own house takes a lot of optimism and trust. Healthy caution and insurance help fill out the package. Many lenders will require that you have certain types of coverage to safeguard their investments. Some types of coverage are optional, but definitely recommended.

Workman's compensation insurance covers people injured while working on your home. It not only pays for medical expenses, but for lost work and recuperation time as well. In many states it is mandatory and you cannot get your permit until you present proof that you have taken out a policy on the project. In any case, it is wise to have coverage for your workmen, yourself, your family and friends. One injury can cost a fortune in hospital and doctor bills and lost work. If you have workman's compensation for everyone working on the site, both paid and unpaid, you are protecting them in the event that something happens. If you do not have this insurance and something does happen, there is a good chance that you will be sued and lose, since it is negligence on your part not to have work people covered by workman's compensation.

Aside from protecting your workers, it is wise to cover the job site with liability in case anyone who is not a worker should get hurt. This is a blanket policy that covers everyone from delivery people to children who wander onto the job site. It is worth the money.

The type of property insurance you need is called a "course of construction" policy. Depending on what you need and how you and your agent write the policy, you can be covered for fire, theft and vandalism during the construction process. It is possible to have supplies and materials covered before they are actually attached to the structure. Your agent should be able to help you decide just exactly what kind of coverage you need.

If you are borrowing money to build the house yourself, much depends on you. Because of this, lenders may require life insurance. Should you die, they would then have enough money to hire people to finish the project.

You may want to cover yourself by both injury and life insurance. If something happens to you, money will be available to finish the project or help you if you are injured.

If you are remodeling your home, check with your insurance agent to see if you need to extend your current coverage. If you are working at a site that is removed from your home or other insured property, check with your agent to see if he can offer you the appropriate policies for the construction. Be sure that you talk to an agent that is knowledgeable in the field of construction insurance.

An investment in prevention can save time and money in the long run.

---

1. Based on *Before You Build*, by Robert Roskind (Ten Speed Press, 1981).

Purchasing

When you are planning major purchases for building, an organized approach pursued in a disciplined and professional manner can save both time and money. It is helpful to think of materials purchasing as involving four elements: budgeting, accounting, bidding, and accepting deliveries.

BUDGETING

1. Assume a total budget for your project, i.e., how much you have available to spend on the project.
2. Break the total budget into categories, e.g., lumber, sheetrock, nails, rebar, etc. This process must be done in conjunction with a "take-off" list from your building plans. The take-off tells you how much of each item will be needed. Take-offs can be obtained from architects, consultants, contractors or you can figure it out yourself. It is very important at this point to identify discrepancies between material needs and budget limitations; it is much easier to adjust your plans at this stage than later on.
3. The total of all budgets for each category must equal the total budget.
4. Budgets must include the *timing* of purchases. This is especially useful as it allows you to project your cash needs at each stage of building.

ACCOUNTING

1. Make a list of all categories of purchases.
2. Prepare a control sheet for each category. This is simply a piece of paper on which you will list all purchases within the category.
3. Code *all* checks and invoices for the category of purchase. There must be an invoice or receipt for all checks, except for those made out to "cash." "Cash" checks should still be coded for applicable categories. If your receipts and invoices and "cash" checks equal the total amount of checks written, you have a "balanced" system with no uncontrolled expenses.
4. Keep each category control sheet up to date and sub-total as often as possible. (It helps to sub-total with a different colored pencil. That way, you won't be adding in total figures and you won't have to re-add columns.) This process allows you to know when you are going over budget in a cost area and allows you to make adjustments as needed.

BIDDING

1. The first rule of getting bids is that you must get at least 3 competitive bids for each major area of purchase. This may not be worth it for small items, as there is a lot of effort involved, but it is certainly necessary for larger purchases where you want to be confident that you have gotten the best possible price.
2. Bids should be analyzed for: specifications, quantity, price, and delivery charges and dates. This is a screening stage for reviewing bids and it is here that you make sure you are comparing "oranges with oranges."
3. Make determination of factors other than initial costs, such as total costs; related costs; status of vendors; and vendor's rating and past history as to reliability, quality and performance. You should also give some consideration to the vendor's technical competence, maintenance of delivery dates, and overall stability.
4. Purchase materials at the lowest bid cost within the standards set for quality and service.

ACCEPTING DELIVERIES

1. Check materials for specification conformance and verify the invoice and/or shipping order. *Don't trust anyone!* The deliverer may be a great guy, but he did not pack the cartons or prepare the shipping tag. Examine the cartons carefully *in the driver's presence* for signs of damage, handling abuse or tampering. Check the contents against the shipping tag. Do it quickly, the driver is in a hurry. Ask the driver to note, date and sign for any evidence of damage or discrepancies in count. Be polite, but firm.
2. Make adjustments with the vendor for non-conformance to specifications, defective materials or rejects.

TIPS

1. Payments should always take advantage of "cash discounts" or "early payment discounts." If, for example, the terms of sale are 2/10 Net 30, this means that there is a *2%* discount if you pay within *10* days from the date of the invoice and that the whole amount is due in *30* days from the date of the invoice. A notation of "E.O.M." means

"end of month," so "10 E.O.M." means payment is due 10 days from the end of the month of the invoice. You should always take advantage of these discounts; they represent actual reductions in the price. A 2% reduction across the board in the price of materials for your project can have a large impact on the rest of your plans.

2. When dealing with salespersons, phone orders, shipments, public offices, etc., get their *name* and *write it down.* These people will be more responsible if you know their name. You can also save time and hassles by going back to the same person; they will already know your problems and needs.

3. When calling manufacturers or vendors long distance, ask them to call you back or if you can call them collect. Many companies have toll-free numbers for incoming calls or WATS lines for return calls. It pays to ask.

Supplies

Different owner builders have different degrees of knowledge about purchasing the supplies needed to build their home. Yet no matter what your level of expertise, you will find invaluable the advice of a reliable supplier you can trust.

It is, therefore, a good idea to get to know the people you will be dealing with. Go into the store a few times and make some small purchases to become acquainted with the counter people. Learn their names. They are more likely to be helpful and give discounts to someone they recognize.

There are advantages to dealing with a few, well-known suppliers. Convenience is one. Dealing with a few suppliers will make your paperwork simpler. Deliveries will run more smoothly. It will be easier to return faulty or extra materials or to order special materials the supplier does not ordinarily stock. In fact, this should be a very important factor to consider when you choose a supplier: pick one who gives you good service and one you trust. Even if the prices are a little higher, the comfort of dealing with people you like may make it worthwhile.

You will need to turn to a lumber yard, plumbing and electrical suppliers, and perhaps suppliers of tile, flooring, roofing, paint and appliances. All-purpose, do-it-yourself stores will offer you the convenience of location, counter knowledge and the display of their products. Large specialty houses, on the other hand, may offer more flexibility in prices and a greater depth of stock. Check to see if an all-purpose store has a "contractors' window" where you can get a better price for your larger orders.

When you are looking for your basic suppliers, follow a few sound principles. Make a complete list of the supplies you will need from that supplier. Make several copies and give them to a minimum of three suppliers to get fair price comparisons. Ask the suppliers for a total price, itemized piece by piece. When you get your lists back, be very careful. Do not look at the bottom lines only. Check each item carefully to make sure nothing has been omitted and that the prices are reasonable across the board. Sometimes savings are concentrated in a single category, e.g., rough lumber, sheetrock, hardware, windows, etc., while the other categories are more expensive than in other bids. Be careful to shop by category; you may lose your savings in the transportation and time involved in item-by-item shopping. Ask about refund policies, particularly if you are buying seconds or at a discount.

There are a lot of ways to save money when shopping for materials. One of them is the contractor's discount, which you may be eligible for since you are buying a large quantity of supplies to build a house. The amount of the discount you receive will depend initially upon your relationship with the supplier and how large an order you make. Attitude is important. Be honest. You do not need a fake contractor's license number, although it might be a good idea to have a business checking account (this will also make your record keeping easier) and a business card. When you go into the shop, lay your business checkbook on the counter. Let people know that you are serious, that you need to spend some money. If the person you talk to cannot give you the discount, ask to speak with someone who can—the manager or the owner. Be friendly and firm. Remember, you have nothing to lose and much to gain.

Consider setting up an account with the supplier if you are going to spend a lot of money there. Not only will it help them to see you as a credible customer, it will help you keep track of your purchases. Most suppliers will give you a 2% discount if you pay your bills by the tenth of the month. Check for discounts if you pay cash. Some suppliers will give up to a 10% discount for cash since it will save them paperwork and help them avoid bad accounts.

It may be possible to get together with another owner builder to buy supplies. Together you can make larger purchases and your discounts will be greater. Plus, between the two of you, you can cover more ground. You can seek out more bargains and share knowledge about prices and other important aspects of buying. A contractor might be willing to add your order to his, automatically giving you a discount. Sometimes it is possible to buy materials from a contractor who is doing installation work for you, like a roofer.

There are many ways to get good deals on supplies, but you need to be careful. The more you know about what you are buying, the better the odds you will actually be getting a bargain. Keep in mind there will be a break-even point between the money you save by looking around and the time you spend doing it. Often you can save about 15% of the total construction cost by hustling.

Find out where the price breaks are for materials. You may be able to save money by buying in quantity rather than buying just what you need. Nails, for example, usually come in 50-pound boxes. If you need 30 pounds, you may end up paying more if you buy 30 pounds loose than if you bought a box. You can always use, sell or give away the leftovers.

The wholesalers, distributors, and manufacturers of certain supplies may be willing to sell directly to you. They may have seconds or semi-damaged materials in their yards that you can use. It is possible to save enormous amounts this way, but you have to know what you are doing.

Another idea that might be fruitful, if you have the time and are making a considerable purchase, such as lumber, is to travel out of your immediate area to look for better prices. There are rural areas where the economy is depressed and goods are less expensive. You would either have to truck the supplies back yourself, which can be expensive if you do not have a truck, or pay freight and storage. Be sure to send out your supply list and compare quotes to those of local dealers.

A big area of potential savings is the use of recycled goods. Auctions are also a good source of materials. You can find notices of auctions in the papers. However, when you buy at an auction, make sure it is a good deal. Know what the materials are, what their quality is and what the going rate on the open market is. Sometimes people will actually bid above the market price. Even though you may not be able to buy all of the supplies you actually need (or you may have to buy more), you can still save money. Just be aware of what you are doing.

It is also a good idea to check the classified ads for special deals. You never know what might turn up. It is possible to find situations at job sites where a contractor might be willing to sell extra materials for a good price if he cannot use them on another job.

The name of the game is knowing what you need and where to find it. A friendly trusted supplier can be of great help to both the beginner and the more experienced owner builder.

PRICE VS. QUALITY

When building or remodeling your home, there is a strong desire to use the highest quality materials to produce the best results. Often we identify high quality with high prices. Yet with most materials, there is a certain point at which you are getting the best product for the money. You need to learn where the quality-vs.-price breaks are for different items.

For instance, foundation and framing materials are by-and-large standardized, i.e., they must conform to regulated or industrial standards that are universal. As long as they meet those requirements, you are not going to get a much better product by spending more. At the same time, you cannot replace your foundation or framing once the house has been finished, so you want to build it right the first time. It is the quality of the *work* that counts in this instance.

On the other hand, you will want to put money into quality materials when you get to the finishing stages, for this is what you will see for the rest of your stay in the house. So you may want to pay a little more. But be careful. There is still a quality line. For example, 3-×-4-foot windows may range from $30 for a cheap aluminum frame up to $140 for a double-paned, wood framed window. It may be that, after spending $90 on a window, the quality for the more expensive one does not increase as much as the price does.

Sometimes you may be able to substitute less expensive materials for the more traditional ones for certain jobs. You may, for example, find a good load of foundation grade redwood for a deck, rather than buying more expensive grades.

If you are working on a tight budget, you may be better off scaling down your plans rather than cutting down on the quality of materials you use. If you do not have the money initially, put up a good frame and do the finishing work as you can, and then replace inferior materials with those of higher quality later on. Or you can design your house so that you can build a portion of it now, move in, and add more as you can afford it.

The important thing is to learn to judge when the quality gained is worth the extra money.

SALVAGE

Looking for building materials at a price you can afford? If you take the time to learn the ins and outs of the salvage network in your area, you may be richly rewarded. With the evolving building codes, the constant changeover of owners and just changing needs, there is a lot of remodeling done. Old elements are often torn out to make way for new ones, and there are many occasions when new things are removed and the old elements restored.

Remodeling almost always begins with a certain amount of demolition. Depending on how skillfully this is done, some real prizes may be preserved for later use. Arched or stained glass windows, hardwood mantles, long lengths of redwood or other old-growth lumber, tile, ornate light fixtures, pedestal sinks and clawfoot tubs are often set aside in this way. These are examples of the "lucky finds" that make fleeting appearances at salvage yards before being taken to their new homes. The chance that you will discover something uniquely fitting and intrinsically valuable is what gives salvage shopping its spice.

Many contractors and owner builders search out salvaged materials because they are looking for a bargain. They know from experience that used items are generally less expensive than new versions of the same thing. One factor in the low price is the assumption that a lot of work will have to be done to bring the article to a usable condition. Sometimes prices are low because the item has cost little in money, time or skill, or because there is an oversupply with little buying pressure.

There are exceptions to this. Brick is an obvious one. The price of used brick in some areas ranges from the same to double the price of new brick. Lumber is another exception. Clean and square used lumber can cost 10% to 50% more than certain grades of new wood with the same nominal dimensions. Part of the higher price of used lumber may be traced to superior quality, since old-growth wood is frequently harder, denser and consequently stronger than new wood and it often has an extra $1/16$ to $1/8$ of an inch of material in each direction.

Another case in which used materials are more expensive is when much labor has been put into recovering or restoring the materials. The less the restoration, the lower the price. Finally, there is the possibility that the material is very scarce in relation to effective demand. In the case of used brick, this is probably the largest single element in the price. The seller knows that if *you* do not buy it, someone else will.

This is not to say that used materials are necessarily superior to new materials. Apart from any intrinsic quality the used item might have had when it was first made, anything old has been subjected to varying degrees of stress. This stress takes many forms, but its common result is to leave the item in a debilitated condition. Doors and windows, for example, are subject to dry rot in the joints and along the upper edges of any horizontal wood surface. Evidence of this malady includes shrinkage, cracking, separation of horizontal and vertical elements at the corners, metal reinforcing braces or plates, and softness or wastage of material. If in doubt, poke the suspicious area with a screwdriver or knife point. If the blade goes in easily, the wood is punky and unsuitable for any structural use. Wood that is merely dry can be strengthened by multiple coats of linseed oil which soaks into the wood, swelling and filling it out again.

To help you know what to look for in used materials, here is a list of the major categories and common problems that you may find.

WOOD: dry rot; powderpost beetled (tiny round holes); splits, cuts, other damage; knots

PIPE: rust deposits, plugs, bends and kinks; bent or crushed threads

DOORS: warping; broken glass; dog damage (deep grooves or bites taken out of edges); dry rot; broken panels; veneer separation of styles from rails, mullions from other elements, etc.

TOILETS, OTHER CHINA: cracks, chips, crazing (can make the item more valuable, as in old toilet bowls with a fine, lacey network of tiny cracks in the surface glaze)

CAST IRON TUBS, SINKS: chips, "rust stars," discoloration and stains, pitting, erosion of enamel by acidic water

WINDOWS: dry rot, cracked or broken glass, putty out, points missing

CABINETS: warped doors, missing hardware, veneer separations, dry rot

The building materials salvage network is an important resource for the owner builder. Learning what salvage has to offer can be enjoyable and educational due to the stimulating exposure to so many styles and potential uses. There is nothing quite like a sunny afternoon in a salvage yard to get the creative juices flowing!

DELIVERIES

In materials delivery, as in most aspects of building, organization pays off. It costs money to deliver, whether the cost is figured into the price of the materials, added on to the price or you pick it up. You do find some suppliers that will deliver for free if they have regular delivery routes that your site falls on, but generally you are going to pay to have things delivered.

Ask the supplier what their charge is. Most suppliers figure that it costs $25 to $40 per hour to deliver. If they say there is no charge, ask if they will give you a discount if you pick up the materials yourself. It may be worth your while, if you have a truck and the time. If you do not have a pickup, you may want to buy a cheap one for the duration of the job.

Ask the suppliers their delivery policy before you buy. Make sure that they will deliver near the job site, not on the street. If you have to carry the supplies all the way across your lot, you are going to waste valuable time and energy. If you are buying roofing material, make sure that they will deliver to the roof so you won't have to carry it up a ladder. Ask the suppliers what kind of truck they use. If they have a truck with a bed that will drop the whole load on the ground, then you and your help won't have to spend hours unloading the truck only to move all the material a second time to the job. If you are having a major order delivered, have them stratify the supplies so you won't be moving half the order off the materials you will use first. If your lot is on a hillside, arrange to have the goods delivered at the top. If you are getting small, frequent deliveries, have them planned out so that you don't end up receiving materials you are not ready to use and waiting for those you need.

When you are accepting a delivery, count it, inspect it, and double check it before it gets off the truck. If you are picking up supplies, count and inspect them before you load them. Once you have the load on the ground or in your truck, it will be harder to send anything back. People make mistakes. Check the price again to make sure it is the one you initially agreed to.

Be extra careful when accepting delivery or picking up bargains, since you may have a problem returning them. Inspect finishing and processed materials carefully. There is little room for error or waste with these products. If you are not sure about the goods, check with a professional. There is no guaranteed immunity from receiving bad materials. Prominent contractors who have been buying from reputable suppliers for years occasionally end up with something wrong. You are not going to offend anyone by checking everything carefully. You are more likely to surprise them if you do not.

You are going to need to pick up supplies as you go along. Running errands can run up the cost. Plan ahead to keep trips down to one a day. Consider installing a phone on the job site and let your fingers do the walking. A little organization can save a great deal of time and money.

STORAGE AND SECURITY

The most important aspect of storage is security. Most of your supplies will not suffer weather damage if they are covered properly. Wood and piping can survive, and while insulation and wiring should not get wet, you can find ways to keep it dry.

What you may run into trouble with is theft. No neighborhood is entirely safe. Know the area where you are building. If you have neighbors, meet them and make friends. Let them know what you are doing. Ask if they can help you keep an eye on your lot and your materials.

If possible and not too expensive, have minimum deliveries made. Stagger them as best you can so that your supplies do not pile up and present more of a temptation. Be extra careful not to leave your tools on the job site. If you have to buy your supplies in big lots, make other arrangements. If you are remodeling, use your garage for storage, making sure it is weatherproof and secure. If you have a neighbor near your site, ask about renting their garage, or consider renting space elsewhere, even if it's not near the job site. Another idea is to build a storage shelter that you could use later, or build your garage first to use for storage during construction. You can also build one section of the house first, make it tight and use it for storage while you are working on the rest of the house.

Present as little temptation as possible. The cost of prevention is worth avoiding the loss of tools and materials.

TIPS ON LUMBER

The quality of your workmanship will depend on five factors: 1) accuracy of your tools, 2) your skill, 3) the standards of quality you set towards your work, 4) your knowledge and 5) the quality of your materials. The tools will be discussed in Chapter 3. The skill should develop as you work, and you should make a *conscious* effort to improve it. The standard of quality, we discuss in the next section. The knowledge, I hope to impart to you in these volumes. Let us now take a closer look at the material.

Wood is a very pleasurable medium to work in. It is flexible, live and pleasant to the touch. It is beautiful and strong and has a certain integrity that man-made products often lack. If you are buying new lumber, try to find a lumber yard that has a high-quality *air- or kiln-dried lumber.* This is getting somewhat harder to locate and often there is an extra expense—5% to 15% for dry lumber—but it is worth it. Most of the lumber today comes straight from the forest to the yard to the job site. The stud you set in the wall may have been part of a pine tree in Oregon two weeks ago. Wood is made up with the same main ingredients as commercial plastics—lignin and cellulose. Lignin is an adhesive which gives strength and rigidity to the wood; cellulose is nature's strong material. It is made up of long chains which run the length of the tree, which accounts for wood splitting along its grain. The moisture in the wood is not held within these molecules, so much as between them. When evaporation occurs, this moisture is lost and the molecules pull closer to each other, which is why wood shrinks much more along its width (laterally) rather than its length (longitudinally).

Wet lumber has many disadvantages. *Nails lose three-fourths their holding power when driven into wet lumber,* as the lumber shrinks away from the nail, reducing the friction between the wood and the nail. There is also a deterioration of moist wood due to the formation of iron oxides on a nail in the presence of wood acids. If dry lumber is not available or you cannot afford the added expense, you may offset the disadvantages of wet lumber by doing two things. First, use threaded nails throughout the house. The Virginia Polytechnic Institute found that *a house built with threaded nails and green lumber could withstand four times the racking load as a house built with green lumber and plain shank nails.* This is also an excellent reason to use threaded nails in earthquake areas. These are sometimes difficult to find but keep looking; they add only about $20 to the cost of the house. The second thing to do if you are using green lumber is to allow the house to season for 6 months to a year so that it will finish drying

before you put on your finish material. So you could close the house in and wait awhile before doing finishing work. If you did this before the wood dried, the finishing boards would be pulled off as the wood shrunk.

Wet lumber has other disadvantages. It is much heavier and therefore harder to handle. This can be quite a problem when you are lifting and erecting your rafters. It is stickier and leaves a resin on the saw blade. (Keep some lacquer thinner on a rag near the saw to remove this resin.) Dry lumber holds paints and preservatives better and is more resistant to attack by fungi and insects. The main problem with wet lumber is that as it dries it shrinks, twists, and bows and thereby weakens your structure. This also throws off your finishing work.

Choosing your lumber

Most lumber comes stamped with the species, grade, moisture content and the producing mill. In each species of trees, there are different qualities in the wood. Usually in each area of the country the lumber yards take construction-grade lumber used for the framing from whatever local species of tree is most accessible. In the West, it is Douglas fir, ponderosa pine and spruce. In the East, it is white and yellow pine. Framing wood comes in 2-foot intervals and is easily available up to 16 feet. From 16 to 20 feet it is harder to find and is sometimes 10 to 15% more.

Above 20 feet it usually has to be specially cut. As you design the house, take this into account; order your lumber so that there will be as little waste as possible. Find a yard that has the wood you need at a good price and one that will let you pick your lumber. This is sometimes hard to do and the lumber company will want you to take the good with the bad. It is not uncommon for 20 to 30% of a stack of studs to be unusable. No matter what the lumber company says, there is no reason to have to buy anything that you cannot use. Sometimes there is a slight charge for picking your lumber. If they will not let you do it for free, pay the charge. Pick good straight boards that are not badly bowed, warped or twisted. At least one end should have a good straight cut. Their length is usually a few inches over the measurement to allow for an uneven cut end. No board will be perfect—it is not the nature of the material, but try to use judgment as to which can be used and which ones can't. Framing lumber is Number 2 or 3 grade, construction or better. Blocking and sheathing can be Number 4 grade.

Stacking lumber

If your lumber needs to be stored for more than a week, stack it in the following manner to allow air to flow throughout the stack, thereby helping it dry and keeping it from getting wet and rotting. Be sure it is supported at least every 4 feet and is level and that it is well weighted down so that the boards don't curl as they dry. Cover them well so that they will not get wet if it rains.

Sawhorses

Before starting your framing, build some sawhorses. Hardware stores sell metal brackets that 2×4s slip into or you can cut the boards yourself. Their height should be about ½ your height or whatever works for you. Be sure no nails are placed where the saw blade might hit them, as it will frequently cut into the top board. Drive a nail on each side to hang your tri square on.

Other fasteners

If you are not using threaded nails, be sure to use coated nails. These are coated with a coat of cement, increasing the holding power of the nail. Metal fasteners, now available at a very reasonable cost, are highly effective and have a much greater holding power than nails. These can often make the work go much quicker and can make certain framing situations much simpler as we will see in the floor-joist system. *In earthquake areas they are highly recommended because of their increased strength, especially in situations where the ground is moving laterally.*

Ordering and delivering the wood

If possible, try to order all your framing wood at one time, if you will be building constantly. If you are working only on weekends you might just want to order your floor joists, then the wall framing, and then the roofing lumber. This will prevent the boards being left at the site unprotected from thieves and the weather. When the lumber is brought to the site, decide on where and how it should be stacked to allow your work to go most efficiently. Be sure you have access to the lumber you will need in the order in which you will need it. If there is any fungus growing on the wood, be sure that there are proper air spaces between the different layers in the stack, even if it will be stacked only for a few days. Fungi can grow very fast and discolor the wood.

Some Thoughts on Work Habits and Attitudes

In ways that we may never realize, the attitude of the builder strongly affects the final outcome of the home. A house built with love and care will reflect it, and return the same to the dwellers. It is as simple as that. We have a chance, in building our own shelters, to do something few Western men or women do anymore. If we can keep this awareness throughout the job and find joy and satisfaction in each step of the work, then the work will become effortless and the house, and the experience of building it, nurturing. It is easy, with financial hassles, late scheduling problems, manpower shortages and all the other things that arise when building a house, to lose sight of this and be working only to finish. Before you begin each day's work, sit down and become aware of what it is you are doing, look at the ramifications it has in your life, realize the opportunities for growth and satisfaction creating your own environment is offering you, and when you feel that joy and excitement begin to rise (even on the 266th work day, after two weeks of rain, a broken Skil saw, and your third smashed thumb), begin your work.

It is a good idea to stop a little early each day and store and properly clean all tools, extension cords and materials. Clean up all the scraps and clean the entire work area. It is good to start each day in an orderly clean area and it can have an effect on your workmanship. A sloppy work area can mean sloppy work. Denail all boards as soon as the situation arises and keep your tools in an easily accessible box or hung on nails. This is especially important when a few people are using one set of tools. I have probably spent 10 hours work time over the last 10 years searching for my pencil, usually to find it stuck behind my ear. So have a set place for each tool; it keeps them from being stepped on, makes them accessible and gives the job a well-organized, professional feel. Learn to respect your tools and how to use them properly in the beginning and it will save you many cuts and perhaps a finger or two. Your power saw will become a very familiar tool to you after awhile, but do not allow this familiarity to lead to laxity. It has a sharp steel blade turning 6000 times a minute and is going to violently cut into anything that it touches, including you. When using a tool, *DON'T EVER LOSE TOUCH WITH WHAT YOU ARE DOING; YOU MAY LOSE A FINGER.*

How to Use This Book

This book was written for one purpose: to assist people who are building their first and probably last home. It is not meant to be a training manual for someone seeking to make housebuilding their profession (though I think it would be of great value to these people). If you were learning the skills to use for a lifetime as a profession, I would have taught some of these procedures differently. I would have stressed more production and speed-oriented techniques that are not really needed by someone building just one or two homes.

Also, know that this is definitely not the final word. No such thing exists in the trades. Ask 10 tradespeople for the right way to do something and you are likely to get 11

Photo 1-1. Safety: Never use a cutting tool so that it is being forced towards you. If it slips, a nice cut is possible. Remember too that well sharpened tools are much safer than dull ones.

Photo 1-2. Safety: Surprisingly enough, one of the most common accidents is leaving a tool up high, on a ladder or a wall, only to remember, painfully, where you left it.

that you understand how all the processes fit together. Since the housebuilding process is a matter of getting many different systems to blend together in time and space, you need to have an understanding of the whole house, all of the systems, before beginning. You should also read about electrical, plumbing, heating and finishing systems that are not mentioned in this book.

After you have finished your first reading, you can begin process by process. Before beginning the process, read the chapter all the way through in detail. Do not just start the process as you read along. Something mentioned late in the chapter might affect your entire approach. Underline or make notes of anything in the chapter that you think you will need to keep in mind during your construction. You may also want to check with your local builder to be sure that there is not some better way to do it in your area. Be sure that you are meeting all the local codes. This can be done by checking in your code handbook or by asking the inspector.

The *Most Common Mistakes* are mentioned to help you avoid them. Usually these mistakes are learned only after years at the job site and having made each one at least once. You can avoid all of these by understanding each mistake well and being sure that you avoid it. You still will make your share of mistakes, but this will help you in avoiding the larger ones.

The *Margin of Error* is there to let you know when you have done good work, work that does not affect the structural quality of the house and will not detract from it cosmetically. A lot of new builders go to great lengths to get everything perfect and spend way too much time doing the job. They can add months to the length of the project. Remember, you are not building a piano and good quality work is not perfect. Try to make each cut and measurement perfect, but use your margins of error and do not correct work that will not affect the integrity of the house either structurally or cosmetically. You just do not have the time to be that exact.

answers, and we are all sure we are right. On top of that, what might be right for one area of the country will not be for another. Be open to receiving different approaches than those laid out in this book and evaluating them as perhaps being better. Question others deeply as to why they think their approach will work better and if you agree, use it. Some of the best approaches have come from novices who had no preconceived ideas as to how something should be done, so don't discount your own common sense. On the other hand, many brilliant new ideas in construction often have a fatal flaw, so if you are trying a radically new approach of any impact, run it by a local professional first.

I think every owner builder should couple themselves with a local professional to act as their mentor and advisor during the construction process. A construction guru if you will. Pay them by the hour to advise you on key points. They can inspect the forms before the pour, inspect the framing, help with complicated roof framing, solve problems, correct mistakes, etc. The money will be well spent.

I advise reading the *entire book* before beginning construction. You do not have to read it in detail at first, but just so

Photo 1-3. Safety: This may look comic, but hauling around long boards is dangerous, especially at a crowded site. Carry the boards low or call a general alert when passing through the site.

Photo 1-4. Safety: Distractions are a major cause of accidents. An accident will occur before you even realize you were getting lax.

The *What You'll Be Doing, What to Expect* section should help you conceptualize the process you are about to begin. It will also let you know what you can expect the procedure to be like for the first time. It might be frustrating, boring, easy, etc. Somehow, being told it will be frustrating makes the frustration easier to deal with when it happens.

The *What You'll Need* section will help you begin the construction procedure with all the needed tools, materials, permits and information. It will also tell you when you will need more than the information given in this book.

The *Reading the Plans* section should bridge the gap between the plans and the actual construction. It will show you how to get the needed information from the plans. On the plans only the information needed for that particular chapter has been shown in bold with unneeded information in the background.

The *Safety and Awareness* section is to remind you of the main things both about construction and safety that you need to keep in mind during the construction of that part of the process.

The *Worksheet* and *Daily Checklist* at the end of each chapter are fill-the-blank sections that allow you to take account and calculate the amount of materials needed. It's also useful in checking off tools and the number of workers you will need. The Daily Checklist can be photocopied and placed at the job site for your convenience.

GOOD LUCK! I hope all this works well for you and you have a safe and successful project.

Construction Site Safety

Since the construction site is unfamiliar ground for most of you, and since you will be concentrating on what you are learning and doing, the hazards around you are multiplied

considerably. It will be constantly necessary for you to remind yourself to maintain an active mental awareness of your immediate environment while working—beside you, behind you, above you, below you!

GENERAL

Be patient. If anger and/or frustration becomes a problem, stop, take a break and reassess the situation once you are calmer.

Working while under the influence of alcohol or other drugs is dangerous to yourself and those around you.

Be careful of sunstroke, sunburn and heat exhaustion.

POWER TOOLS

Power tools and many hand tools as well as construction operations are dangerous when being used by those lacking proper knowledge and experience. IF YOU HAVE ANY DOUBTS OR FEEL YOU NEED MORE INSTRUCTION: STOP! GET IT BEFORE MISTAKES ARE MADE.

Wear protective goggles *at all times* when power tools are in use.

Don't use power tools when standing in water—it can be a shocking experience.

If changing a blade or adjusting the cut, be certain the tool is unplugged.

Watch your cord placement when using the circular saw to be certain it is out of the way.

Set the circular saw blade to the appropriate depth.

There are specific safety rules for each power tool. Familiarize yourself with these rules prior to use.

Photo 1-5. Safety: One of the most dangerous situations is working with a saw when the blade guard is tied back and having the moving blade brush against some part of your body. ALWAYS know where the blade is.

PROTECTIVE CLOTHING AND EQUIPMENT

On the job site, WEAR HEAVY SOLED WORK BOOTS (steel toes if available). Tennis shoes and other soft soled shoes are dangerous to the wearer. Use rubber soled shoes when working on the roof.

Wear gloves while handling lumber, metal or other materials capable of injuring your hands for extended periods. NON-POROUS GLOVES SHOULD BE WORN when handling or using solvents, preservatives or corrosives.

Safety glasses, goggles or face shields should be worn during any operation where there is an inherent probability (or even possibility) of eye injury from flying or falling particles, or from spraying or splashing of liquids. WEAR EYE PROTECTION WHEN USING POWER SAWS.

WEAR HARD HATS AT ALL TIMES WHEN WORKING UNDER OR AROUND OVERHEAD OPERATIONS OF ANY KIND.

Be sure long hair is tied back so it does not get caught in power tools.

SITE

Scrap lumber and debris should be kept reasonably cleared from all work surfaces, as well as normal foot traffic areas. Never leave lumber in a vertical position; stack horizontally in neat piles.

Within 6 feet of the building under construction, the ground should be kept reasonably free of irregularities and debris.

Place materials in stable stacks to prevent materials from falling, slipping or collapsing.

ANY BOARD OR OTHER MATERIAL THAT HAS NAILS PROTRUDING FROM IT SHOULD BE DE-NAILED OR THE NAILS BENT OVER FLAT in such a way to prevent punctures or other accidents—BEFORE THE PIECE IS DROPPED OR DISCARDED.

HAND TOOLS

When not using tools, keep them picked up and in a box. When using tools, keep track of them. Don't use tools which are dull or in poor condition—check the handles for looseness.

Select the appropriate tool for the job.

Hold edge tools (planes, chisels) so the cutting action is away from you. Beware, as edge tools will be quite sharp!

Don't throw or drop tools.

Don't leave tools on ladders, scaffolding or high areas— they are potential missiles. Avoid walking beneath ladders or scaffolding where people are working.

Don't carry sharp tools in your pockets.

LIFTING, CARRYING AND BENDING

Stand close to your load, bend your knees and lift from your knees, not your back. Reverse this technique to set an object down.

Photo 1-6. Safety: Cutting a board between two supports will often cause the boards to bind on the saw blade and result in the saw kicking back. Always cut with the board cantilevered over a support.

Do not twist or turn your body when lifting or carrying a heavy load.

Carry the load close to your body and at waist height.

Work at a level which avoids constant bending at the waist. When working at a low level, bend at your knees. Have a work bench or saw horses at a level which minimizes back strain.

If you anticipate an object being heavy, test it prior to lifting.

If an object is too heavy, get help!

When placing a heavy object down—do not drop it. Your fingers and your partner's fingers are at stake! If you drop lumber, you can crack it.

If you are over 5 feet high on a ladder, have someone hold the ladder.

Photo 1-7. Safety: Never place your hand in the path of any saw blade, but especially not a radial arm saw, which is known to kick back.

Enjoy Your Work

Drudgery creates accidents. Hard work can be basically good and healthy, but don't get exhausted.

Be your own barometer as to when to rest or change to something different.

Take your time. Don't be afraid to just stare at the work a while before making your move.

Make it a *good* experience.

Don't fight your work. Arrange your immediate work area so that you're not reaching, straining, struggling. Move saw horses, pick up scraps under your feet, arrange the work for yourself.

THINK SAFETY

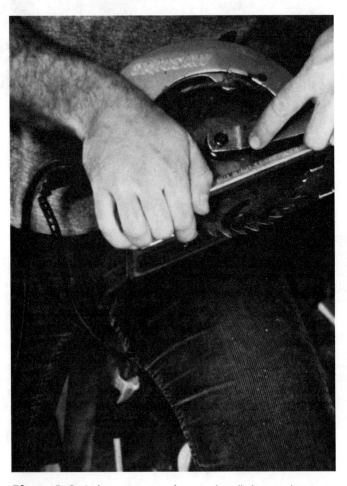

Photo 1-8. Safety: Many professionals still change their saw blades with the saw plugged in. Many professionals are also missing finger digits.

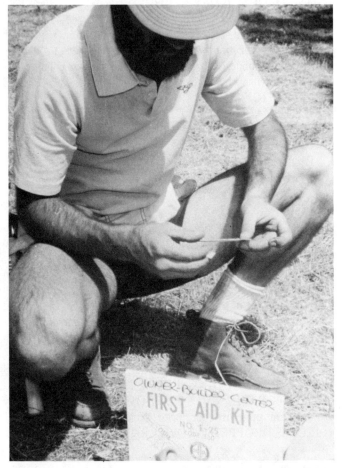

Photo 1-9. Safety: Keep a well-stocked first aid kit and booklet at the site at all times as well as emergency phone numbers.

Construction Schedule

by Charley Huddleston

THIS SCHEDULING GUIDE can be adapted to your project and circumstances. It follows a typical home-building project for the construction of a 1,500-square-foot one-story house with a perimeter foundation on a level site using standard wood-frame construction techniques. Note how certain tasks arrange themselves in clusters and that some activities must be successfully completed before you can proceed with subsequent jobs. This guide will also help you coordinate loan disbursements, ordering materials and inspections. You will need to schedule your work accordingly.

1. Submit copies of your house plans to your building department for the appropriate permits.
2. Deliver your plans to subcontractors for estimates and, if possible, firm bids.
3. Deliver plans to suppliers for quotes on materials. You're likely to need bids from subcontractors for the

following jobs: trenching, foundation, framing, plumbing, heating, sheet metal, electrical, wallboard installation and finish, roofing, finished flooring, tiling, painting, concrete walks and insulation. You can obtain quotes from suppliers for the remainder: cabinets, windows and doors, mirrors, countertops, hardware and fittings, appliances and a fireplace.

4. Apply for construction or mortgage loans at your bank. When contracting your own house construction, your application will probably include a personal financial statement, house plans (including elevation and lot drawing), a preliminary title report, copies of written bids and quotes and a lending institution Cost Breakdown sheet.

5. Contact and arrange with local utility companies for electrical, gas, water and telephone service.

6. Arrange for temporary facilities on the building site. These might include a chemical toilet, a temporary power pole, a construction shack, a telephone and living quarters.

7. Pick up your initial building permits.

8. Check with your bank for confirmation of your construction loan.

9. Complete loan arrangements with the bank and record your deed of trust.

10. Sign and return the contracts to your subcontractors. Set up tentative dates to start their services. Establish supplier orders and delivery schedules.

11. Get a surveyor to locate the lot boundaries.

12. Set the temporary power pole.

13. Have the electrical inspector inspect your power pole.

14. Have the utility company hook up power to the power pole.

15. Foundation contractor lays out the site for trenching, footings and foundation.

16. Now the foundation can be dug.

17. The foundation contractor installs the forms for the concrete.

18. Call for a foundation form inspection by the local building inspection department.

19. Order the framing lumber from the lumberyard.

20. The foundation contractor pours the concrete and later strips the forms.

21. The framing contractor lays the sill and joists.

22. The plumbing, electrical, and heating contractors do their underfloor work. The local building department makes an underfloor inspection (Uniform Building Code areas).

24. The framing contractor lays the subfloor.

25. If your bank uses a draw system to finance construction payments, you can call for your first disbursement, usually about 20%.

26. The framing contractor frames the walls.

27. The contractor frames the ceiling and roof.

28. Order the delivery of the windows and the exterior doors.

29. Carpenters install wall and roof sheathing, windows, siding and exterior doors.

30. With the house framed and the siding installed, you can install sheet metal and flashing.

31. The roofing contractor installs roofing.

32. At this stage your rough plumbing, electrical, heating, telephone pre-wiring, cable TV, etc., should be completed and ready for inspection.

33. Contact the local building department for a close-in inspection. You'll need this permit before covering any in-wall components of the electrical, plumbing and heating systems.

35. The insulation contractor installs insulation between wall studs and ceiling joists.

36. Call for second disbursement from the bank, usually about 30%.

37. The drywall contractor installs the wallboard.

38. At this stage you may also need to have a wallboard nailing inspection.

39. Order the delivery of interior doors and millwork trim.

40. Order and arrange for delivery of kitchen cabinets and bathroom vanities.

41. Carpenters can now install the garage door.

42. Arrange for the subcontractors to finish their plumbing, electrical and heating work.

43. Order appliances and electrical fixtures.

44. Call for a third disbursement from the bank, usually about 15%.

46. Various materials, finishes and household elements can now be ordered. These include mirrors, shower doors, tile, linoleum, carpeting, countertops and weatherstripping.

47. Painting contractor paints interior walls and trim, starts exterior.

48. Lay the resilient flooring.

49. Mechanical services are completed by the plumbing, electrical and heating contractors.

50. Install tile and countertops.

51. Install mirrors, shower doors, carpeting, weatherstripping and finish hardware.

52. Call for a final building inspection. This step allows you to establish electrical service.

53. Obtain a notice of completion and file with county recorder. The bank will make its own final inspection about this time. The lien period (usually about 60 days) begins, during which time your subcontractors still have lien rights on your construction.

54. Request your utility company to hook up electrical service.

55. You will receive another disbursement from the bank, usually about 15%.

56. Pay the final bills as they come due and take discounts on materials.

57. Have your subcontractors and suppliers sign lien releases as they are paid.

58. Receive the final disbursement from the bank, usually about 20%, as the lien period ends.

59. Move in.

60. Congratulations for hanging in there!

2 Types of Construction

Photo 2-1. A modular wall section of a manufactured stud house being assembled in the factory with pneumatic tools.

MANY NEW BUILDERS do not realize that there are many different types of construction they can choose from. Most builders proceed building the standard stud-constructed house, never stopping to consider their other choices. This chapter will explain the most common types of construction methods used in the United States today. Your choice in the type of construction you will use should be well thought out. Your decision will impact your cost, your design, the feel of your home and your building process. There should be definite reasons for choosing one type of construction over another.

Along with your decision on the type of construction you will use, you also will need to decide whether to use a pre-fab kit home or build the entire house yourself at the site (a site-built home). This is a very important decision too; it can greatly impact your building experience. Let's discuss this building issue first.

The Site-Built Home

Until a few decades ago, almost all houses were site-built homes (except for those ordered from the Sears catalogue). Most owner builders have avoided factory-built homes, feeling that they could not get the design or quality they wanted from a kit. This is really no longer the case. You still may, however, choose to build the entire home yourself for several reasons. Needless to say, you do have more control over your home should you decide to build at the site. You can choose and inspect every piece of material and keep the quality of construction at whatever level you want. You are also able to make more design changes during the course of construction since the house is being cut and assembled as you go. Some types of designs may not be available in a kit home and you will need to build the entire house yourself.

Photo 2-2. A panelized wall section of a manufactured stud house being lifted into place by a crane. The entire house might be completed in a week or two.

Sometimes there is a certain feel you want to instill in the house, one of handcraftsmanship or maybe high tech, that kits do not offer. Finally, many people just want the satisfaction of knowing they built it themselves.

Manufactured Housing

(*Photos 2-1–2-3.*)

Until several years ago, I, like many other people, had a certain attitude about manufactured houses. Since I began as a custom builder, I felt manufactured houses limited people's creativity and design and often produced an inferior product. In the last few years, I have made a 180° turn. Most all of the existing manufactured housing companies, especially those that have been in business for some time, offer high-quality products and the design options are limitless. On top of that, it is often a less expensive way to create the same quality house you would build for yourself. Here are several of the advantages to manufactured housing.

One of the greatest advantages to the owner builder is that you are linking yourself with a support network, the manufacturer and your local dealer, who will assist you through all stages of construction—from getting your permit, to getting finances, to getting the house built, etc. This support system can be of great value to a novice builder.

Your construction time is greatly reduced since a lot of the work is done at the factory. And if you are working on a limited time budget, this can be very helpful to you. A lot of the work is done by the manufacturer; the amount of knowledge and information and work you will have to do is limited. Often, a manufactured home can go up in a third of the time of a job-site-built home. This reduced time can be translated into dollar savings since your construction loan, which is often a few percentage points over your mortgage loan, will be reduced. If you own another home and are paying a mortgage while you build, you will be able to move into your new home sooner, eliminating the cost of two mortgages.

Manufacturers are able to buy in large lots and can get superior-quality materials at a lower price. This saving is often passed on to the owner. Since factory labor is a lot less expensive than hired carpenters, the work done on the house is less costly. This is passed on to the buyer.

For the most part, a house using high-quality materials can often be had more cheaply from a manufacturer than one built by yourself at the job site.

Photo 2-3. A modular house being delivered to the site in several large sections.

There is one other added advantage. If you are building a home in a remote area where labor is expensive and unavailable, you can solve many of your problems by using a manufactured house.

A few problems with manufactured housing are that you may not always be able to get the design you want from every manufacturer, and occasionally there may be code problems in your local area with some manufactured housing. However, most of the larger manufactured housing companies have ICBO (International Congress of Building Officials) numbers, which will assist you in getting whatever permits you need to build the house in their area.

There are many different types of manufactured housing. Almost every style of home, including domes, logs, laminated timbers, stud, pole, etc., comes in a manufactured housing option. Some manufacturers simply provide the pieces for the weather-tight frame of the home. Sometimes the entire interior finishing materials are supplied as well. In some panelized packages, the entire wall section, including the interior finishing boards, the exterior walls, the plumbing and electrical fixtures, the frame, and insulation, are put together in panelized sections, shipped to the site and assembled (usually with the use of a crane). Sometimes the pieces are numbered, and you erect the entire thing like a giant erector set. Other modular homes have the entire house in two or three large sections with the carpets down, the appliances in, and the plumbing and electrical fixtures in, that they bring to the site and bolt together.

I highly recommend that you explore the manufactured housing alternative for any style house you are planning to build. Here are a few tips to consider before choosing whether to use this alternative and, if so, which manufacturer to choose.

1. Be sure the manufacturer's package will comply with the local codes.
2. Investigate the company. What is their credit rating? How long have they been around? Do they have a record with the Better Business Bureau? Have they ever been taken in front of a consumer affairs board? Have they ever been bankrupt?
3. Ask for references of other customers who have recently built and lived in one of their houses.
4. Ask to see all of the instructional materials and educational pamphlets.
5. Be clear as to what the package includes and what it does not include. Make sure you have worked this out in detail and know exactly what you are getting for your money and what you will still have to go out and purchase or subcontract. Often a lot of problems lie in this area. It is hard to compare one manufactured housing company to another unless you know they are both offering the same types of materials and services.
6. Be sure that you will be able to re-sell this style of home in your area should you ever move.

7. Investigate whether or not you will be able to make design changes or design the house exactly as you want it.

8. Find out what other assistance the company will provide. Will they assist you with financing? Will they assist you with permits, with site choosing, with site improvement, with construction, with finishing?

Standard Stud Construction

(Photos 2-4–2-8.)

Most of the houses built in the U.S. today are built using a standard stud construction. There was a time when almost all houses were either post and beam or log, but stud construction caught on with such a fury that, until recently, all others were almost forgotten. This did not come about because stud construction was, across the board, a better way to build, but it was quicker and easier, much as white bread replaced whole grain. The old construction method of post and beam makes use of large structural framing members, and therefore fewer timbers are needed, but construction usually required the skill of a highly trained joiner since a small number of joints carried the entire weight of the building. Because of this, each joint had to be exactly fitted. At the turn of the century there was a switch to stud construction; the work was quicker and took less skill. As cities grew, buildings needed to go higher in order to make better use of the expensive land. With the old post and beam method you would need longer and longer timbers in order to go higher. With stud construction, you simply stack one story on top of another, never needing a wall member over 8 feet long.

To build with stud construction, you first build a foundation, then on this you build a floor frame. The floor frame is built with 2-inch-thick construction-grade lumber (2×6, 2×8, 2×10 or 2×12) called floor joists. A floor joist is one of a series of parallel framing members that run underneath and support the floor. These are usually placed on 16- or 24-inch centers. After the joists are in place, you apply the subfloor (usually plywood) and then use this platform on which to build the rest of the house (hence the name platform building, as it is still occasionally referred to). The walls are built with studs, which are 2×4s or 2×6s that are about 8 feet long and again are placed on 16- and 24-inch centers. Where the structural integrity of the wall frame is violated by an opening for a door or window, a larger header spans across the top of the opening to carry the load to either side of the opening. Since the walls are carrying the roof load, these headers are essential. The roof frame is made up of roof rafters, which are also two-inch-thick stock that support the roof sheathing and roofing. These rafters rest on top of the walls, and the walls carry the load into the floor and onto the foundation and into the ground. If there is a second or third floor, you simply build your first-floor walls, place your second floor on top of

Photo 2-4. The floor joist system of a stud house. In this case, the joists are cantilevered as a design feature.

Photo 2-5. A stud frame house under construction. Note that the platform is built and walls are going up.

Photo 2-6. A stud house under construction.

Photo 2-7. A stud house using some post and beam in the front section. Note that large framing members are used for the wall, but the rafters, since they will not be exposed to the interior, are 2×10s.

Photo 2-8. A stud house with some post and beam construction.

Photo 2-9. A post and beam house built by students at Heartwood Owner Builder School in Washington, Massachusetts. Note that the horizontal beams and vertical posts shown constitute the entire structural framing system.

them and then build your second-floor walls. The third floor is added in the same way. So the roofing is supported by the rafters, which are supported by the walls, which are supported by the floor frame, which is supported by the foundation, which is supported finally by the ground.

There are many advantages to this type of building, especially for the novice builder. Everything in the construction world, at least as far as residential construction is concerned, is set up around this type of construction method. The materials and information are readily available and it will meet all local codes. In addition, since many different small pieces of wood make up the frame of the house, the load is spread over many joints and many pieces of wood. No one joint is essential and therefore a ¼-inch margin of error is allowable at the framing stages, taking the burden off the builder to make exact cuts. Finally, many of the building materials are provided in 4-×-8-foot sections: plywood, paneling, sheetrock, etc. These accommodate the 16- or 24-inch centers of the framing members. Heaters, ductwork, medicine cabinets, etc., are made to fit between the framing members.

Post and Beam Construction

(Photos 2-9, 2-10.)

Post and beam construction, which is sometimes called plank and beam construction, was used in the 18th and 19th centuries and was the dominant type of construction before stud construction was introduced in the United States.

This type of construction involves large timbers, usually 4 to 12 inches wide, that are placed both vertically and horizontally. The vertical timbers are called posts and these support horizontal timbers called beams. The load of the roof is carried onto the horizontal beams, then over to the vertical posts and onto the ground. The walls themselves do not carry the loads; they are used only to hang the siding, the doors and windows. The posts and beams carry the entire load. Therefore, fewer but larger pieces of framing materials are used than in the standard stud construction. Usually in this type of construction, the foundation and floor system are built as in conventional stud construction and then the posts

Photo 2-10. A metal bracket used to hold the post and beams together in earthquake areas.

Photo 2-11. Large timbers are bolted to poles in this pole house. Note how the house is resting on these timbers.

and beams are erected on the floor platform. Many times post and beam construction is used in certain areas of a house. For instance, highly exposed areas such as the bedroom or the livingroom might use a large post and beam type of construction, and the rest of the house may be stud. Four-inch-wide beams are used for the roof rafters and these are left exposed to the room below.

The greatest advantage of post and beam construction is the sense of solidity, character and integrity that the large exposed timbers lend to the structure itself. A home done with a stud construction, without the large exposed framing members, will feel quite different from the same house built with large exposed framing members. Where posts and beams, rather than the walls, carry the load of the roof, you can also have larger and more frequent openings for doors and windows, and large interior spaces. Post and beam houses can be designed to fit almost any style. Usually 4 to 5 people and perhaps even a crane may be needed during the frame-construction period.

The disadvantages in post and beam construction are few. In some areas, engineering may be required, but this is usually not too costly. It can also be difficult to find high-quality larger timbers. Since there are fewer framing members and each one carries a greater load, the cuts and your general work must be more exacting than in stud construction, where many small framing members carry the entire load.

In earthquake areas, as well as in hurricane and tornado areas, where the house stands a lot more stress and strain than in areas where these natural disasters do not occur,

houses have to be better built. Because of this factor, post and beam homes often have to be connected with large metal brackets. This is especially true in California. In this case, your work does not have to be as exacting since the joints are not made of wood but of metal brackets, bolted to the wood and framing members. Yet even this can have a very distinctive appearance which should be considered. As in all other types of construction, post and beam packages are available from a number of different manufacturers.

Pole Construction

(Figure 2-1, Photos 2-11–2-20.)

Pole construction involves vertical load-bearing poles that are embedded in the ground sometimes up to 6 or 8 feet deep. These poles continue up and support the floor frame, the second floor and the roof. The floors and the roof are attached by horizontal boards that are bolted and often notched into the vertical poles. This type of structure is becoming more and more popular. In the past, it has often been used for agricultural and farm use where the dirt floor between the poles was used for equipment and a place where livestock could move around within the building. Given some of its unique advantages, pole construction is now having somewhat of a renaissance.

Perhaps the greatest advantage of this type of construction is its practical use on a sloping lot. Often on sloping lots

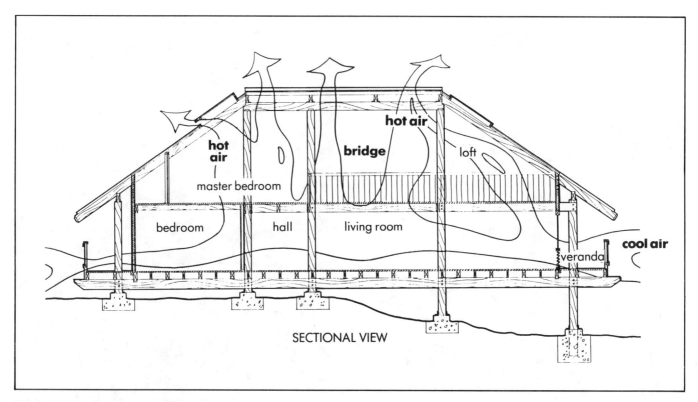

Figure 2-1. Since pole houses do not require as many interior bearing walls as standard construction, they are very well suited for natural ventilation in summer and transfer heat easily between rooms in passive solar homes. (Diagram courtesy of Pole House Kits of California, Irvine, California.)

Photo 2-12. A pole house in progress. Note how the walls are framed in typical stud fashion.

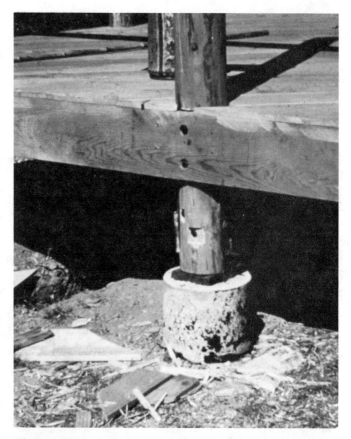

Photo 2-13. Poles for this pole house are kept out of the ground by fastening them to concrete piers. Note the small redwood sill block.

Photo 2-14. A pole house under construction. Note how few framing members are actually needed for the structural components of the house. The large poles serve as foundations and support the floors and roofs. Standard-size framing members will be added between the poles to support windows and doors and attach interior and exterior skins. The roof was added to protect the home early in construction. (Photo courtesy of Pole House Kits of California, Irvine, California.)

foundations can be very expensive; as the lot slopes, the foundation must become higher and higher to provide a level plane. With pole construction, however, longer poles are used at the lower end of the lot and shorter poles at the higher end to make adjustments for the foundation. This can save you many thousands of dollars in construction costs. A pole house also performs very well in hurricane, tornado and earthquake areas since the house is tied well into the ground with the long poles acting as the foundation.

Like post and beam construction, it uses some large framing members to give the house a sense of strength and solidity, but the exactness of post and beam work is not required with the round poles. The house can go up rather quickly and the roof can be put on before the walls are completed, thereby providing a protective work area as you finish the inside of the house.

Often it will take several people and perhaps even a crane to erect the large poles, but after this the work goes rather quickly. It is best to use some type of pressure-treated poles so the wood will not rot in the ground, or to build a system where the poles sit on top of a concrete pier foundation and are bolted to this foundation. This will also keep the wood out of contact with the ground.

Perhaps the greatest advantage of the pole house, aside from the strength and solidity of the large poles, is the openness it can allow. Load-bearing walls are not needed, as the poles carry the weight, and both large interior and exterior openings are possible. Also, large sweeping verandas are very simple to implement in your house design.

Though in the past most people have chosen to build their own pole house, nowadays there are a few kit companies available. If you are planning to build a pole house, it may be a wise decision to investigate one of these kit homes to see if there is a labor and money savings.

Photo 2-15. Pole houses are especially well suited for sloping sites, where the longer poles are used on the lower part of the slope. The savings over traditional foundation systems can be considerable. (Photo courtesy of Pole House Kits of California, Irvine, California.)

Photo 2-16. A finished pole house. Once again notice its application on steep slopes. (Photo courtesy of Pole House Kits of California, Irvine, California.)

Photo 2-17. Pole construction used for a commercial building. Note how well the poles work on a sloping site.

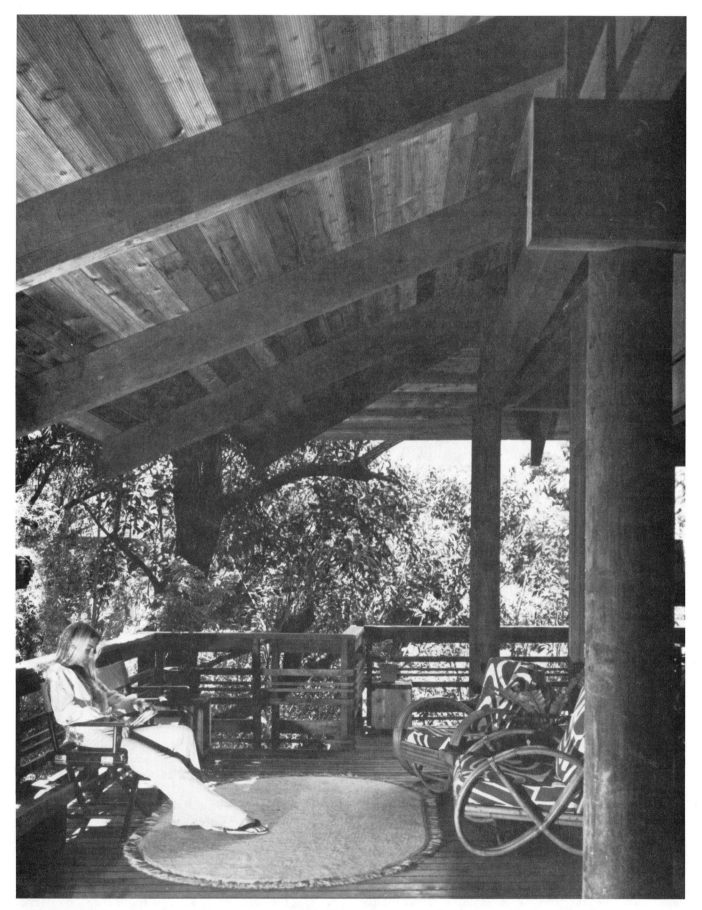

Photo 2-18. Pole houses are conducive to implementing wide-covered verandas as shown here. Note stringer attached to pole at upper right. (Photo courtesy of Pole House Kits of California, Irvine, California.)

Photo 2-19. Pole houses allow for open spaces and cathedral ceilings. The poles carry the load and can allow for large open interior areas without interior bearing walls. (Photo courtesy of Pole House Kits of California, Irvine, California.)

Log Homes

(*Photos 2-21–2-24.*)

Log homes were one of the first types of construction to come to the United States. All of us were familiar with the log homes built by the pioneers and our ancestors when they founded this country. Today there are still over 80,000 log homes built each year in the United States.

Log homes have a feel different from almost any other type of structure. Their massiveness and strength are apparent as soon as you walk in them or view them from the outside. A house built with a stud construction will feel entirely different from a house of the same design built from logs.

Log kit homes come in several different types. One type includes the walls only. This is usually made up of precut logs and does not include a roof system, doors, or windows. Another type of kit includes the logs for the walls, the roof system, the doors, and windows, providing therefore a weather-tight shell. A third system includes the weather-tight shell, the floors, the interior walls, counters and stairs. And finally, the last system includes everything you need for the completed house.

Log homes are usually rather simple to erect and require less skill and exactness of construction than many other types of homes. It is really just like putting together a large lincoln-log set that we used when we were children. One great advantage of erecting a log home is that as the logs are erected, you are not only framing the house, but you are also insulating the house and finishing off the interior and exterior walls. As a bonus, log homes require little maintenance, usually just some wood preservative every few years.

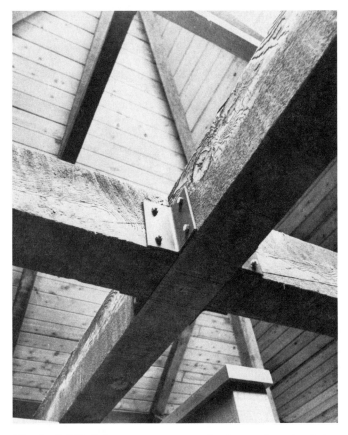

Photo 2-20. Pole construction can also be combined with the beauty and strength of post and beam construction, as shown here. (Photo courtesy of Pole House Kits of California, Irvine, California.)

Photo 2-21. A hand hewn log building. This type of structure can be inexpensive to build and of greater strength and quality than typical stud construction.

Photo 2-22. A manufactured log house kit. Beautiful and solid.

Photo 2-23. The logs from a kit home stacked and ready for assembly.

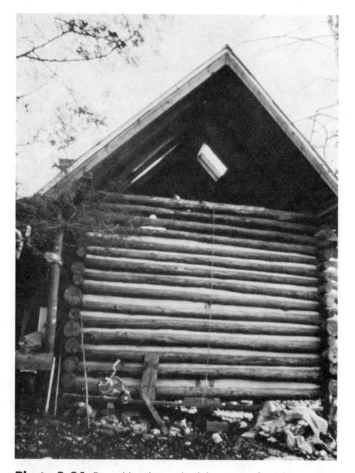

Photo 2-24. Round log home built by owner from logs cut at the site.

There are many, many different log-home manufacturers and the design variations have multiplied considerably in the last few years. Log homes, being easy to assemble, usually require no more than 2 or 3 people and very novice skills.

Many people are concerned about the energy efficiency of a log home. Wood has an R factor of about 1.5 per inch, whereas good insulation can have an R factor of anywhere from 4 to 6.5. (R=Resistance to heat loss; the higher the R number, the greater the insulating property of the material.) Therefore, the R factor of a typical log wall is often no more than 8 to 10 while that of a stud home can be 11 to 14. This has discouraged some people from building a log home. You may want to consider building a laminated timber home, mentioned in the next section, which gives you the advantage of a solid-wall wooden home and at the same time provides the increased R factor of 23 or even higher. However, many people who live in log homes say that they are very comfortable in winter and summer and that the R factor of a true log home is not the only thing to be considered. The cellular nature of the solid wood acts as a much greater natural insulation by trapping air in the cells, making a log home more comfortable than the R factors would indicate.

Before choosing to build a standard log home, be sure that it fits all local codes. Usually this will not be a problem since log homes can exist anywhere. It should blend-in in your area. If you are building in the urban or suburban area, often

times your design style will not fit in with your neighbor's.

Try to choose a dealer who can transport the heavy logs to your site without a tremendous increase in transportation costs. And, above all, be sure that you feel comfortable in the solidity and strength of a log home and that the tremendous amounts of exposed wood will go with your decorating scheme.

Laminated Timber Construction

(Photos 2-25–2-33.)

In the past few years, a new manufacturing process has been developed which gives the solidity, quality and strength of a solid log home or solid wood home, and at the same time gives a greater insulating factor than typical stud construction. The process involves laminating boards to both sides of styrofoam (or other types of insulating foam) core. Usually 2 inches of cedar are used on each side of a 2-inch-thick foam core. The R factor of this wall can be anywhere from 19 to 23 as compared with an R factor of 13 for a typical stud house.

These houses have the advantage over log homes in the sense that they provide a greater insulating property while still offering all the advantages of solid wood. They have an advantage over a hollow-wall stud home in that they are solid and add a much greater sense of stoutness and strength to the house and the hollow core of a stud home.

Usually they cost little or no more than a similar house of the same quality built in a stud or log construction. Another advantage of these houses is that, as you close in the house, you are finishing the exterior and interior walls, framing the home, and insulating it all in one process, much as you do with the stud home.

The sound transmission control, which represents the abil-

Photo 2-25. Mock-up of intersecting laminated walls. Note that the insulating foam core, sandwiched by cedar planks, offers a solid wall with good insulation. (Photos courtesy of Pre-Cut International, Woodinville, Washington.)

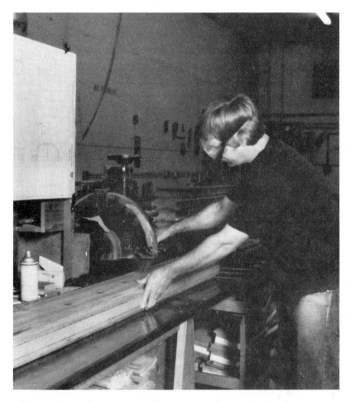

Photo 2-26. Cutting the laminated logs in the factory from a customer's design. Each house is cut according to the customer's own plans and then marked as to its location in the wall. (Photo courtesy of Pre-Cut International, Woodinville, Washington.)

Photo 2-27. Electrical wires are run through the bottom few courses of a laminated timber home. (Photo courtesy of Pre-Cut International, Woodinville, Washington.)

Photo 2-28. A laminated insulated timber home under construction. Note how no trimmers or headers are needed around the openings. (Photo courtesy of Pre-Cut International, Woodinville, Washington.)

Photo 2-29. A laminated timber house under construction. Logs are cut at the factory from the owner's plans. (Photo courtesy of Pre-Cut International, Woodinville, Washington.)

Photo 2-30. The interior of a laminated timber home. Interior walls look like walls covered with tongue and groove cedar planks. Interior walls can also be covered with traditional wall coverings. (Photo courtesy of Pre-Cut International, Woodinville, Washington.)

Photo 2-31. Finished solar home built from laminated insulated timbers. The exterior appears as a home sided with tongue and groove cedar boards. (Photo courtesy of Pre-Cut International, Woodinville, Washington.)

ity of the house to reduce the sound from within and without, is much greater because of the solidness of the home and the foam core. Its shear strength and wind-load factor is superior to that of the stud home. The wood also provides natural beauty to the home, and since wood breathes, it acts as a humidifier and dehumidifier. It is easier to maintain, requiring only a wood protection in the beginning and a light coating of a wood preservative every few years after that.

Energy-wise, it saves tremendous amounts of energy due to the increased R factor and the continuous insulating membrane provided by the solid home. Where a typical stud house uses 5,000 to 7,000 board feet of common-grade wet lumber, a laminated timber home uses 18,000 to 22,000 board feet of kiln-dried timber. This wood has minimal shrinkage and more strength.

The house can be designed according to your design plans, or it can be chosen from the manufacturers. You can design whatever style house you would like, anywhere from a southern mansion to a modern contemporary home, and it can be cut to fit this style. Should you choose to paint the outside of the home, it would only appear as if the house was sided with 1-×-8 siding boards put on horizontally. On the inside, the interior partition walls can be made out of sheetrock and even the interior surfaces of the exterior walls, which are usually made out of cedar, can be covered with sheetrock in order to make the house have a more traditional look. Both the exterior walls and interior walls can be left with the cedar exposed, giving a more rustic appearance.

Most of these houses are approved by the International Congress of Building Officials and will have no problems passing your local code.

In many ways, this is a superior building style. It gives you the solidity and strength of a solid timber home without the drawback of a log home, the lack of an insulating property. At the same time it allows you a tremendous amount of design flexibility and can appear to be a typical house built like any other house. It costs you the same price, but ends up to be a much higher-quality home.

Photo 2-32. Completed laminated log home.

Photo 2-33. A laminated timber home in traditional style. Exterior and interior look like T&G cedar siding. (Photo courtesy of Pre-Cut International, Woodinville, Washington.)

Photo 2-34. A dome shell under construction. A shell can be erected from a kit in a day or two. The triangular pieces are bolted together to form a pentagon which is then bolted in place to other assembled pentagons. (Photo courtesy of Cathedralite Domes, Medford, Oregon.)

Domes

(*Photos 2-34–2-39.*)

Domes are free-standing structures which need no load-bearing interior walls to carry the weight of the roof or the structure itself. They were developed in 1956 by Buckminster Fuller and Al Miller.

Domes have several advantages. For one thing, the structure encloses the maximum amount of living space with the least amount of exterior surface area for its volume. Also, domes are now accepted by most code offices throughout the United States and dome manufacturers usually have an ICBO (International Congress of Building Officials) number that allows them to pass all local codes. Presently there are over 200,000 domes in use world-wide and it is predicted that over one million domes will be erected during the 1980s.

There are two different types of dome kits: the panelized and the hub and strut systems. The panelized dome kit is made up of triangular panels, usually made of plywood and 2×4s or 2×6s, with struts on all three sides and exterior skins already in place. These plywood triangles are usually one of two sizes and are joined together in pentangles which are then lifted into place. Usually 3 to 5 people are needed

and scaffolding is erected on the dome floor to lift these pentangles into place. Often a riser wall, which is a vertical wall 3 to 5 feet tall, is built and the dome is erected on top of it. This gives the house some vertical spaces and also allows for a larger home. Openings for doors and windows are placed in different areas around the dome and skylights can be added by simply leaving out one of the triangles in the dome surface itself.

Another system, though not as commonly used, is the hub and strut system, developed in Arizona in the mid-1960s. In this type of system the frame of the dome or the skeleton is first erected similarly to that of a stud house. The frame is usually made up of 2×4s or 2×6s bolted together with metal hubs or plywood hubs. The external skin, which is usually plywood, is then applied just as the sheathing for a stud house would be applied over its frame.

Both kits usually contain only the shell with the interiors, the foundations and the finishing work being supplied by the owner.

Dome homes are some of the most energy-efficient homes

Photo 2-35. Domes can be used for commercial and industrial application as well as residential. (Photo courtesy of Cathedralite Domes, Medford, Oregon.)

Photo 2-36. A completed dome at the seashore. (Photo courtesy of Cathedralite Domes, Medford, Oregon.)

Photo 2-37. A completed dome built above a full-size first story with a slab foundation. (Photo courtesy of Cathedralite Domes, Medford, Oregon.)

Photo 2-38. The interior of a residential dome. Note how the shell can span the entire house without the use of interior bearing walls. (Photo courtesy of Cathedralite Domes, Medford, Oregon.)

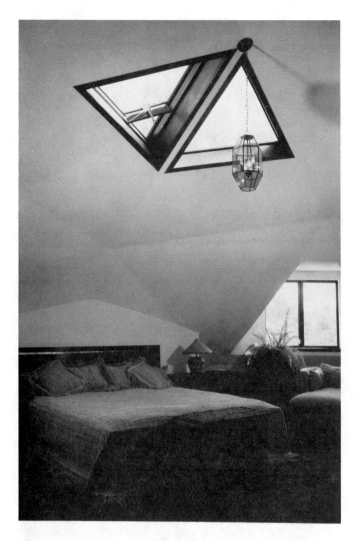

Photo 2-39. The upstairs interior of a dome. Again note vaulted ceiling's interior partition walls. (Photo courtesy of Cathedralite Domes, Medford, Oregon.)

Photo 2-40. The floor system of a hexagon is a series of radiating 4-inch-thick floor beams. (Photo courtesy of Honeycomb Systems, Inc., San Juan Bautista, California.)

that you can build. Since the maximum amount of space is enclosed by the minimum amount of surface, the heat loss is cut to a minimum. Dome manufacturers claim that they will out-perform any other type of structure with a comparable amount of insulation. Domes provide natural air circulation, they have good acoustics, and they require less maintenance, since there are no corners for moisture or dry rot to build up in. Unlike many types of homes, no interior walls are needed to support the roof. Indeed, the entire dome can be one open room. Because of this you have a much greater design flexibility. Often the shell can be put up in a day or two and allow you to work inside with protection from the weather. Domes can also withstand a great amount of wind and snow and, because of their stable shape, they are very earthquake resistant.

The structure of a dome is entirely that of one large roof rather than walls and roofs as in many types of construction. Roofing, therefore, must be done properly to avoid leaks. Almost all manufacturers have developed good roofing techniques and this is no longer a problem, but be sure you do the roof properly. Since there are few vertical walls but many

sloping walls and angles, decorating can be a challenge in a dome home.

One problem with dome homes might be that financing may be difficult to obtain. However, more and more banks are getting used to seeing this type of construction, and if it is a problem with your local bank, with the help of your manufacturing company and perhaps some other local dome owners, you should be able to convince them to finance the home.

Before deciding to build a dome home, go and visit several different domes. From my experience in dealing with owner builders, I have found that most people who build a dome know almost instantly upon going in their first dome that this is the type of housing they want to build. They feel more comfortable with the angles and the sloping walls than they do with the true vertical and horizontal planes and the 90° angles that most other houses offer. In making this important decision, ask yourself these questions: How does the dome feel to you? Does it make you feel at peace? Do you feel more at rest in a dome, as opposed to a conventional type of structure?

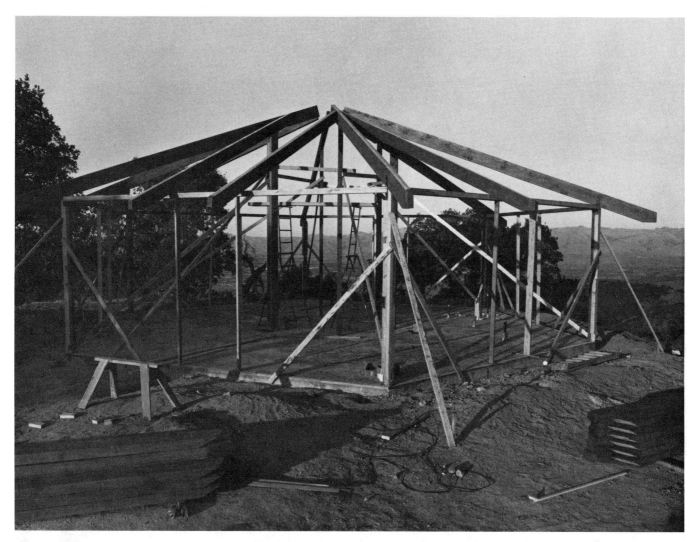

Photo 2-41. The completed framing of a hexagonal home. (Photo courtesy of Honeycomb Systems, Inc., San Juan Bautista, California.)

Hexagonal Homes

(*Photos 2-40–2-45.*)

Another type of construction that is available in kits in the United States is hexagonal construction. As the name implies, this type of construction involves 6-sided buildings. This structure creates a rather unique living space with almost no right angles anywhere in the structure. Because of this and the fact that the structure needs no interior supporting walls, your design parameters and the feel of the house can be quite different from other types of construction.

The foundation system is built in a hexagonal shape. The floor system is built on top of this using beams that radiate in a hexagonal shape. A subfloor is applied and posts are erected around the exterior of the house. The posts will support the large roof beams. At the center of the home these roof beams are supported either by more vertical posts or by a "truss ring"—no vertical posts are needed in the center of the home. Walls constructed between these posts simply serve the purpose of attaching the siding, doors, windows, insulation and interior wall covering. Like the dome,

the hexagonal structure uses the strength of the triangle to give it stability and flexibility. It is a series of interactive triangles from which it derives great strength.

Hexagonal homes are available from several kit manufacturers or can be built by the owner from scratch. Since the pieces are all cut from patterns and the design is a simple one it is easy for the novice builder to build. Materials are easily available and it will usually meet all local codes. Since the weight of the roof is carried by the wall posts and not the walls themselves, windows and doors can be easily added and deleted. The buildings can be built up to three stories high or can be clustered together in a series of small hexagons. This allows you to add space as it is needed or can be afforded. Because of the vaulted ceilings and lack of right angles, the interior spaces can often feel larger than they really are. In many ways these homes reflect a certain change in lifestyle, one that is individual and yet strives for unity and order.

Photo 2-42. Hexagonal buildings have a good view from all sides. (Photo courtesy of Honeycomb Systems, Inc., San Juan Bautista, California.)

Photo 2-43. Hexagonal buildings can be built in clusters. This makes it easy to add on as the family grows or more funds become available. (Photo courtesy of Honeycomb Systems, Inc., San Juan Bautista, California.)

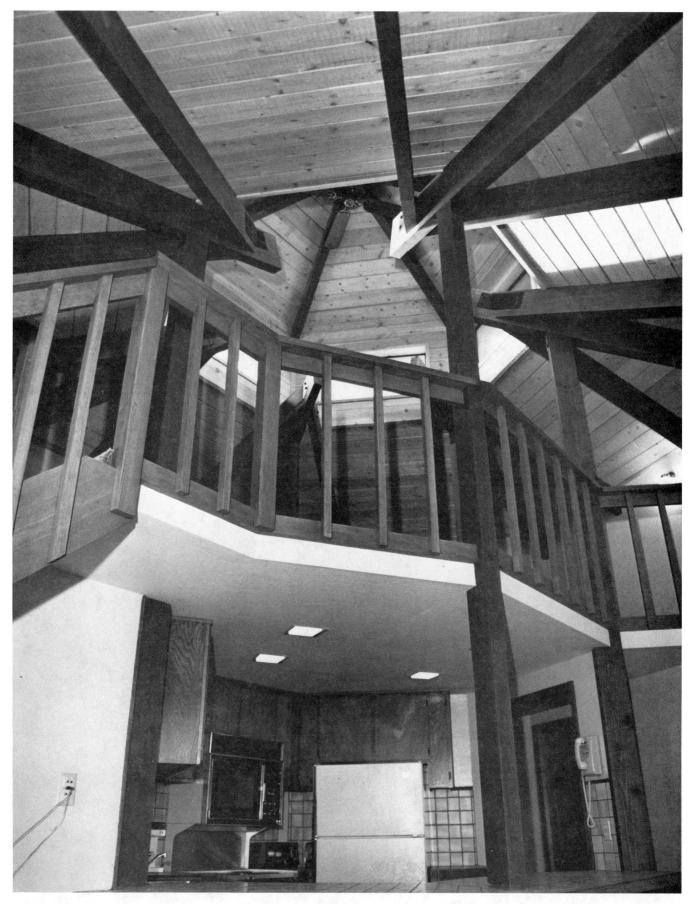

Photo 2-44. The interior of a hexagonal home. The large ceiling beams rest on the structural thrust ring, a feature which provides integral strength and flexibility to the hexagonal home. (Photo courtesy of Honeycomb Systems, Inc., San Juan Bautista, California.)

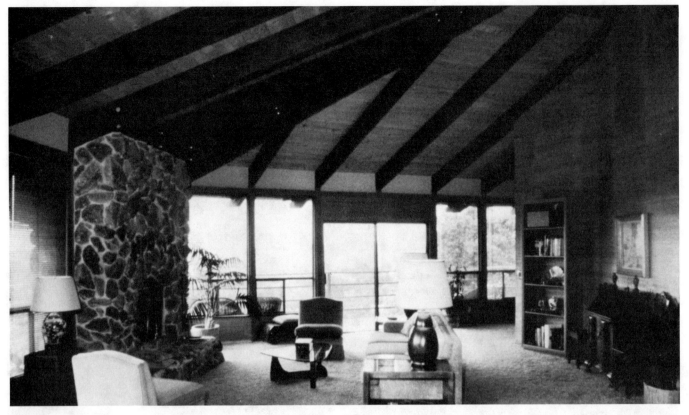

Photo 2-45. The interior of a hexagonal structure. Note the open spaces and the lack of right angles. (Photo courtesy of Honeycomb Systems, Inc., San Juan Bautista, California.)

Included in this chapter are pictures (Photos 2-46–2-51) of various styles of homes popular in different parts of the country.

Photo 2-46. Natural stone houses are rare, but permanent. These houses are labor-intensive, but beautiful.

Photo 2-47. Partial cut stone and post and beam structure.

Photo 2-48. Brick structures are common in some areas. Often stud frame houses are covered with a brick veneer.

Photo 2-49. Concrete block buildings are common in many areas. This one is in Florida where termites would pose a threat to wood frames.

Photo 2-50. A-frames are a quick, easy and inexpensive type of construction. I built this one in North Carolina in 2 months. It is 1200 square feet.

Photo 2-51. A house I built from a large wine barrel. Six inches of wine was left in it to create a "wine cellar."

3 Tools

The following section on tools was written by Mel Berry. Mel has taught people to remodel their homes for many years and is a licensed cabinet maker.

THE FIRST CONSIDERATION, before starting to build portions of a house, should be to get good quality tools and understand how to use them. Frequently those who have not done a large construction project have gathered a collection of "used" tools made up of other people's cast-offs, slightly broken and usually dull. They have been satisfactory for putting a door back on its hinges, cutting firewood, replacing a stair tread or a piece of decking, but now the greater task of many hours in housebuilding demands a careful evaluation of tools available and their condition. The most highly skilled craftsperson would not be able to do satisfactory work in a reasonable period of time if his tool collection was not as carefully developed as his work habits and practices. The pleasures of building and creating as a craftsperson will change to frustration if dull screwdrivers tear out screw slots; dull chisels cause errors and even injury because of excessive pressure and force; dull hand saws leave one's arm aching and hand blistered; and dull power cutting tools smoke, burn and kick back.

Buying Tools

A builder should get the best tools he can afford. Choosing well-known brands is probably safer for a novice. In comparing both power and hand tools, consider balance, weight, comfort and durability. An electric drill with too small a handle feels "top heavy." A 32-ounce framing hammer for a large person will drive nails quickly, but would be too much for a smaller person. A chisel with an all-plastic handle will not take as much pounding as a chisel with the steel of the blade extending all the way through the handle. In most cases the better tools will cost more, but it is a necessary expense and actually small, considering the size of the housebuilding project. Also, better tools frequently carry manufacturer's warranties and even lifetime guarantees. Once sharpened, good cutting tools keep a sharp edge. (Photo 3-1.)

Sharpening Tools

Most carpenters today have their saws sharpened by professional sharpening companies, but they sharpen their own plane irons, knives, screwdrivers and chisels. Regrinding plane irons, knives, and chisels is not usually needed unless the tool has hit a hard object during use and has chipped. If regrinding is necessary, it can be done by some saw sharpening shops or the carpenter can re-do the shape if he has his own bench grinder. For routine sharpening of tools, a craftsperson needs metal files, a combination bench stone and honing oil. Metal files are used for reshaping screwdrivers, hatchets, shovels, chainsaws and other tools. For some tools, filing is satisfactory sharpening. Other tools need honing on a bench stone.

A combination bench stone has a coarse side and a fine side. Use the same procedure for sharpening chisels and plane irons. With the bevel at the angle of the original grinding, move the tool in a figure 8 pattern over the surface of the stone until the edge is improved, usually about 30 to 40 strokes. Honing oil applied to the surface of the stone keeps the metal from filling the pores of the stone. Then turn the stone over and continue honing, using the fine side of the stone. The back or flat side of the tool is rarely ground or stoned, except for a few light strokes occasionally to remove

Photo 3-1. Avoid cheap tools. They can be dangerous when they fail.

the metal that curls over during sharpening, creating a burr. The figure 8 pattern on the stone is not essential, but helps to keep the oil distributed. If the stone gets "dirty," or clogged with sawdust, it must be cleaned with a solvent, such as kerosene. Other stones that can be used for fine honing include the natural Arkansas stones and Japanese water stones. After sharpening, a tool should be stored in a protective covering to keep its fine edge.

Basic Tools

These basic tools should be collected before attempting to build. They will all be needed frequently.

Combination stone	Nail sets
Metal files	Framing hammer
20- or 25-foot tape	Screwdrivers
Plumb bob	Phillips screwdrivers
Chalkline	Pliers
Pocket knife	Adjustable wrench
Utility knife	Block plane
Carpenter's pencil	4-in-1 file
Carpenter's square	Flat bar
Combination square	Nail claw
2-foot, 4-foot level	Twist bits
Crosscut saw	Spade bits
Rip saw	Circular saw
Coping saw	Sabre saw
Hacksaw	⅜ variable speed reversing
Wood chisels	belt sander
Cold chisels	Finishing sander
Diagonal cutting pliers	Heavy duty extension cord
Finishing hammer	Power drill
Speed Square	

Secondary Tools

Secondary tools have less frequent usage than the basic tools, but most of them should eventually be added to a builder's toolchest. Until then, they will have to be borrowed or rented when they are needed.

Bench grinder	Router and bits
50- or 100-foot tape	½-inch right angle drill
Builder's level or transit	Reciprocating saw
Sledge hammer	Power miter saw
Bit brace	Power plane
Hand drill	Com-a-long
Power auger bits	Rabbet plane
Forstner bits	Nail shooter
6-foot level	
Aviation snips	
Assorted files	
Ripping bar	
Countersink	

Specialized Tools

Specialized tools are infrequently needed tools, or an expensive purchase that can only be justified with a great deal of use on a single job or repeated professional usage.

Laser level	Pneumatic stapler and
Foundation stake puller	equipment
Hardwood flooring nailer	Radial arm saw
Shingle ripper	Table saw
Battery powered drill	Tool specialties from various
Pneumatic nailer and	trades
equipment	

Photo 3-2. Metal tapes are an essential. I recommend a 20- or 25-foot tape with a 1-inch blade.

Photo 3-3. Here is an example of using a plumb bob to see if a post is plumb. Note that a block is used at the top and bottom of the string to see if it is an equidistance from the post. Plumb bobs are also used to locate points directly below other points.

Layout Tools

STEEL TAPES (Photo 3-2) have largely replaced the folding wood rules for most people. The usual lengths are 20 or 25 feet for general measurement, and 50 or 100 feet for larger layout jobs. The most desirable width for rough carpentry is 1 inch, since it allows the worker to extend the tape further before it "buckles."

A PLUMB BOB (Photo 3-3) is necessary to determine a reference of straight up and down or right angles to the earth. While any heavy object suspended on the end of a string will determine this reference by gravity, usually a craftsperson will purchase a machined plumb bob for greater accuracy. The heavier a plumb bob is, the less it will be affected by the wind while it is being used.

A UTILITY KNIFE (Photo 3-4) should be of high quality steel and fit comfortably in your pocket. Some craftspeople, however, prefer to have a larger knife and keep it in their tool pouch or on their belts. The choice is yours, of course, but a knife is necessary to cut cord, mark closely around hinges for mortises, sharpen pencils, etc. Most craftspeople will also have a utility knife for general use.

The CARPENTER'S PENCIL (Photo 3-5) is a flat pencil with large lead. It is easy to sharpen, draws broad lines that are easy to see and it won't roll away.

The T-BEVEL (Photo 3-6) or bevel square has an adjustable blade which can be set to any angle. It is usually used to transfer angles from the work spot to the cutting tools.

The COMBINATION SQUARE (Photos 3-7, 3-8) has several uses. Frequently it is used to mark a 90° line across a board to follow when cutting or when joining another board to it. It will also measure a 45° angle, check for square, and measure and transfer depths and distances.

Photo 3-4. Utility knives are needed in many processes during construction, from cutting the layout strings to scoring the drywall. Be sure to get one that has a retractable blade; extra blades are stored in the body.

Photo 3-5. Carpenter's pencils are a must. They come in broad and narrow leads. Keep a supply on hand.

Photo 3-6. Using a sliding T-bevel to find an angle. This angle can then be transferred to the board you are cutting.

Photo 3-7. Using the combination square to mark a board at a 90° angle. This square can also be used to mark a 45° angle and to scribe the length of the board.

Photo 3-8. Using the combination square to mark a straight line down the length of the board. This method ensures that the line you are marking is an equidistance from the edge of the board even if the board is not straight.

Photo 3-9. Using a framing square to lay out a stair tread. Framing squares are used throughout the housebuilding process. Get a good one and be careful not to leave it lying around where it could get stepped on and bent. It is of no use once it is bent.

Photo 3-10. A chalkline is used to mark straight lines.

Photo 3-12. A torpedo level or 1-foot level comes in handy. It's being used here to level a pier block.

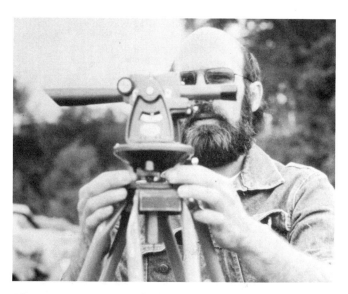

Photo 3-11. Using a 6-foot level to check the plumb of a post. Note the clips at the top and bottom of the level. These clips keep the level off the board which will have many irregularities and make it hard to determine true plumb. You will need a 2-foot and 4-foot level, and a 6-foot or 8-foot is advised.

Photo 3-13. Transits, or their cousins the builder's levels, are needed during the layout. You can rent these, but if you can afford one, they are very useful during many states of construction in checking for level and plumb.

The large CARPENTER'S SQUARE or FRAMING SQUARE (Photo 3-9) has many uses in addition to measuring squareness of work, as mentioned in other chapters of this book. Today most carpenters choose aluminum framing squares since they are lighter to handle. Some squares have one special scale measured in 12ths of an inch for reading scale drawings.

A CHALKLINE (Photo 3-10) is used to lay out straight lines for reference and assembly. It can be a length of line and a block of carpenter's chalk, or it can be a line inside a chalk box that applies powdered chalk as the string is drawn in and out.

Levelling Tools

A 4-FOOT LEVEL is used for spot checks of plumb and level. For more accurate measurements, a 6-FOOT LEVEL (Photo 3-11) is necessary. Some craftspeople extend the use of the

2-foot level by putting it on a longer straight edged board. A 1-FOOT LEVEL (Photo 3-12) can be used for levelling smaller surfaces.

A BUILDER'S LEVEL is not part of every carpenter's tool collection, but is essential for efficient layout of footings and foundation walls. The builder's level establishes a level line of sight; all points along that line of sight are the same as any other point.

The TRANSIT (Photo 3-13) has one more operating mode than the builder's level. It pivots up and down in a vertical plane and enables the operator to measure and transfer points in that plane. It can also be used to plumb work. These tools are expensive for one-time use and can be rented. (For an explanation on the use of a transit, see *Layout* chapter.)

A newer levelling device, the LASER LEVEL, projects a beam of coherent light onto surfaces for a reference indication. Laser levels, however, require electrical power, which may not be available in the initial layout of residential homes.

Photo 3-14. There are several different types of hand saws; their use depends on whether you are cutting across the grain (crosscut saw) or with the grain (rip saw). A finishing saw has teeth that are set closer together. You may want to buy a general combination saw that can cut in either direction.

Photo 3-15. Chisels are a must. I advise a ¼-inch, ½-inch, ¾-inch, 1-inch and a 1½-inch. Get the kind where the metal shaft extends all the way to the butt, as shown on the left. The metal shaft on the right is embedded in plastic and will not last as long.

Photo 3-16. Several kinds of hammers are needed during house construction, i.e., a framing hammer, finishing hammer, drywall hammer, etc. Use ones with fiberglass or wood handles.

Cutting Tools

SAWS (Photo 3-14). Today's craftsperson cuts mostly with electric tools, but a crosscut saw, with about 8 knife-shaped teeth per inch, is used when power is not available or convenient and when the round-cutting pattern of a circular saw is not acceptable. When cutting stair stringers for example, the circular blade will not cut completely into the corner of the layout (see section on stairs). A sharp crosscut saw may also outperform the circular saw if lengthy extension cord layout is necessary. A blade cover should be purchased or fabricated to prevent damage to the teeth. Finish saws are usually slightly shorter and may have up to 12 teeth per inch.

A RIPSAW cuts with the grain of the wood and has chisel-shaped teeth to keep the saw from following the grain. Nearly all ripping cuts today are done with a circular whenever possible.

A COPING SAW or hand jigsaw is used especially to shape moldings to fit. Its fine blade allows intricate cuts over short distances.

A HACKSAW is necessary to cut metal stock and can be used for wooden moldings.

WOOD CHISELS (Photo 3-15) from ¼ inch to 2 inches in width are necessary to remove stock for hinges, shaping openings and patterns. High quality steel is necessary to keep a sharp edge longer. Strong handles that will take hammer blows are essential for a carpenter since mallets are rarely available. A cold chisel is necessary to cut through nails and undesired metal pieces.

Assembling Tools

A HAMMER (Photo 3-16) is probably one of the first tools associated with carpenters. Many carpenters have several hammers for different purposes and enjoy their unique features.

FRAMING HAMMERS are available in weights from 16 to 32 ounces with ripping and curved claws. Although few people find the heaviest weights comfortable, choose the heaviest hammer that can be used without tiring. The straight or ripping claw is useful for driving between pieces and as a lever. The curved claw gives more nail-pulling leverage. Framing hammers are also available with waffled faces to prevent slipping from the nail. FINISHING HAMMERS have smooth faces and range in weight from 7 to 16 ounces. Curved and rip claws are available. A general purpose hammer that could be used for both framing and finish work would have a smooth face and a 16-ounce head.

SCREWDRIVERS are necessary for both Phillips and slotted screws. Various sizes of each screwdriver are also necessary to fit all the screws used in construction. Standard screwdrivers are sized by the length of the blades and the size of the tips. Phillips screwdriver sizes refer to the size of the tips and are numbered from 0 to 4. A Number 2 Phillips screwdriver is the most common and will fit most Phillips screws, but other sizes will eventually be necessary to insure a proper fit on all screws.

Photo 3-17. This tool works much like the plane.

Photo 3-18. Above are various types of nail-pulling tools. Needless to say, it is highly recommended that all novice owner builders have a complete assortment as shown here. They will be well used. From left to right: large flat bar (wonder bar), small crowbar, cat's paw, small flat bar and a large and small set of nail clippers.

Photo 3-19. Shown here are some large wrecking and timber moving tools. It is a good idea to have the full assortment at the job site. From left to right: a hand winch (com-a-long), a sledge and a large crowbar.

Pliers and Wrenches

PLIERS are needed to hold steel pieces and fasteners during assembly.

For careful construction, nuts and bolts should have wrenches of appropriate size; however, a high quality AD-JUSTABLE WRENCH is very valuable in holding a variety of pieces.

Smoothing Tools

The BLOCK PLANE is necessary for jobs such as shaving small amounts from a door, window, or a finish piece of wood. While power planes are replacing the larger sizes of hand planes, the control necessary for small adjustments and shaping makes it important to always have a block plane handy. (Photo 3-17.)

Several files of various shapes, sizes and coarseness are desirable. The most universal file for wood is a 4-IN-1 FILE. This file has 4 different surfaces which are quickly available in one tool, and it is easily carried in a tool belt. One side has coarse and fine flat surfaces. The other side has coarse and fine curved surfaces.

Prying and Wrecking Tools

The RIPPING BAR, also called a wrecking bar or pry bar, is used to pull previously nailed pieces apart, withdraw nails and lever pieces into place.

A FLAT BAR is used to remove trim and molding, separate previously nailed framing pieces, and withdraw nails. It can be driven between pieces with a hammer and pried straight back or to the side to separate pieces.

The NAIL CLAW, also called a CAT'S PAW (Photo 3-18), is driven into the wood under the head of a nail to start to pry it out. Further prying is done with a hammer, flat bar or wrecking bar. Both novices and pros make mistakes, so have one of these in your tool box.

SLEDGE HAMMERS (Photo 3-19) are necessary to drive stakes, wreck or move framing.

Boring Tools

Most holes are drilled with ELECTRIC DRILLS today, and some drill motors are battery powered. Bit braces and hand drills are useful only when electricity is not available or convenient. The type of hole necessary determines the bit that is used. For holes up to ½ inch in diameter, machine or twist bits are frequently used. These bits are useful for metal or wood cutting. For larger holes, spade or power bore bits can be used. However, to cut a truly round hole, remove chips quickly, and drive easily, a power auger bit is used.

POWER AUGERS are used with large drill motors at lower speeds. When very accurate holes with crisp edges are needed, as for exposed dowels or plugs, a craftsperson can use FORSTNER BITS. When screw heads must be flush or below the surface, holes are first drilled with a countersink (Photo 3-20).

Photo 3-20. Nail sets or nail punches are available in different sized tips to countersink different sized nails.

Photo 3-21. Metal legs for saw horses are easy to use and more secure than wooden legs.

Power Tools

The CIRCULAR SAW (Photo 3-22–Photo 3-27) is usually one of the first power tools purchased. It is necessary to efficiently cut framing pieces. Since the saw will be used frequently it is important to choose a high quality tool that feels comfortable. The blade must always be sharp to prevent overloading the tool, damaging the work or causing a kickback toward the operator. To keep a sharp blade on the tool, some craftspeople choose carbide tipped blades which keep their keen edge longer. However with the rough service sometimes demanded of a blade, you may choose to have many less expensive steel blades to change frequently and have some at the saw shop for resharpening. Resharpening costs for steel blades are less.

Most Common Mistake

Setting a board *between* two supports to be cut. As the board droops during the cut it binds the blade and causes the saw to kick back.

Photo 3-22. Circular saws have come a long way from this original one.

Photo 3-23. The power circular saw is perhaps the most commonly used power tool during the housebuilding process. Be sure to choose one that will last and that feels comfortable to you. The model above is referred to as a "sidewinder" as opposed to a "worm drive" model. Try them both and see which feels more comfortable.

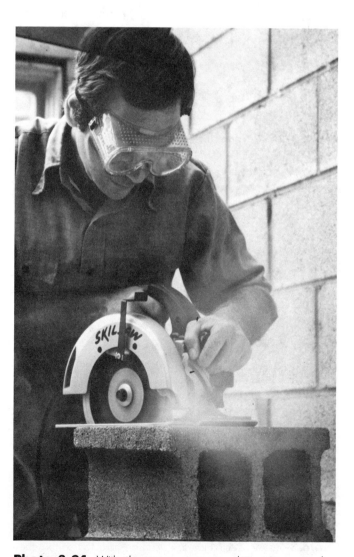

Photo 3-24. With the proper masonry bit, power circular saws can be used to cut concrete block and brick.

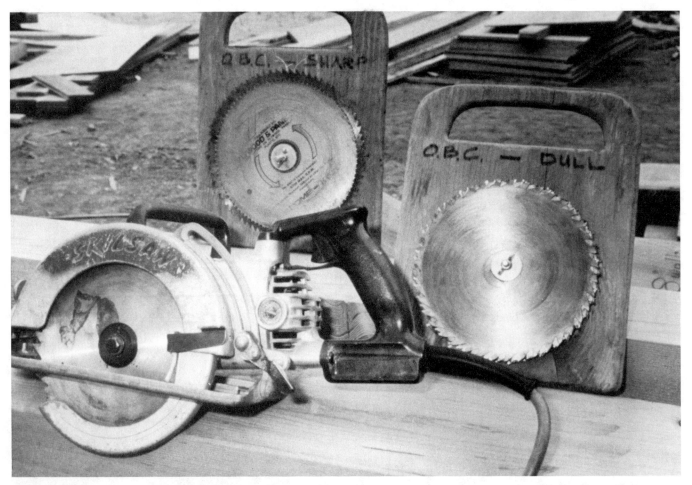

Photo 3-25. A worm drive saw with blades. Note how dull blades are separated from the sharp blades on plywood boards. Have a good assortment of blades, both carbide tipped and standard.

Photo 3-26. Most circular saws can be adjusted so that the saw is at an angle to the cutting platform. This allows you to bevel cut the board up to 45°.

Photo 3-27. This 5½-inch circular saw is good for cutting paneling, siding and trim. Not necessary, but useful if you can afford it.

The SABRE SAW (Photo 3-28) is a portable jigsaw used for cutting a variety of materials and shapes. Blades are available for cutting wood, plywood, metal and plastics. The tool is useful for making cutouts in the center of building materials, including sheets of plywood and laminated countertops. Because the sabre saw has a very small blade, it is also very useful in making curved cuts.

Helpful Hints and Most Common Mistakes

☐ Finished surfaces such as plastic laminates can be scratched by the base of the sabre saw. Covering the base of the saw with tape will prevent damage.

☐ Be careful not to pinch a finger between the blade chuck and the body of the tool while it is operating.

☐ Choose the appropriate saw blade to insure a fast and smooth cut.

ELECTRIC DRILLS (Photo 3-29–Photo 3-31). The most universal drill for a carpenter is a ⅜-inch, variable speed, reversing drill. This tool allows bits up to ⅜ inch to be used for drilling. Occasional larger holes can be done with wide power bits with smaller shanks. For continued large hole boring and heavy-duty use, a more powerful ½-inch drill is more appropriate. As chuck capacities go up, drills are designed to turn more slowly to produce more torque with less likelihood of operator injury if the bit should jam.

It is also possible to use this ⅜-inch drill with a screwdriver tip (usually Phillips) in the chuck to make it a power screwdriver. The variable speed trigger plus forward and reverse features provide ample control.

Photo 3-28. A jigsaw is very useful at most building sites. It can cut curves and angles and fancy scrolls.

Photo 3-29. ¼-inch drills are handy for smaller projects, but usually ⅜-inch or ½-inch drills are used for larger jobs.

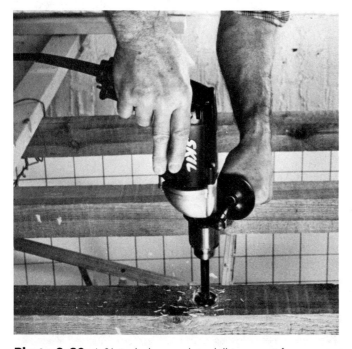

Photo 3-30. A ⅜-inch, heavy-duty drill is a must for anyone planning to do their own plumbing and electricity.

Photo 3-31. Cordless, rechargeable drills are handy during all stages of construction.

Photo 3-32. Small cordless screwdrivers are a new tool on the market. They come in very handy in many phases of building.

The BELT SANDER (Photos 3-33, 3-34) has a cloth-backed abrasive belt that travels between the two wheels of the tool. The base of the tool is flat steel and if the tool is held level, it will remove uneven and rough material, and create a surface ready for finish sanding. Practice and skillful handling are essential to the operation of this tool, so get a "feel" for the tool on a piece of scrap stock before sanding the finish piece.

Sanding should always be done by using progressively finer grits of abrasive belts and paper. Each finer grit removes the scratches of the previous grit until the desired finish is achieved.

Helpful Hints and Most Common Mistakes

☐ Belt sanders must be held level to achieve good results. Often it is necessary, when doing surfaces with pieces cut out of them, to imagine a completed surface and hold the belt sander to the imagined plane. Dipping the sander into the openings or applying more pressure to the corners will cause gouging of the work.

☐ Belt sanders must be kept moving from area to area or the belt will dig in.

☐ Sanding belts are usually directional and putting belts on backwards tears the seams. Some non-directional belts, however, allow additional sharp usage by reversing them.

Photo 3-33. A heavy-duty belt sander like this is usually not needed in a typical housebuilding process. It is used for large sanding jobs where the weight of the machine is needed to make sanding easier.

Photo 3-34. The belt sander is used for larger sanding jobs. Wearing safety glasses as shown is recommended whenever you are using any power tool. If you wear glasses, use hardened glass or plastic.

The FINISHING SANDER or PAD SANDER (Photo 3-35) is useful in smoothing away tool marks and wood fillers. Some are available with orbital and "in-line" motions. Orbital action removes stock more quickly, while "in-line" action allows sanding with the grain of the wood for a smoother finish. Finishing sanders have a cushioned base of felt or rubber, and are designed for smoothing. To remove a lot of material and make a flat surface the belt sander is used.

Helpful Hints and Most Common Mistakes

☐ Different level wood joints sanded to flat with a finish sander will be smooth, but not flat and straight.

☐ Trim wood should be sanded with a grit of sandpaper as high as 220 to remove machine marks that will be evident when the stain is applied; but sanding with too fine a grit can burnish the wood cells closed and cause a blotchy stain effect. The highest sanding grits are used between coats of finish.

Additional Tools

ROUTERS (Photo 3-36) are basically edge-forming tools, but with additional guides they can be used to cut grooves, rabbets, dadoes and mortises for hinges. A collection of bits for routers can frequently exceed the cost of the router itself. Bits are available from high-speed steel or carbide-tipped steel. When pilot tips are part of the cutter, steel bits have a fixed pilot and carbide cutters usually have ball bearing pilots. The carbide cutters stay sharp longer, cut more cleanly, and the ball bearing pilots do not burn the wood. For infrequently used profiles, the steel bits allow a greater variety of cutters at a more economical price.

Helpful Hints and Most Common Mistakes

☐ The base of the router must be kept flat to the board during use to insure profile accuracy.

☐ Since the cutter revolves in a clockwise direction (as seen from the top) the router should be moved from right to left to move the cutter into the work. A full-depth cut from left to right will cause the cutter to "climb" the wood and start to self-feed; however, a shallow precut from left to right followed by a full depth cut from right to left will prevent splintering on difficult woods.

☐ Rapid movement can cause splintering of the wood. Slow movement with solid steel pilots will cause the cutter to burn the wood. Practice on a scrap of wood to develop the proper technique.

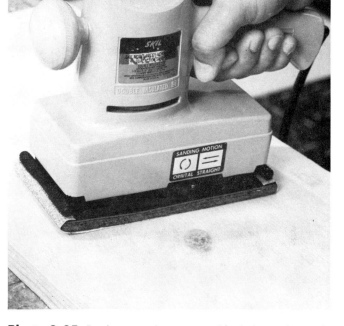

Photo 3-35. Finishing sanders are used for lightweight sanding such as furniture refinishing. Many people use them when sanding dry wall as well.

Photo 3-36. A router is an excellent finishing tool. It can round edges, make different types of grooves, finish formica, etc.

Photo 3-37. A heavy-duty extension cord with a four-way junction box is essential.

Photo 3-38. Many professionals use a locking plug as shown here. This male plug takes a corresponding female adapter. Once inserted and twisted, the plugs are locked together and will not pull apart. You may want to consider changing your regular plugs on your commonly used tools to this style.

HEAVY-DUTY EXTENSION CORD (Photos 3-37, 3-38). Along with the purchase of your first portable power tool should come the purchase of a heavy-duty (large wire diameter and heavily insulated) extension cord. When power must run a long distance to the tool, it loses effectiveness with small cords and can damage the tool. Nor will a small cord stand up to the wear and tear of use on a job site. Local safety requirements may dictate that the cord and tool be outfitted with twist-locking plugs, as shown, for secure connections.

A heavy-duty ½-INCH DRILL is essential for those who do their own plumbing and electrical work, and very desirable for boring long or frequent large holes for bolts and other fasteners. A right angle drill allows the operator to get in between framing members easily.

Helpful Hints and Most Common Mistakes

☐ Many bits used for drilling large holes have self-feeding pilot screws that assist in drawing the cutting edges into the wood. Care should be taken to keep face and hands clear of projecting handles. Frequently, injuries occur when a bit binds in a hole and the tool is wrenched from the operator's hands.

☐ Bit extensions and long bits are available to drill through several studs in one pass.

☐ When drilling deep holes, withdraw the drill bit occasionally to clear the chips.

The **RECIPROCATING SAW** (Photo 3-39) is similar to a sabre saw but much heavier in construction. It is the surgery tool of house construction. It is used to carve out holes for vents, cut openings for lights and other objects, notch studs for plumbing or electrical wires, and modify existing framing. Metal blades will cut nails, pipe, conduit and other pieces. It is an all-purpose saw, and its long-bladed snout allows the operator to reach into otherwise inaccessible areas.

Helpful Hints and Most Common Mistake

☐ Reciprocating saws bounce less and break fewer blades if the saw guide of the tool can be held tightly to the material.

POWER MITER SAWS (Photo 3-40) have largely replaced hand miter boxes in the woodworking shops and at construction sites. Nicknamed "chopsaws," they easily cut through material as thick as framing stock, bringing cabinet shop accuracy to the field, for clean miters on casings, handrails and all moldings. By setting a block to butt against, power miter boxes can be used to cut many pieces to the same length or angle without repeating measurements.

Helpful Hints and Most Common Mistake

☐ The power miter saw should not be overused. Straight cuts for framing that do not require this accuracy should be made with the circular saw at the spot they will be used. This saves time and handling effort.

A **POWER PLANE** quickly smoothes surfaces and trims materials to size. It is operated in the same manner as a hand plane, but since the rotating cutters smooth the surface, the tool moves more easily and the motion is not affected by knots or irregular grain.

Helpful Hints and Most Common Mistakes

☐ The blades are exposed on the bottom of a planer and subject to damage if they come in contact with a hard surface, while running or not.

☐ When starting cuts, pressure should be applied more to the front of the tool. When completing cuts, pressure should be applied more to the rear of the tool.

Photo 3-39. The reciprocating saw has a knife-like blade that protrudes from the front of the saw and cuts in a back-and-forth direction. When you need this tool, nothing else will do.

Photo 3-40. A power mitre saw (chopsaw) is a professional tool used for finishing work. You may want to rent one or buy one if you are building a large custom house.

Photo 3-41. Pneumatic tools, powered by compressed air, make many jobs quicker and easier. A professional tool, they can usually be rented at certain phases of construction.

Photo 3-42. A radial arm or contractor's saw is useful both during the framing and finishing stages. It is expensive and not necessary for a one-house project, but very useful if you can afford it.

PNEUMATIC TOOLS (Photo 3-41). Pneumatic (air driven) tools such as staplers and nailers are available to increase production. When a good hand rhythm is achieved, work goes quickly and smoothly. To operate pneumatic tools, the tool must be connected with an air hose to a compressor. This air hose "umbilical" is restrictive and of questionable value, especially considering the investment necessary for a single house.

Some contractors find pneumatic tools useful, however, for multiple units and large square footage jobs such as siding and roofing, and some framing sub-assemblies. The decision to use pneumatic tools or not depends on the job conditions, craftspeople, project design and total square footage. Pneumatic tools are enjoyable to use, less tiring, fast and effective, but not essential.

RADIAL ARM SAW (Photo 3-42). One of the first stationary power tools for many people is the radial arm saw. It is useful on the construction site for cutting beams, repetitious framing pieces, angles and compound angles. This saw is basically designed to draw the blade across (crosscutting) the wood. Ripping (cutting with the grain) in the long direction of a board is usually done with a portable circular saw or table saw.

Most Common Mistake

☐ Since the radial arm saw is a stationary tool the work must be brought to the tool. Making too many cuts with this saw, especially when work must be transported from another floor, is very time-consuming. Unless there is unusual thickness or angles, or a need for extreme accuracy is involved, the circular saw should be used for framing.

The TABLE SAW (Photo 3-43–Photo 3-46) excels at cutting sheet stock such as plywood, and cutting the long way of a board (ripping). It is more difficult to cut across the grain (crosscut) on a table saw since the whole board must be moved across the blade. For carpenters who will be doing their own cabinets and built-ins, a table saw will be very useful.

Most Common Mistake

☐ The table saw is outfitted with two guides to use in cutting stock, a miter gauge used at angles to the blade and a rip fence which is parallel to the blade. When cutting stock, choose the guide that will allow the longest edge of the stock to be against the guide. Do not have the stock touching both the miter gauge and the rip fence while cutting, or binding and kickback may occur.

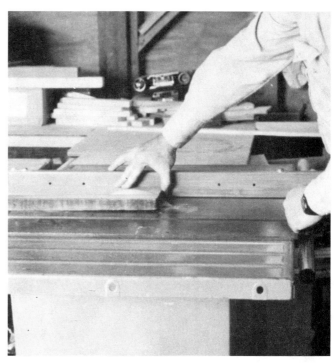

Photo 3-43. Table saws are excellent for doing trim and finishing and cabinet work. They are not a required tool for the one-time owner builder, but are useful if you can afford them. The one above is a smaller homeowner's model. It should be all that is needed for a one-house project.

Photo 3-44. Large bench saws are not essential, but very useful if available.

Photo 3-45. Table saws can use dado blades to make grooves like these. Many other blades are also available.

Photo 3-46. Band saws are used mostly in finishing and sculpturing work. They are useful for cutting angles and curving pieces of wood. You can probably get by with the hand-held equivalent, the jig or sabre saw.

Photo 3-48. Shop vacuum cleaners are useful, especially during construction stages.

Photo 3-47. This "Xtra-tool" is several tools in one. It can serve as an electric screwdriver or drill, as well as a hammer-drill, or hammerchisel. It can drill into brick or concrete, chisel or gouge wood, and be used to remove paint or linoleum as well as chip concrete. A useful tool.

Specialized Tools

Specialized tools are not part of everyone's toolchest. They have specific purposes and are seldom needed, but essential when they are needed. You may want to buy, borrow or rent these tools. Also a tour of the local tool rental shop may find a tool you would like to have occasionally. A FOUNDATION STAKE PULLER saves time and money, for instance, but is a one-day need.

Other tools to consider are the com-a-long and hardwood floor nailer. A COM-A-LONG is a device with a cable and ratcheting handle used to pull framing sections into square and plumb. The FLOOR NAILER holds and aligns the nails along the edge of hardwood flooring. It drives a nail when struck with a hammer or mallet.

Additional hand tools with specialized purposes are the SHINGLE RIPPER for removing nails during roofing repairs, RABBET PLANE for shaping rabbet cuts in wood and a NAIL SHOOTER for driving nails in difficult spots.

Hundreds of tools also exist that are used for special trades only. Drywallers, carpet layers, tilesetters, roofers, plumbers, electricians and others have occasional need for more specialized tools. To become familiar with all the tools available, visit the trade supply distributors. While a one-time need will not justify a complete extension of your tool collection for every trade, some special tools may be helpful. (Photos 3-47, 3-48).

Layout

Figure 4-1. Example of a typical layout and its relationship to the foundation (dotted lines). Layout lines occur directly above the exterior edge of the foundation wall and over the interior foundation piers.

What You'll Be Doing, What to Expect

THE LAYOUT OR FOUNDATION LAYOUT, as it is sometimes called, is a process of suspending strings in the air over the building site. (See Figure 4-1.) These strings, called layout lines, indicate the exact edge of the future foundation walls as well as their exact corners. In addition to demarcating the perimeters and the corners of the foundation, the lines are all exactly level, thereby superimposing a level line on an otherwise irregular site. These lines are then used to build the foundation level. The structures that support these lines are called batterboards. Additional lines are run to indicate any interior foundation piers or walls. Lines are also used if you are planning foundation piers for the exterior walls instead of a continuous foundation. (See Photo 4-1.)

This process is one of the more mentally demanding processes in building, so be sure that you understand it well before beginning. Physically, it is a rather simple process, except for hammering the vertical supports into the ground, which can be difficult if the ground is hardpan. (In this case, some builders use round metal stakes as vertical uprights for the batterboards.) Mentally, the process is rather trying because it is essential that the layout be accurate as the foundation will be built from these lines. The process is one of trial and error and demands you keep working with it until the lines are level and accurate.

Since the batterboards and strings will eventually be taken down, there is a tendency not to do a good job or make the batterboards stable. Be careful of this tendency; the foundation will be off if the batterboards shift at all. Besides, you want to set healthy, high-quality building standards for yourself from the beginning.

Photo 4-1. A job site with the batterboards and layout lines in place and the foundation trenches dug.

Jargon

BATTERBOARDS. Temporary, wooden framework on which the layout lines or strings are attached.

BENCHMARK. A permanent mark on a stable object, such as a tree or the side of a building, to be used as a constant reference from which to compute elevations or levels.

BUILDER'S LEVEL. Telescope mounted on a tripod used in levelling and determining angles of wall.

CROSSMEMBER. The horizontal piece of the batterboards.

DUPLEX or FORM NAIL. A doubleheaded nail used in situations where the nails will be removed.

FOOTING. Concrete pad or support under the foundation wall or pier.

LAYOUT LINES. Strings suspended in the air, used to locate the perimeter and the corners of the foundation and as a level reference.

LEVEL. Perfectly horizontal.

PLUMB. Perfectly vertical.

PLUMB BOB. A heavy pointed weight on a string used to determine plumb or true vertical.

SETBACK. The regulated distance that a building is allowed to be built from the property line, easement line, road right of way, etc.

TRANSIT. Same as the builder's level but can also tilt up and down.

Purposes of the Layout

1) To locate the exact perimeters (outside edges) and corners of the foundation
2) To superimpose a level line on an otherwise sloping irregular site which will be used as a level reference during construction of the foundation
3) To assist in determining correct angles for intersecting walls
4) To serve as a guide for digging foundation trenches and erecting foundation form boards

Design Decisions

Before beginning your layout process, there is much to consider as to the exact location of the house. The subject of setting a home can fill a book on its own. Much has to be taken into account: solar, wind, privacy, view, setback requirements, parking, etc. Do not shortchange the setting process of the home; it is a crucial decision. Since I have discussed this subject thoroughly in our first book, *Before You Build* (Ten Speed Press, 1981), I will not go into it here. You must, however, be sure to consider all facets of the decision well before layout.

What You'll Need

TIME   24 to 32 person-hours per 1000 square feet of floor space on a relatively flat site, with a relatively simple house design.

PEOPLE   2 Minimum (1 skilled, 1 unskilled); 4 Optimum (2 skilled, 2 unskilled); 4 Maximum (1 skilled, 3 unskilled).

TOOLS   Levelling tool (builder's level, water or hydro level), hand or power saw, framing hammer, 3 metal tapes (one 100-foot tape), 4-foot level, knife, plumb bob, sledge hammer.
RENTAL ITEMS: Transit (optional)

MATERIALS   2-×-4 vertical supports, 1-×-4 horizontal cross members, short 2-×-2 pointed stakes, nylon string, 8d duplex nails, 8d standard nails.

INFORMATION   This chapter should give you everything you need for a typical house layout.

PEOPLE TO CONTACT   You may need to contact work people or suppliers you plan to use in the upcoming stages of construction.

INSPECTIONS NEEDED   Some subdivisions or local permit agencies may want to check your layout before you start to dig to be sure it does not encroach into setbacks or present other problems as to the siting of the house.

Reading the Plans

Your plans will tell you all you need to know about your foundation and thereby your layout. Your site plan will tell you the location of your house on your site. Be sure you have met any setback requirements as to frontyards and backyards, there is enough distance between the house and the septic tank or well, and there is room for parking and the driveway. It is imperative to know exactly where your property lines are if you are building close to your borders. I know a couple who spent $1200 for a 2-×-100-foot piece of their neighbor's lot because they inadvertently built too close.

In addition to the site plan, the floor plans, foundation plans and structural plans will provide all the information you need for the layout.

Safety and Awareness

SAFETY: Be careful using the sledge, especially when someone is holding a vertical stake for you. Have them wear a hard hat and hold the stake a good distance below the top. Using gloves to hold the stake is also advised. Warn the person holding the stake not to look at the top in case there are flying splinters.

AWARENESS: Exactness is required throughout the process. Take your time. Be exact. Be careful not to upset the transit or batterboards once they are set. Be sure the batterboards are securely built. Remember it is a process of trial and error.

Overview of the Procedure

Step 1: Check the property lines
Step 2: Establish corner "A"
Step 3: Set up transit over corner "A"
Step 4: Locate approximate corner "B"
Step 5: Build batterboards behind corners "A" and "B"
Step 6: Run string directly over corners "A" and "B"
Step 7: Transfer corner "A" to string
Step 8: Measure along string "AB" to exact corner "B"
Step 9: Sight transit along string "AB"
Step 10: Rotate transit 90°
Step 11: Locate approximate corner "D"
Step 12: Build batterboards behind corner "D"
Step 13: Locate where string "AD" crosses batterboards at corner "D"
Step 14: Locate exact corner "D"
Step 15: Check intersecting lines using a 3-4-5 triangle
Step 16: Locate approximate corner "C"
Step 17: Build batterboards behind corner "C"
Step 18: Move transit to corner "B"
Step 19: Sight along wall "AB"
Step 20: Locate where string "BC" crosses batterboards at corner "C"
Step 21: Run string over corners "B" and "C"
Step 22: Measure along string "BC" to locate exact corner "C"
Step 23: Run string over corners "C" and "D"
Step 24: Check by measuring the diagonals
Step 25: Do layout for interior piers or walls

36.00'   34.18'

C   30' front setback

north

solar north

plan north

property line to front wall of house

56'0"

driveway

34'

32'

30'

28'

26'

existing contours

18" oak

20'

parking for 2 cars

20'

graded contours

24'

22'

A   5' side setback

5' side setback

150.54'

HOUSE
finished floor + 25.00'

E

roof overhang dashed

148.00'

D   7'6" drain easement

20'

12'0" to house

30" oak

6" oak

6" oak

18'

lot #672

lot #671

16'

B   23' rear setback

pedestrian & drain easement

80.69'

A side setback
B rear setback
C front setback
D easements
E roof overhang

Figure 4-2. Transit.

Using the Transit

Before beginning the layout, it might be useful to become acquainted with the transit. This section has been added to show you how to use a transit and make you feel more comfortable with the idea of using one if you have never worked with one before.

Diagrams: Figures 4-2, 4-3.

Photographs: Photos 4-2, 4-3, 4-4.

The builder's level and the transit are very similar instruments, with the transit scope having the added capability of tilting. In our example, we will be using the transit and you will see how this ability to tilt comes in handy during the layout. If you are using a builder's level, you will have to make some adjustments at certain places where a tilting scope is needed; otherwise their uses are identical.

When using either instrument, first set the tripod on the ground. Adjust the sliding legs until the mounting plate is relatively level. Be sure that the pointed legs are securely embedded into the earth. If the instrument moves during the layout, it must be reset.

After the tripod is securely in the ground, attach the transit to it. You are now ready to adjust the transit so that the telescope is exactly level in any direction it is turned. Begin by turning the telescope so that it is directly over two of the adjusting screws. Now, turning the screws slowly and both at the same speed, either towards each other or away from each other, adjust them until the spirit level is exactly level and the feet of both adjustment screws are on the transit base. (See Photo 4-2.)

After the scope is adjusted over these first two screws, turn the scope 90° to the other two screws and adjust them in the same way. Turn the scope and adjust until both spirit

levels read exactly level in any direction the scope points. This could take some time, so be patient. Never force the adjusting screws as they strip easily. Never tighten them too much; you can warp the base plate.

Experiment with the transit. Looking through the scope you will note crosshairs. Look at an object and adjust the focus as if you were to drive a nail into that object exactly where the crosshairs meet. Swinging the scope to a new object, do the same. The two nails should be exactly level to each other. In this way, the transit is used to find exactly level points.

The transit can easily be used to find true right angles of intersecting walls. To use it, first twist the horizontal circle until it is at 0°, using the zero line of the index pointer as the mark. Turn the telescope and you will be able to see what

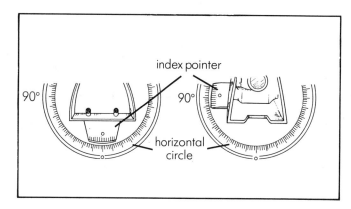

Figure 4-3. Rotating transit 90°, as viewed from above.

angle from the original line of sight you have turned by reading it on the horizontal circle, using the zero line of the index pointer as the mark. Locate a mark on an object using the scope and the crosshairs. Set the horizontal circle at zero and turn the scope until the zero lines of the index pointer read 90° on the horizontal circle. Look through the scope at another object and set a mark at the crosshairs. Lines coming to the transit from these points and intersecting at the transit would be at right angles. In this way, the transit can be used to find any angle size.

There are some other knobs and gizmos on the transit for fine turning and locking the instrument in place. Get acquainted with these before you begin the layout. If you are renting or borrowing a transit, check to see if it has been recently calibrated. If it has been badly taken care of, it will give inaccurate readings which can greatly affect the quality of your work. Be sure to treat the transit gently and with care at all times. It is a precision tool and can easily become misaligned if badly treated.

You might consider buying one of these tools, or at least having access to one, as they are useful for finding exact levels throughout the construction of the house.

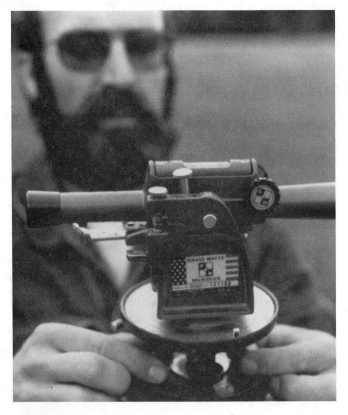

Photo 4-2. Level a transit by adjusting 2 opposing levelling screws. Note bubble level on top of transit.

Photo 4-3. Making fine adjustment on the transit.

Step 1
Check the Property Lines

Before beginning the layout, make one final check of the house's location on the lot. Be careful to inspect any property line setbacks if you are building close to the borders of the property. If there are setback requirements by the inspection office or subdivision, are you within these? Do they refer to roof overhangs? Decks? Foundations? (Your house could look funny with all the eaves hacked off on one side.) Are you properly aligned for solar use? For view? For shade? Give it one final review. A total site evaluation should have been done before this. Some permit offices or subdivisions will want to check your layout lines before you begin to dig. See if this is so in your area.

Step 2
Establish Corner "A"

Margin of Error: Exactly where you want it.

Most Common Mistakes: Not starting at highest corner; not siting house properly.

Diagram: Figure 4-4.

Determine exactly where corner "A" will be. At this point drive a 2×2 stake securely into the ground with a nail in the center of the stake. This nail will mark the exact corner "A." It is usually best to choose the highest corner to begin with, so you will not run into the ground elsewhere in the layout. *You now have one definite corner, corner "A."*

Photo 4-4. The index pointer and horizontal circle are both set at zero before rotating transit 90°. Be very exact.

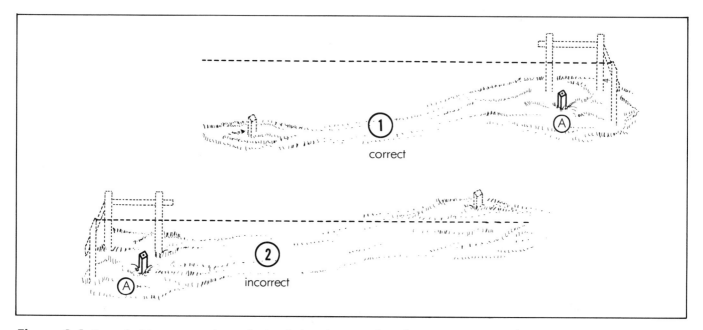

Figure 4-4. Example 1 is correct as layout lines will clear the ground at all points. Example 2 is incorrect as lines are too low at high corner.

Step 3
Set Up Transit Over Corner "A"

Margin of Error: Exactly over the point and exactly level.

Most Common Mistakes: Transit not level; transit not directly over nail in stake "A"; tripod legs not set securely into ground.

Photograph: Photo 4-5.

Set the transit up exactly over corner "A," aligning the point of the plumb bob that hangs from the center of the transit with the nail in stake "A." Using the method shown in the section called "Using the Transit" at the beginning of this chapter, level the transit and lock in place.

Step 4
Locate Approximate Corner "B"

Margin of Error: Approximate corner, but you are fixing wall "AB" permanently.

Most Common Mistake: Not fixing wall "AB" where you want it.

Diagram: Figure 4-5.

Determine which wall you want to lay out first (wall AB). Using a long steel tape and beginning at the nail in stake "A," measure out the distance along the wall line "AB" to your approximate corner "B." Drive a stake into the ground at this point and drive a nail into the top of the stake. This corner is approximate because you have no way as of yet to ascertain if you are holding the tape exactly level. This can throw your

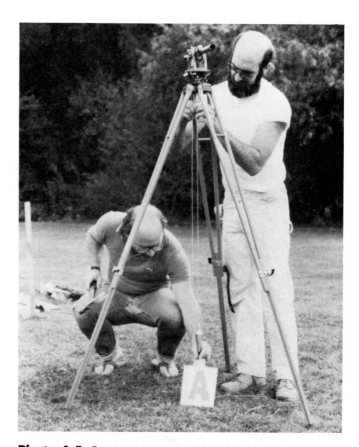

Photo 4-5. Positioning a transit directly above corner "A." Usually you set up the transit and then locate corner "A" directly below.

measurement off. You are, however, fixing wall "AB" by setting this point. Exactly where along this wall corner "B" will fall is still undetermined. *You now have a definite corner "A," an approximate corner "B," and a definite wall "AB."*

Figure 4-5. Locate the approximate corner "B" by measuring the distance of wall "AB" from point "A." Hold the tape as level as possible.

Figure 4-6. Typical 2-section batterboards used when digging with heavy equipment.

Step 5
Build Batterboards Behind "A" and "B"

Margin of Error: Horizontal cross members of the batterboards must be exactly level and all at the same level. The vertical stakes of the cross members do not have to be exactly plumb but they must be securely set.

Most Common Mistakes: Cross members not level with each other; batterboards too close to the corner; batterboards not securely built.

Diagrams: Figures 4-6, 4-7, 4-8, 4-9, 4-10.

Photographs: Photos 4-6, 4-7, 4-8.

The diagrams show different aspects of a typical batterboard. You will be building these behind all corners of the house using the same procedure as shown here. Note that these batterboards use 2×4s for the vertical pieces and 1×4s for the horizontal members. This is fairly typical. Two-section

Figure 4-7. Typical 1-section batterboards used for hand digging or a careful backhoe operator.

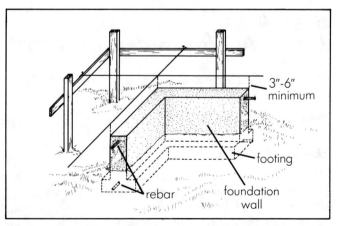

Figure 4-8. Note that layout lines are at least 3"-6" above foundation wall at its highest point. Forms and foundation will be built below these lines. Note lines directly above exterior edge of wall.

batterboards are often used to keep batterboards well behind foundation trenches, especially when using heavy equipment for digging.

The most essential part of building the batterboards is that all the horizontal cross members be exactly the same level. This is where the transit comes into play. First you must determine at what level you want the top of the cross members to be. Your layout strings will be running over the top of the horizontal cross members so the cross members will determine the level of the layout lines. If all of the cross members are at the same level, the layout strings will be level.

The layout strings should run at least 3 to 6 inches higher than the top of the proposed foundation wall; out of the way, but close enough so they can be used throughout construction of the foundation as a guide to check the level and location of the foundation forms. The foundation should be at least 18 inches above the ground at the highest corner. Check your local code on this. (I recommend increasing this minimum distance to 24 inches; it protects the wood of the house better and allows for a higher crawlspace in which to work beneath the house.) If your foundation has to be at least 18 inches high at the highest corner "A" and the layout lines run, say, 4 inches (minimum) above this, then the tops of the cross members have to be 22 inches above the ground at corner "A." Use an easily remembered number.

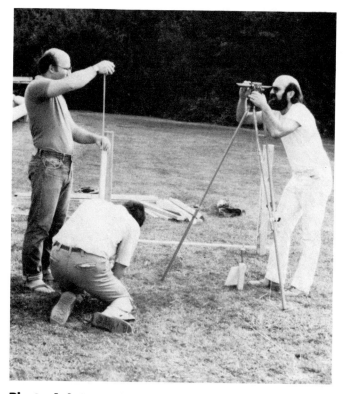

Photo 4-6. Using a transit to mark the location of horizontal cross members on vertical stakes at corner "A."

Photo 4-7. Marking the level points on vertical pieces of batterboards in order to locate level horizontal cross members. Batterboards are in place at corner "A."

Photo 4-8. Using a sledge to stabilize a vertical stake while nailing the horizontal cross member. Note how the top of the horizontal cross member is level with the mark on the vertical stake.

Figure 4-10. A bowed cross member throwing lines off level.

Figure 4-9. Locate the horizontal cross members on the vertical stakes. Be sure the top of the cross member is at least 3 to 6 inches above the foundation wall.

Using a tape or a graduated stick or rod, provided with the transit, determine how low below the crosshairs of the transit scope the tops of the horizontal cross members need to be in order for them to be a minimum of 3 to 6 inches above the foundation at corner "A." In our example, they will be exactly 36 inches below the crosshairs. Using this exact measurement, the top of the cross members at all batterboards can be located.

After you have driven in the vertical stakes of the batterboards in their proper locations and approximately plumb behind corners "A" and "B," use the transit to mark on these vertical stakes a point exactly 36 inches below the crosshairs. Mark each piece by having someone hold a tape or graduated stick exactly plumb until the crosshairs are at 36 inches. (You can tape your tape measure to a 4-foot level *or* mark the distance directly on a 4-foot level.) These points will fall at equidistant points below a level plane and will therefore all be level. By lining up the top of each cross member to these points, the tops of the cross members will also be level. Consequently, when the string is run over the tops of these cross members, the strings also will be level. Easy, isn't it?

Mark the vertical stakes, but be sure they are securely set into the ground. (If they ever move they will throw your entire layout off.) Mark all the vertical stakes.

Select a cross member and be sure that it is good straight stock, as any bow in the board will throw the lines off. Do this by looking down the piece to see if it is straight. Using your sledge to steady the vertical stakes, nail the cross members on so that their tops are on line with the marks. You will be repeating this process at each corner. Use double-headed (form) nails or regular nails not driven all the way in so you can take the batterboards apart after the foundation forms are finished.

Build these batterboards behind corners "A" and "B," using either 1-section or 2-section batterboards as described earlier.

Step 6
Run String Directly Over Corners "A" and "B"

Margin of Error: Exactly over the nail in each stake.

Most Common Mistakes: String not exactly over corners; using cotton string; throwing horizontal cross member off level when nailing.

Photographs: Photos 4-9, 4-10.

Diagram: Figure 4-11.

Using a plumb bob and nylon string, run a line that passes directly over the nails in each stake and tie the string taut by driving a nail at the top of the cross members at each corner. You can locate the exact point of the cross member at point "B" by sighting with the transit aligned exactly along wall "AB." (See "Step 9.") It is wise to support the cross member from underneath with a sledge placed between the cross member and your knee. This keeps the cross member from being thrown off level as you nail. An alternative to nailing a nail into the top of the cross member (which may throw the cross member off level) is to place the nail on the backside of the cross member as shown in Figure 4-11. This also allows you to make fine adjustments in the strings by placing knife notches in the top, backside of the board to move the string as needed. You now have a level line that is running exactly along the exterior edge of foundation wall "AB." This may be a good opportunity to let your children (if you have any) help. There is an old Russian adage: "Kids don't trample the wheat they sow."

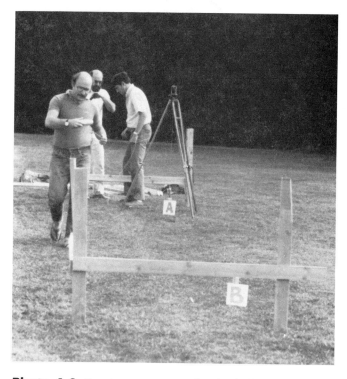

Photo 4-9. Running out a string for the layout line that will pass directly above corners "A" and "B."

Figure 4-11. Use nails on the backside of the cross members and notches on the top to hold the string in its proper place.

Photo 4-10. A line passing directly above corners "C" and "B." Note line is touching the plumb bob line.

Step 7
Transfer Corner "A" to String

Margin of Error: Exact.

Most Common Mistake: Not transferring corner "A" *exactly* to string.

Photograph: Photo 4-11.

Using the plumb bob, transfer the exact corner "A" to the string by aligning the tip of the plumb bob directly over the center of the nail at stake "A." Tie a small piece of string at this point on string "AB." You have now transferred the exact corner "A" onto string "AB."

Step 8
Measure Along String "AB" to Exact Corner "B"

Margin of Error: Exact.

Most Common Mistake: Not measuring accurately.

Diagram: Figure 4-12.

You now have a level line along which to measure from point "A" to the exact corner "B" (which has been an approximate corner up until now). Simply use your long steel tape and have someone hold it at the piece of string on line "AB" that marks corner "A" and measure out the prescribed distance of

Figure 4-12. Measure the exact distance of wall "AB" and determine the exact corner "B." To hold the tape level, use the layout line for reference.

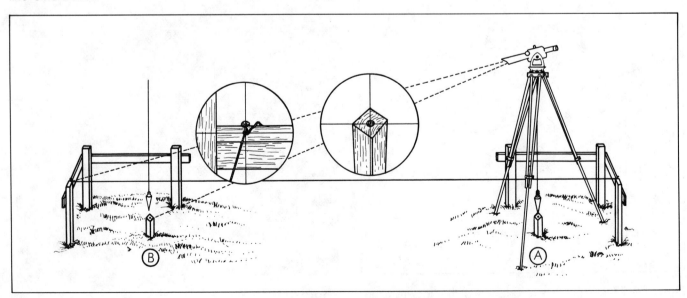

Figure 4-13. Sight the transit along wall "AB" by sighting the nail on the final stake or the nail on the cross member.

the wall (in our example 25 feet). Tie a string at that point. You may want to have someone support the tape midway to correct for any dip in the tape. This piece of string represents the exact location of corner "B." Reset stake "B," using your plumb bob, so that the center of the nail in the stake is directly below the piece of string. Check to be sure this final corner "B" is within your setback requirements. *You now have two definite corners, "A" and "B," and a definite wall "AB."*

Step 9
Sight Transit Along String "AB"

Margin of Error: Exact.

Most Common Mistake: Improper sighting.

Diagram: Figure 4-13.

Sight the transit along line "AB" and then rotate the transit 90° to locate wall "AD." At this time your transit is still directly over point "A." Before proceeding, check the transit. If it is not level, reset it. If you have to reset the transit, you will have to use new measurements—the transit has moved. The transit need not be exactly at the same level as the original sighting (36 inches above the string in our example). You need to know, however, how far above or below the original plane the new level is and adjust the measurement accordingly. If, for example, after releveling the transit, you are 34 or 37 inches above the previously set cross members, use this measurement for the remaining cross members.

Once the transit is level and is directly over corner "A," tilt the scope and sight the crosshairs either on the nail in the stake at corner "B" or on the nail holding string "AB" at the cross member behind corner "B." This means your transit is sighted directly along wall "AB." If you are using a builder's level which will not tilt, have someone hold a carpenter's level, exactly plumb, from one of these nails and sight on the side of it.

Step 10
Rotate Transit 90°

Margin of Error: Exact.

Most Common Mistake: Not rotating transit exactly 90°.

Photograph: Photo 4-12.

Diagram: Figure 4-14.

In order to find the intersecting wall "AD," which is at a right angle (90°) to line "AB," rotate the scope 90°. All points along the crosshairs in this new direction will be at a right angle from the original sighting on line "AB." Before rotating the scope, twist the horizontal circle until it is at 0°, using the center line of the index pointer as the mark. Be exact. Then turn the scope until you are reading 90° on the horizontal circle. (See "Using the Transit.") Lock the scope when this is done so it will not turn. You are now sighting at 90° from wall "AB."

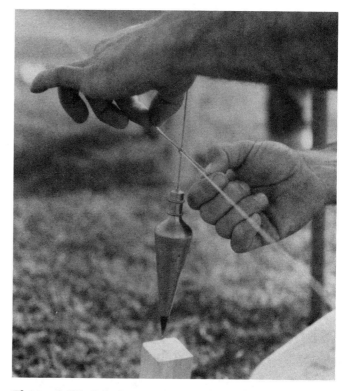

Photo 4-11. Transferring corner "A" directly above to string "AB." Use a small piece of string to mark "A" on line "AB."

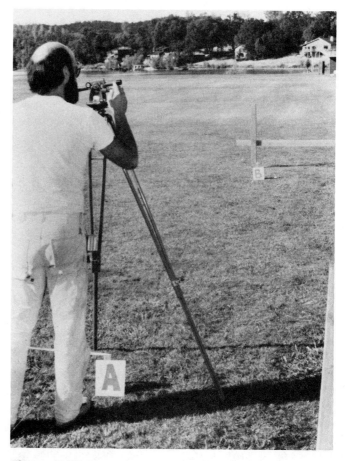

Photo 4-12. Rotating a transit 90° from wall (line) "AB" to locate corner "D."

Step 11
Locate Approximate Corner "D"

Margin of Error: Approximate, within 1 or 2 feet.

Most Common Mistakes: None.

Diagram: Figure 4-15.

Run your steel tape out along wall "AD" until you can see it in the scope of the transit. Drive a stake at the measurement corresponding to the length of wall "AD." This stake is only approximate as you have no way of knowing if you were measuring along a level plane. *You now have two definite corners, "A" and "B," one definite wall, "AB," and a third approximate corner, "D."*

Figure 4-14. Rotate the transit 90° from wall "AB" (1) to sight along wall "AD" (2).

Step 12
Build Batterboards Behind Corner "D"

Margin of Error: Member must be exactly level with others.

Most Common Mistakes: Vertical stakes not securely set into ground; horizontal cross members not level with those of other batterboards.

As you did in "Step 5" for corners "A" and "B," build batterboards behind corner "D." Be sure that they are secure and can remain so throughout the construction of the foundation. Most important is that the tops of the horizontal cross members be at the exact same level as the tops of the cross members at "A" and "B." You will be using a point 36 inches below the crosshairs in our example unless you have changed the level of the transit and you need to compensate for this.

Figure 4-15. Locate the approximate corner "D" by rotating the transit 90° and measuring out the approximate length of wall "AD."

"D," however, is not yet set. *You now have two definite corners, "A" and "B," two definite wall lines, "AB" and "AD," and an approximate corner "D."*

Step 13
Locate Where String "AD" Crosses the Batterboard at Corner "D"

Margin of Error: Exact.

Most Common Mistake: Sighting improperly.

Photograph: Photo 4-13.

Using the transit which has been turned at an exact 90° angle from wall "AB" (or a builder's level and a level-held plumb), sight the crosshairs on the horizontal cross member at corner "D." Drive a nail at this point. Run a taut string from this nail to a nail at the cross member at corner "A" so string "AD" crosses directly over corner "A." This string should be level with string "AB," at right angles to it, and passing directly over point "A" and over stake "D." The final location of stake

Step 14
Locate Exact Corner "D"

Margin of Error: ⅛ inch.

Most Common Mistake: Improper measurement.

Photograph: Photo 4-14.

To find the exact corner "D," measure from where the two lines "AD" and "AB" intersect at corner "A." They should be intersecting directly over corner "A" or something is amiss. Measure along string "AD" the prescribed length of wall "AD" (in our example 25 feet) and tie a small piece of string there. Reset your stake so that it falls directly underneath this string. *You now have three definite corners, "A," "B" and "D," and two definite walls, "AB" and "AD."*

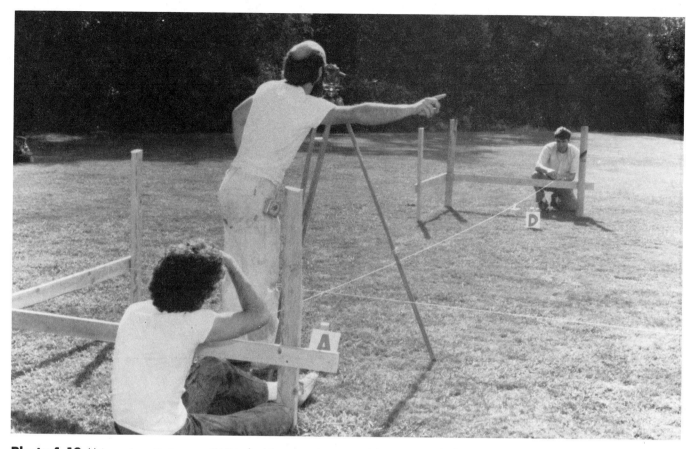

Photo 4-13. Using a transit at corner "A" to find the exact location of the string on the horizontal cross member at corner "D."

Photo 4-14. Using a tape to find the exact location of corner "D" along line "AD." Note the woman holding the tape in the middle to avoid slack in the tape. Mark "D" with the string on the layout line.

Figure 4-16. Using 3 tapes to check for the right triangle using 3-4-5 triangle (12-16-20). Be sure the strings cross *exactly* over corner "A."

Step 15
Check Intersecting Lines Using a 3-4-5 Triangle

Margin of Error: Within ¼ inch of true measurement when using a 12-16-20 triangle.

Most Common Mistake: Inexact measurements.

Diagram: Figure 4-16.

It is a good idea to check your walls to be sure the lines are definitely a right triangle. You should know this checking technique in case you do not have access to a transit or builder's level. It is a simple way of determining when lines are at a true right angle.

It is based on this mathematical principle: in a right-angle triangle the square of the hypotenuse (the side across from the right angle) is equal to the sum of the squares of the other two sides. This is also called a 3-4-5 triangle with 5 being the hypotenuse and 3 and 4 the two sides. Accordingly, 5 squared (25) = 3 squared (9) + 4 squared (16). This also applies if you multiply each number, 3, 4 and 5, by the same number.

To use this in checking your lines, measure out from corner "A" 3 feet (or a certain multiple thereof) in one direction, and 4 feet (or the same multiple thereof) in the other direction, and see if the distance between these two points is 5 feet (or the same multiple thereof). It is best to use the highest multiple the walls will allow, as this makes for greater accuracy. Builders usually use 12-16-20 feet. The diagonal should fall within ¼ inch to ½ inch of 20 feet, if the strings are at a true right angle.

Step 16
Locate Approximate Corner "C"

Margin of Error: Approximate, within a foot or two.

Most Common Mistakes: None.

Diagram: Figure 4-17.

Using two tapes, each at the measurement of the prescribed walls, locate an *approximate* corner "C." *You now have 3 definite corners, "A," "B" and "D," two definite walls, "AB" and "AD," and one approximate corner "C."*

Step 17
Build Batterboards Behind Corner "C"

Margin of Error: Cross members must be exactly level to other cross members.

Most Common Mistakes: Batterboards not secure; cross members not level.

Using the same method as explained in "Step 5," build batterboards behind corner "C." As before, be sure that they are well built, that the horizontal cross member is straight with no bows and that it is exactly level to the other cross members.

Figure 4-17. Using 2 tapes to locate the approximate corner "C."

Photo 4-15. All four batterboards are in place and the transit was moved to corner "B."

Figure 4-18. Sight along wall "AB" after moving the transit to corner "B." Rotate the transit 90° to locate wall "BC."

Step 18
Move Transit to Corner "B"

Margin of Error: Exactly over corner "B."

Most Common Mistakes: Transit not level; not compensating for new level.

Photograph: Photo 4-15.

Move the transit from corner "A" and set it up over corner "B." Adjust the transit *exactly* over corner "B" and level the transit. Use a previously set cross member to find how far above or below you are from your original level. Compensate for this in building your remaining batterboard. If your new level is now 32 inches above a previously set batterboard (distance from top of batterboard to center of crosshairs), use 32 inches to locate cross members set from this setting and forget the previous 36-inch measurement.

Step 19
Sight Along Wall "AB"

Margin of Error: Exact.

Most Common Mistake: Inaccurate sighting.

Diagram: Figure 4-18.

Now sight back to the nail holding the string at corner "A" so that the transit is again directly sighted to wall "AB." You are now looking for wall "BC," which is at a right angle to wall "AB," so simply rotate the transit 90°.

Step 20
Locate Where String "BC" Crosses Batterboards at Corner "C"

Margin of Error: Exact.

Most Common Mistake: Inaccurate sighting.

As you did in "Step 13," locate where string "BC" crosses the horizontal cross member. Drive a nail at this point.

Step 21
Run String Over Corners "B" and "C"

Margin of Error: Exact.

Most Common Mistake: Strings not running exactly over "B" and "C."

Diagram: Figure 4-19.

Run a string passing directly over corner "B" to the new nail at corner "C." This new string should represent the exact outside edge of the foundation wall "BC." Again check to see if it is running directly over corner "B." Use the 3-4-5 triangle to be sure you have a right triangle.

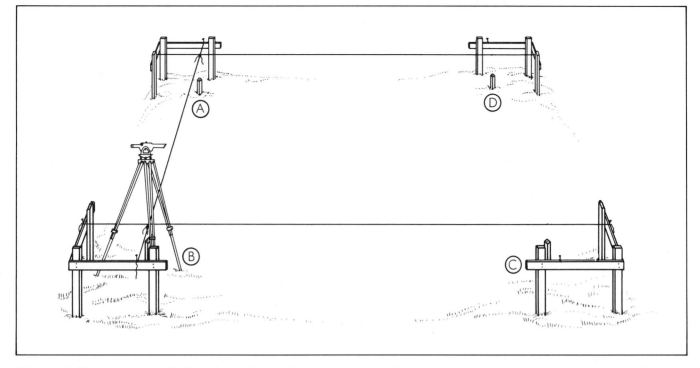

Figure 4-19. Run string "BC" from the nail set in the cross member behind "B," crossing directly over corner "C," to the nail behind corner "C."

Step 22
Measure Along String "BC" to Locate Exact Corner "C"

Margin of Error: Within ⅛ to ¼ inch of exact distance.

Most Common Mistake: Inaccurate measurement.

As you did in "Step 8" and "Step 14," measure along string "BC," from where it intersects line "AB" at point "B," the prescribed distance of wall "BC" to locate corner "C." Tie a string at this point and reset stake "C," driving a nail in the stake at the exact corner. *You now have four definite corners, "A," "B," "C" and "D," and three definite walls, "AB," "AC" and "BC."*

Step 23
Run String Over Corners "C" and "D"

Margin of Error: Exactly over these corners.

Most Common Mistakes: None.

Diagram: Figure 4-20.

Run a line, using your plumb bobs, directly over corners "C" and "D." When measured, this line should be the same as the distance prescribed for wall "CD." If not, something is off and you need to find out where.

Step 24
Check by Measuring the Diagonals

Margin of Error: ½ to ¾ inch over each 35 feet of diagonal.

Most Common Mistakes: Allowing too great a margin of error; improper measuring.

Diagram: Figure 4-21.

Photograph: Photo 4-16.

After all your lines are in place, you can check the rectangular or square sections of the building by measuring the diagonals. Ideally, the diagonals should equal each other. In practice, that seldom happens, nor does the foundation need to be that exact. If the diagonals are within ½ to ¾ inch over every 35 feet of diagonal, this will be sufficient.

If there is a greater discrepancy, do not be upset. Layout is a process of trial and error and it rarely works out the first time around, so do not expect it to. No matter how accurate you have been, it just never seems to work the first time. You now begin an investigation process of trying to determine where you are off.

Begin by measuring all the wall lengths to determine if they are the prescribed distance. If you are lucky, one may be off and the problem is quickly solved. Once you have checked the distance, use your 3-4-5 triangle or your transit or both to check to see if your corners are all 90°. Continue searching and adjusting until the diagonals work out within the allowable margin of error. Be patient, it may take time and get frustrating, but eventually you will make it work.

Figure 4-20. String "CD" is in place, crossing directly over corners "D" and "C."

Photo 4-16. Checking the diagonals to see if it is a true rectangle. Margin of error is ½ to ¾ inch over 35 feet of diagonal.

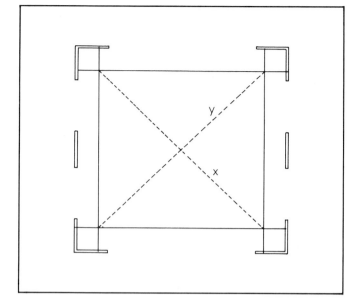

Figure 4-21. Measure the diagonals to check for accuracy of the layout (x=y).

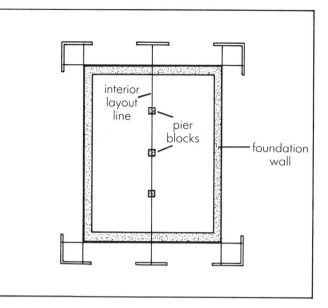

Figure 4-22. Single batterboards are in place to mark the pier blocks used for support girders.

Step 25
Do Layout for Interior Piers or Walls

Margin of Error: Within ¼ inch.

Most Common Mistake: Inaccurate layout.

Diagram: Figure 4-22.

Most houses will have some type of interior foundation as well as the foundation for the exterior walls. If the house is not very wide in some areas, 16 feet or less, intermediate piers and girder may not be required. Check your plans to see if any are needed.

If you have interior piers or full walls, you will need to set lines for them. (See Chapter 6, *Poured Concrete Foundations,* "Step 14B.") Actually, you can omit setting the lines at this stage. You can set them once the form boards are in place for the foundation by attaching them to the inside of the interior form boards. This will require digging the holes for the piers after the forms are in place. Whichever seems to work best for you is OK.

If you decide to dig the holes or trenches at this point, check your plans to see the location of the interior walls or trenches. Be sure you know what the measurement you are reading applies to, to the edges of the piers or wall or to the center of the piers or wall. THIS IS IMPORTANT. Measure that distance in on your perimeter lines and tie a piece of string at this point (in our example 10 feet). Build a single batterboard behind the lines at either wall. Be sure the cross members are level with each other. Run strings over the top of these cross members so they cross the pieces of string. If there is more than one set of interior piers or more than one wall, repeat the process for each one. Your layout is now complete.

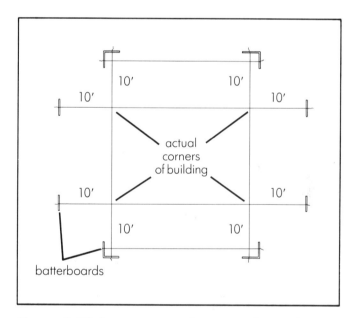

Figure 4-23. Setting strings and corners 10 feet out from the actual corners. Sometimes the batterboards are built further from the actual foundation to allow equipment to move without upsetting the batterboards.

Special Situations

Offset Hubs

Sometimes offset hubs are used instead of a standard layout. This is a process of setting the strings and corners a good distance, 10 feet or more, back from where the actual corners will be. Two-section batterboards are used instead of 1-section. You may want to consider using this process when you plan to use heavy equipment to dig your trenches in order to keep the batterboards a good distance from the equipment and digging. (See Figure 4-23.)

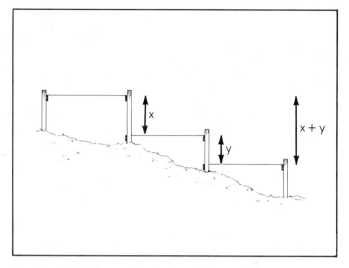

Figure 4-24. Stepped batterboards for steep slopes.

Figure 4-25. Bracing.

Figure 4-26. Bracing batterboards.

Figure 4-27. Less expensive hydro- and water levels that replace the levelling function of the transit.

Steep Slopes

Where steep slopes are involved, you may need to build several intermediate batterboards as batterboards are hard to stabilize if they are over 6 feet high. In this case the foundation will be stepped (see Chapter 6, *Poured Concrete Foundations,* "Step 2") and it is not essential that all the lines be at the same level, since the foundation will not all be at the same level (see *Knee Walls* chapter, "Purposes of the Knee Wall"). Since you can calculate the vertical distances between the strings, you can keep the different sections of foundation walls level. (See Figure 4-24.)

Braced Batterboards

If the batterboards are high (over 4 feet) you may need bracing as shown in Figures 4-25 and 4-26.

Water Level and Hydro Level

If you cannot afford a builder's level or transit and do not have access to one, you can buy a less expensive hydro level or water level that can serve the levelling functions of the transit or builder's level. These tools use water in clear tubes to level, on the principle that water always seeks its own level. In using these tools, be sure they are always in the shade or always in the sun when not in use. Changes in the temperature of the water can cause expansion and thereby change the water level. (See Figure 4-27.)

Digging Trenches or Excavating Before Final Layout

In some cases, where lots of excavating is involved, such as with basements, rough layout lines are set to show the backhoe operators where to dig. After the excavating is completed, exact layout lines are set up. In houses with standard foundations, some builders choose to set rough lines first, dig the trenches and then set up exact layout lines for building forms. This is done to keep the batterboards away from the digging.

Worksheet

ESTIMATED TIME

_____

_____

_____

_____

CREW

Skilled or Semi-Skilled

_____ Phone _____

_____ Phone _____

_____ Phone _____

Unskilled

_____ Phone _____

_____ Phone _____

_____ Phone _____

_____ Phone _____

_____ Phone _____

MATERIALS NEEDED

2×4s, 1×4s, 2-×-2 stakes, nylon string, and nails.

ESTIMATING MATERIALS

2×4S:

_____ feet long: Quantity _____

1×4S:

_____ feet long: Quantity _____

2-×-2 STAKES: Quantity _____

NAILS:

_____ lbs. of 8d duplex

_____ lbs. of 8d standard

STRING:

_____ feet of nylon string

COST COMPARISON

2×4S:

_____ Store: _____

Cost per foot _____ total $ _____

_____ Store: _____

Cost per foot _____ total $ _____

_____ Store: _____

Cost per foot _____ total $ _____

1×4S:

_____ Store: _____

Cost per foot _____ total $ _____

_____ Store: _____

Cost per foot _____ total $ _____

_____ Store: _____

Cost per foot _____ total $ _____

PEOPLE TO CONTACT

Concrete Supplier _____

Phone _____ Work Date _____

Concrete Pumper (if needed) _____

Phone _____ Work Date _____

If underfloor utilities need to be installed before floor framing:

Electrician _____

Phone _____ Work Date _____

Plumber _____

Phone _____ Work Date _____

Heating and Air
Conditioning _____

Phone _____ Work Date _____

Gas _____

Phone _____ Work Date _____

Daily Checklist

CREW:

_____ Phone _____

_____ Phone _____

_____ Phone _____

_____ Phone _____

_____ Phone _____

_____ Phone _____

TOOLS:

☐ builder's level

☐ water level or hydro level

☐ sledge hammer

☐ hand or power saw

☐ hammer

☐ three metal tapes (one should be 100-foot)

☐ 4-foot level

☐ knife

☐ plumb bob

RENTAL ITEMS:

☐ sledge

☐ transit

MATERIALS:

_____ ft. of 2×4s

_____ ft. of 1×4s

_____ no. of 2-×-2 stakes

_____ lbs. of 8d duplex nails

_____ lbs. of 8d standard nails

_____ ft. of nylon string

DESIGN REVIEW:

Be sure you have taken into consideration all the crucial factors in choosing an exact location before beginning layout.

INSPECTIONS NEEDED:

Inspector's name _____

Phone _____

Time and date of inspection _____

WEATHER FORECAST:

For week _____

For day _____

5 Types of Foundations

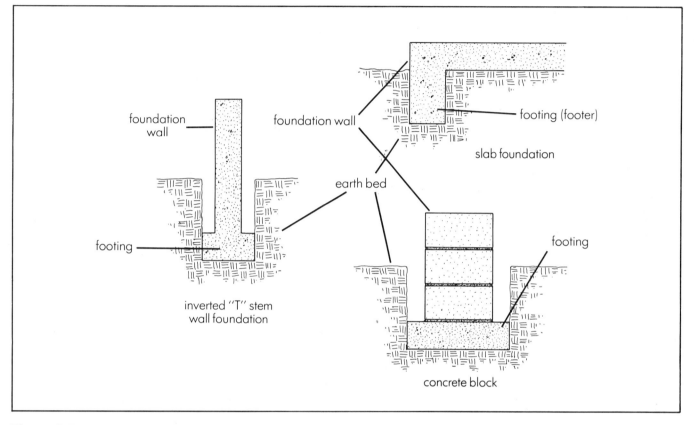

Figure 5-1. Parts of a foundation.

Introduction

BEFORE GETTING INTO the actual construction processes of various foundations, I thought it best to spend some time discussing what the different possibilities are. Often there are several options open to you, and a wise decision here can save you time, money and energy once construction begins. Other times, due to site, design or code specifications, no options are available and you will have to build one particular type of foundation. If the latter is the case or if you already have definitely decided what foundation you are going to build, you can skip over this section.

I have divided this section into three main areas: pier foundations, continuous-perimeter foundations (including basements) and slab foundations. Under each of these headings are examples with short descriptions of the construction details and a list of the advantages and disadvantages of each. Chapter 6, *Poured Concrete Foundations,* describes, in detail, how to build a concrete continuous-perimeter foundation.

Contracting Out the Foundation

Except for the most complex, hillside foundations, most foundation construction is well within the reach of the novice or first-time builder. It is not very difficult to understand, but it does require a greater accuracy than some wood construction; once it is poured, correction requires a lot of work. This factor often intimidates many owner builders, but if you know what you are doing and check everything out before the concrete is placed (poured), it need not present any real problems.

Some owner builders choose to contract out the foundation in order to save the time and energy involved in its construction. If it is a very complex or an extremely large foundation, I would recommend that you consider contracting it out. If your time is limited (or your energy) and you have allotted some money for labor, this may be the place to spend it. Building a foundation with a small, novice crew (like the lone owner builder) can take a long time and a lot of energy, but personally, I have always found a sense of satisfaction in preparing foundations for my houses.

Whether you do it or you contract it out, be sure that it is done properly: square, level and the proper dimensions. Inaccurate or sloppy work at this stage can cause problems throughout the building process and, if the work is poor quality, it can threaten the entire home.

Foundations

Almost all foundations (except slabs) have three main parts: the earth bed, the footing and the foundation wall. The earth bed is the final resting place for the weight of the house. The type and strength of the soil can have a bearing on the type of foundation chosen and its construction. (See Figure 5-1.)

The foundation footing spreads the weight of the house over a larger area of the earth so that a great load will not be concentrated on a small area.

The foundation wall lifts the house above the moist ground and provides a level building plane. It also serves to carry the load of the house down to the footings and from there to the earth bed. The main purposes of a foundation are:
1. To anchor the house to the ground;
2. To provide a level building plane on an irregular sloping site;
3. To carry the weight of the house down to the soil;
4. To keep the vulnerable wood away from the moisture and insects that might attack it.

Before we get into the different types of foundations, consider the following factors as you determine the type of foundation that you plan to use.

Factors to Consider in Choosing a Foundation

The Soil

The type and strength of the soil directly below the foundation must be considered. Weak or unstable soils may require larger footings or even engineered foundations. Some soils are so weak that a slab may be required to spread the weight over the greatest possible area. Know your soil, especially if there is a history of soil problems in your area, before you begin.

Codes

Codes can be very restrictive when it comes to foundations. In areas covered by the Uniform Building Codes, all houses must have continuous-perimeter foundations; many types of pier foundations are not permitted unless engineered. Some areas require reinforcing bars (rebar) in the foundations, others do not. Codes regulate the size and thickness of the footings and foundation walls, the depth of the footing, and other construction factors in foundations. Before beginning, be sure that you are clear on what the code requirements are in your area.

Slope of the Site

Steeply sloping sites may require high foundation walls at their lower ends. Unless you are using piers or a pole constructed house, this can be very costly. You may want to consider a half basement on steep lots. This would affect the type of foundation to be used. Long foundation walls running across a slope can create big drainage problems. Drain tile is recommended.

Weather

In colder climates, you may want to use a solid perimeter foundation instead of an open pier foundation to keep the area directly under the house warm and protected from cold winds. If you are using a pier foundation in cold climates, it is recommended that you insulate the floor. In areas having heavy rainfall, slabs may not be a wise decision, due to possible flooding in low areas.

Seismic Areas

In the event of an earthquake, the foundation will receive the brunt of the quake and therefore needs to be built much stronger than foundations built in non-earthquake areas. It is often recommended that these foundations be continuous foundations so that the entire foundation will move as one unit should an earthquake hit. In earthquake areas, local code offices should be consulted for requirements not found in the national codes.

Passive Solar Systems

Very often concrete foundations are used for heat storage in passive solar systems. This is especially true of slab foundations. Continuous-perimeter walls can also be effectively used as storage areas (if they are within an enclosed solar greenhouse, for instance). Consider this as you choose a type of foundation.

Local Foundation Problems

Many areas of the country have specific problems that often affect the type and design of foundations used. In many areas of Maine, for instance, bedrock is encountered a few feet below the ground and the footings need to be anchored to the rock by inserting steel stakes into holes drilled into the rock. Areas of Florida have sand to a great depth and long poles need to be used. Check with local builders or the code office about any problems in your area.

Cost Factors

Your decision as to the type of foundation you plan to use can make the difference of hundreds (and in some cases thousands) of dollars. Research well the difference in costs before you make your decision; otherwise you are making it with incomplete data, and that can be dangerous. Pier foundations are much less expensive and easier and quicker to build than continuous-perimeter foundations. If allowed by code, the pier foundation can serve just as well as the continuous foundation, which is greatly overbuilt to begin with. The floor can be insulated to help with the energy efficiency; and it allows

Photo 5-1. Natural stone piers (dry laid). This foundation is not allowed in code-enforced areas.

the crawlspace greater ventilation and access, which to me is a great advantage.

Slab foundations serve as not only the foundation but the first floor as well. This saves you the cost of having to build a floor frame and subfloor. The savings can be considerable in time and labor as well as money. Their great drawback is that they keep the house close to the moist ground.

Aesthetics

In choosing the type of foundation, consider the impact the foundation will have on the looks of the home. This is especially important if there are to be any high foundation walls. Houses built close to the ground on slabs will appear different than those built on foundations that raise them above the ground a certain distance.

Pier Foundations

Natural Stone

This type of foundation was the most common before the advent of concrete. Many older homes and barns are still standing, level and secure, on natural stone piers. Few new homes are built this way, but if no codes exist it can be considered in some areas. It is simple, inexpensive and, to some, aesthetically pleasing. I built a home a few years ago in North Carolina using this type of foundation and as yet there have been no problems. It can be laid with mortar or dried-laid stone (no mortar). In earthquake or code-enforced areas it is not allowed. (See Photo 5-1.)

Advantages
Inexpensive
Aesthetically appealing
Easy to build

Disadvantages
Not allowed by many codes
May affect resale value
Not advised in earthquake, hurricane or tornado areas
Large, flat stones are hard to find

Wood Columns

Though more common than stone piers, these are seldom seen except in rural buildings. If they can be approved by the code office, you may want to consider using these. Using any type of wood for a foundation is an "iffy" business. Even the new pressure-treated woods are only guaranteed for 20

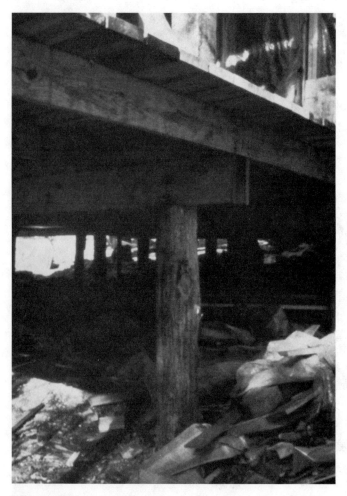

Photo 5-2. Wood posts used as foundation piers. Use a rot-resistant wood.

years (some manufacturers swear they will last 50, but this is still not a long time for a foundation). (See Photo 5-2, Figure 5-2.)

Advantages
Inexpensive
Easy to build
Can use on steep sites by using longer poles on lower areas

Disadvantages
May not be allowed by codes
Lower resale value
Wood is prone to rot

Brick

Brick piers offer the permanency of stone with the low cost and ease of construction of pier foundations. (See Figure 5-3.) Brick piers are often seen on older and sometimes newer homes in the East, especially the Southeast. (See Photo 5-3.) In earthquake areas they are prohibited, since they are likely to fall apart in a good shake. You may want to consider them if the code will allow.

Advantages
Easy to build
Inexpensive
Attractive

Disadvantages
May not be allowed in some areas
May affect resale value
Not advised in earthquake, hurricane or tornado areas

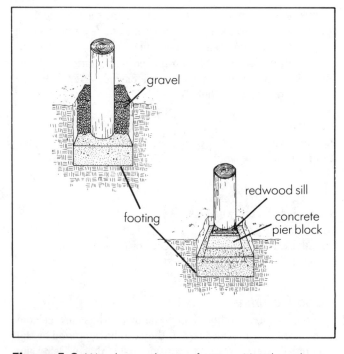

Figure 5-2. Wood piers showing footings. Note how the use of a pier block on the right keeps the piers out of contact with the moist ground.

Figure 5-3. Brick pier.

Photo 5-3. Brick piers used for foundation.

Concrete Block

Piers of concrete block are still quite prevalent in the building trade. (See Photo 5-4.) They are used for foundations constructed totally from piers as well as piers for girders between continuous-perimeter wall foundations. Pier holes need to be dug accurately so that all the piers will be the same height when completed. In earthquake prone areas, they are not advised for the perimeter foundation but can be used for interior piers. In this case it is advised (and often required) to run reinforcement bars through the cells of the block and then fill the cells with concrete (grout).

Advantages
Easy to build
Inexpensive
Permanent
Allowed by many codes

Disadvantages
Not allowed in some code areas
May affect resale value

Photo 5-4. Concrete blocks used for foundation piers.

Figure 5-4. A steel I-beam used as a pier.

1 set up tube level
2 place concrete
3 when dry strip tube
4 finished pier

Figure 5-5. Using cardboard tubes as forms for concrete piers.

Steel Columns

Using steel columns for the entire foundation is rarely seen in single-family residence construction. (See Figure 5-4.) Some of the cliff-hanging homes in the California area use these systems, which must be professionally engineered. Steel columns are, however, commonly used as supports for wooden and steel girders in basement areas.

Advantages
Easy to build
Permanent

Disadvantages
Unattractive
Expensive
Not allowed by many codes

Concrete Columns

Concrete piers are also commonly used in construction. A common way of building concrete piers is with cardboard tubes. (See Figure 5-5.) These are cardboard cylinders that come in different diameters and heights. The fresh concrete is poured directly into the tube and then the cardboard is peeled away when the concrete is hard. (See Photo 5-5.) Forms can be built to whatever shapes and sizes you want. I once saw a home that was built entirely on concrete piers shaped like toadstools.

Advantages
Permanent
Easy to build
Inexpensive
Can be built to any shape and size

Disadvantages
May not be allowed by some codes
May affect resale value
Can be unattractive

Pole Construction

Pole construction is basically a different type of construction procedure than those shown so far. (See Figure 5-6.) Large poles are sunk into the ground for the foundation. The floor frames and roof are attached by the use of horizontal girders or stringers that are bolted to the poles. The weight of the building is totally carried by the poles and not by the wall, as is the case with standard stud construction. Studs are placed between the poles to hold the windows, doors, siding and insulation and interior trim.

In the past, pole construction was used mostly in agricultural buildings, where the earth was left for the floor so the tractors and livestock could move around. More recently it has become popular for one-family dwellings and larger buildings as well. It lends itself well to hillside lots, where longer poles can be used in the lower areas. Often the large poles are exposed, giving the house a greater sense of strength than found in stud construction. You may seriously want to

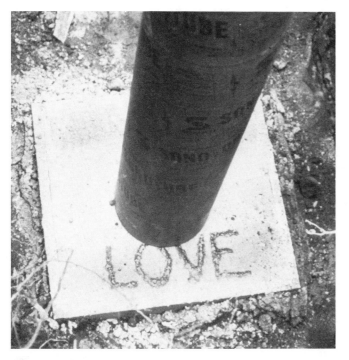

Photo 5-5. Poured concrete pier.

consider this type of construction. Check the bibliography for books available on the subject.

NOTE: One major disadvantage of pole construction in the past was the need to sink wooden poles into the ground for the foundation. These would rot. You can modify the process slightly to prevent this, as shown in Figure 5-6.

Advantages
Inexpensive
Good for steep sites
Allows for large wall openings (up to 14 feet)
Large poles give house a sense of strength
Allowed by many codes
Earthquake resistant

Disadvantages
Trim and finish work around poles may be difficult
Foundation is wood (unless you use an alternate method)
Some engineering may be required

Figure 5-6. Pole construction. "A" shows poles sunk into the ground. "B" shows recommended way that keeps pole out of contact with the ground.

Photo 5-6. Natural stone continuous-wall foundation under mill built in the 1700s. Foundation is still level and intact though no mortar was used.

Continuous-Perimeter Foundations

Natural Stone Continuous Wall

As were their stone pier counterparts, natural stone continuous foundations are common to houses built before the advent of concrete. Many old houses used a natural stone, either pier or continuous. (See Photo 5-6.) These stones were either dry laid, simply stacking the stones using no mortar, or they were laid using mortar. Large, flat rocks, called baserocks, were used for the footings. Many are still standing in excellent shape. Though seldom used in this form in new construction, in the proper conditions and if no codes exist, they can work well and add the beauty of natural stone to your home.

Advantages
Inexpensive
Attractive

Disadvantages
Not allowed by most codes
Not advised in earthquake, hurricane or tornado areas
Large flat stones can be hard to find
May affect resale value
Time consuming to build

Natural Stone Using Forms and Mortar

An adaptation of the natural laid stone is sometimes used whereby forms are built, stones are placed inside the forms and then the spaces are filled with mortar or concrete. (See Figure 5-7 and Photo 5-7.) Sometimes only an interior form is used. It is simpler than laid stone and the rocks do not need to be as flat, since the concrete or mortar will bind them together. Often this system will not pass code, but it is used in rural non-code areas. It offers the permanency and beauty of natural stone without requiring as much effort or as many flat stones as does the laid-stone method.

Advantages
Permanent
Attractive
Inexpensive

Disadvantages
May not be allowed by codes
Not advised in earthquake, hurricane or tornado areas
May affect resale value
Somewhat difficult to build

Figure 5-7. A laid stone foundation. The plywood form will be removed after the mortar has set.

Photo 5-7. Using form (plywood) and natural stone for continuous-wall foundation.

Continuous Brick

Brick foundations are sometimes used in new homes, especially in the eastern states. They can be either solid brick or a brick veneer covering a 4- or 8-inch concrete block foundation. (See Figure 5-8.) These foundations are aesthetically appealing, permanent and allowed by many codes. Bricklaying, for the beginner, can be both frustrating and time consuming. You may want to consider contracting a brick foundation, unless you are ready to accept the challenge of mastering a new skill such as bricklaying.

All-weather Wood

The all-weather wood foundation is new to the building industry. (See Figure 5-9.) It was developed mostly for contractors in the colder regions of the country so they could continue to build year-round, even when the weather was too cold to pour concrete. Since its introduction into the industry, it has been pushed and praised (often by the plywood associations). It is built with no concrete, gravel serves as the footing, and it uses pressure-treated lumber and plywood. This wood is guaranteed for only 20 years, though manufacturers claim it should last longer. Basically, it costs about the same as a poured concrete foundation, but its lifetime is not nearly as long. I would not ever recommend using any type of wood for a foundation.

Advantages
Can be built in freezing weather
Easy to insulate
Easy to build for novice builder

Disadvantages
Limited lifetime (20 to 50 years)
May affect resale value
May not be allowed by some codes

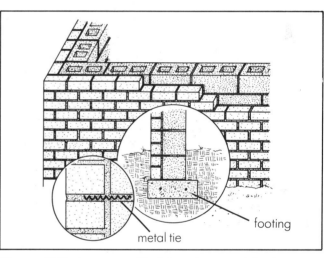

Figure 5-8. A concrete block foundation with brick veneer. Metal tie holds brick to concrete block.

Figure 5-9. An all-weather wood foundation.

Photo 5-8. Concrete block foundation in progress.

Photo 5-9. Horizontal rebar being placed in a concrete block foundation in an earthquake area. Note the slots left in the blocks to receive the horizontal rebar.

Concrete Block

Concrete block foundations comprise approximately 38% of residential foundations. (See Photo 5-8 and Figure 5-10.) They are cost-effective and within the abilities of a novice builder. Their cost is equal to their poured concrete counterpart, though they can take longer to build if you are slow at laying blocks. In areas that are inaccessible to a concrete truck, they may be the best way to go.

Advantages
Within the abilities of a novice
Permanent
Accepted building practice
Cost-effective

Disadvantages
Work can go slowly for novice builder
More costly than pier foundation

Concrete Block (Earthquake Areas)

Using concrete blocks in earthquake areas is a good bit more difficult than in other areas. Should the foundation receive a good shake, the unfilled and unreinforced blocks could easily come loose from the mortar and the foundation fall apart. Because of this steps have to be taken to keep the blocks together in the event of an earthquake. Rebar (reinforcing bar made of steel rods) is run both vertically and horizontally through the cells of the blocks. (See Figure 5-11 and Photo 5-9.) Special blocks, called bond beam blocks, are laid every few courses to allow the rebar to run horizontally. Once the blocks are laid, grout (concrete with pea gravel) is poured in some or all of the cells. (See Photo 5-10.) This holds the foundation together. In essence, the blocks act as a form for the concrete.

Advantages	*Disadvantages*
Permanent	Slow and difficult to build
Cost-effective	
Can be built in remote areas	

Photo 5-10. Filling cells of concrete blocks with grout (concrete with pea gravel).

Figure 5-10. A concrete block foundation.

Figure 5-11. A concrete block foundation for earthquake areas. Note that the rebar (reinforcing bar) is running both vertically and horizontally and that all the cells are filled with concrete (grout).

Photo 5-11. Concrete block basement walls. Walls are waterproofed (black areas) where they are below grade. Note the concrete block piers to support the floor frame system.

Concrete Block (Basement)

Basically, this foundation is similar in construction to the concrete block perimeter foundation except that it is higher, contains more doors and windows, is below grade, and must be well waterproofed. Since the walls are earth, retaining some areas requires rebar and filled cells. The floors are often slabs poured between the walls. (See Photo 5-11.) This type of foundation offers a large challenge to the novice builder and should not be undertaken without careful thought and a complete understanding of what is involved.

Advantages
Cost-effective
Permanent

Disadvantages
Can be difficult and slow for the novice builder
Ground water can cause leakage

Poured Concrete

Poured concrete foundations are by far the most common in residential construction (58%). Their construction involves digging footing trenches, building wooden forms, placing the concrete and then stripping the forms. (See Photo 5-12.) Though it often appears intimidating, it is well within the

scope of the novice builder. If a perimeter foundation is desired or required, either a poured concrete or concrete block is suggested. For owner builders it is recommended that the floor joists be used as the foundation forms to help cut costs. Construction of this type of foundation will be discussed in the chapter to follow.

Advantages
Permanent
Good resale value
Within the scope of the novice builder
Typical code foundation

Disadvantages
More expensive than comparable pier foundations
Takes considerable time and energy
Demands considerable accuracy

Poured Concrete (Basement)

Basically the poured concrete basement wall is similar to the poured concrete stem wall foundation. There are a few differences: the walls are higher, they must be waterproofed, there is a slab floor between the walls, there are more openings for doors and windows and they will be below grade. They are perhaps the most difficult of all foundations to build.

Photo 5-12. Poured concrete basement. Note that the forms are removed as the foundation progresses.

Photo 5-13. A grade beam foundation being poured. The round columns will be joined together with a 12×12 grade beam of concrete and rebar.

Photo 5-14. After the foundation is poured, girders are set on the piers. The joists will rest on top of these or be hung from them. These foundations can be very costly if you need to go very deep into the soil.

Photo 5-15. Slab preparation. Forms are in place and trenches are dug for the footing for both exterior and interior load-bearing walls. Rebar is in and pipes are wrapped where they pass through the concrete slab.

Photo 5-16. Footings are being poured on first pass. Note that the underbed is ready; and the wire mesh, and wooden screed board, to be used in levelling the slab, are in place. A boom pumper is being used.

Photo 5-17. Screed boards and a long float are being used to smooth and level the top of the slab.

Figure 5-12. Three different types of slab foundation. Vapor barriers are sometimes placed on top of the sand or gravel (check local practices).

They involve high forms with tremendous pressure against them from the concrete and accurate slab work as well. It is advised that you consider contracting these types of foundations to a professional (a good one, as they can run into problems). As with all basement foundations, great care must be given to waterproofing and also insulation. Drainage is very important with this type of foundation, so determine how local builders install their drain tiles.

Advantages
Permanent
Adds to the living space
Good resale value
Commonly accepted foundation

Disadvantages
Requires buying or renting tall forms
Very difficult and time consuming for the novice builder
Expensive
Must be properly waterproofed

Grade Beam

The grade beam foundation (Photos 5-13, 5-14) is a rather new addition to the family of foundations. It is often used on the West coast, where there is a chance of earthquakes, to tie a foundation together so that it will move as a unit. Ordinarily, on a steep site, a poured concrete stem wall foundation that is stepped is used. This being expensive and time consuming to erect on a steep lot, a grade beam foundation is often used in its place.

A grade beam foundation is made up of individual round piers connected by concrete "beams" that run below grade and tie the entire foundation together. The beams are made by trenching into the ground along the grade of the slope, placing rebar into the trench and then pouring the concrete into the pier forms and trenches at the same time. This foundation is easier and cheaper than a comparable poured concrete wall foundation, but may require some engineering.

Slab Foundations

Slab foundations are becoming increasingly more popular. (See Figure 5-12.) They help in cutting costs, since no floor frame or subflooring system is required. The slab foundation serves as the floor frame and subfloor. They are also being used more and more as part of direct-gain passive solar storage systems. (See Photos 5-15–5-17.) They are relatively easy to construct once you know what you are doing and are well within the reach of most novice builders. Their two greatest drawbacks are that they make for a hard, unyielding floor and they bring the house very close to the ground. This is not a problem to most builders, who give only a few years' warranty. You, however, may want to take this into consideration for the house you are building for yourself.

Once a wooden house is placed near the ground, the earth, in a very natural and positive way, begins to attack it, causing it to decay and turn to organic topsoil to be able to support and grow yet more trees to make more lumber for yet more wooden houses. The earth uses fungus, insects, moisture, vapor and water to decompose the house. It is a beautiful system, but not one that you may particularly want working on your home. Because of this, be sure you have a good drainage and gutter system if you plan to use a slab foundation.

Advantages
Cost-effective
Lends itself well to passive solar heat storage
Time efficient

Disadvantages
Can crack on unstable soil
Brings house close to ground
Floors are hard and unyielding
Can be problematic if not built correctly

6 Poured Concrete Foundations

Photo 6-1. The house after the concrete has been "placed" and the forms removed.

What You'll Be Doing, What to Expect

THIS CHAPTER WILL discuss the construction of a typical poured concrete stem wall foundation that is stepped (Photo 6-1, Figure 6-1). This type of foundation is common in many areas of the country. We will be using the earth as the forms for the footing, suspending the foundation forms over the earth and then placing the rebar, wedge ties, and anchor bolts inside the forms. The size and location of the rebar change depending on your locale and whether you are in an earthquake area or not. Check your local building practices before beginning, to see if there are any special requirements due to local codes or conditions. More than any other part of the house, foundations vary from area to area.

It is important that this part of construction be very accurate, not only because you are working with concrete, which is difficult to change in case you make a mistake, but also because all the rest of your work, the floors, the walls, the roof, etc., will be built on this. If the foundations are not square at the corners, or if the dimensions are off, or if the tops of the foundation walls are not level at this stage, it can cause tremendous headaches down the line. At the end of this chapter there is a checklist of things to inspect before the concrete is placed. Go over this carefully. If possible, have a professional inspect your work before you pour. Be accurate and careful, it will pay later.

Jargon

ANCHOR BOLTS. Bolts embedded in the concrete foundation used to hold the sill plates to the foundation wall.

CLEAT. A small piece of wood used for reinforcing.

CONCRETE PUMPER. A machine used to pump concrete through a hose.

CROWBAR or PRY BAR. A metal bar used for prying.

DRAIN TILE. Perforated pipes placed near the footing of the foundation and surrounded by gravel used to drain ground water away from the foundation, basement or crawlspace.

FLOAT. A wooden plaster or concrete working tool.

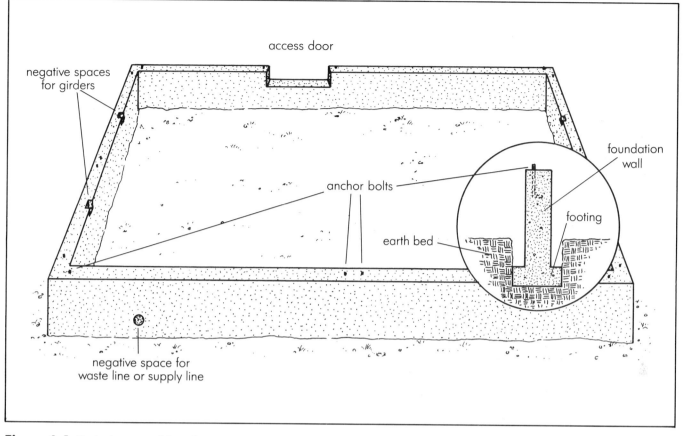

access door

negative spaces
for girders

anchor bolts

foundation
wall

footing

earth bed

negative space for
waste line or supply line

Figure 6-1. Typical stem wall foundation.

FOOTING. Concrete slab at the base or bottom of the foundation wall, used to spread the load over a greater area.

FORM TIES. Metal straps or bars that hold the forms together until the concrete has set.

FOUNDATION. The supporting portion of a building below the first-floor construction.

FOUNDATION FORMS. Wooden, plywood or metal panels that hold the concrete in place until it has set.

FOUNDATION STAKES. Wooden stakes that hold the forms suspended over the ground until the concrete has set.

FROSTLINE. The depth below the surface to which the soil freezes and thaws.

KICKERS. Wooden stakes that hold the forms upright until the concrete has set.

NEGATIVE SPACES. Holes or spaces left in the concrete foundation to be used as passages for plumbing and gas pipes, electrical wires, girder pockets, etc.

PIER BLOCKS. Small concrete foundation blocks, usually used to support wooden posts.

REBAR (REINFORCING BAR). Steel bars that are set in the concrete in such a manner that the two materials act together to resist force.

REBAR CUTTER. A tool used to bend and cut reinforcing bar.

SILL PLATE. A board bolted to the top of the foundation wall, on which the floor joists are attached (see *Sill Plates,* Chapter 7).

SCREED. To form concrete to the desired shape or level by using a metal or wooden tool (float).

Purposes of the Foundation

1) Raise the house above the moist earth
2) Provide a level building plane
3) Anchor the house to the ground
4) Carry the weight of the house to the earth bed

Design Decisions

You will need to determine at this point the manner in which the joists are to be joined to the girders. You need to know this in order to determine the exact heights and locations of the negative spaces. There are several different ways this is done. Each way has advantages and disadvantages. You need to decide at this time which system you are going to use. (Figure 6-2.)

The advantage in System 1 is that the metal fasteners being used help the floor frame hold together in an earthquake. The joists are also on line for the plywood subfloor installation (see *Subflooring,* Chapter 10). Its only real disadvantage is that there is less room in the crawlspace than in the systems where the joists are on top of the girders.

System 2 still allows your joists to be on line and also gives you more room in the crawlspace. System 3 eliminates the need to cut each joist exactly, but adjustments must be made in order to provide nailing surfaces (end joists) for splices in the plywood. System 4 is an older system originating before metal hangers were around. It is not recommended as it

1. Joist hung from girder with metal hanger.

2. Joist sitting on top of girder (butt end).

3. Joist on top of girder (overlap).

4. Ledger used to support joist at girder.

Figure 6-2. Different ways of attaching the joists to the girders. Each affects the level of the girder and thereby the placement of the girder pockets in the foundation wall.

takes too much time to notch each board and the notches weaken the joists. (For more on notching, see end of *Floor Framing*, Chapter 9: "Special Situations—Notching.") Just make your decision before you pour the foundation. (See photos in Chapter 9, *Floor Framing*, "Step 7.")

Review the decision you made for the locations of access doors and other negative spaces. Be sure the final height of the foundation wall is certain. You are finalizing the location of the house, so give it one last thought. You will need to determine the locations of the access door for the foundation, the entrance of any utilities as well as the exit of the sewer lines in order to leave negative spaces for these (see "Step 6," this chapter). See Chapter 5, *Types of Foundations,* to be sure you have chosen the proper foundation.

What You'll Need
Steps 1 to 10

TIME   TO DIG TRENCHES: According to backhoe operator's estimate. TO BUILD FORMS, SET REBAR, TIES AND

ANCHOR BOLTS: 50 to 70 person-hours per 120 linear feet of foundation wall averaging 3 feet in height or less.

PEOPLE   2 Minimum (1 skilled, 1 unskilled); 4 Optimum (2 skilled, 2 unskilled); 6 Maximum (2 skilled, 4 unskilled).

TOOLS   Sledge hammer, framing hammer, levelling device: transit, builder's level, hydro level or water level, steel tape, saw horses, combination square, safety goggles, nail-pulling tools, nail belt, large crayon, pencil, carpenter's level, extension cords, plug junction boxes, saw blades.

RENTAL ITEMS: Transit, rebar bender and cutter, electric shovel (optional), backhoe.

MATERIALS   You are better off purchasing the concrete from a concrete company than mixing it yourself. The form boards can be rented, but most owner builders use their joist stock as forms and clean them and use them as floor joists. Anchor bolts are ½×10 inches (in earthquake areas ⅝×18 inches is recommended) and there are several varieties of form ties that can be used. We will be showing wedge ties in our example.

ESTIMATING MATERIALS NEEDED

REBAR: Rebar is rather simple to order. Just measure the length of the walls and how many levels of rebar there are in each wall. Add 20% to this figure for bends and waste. Baling wire is used to tie the bars together for bends and waste.

ANCHOR BOLTS: You need one anchor bolt for each 6 linear feet of foundation wall (3 in earthquake areas for added protection). In addition, there needs to be an anchor bolt within 12 inches of the end of any sill plate stock.

FORMS: If you are using floor joists, calculate the length and height of the concrete forms to see if the joist stock will be enough for the forms. If not, you can use some of your rafter stock. Have an additional 100 feet or so of 2×4s and 2×6s for cleats and bottom form boards (more, if you are building high forms over 3 feet). Remember, you don't want to cut your floor joists when using them for forms.

STAKES and **KICKERS:** You will need 2 vertical stakes for every 3 to 4 linear feet of form (one for exterior form, one for interior). Also you will need 2 kickers for every 4 to 6 linear feet of wall. Kickers must be long enough to extend from the top of forms, at an angle, into the ground 10 to 12 inches; usually, 1×4 precut stakes can be bought and used.

Also rented metal stakes can be used for kickers and stakes (see "Step 3A: Installing the Vertical Stakes").

WEDGE TIES: Wedge ties usually occur every 2-4 feet along the wall and between each course of form boards.

INFORMATION This chapter is sufficient for building a standard poured concrete foundation. Many of you may have unique situations that are not covered here. You may need to consult a professional or a good book (of which there are few). Many problems you may need to solve at the job site using your common sense. Be sure your solutions will work, pass code and are the simplest solutions you can think of.

PEOPLE TO CONTACT Concrete supplier, concrete pumper. If underfloor utilities are to be placed before the subfloor, you can give any subs you plan to hire notice at this time: plumber, electrician, gas, heating and air conditioning installers, and solar panel installer.

INSPECTIONS NEEDED After the forms are completed and before you pour, you will need to get your rebar and forms inspected.

Reading the Plans

Most plans will provide the details about your foundations and footings. Since this is probably the most important section of the house and since a poorly designed or poorly constructed foundation can cause total house failure, the permit department will probably want detailed foundation specifications.

Plans should include the following:

A) Width of foundation wall
B) Width of footing
C) Height of foundation wall
D) Height of footing
E) Size and placement of reinforcing bar (rebar)
F) Depth of footing trench
G) Location and size of any pier blocks
H) Location of grade, both interior and exterior
I) Location of any drain tile
J) Size and locations of anchor bolts
K) Waterproofing (if any)
L) Any special details
M) Locations of access door and vents

If your plans are not complete, be sure you gather the proper data before beginning. A mistake in this area can be very difficult to correct. (See Figure 6-3.)

Safety and Awareness

SAFETY: Form building is not a particularly dangerous part of the housebuilding process. As always, be careful with the power equipment. Be careful moving the long lengths of rebar around other people. Be careful with the sledge.

AWARENESS: What you are seeking in form construction is accuracy and stability. The tops of the forms need to be high enough above the bottom of the trench to provide the needed footing thickness. The trenches need to be clean, on stable soil and deep enough to place the entire footing beneath the frostline. The forms need to be square and the proper dimension within the allowed margin of error. The rebar and anchor bolts need to be accurately and securely set. All negative spaces must be provided. The forms and dams must be stable so as not to break or fall during the pour.

Overview of the Procedure

Part One: Digging the Footing Trenches and Building the Forms

Step 1: Transfer the batterboard lines to the ground
Step 2: Dig the footing trench
Step 3: Build the forms
Step 3A: Install the exterior vertical stakes
Step 3B: Nail on the exterior form boards
Step 3C: Plumb the exterior forms
Step 3D: Locate and place the interior form stakes
Step 3E: Nail on the interior form boards
Step 4: Place the ties
Step 5: Place the rebar
Step 6: Provide for negative spaces and step dams
Step 7: Set the anchor bolts
Step 8: Oil the bottoms of the forms and stakes
Step 9: Clean out the trench
Step 10: Call for code inspection

Figure 6-3. Plans.

LEGEND

A spacing between piers
B spacing between girders
C width of foundation wall
D location of anchor bolts
E location of access door
F girder notches

G foundation dimensions
H rebar schedule
I width of footing
J thickness of footing
K distance from grade to joist
L distance from exterior grade to top of foundation
M depth of footing/pier trench

FOUNDATION PLAN

FOOTING AND PIER DETAILS

BUILDING SECTION

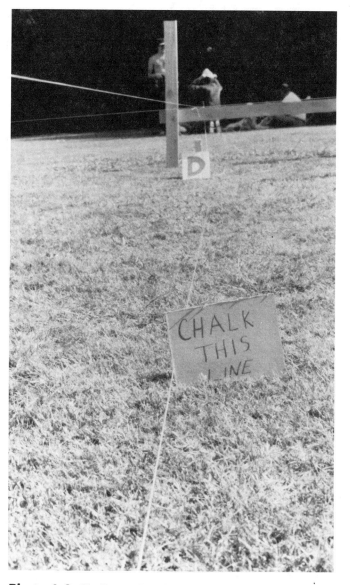

Photo 6-2. Chalking a line on the ground as a guide for the backhoe operator. Here the line represents the outside edge of the ditch and the footing.

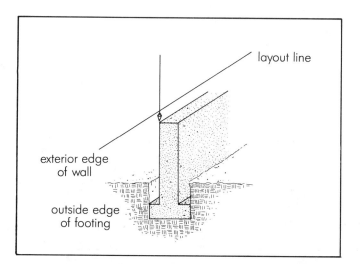

Figure 6-4. Relationship between foundation wall and layout line.

Step 1
Transfer the Batterboard Lines to the Ground

Margin of Error: ½ to ¾ inch.

Most Common Mistake: Forgetting which part of the foundation wall aligns with the layout line.

Diagrams: Figures 6-4, 6-5.

Photograph: Photo 6-2.

At this point your layout lines are up and should be checked for squareness and dimension accuracy one last time. Their accuracy will determine the accuracy of the foundation wall. Once you have the lines where you want them, you need to "transfer" these lines to the ground in order to know where to dig your foundation trenches. Remember, these lines usually represent the exterior edge of the foundation wall, not the interior of the wall or the middle. Also note that the exterior edge of the footing falls to the outside of this line.

To transfer these lines to the ground, simply use a plumb bob to locate each corner of the foundation on the ground, draw a taut string between the corners and mark along the string with lime or powdered chalk. This line will now be your guide for digging your footing trench.

If you want, lines can be run to represent the exact sides of the footing trench.

Figure 6-5. Birdseye view of trench lines marked on the ground.

Step 2
Dig the Footing Trench

Margin of Error: 1 to 1½ inch off alignment with mark.

Most Common Mistake: Not digging deep enough or into stable soil.

Diagrams: Figures 6-6, 6-7, 6-8, 6-9.

Photographs: Photos 6-3, 6-4.

At this point you know where to dig the trench; the next question is how deep. To answer this you must know the frostline in your area. The frostline is the depth to which the moisture in the earth thaws and freezes. This can vary from several feet in the cold states to no frostline in warmer areas where there is no freezing (in these areas a nominal 6-inch frostline is often used). In most areas, the code (as well as good building practices) demands that the *entire* footing be below the frostline. This is needed so that as the earth thaws and freezes, heaves and rises, it will not affect the footing or foundation. The ground below the footing must be stable also and the soil in the area of the frostline is not. So if your frostline is 12 inches and the thickness of the footing is 6 inches, the trench must be at least 18 inches deep to keep the entire footing below the frostline. If you plan to step the footing or foundation (see "Steep Slopes" in Chapter 4, *Layout*, p. 94), to avoid digging deep trenches and pouring lots of concrete, be sure you are still at the proper depth to keep the footing below the frostline. The soil at the bottom of the trench should remain undisturbed and stable or the foundation could sink. Never throw any fill dirt into the bottom of the trench.

It is best to hire a backhoe contractor to dig your trenches. If this is not possible, it can be done by hand. If that is the case, renting an electric shovel is advised. These are jack-hammer-like tools that use a small electric motor and are very easy to dig with. If you are hiring a backhoe operator, be sure he or she understands where you want the trench, where the steps are to be (if any) and how deep to go. Also be sure they are capable of good work or you will have to do a lot of hand digging to adjust for mistakes and perhaps place a lot of wasted concrete. While they are at the site digging the footing trenches, see if there is other work you need them to do, such as driveways, parking pads, septic systems, water, gas or power trenches, stump removal, etc. Be sure all dirt is placed 4 to 6 feet to the outside of the foundation; you want to keep a clearance between the ground and the under parts of the house. The dirt should also be out of the way during the pour.

At this time you can dig any pier holes that are needed. By referring to the plans, run strings over any lines of pier blocks and mark on the ground the outline of the pier footings. Remember, these footings need to be entirely under the frostline. Refer to "Special Situations: Post and Beam" in Chapter 11, *Wall Framing*, p. 250, to see if any piers are needed under load-bearing posts. Cover these holes with plywood so you do not step in them while working. One of our students sprained an ankle that way.

After the trenches and holes are dug, set the batterboard lines back up (they will need to be removed during the digging) by simply rehooking the lines to the nails on the batterboards and test the accuracy of the trench and pier holes. If they are within the margin of error allowed, you are ready to build the forms. Before beginning, clean out the trenches and holes of any debris that could become embedded in the concrete footing and decay, leaving an air pocket. If your soil crumbles easily, you can bevel the sides of your trenches to keep dirt from falling in.

Figure 6-6. Note that the entire footing is below the frostline.

Figure 6-7. Stepped trenches must be dug deep enough to keep the footing below the frostline at all points. Tape determines level of step by measuring from a level line (layout line).

Figure 6-8. Locating, digging and placing pier footings and blocks.

Photo 6-3. Digging the trenches with a small backhoe. These can often be rented.

Photo 6-4. Digging the trenches with an electric shovel. This is a common rental tool.

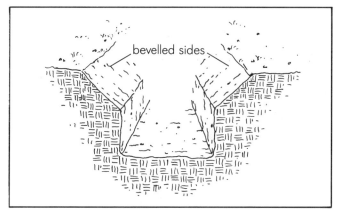

Figure 6-9. Bevel edges of trench in loose soil to keep walls from collapsing.

Step 3
Build the Forms

Diagram: Figure 6-10.

Photograph: Photo 6-5.

Note that the vertical stakes keep the forms suspended over the footing in such a manner that the top of the footing is at the same height as the bottom of the lowest form board. Because of this, the width of the bottom form board must be chosen to allow the footing to come out the proper thickness. The concrete will ooze under the form boards to the trench walls, thus forming the footing. The diagonal kickers keep the forms plumb and properly aligned; the ties and wedges hold the forms together under the pressure of the fresh concrete.

Step 3A
Install the Exterior Vertical Stakes

Margin of Error: ¼ inch off alignment, ¼ inch off plumb.

Most Common Mistakes: Using flat metal stakes; not setting stakes back from layout lines the thickness of a form board.

Diagram: Figure 6-11.

Photograph: Photo 6-6.

After the layout lines have been set up and rechecked for their accuracy, you can begin to install the exterior vertical stakes. You can use wooden stakes (either 2×4s or 1×4s) or metal stakes (either flat or round). The metal stakes can be rented if you do not need them for too long; stake pullers are made for the round stakes which make stake pulling very easy. The flat metal stakes are much harder to pull out of the footing concrete and therefore are not recommended. The 2×4s work pretty well if the ground is not hardpan; if it is, switch to the metal stakes.

The stakes are usually 3 to 4 feet high and are spaced 3 to

4 feet apart. They are set back from the layout line (the outside edge of the foundation) the thickness of 1 form board (in our example 1½ inches).

Locate the 2 corner stakes, run a string between them and place the remaining stakes along the string. Do not push the string out of line with the stakes.

Photo 6-5. The house with trenches dug and forms beginning to be installed. Note: the batterboards and layout lines are used for reference in building the forms.

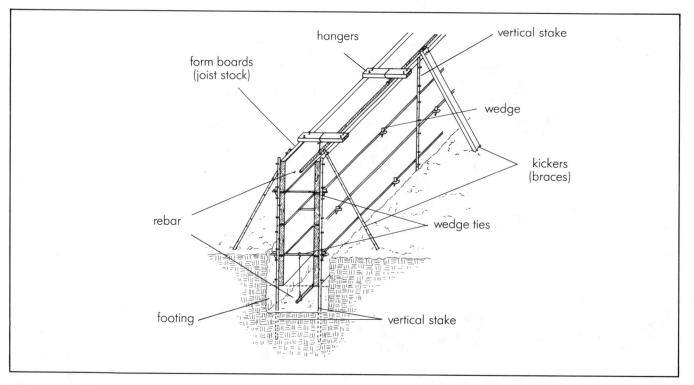

Figure 6-10. Cross-section of typical stem wall form.

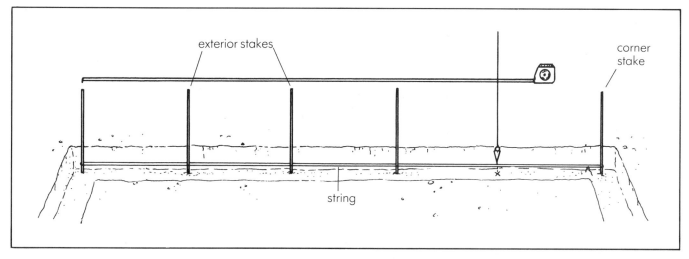

Figure 6-11. Locating corner stakes and running string between these to locate other stakes.

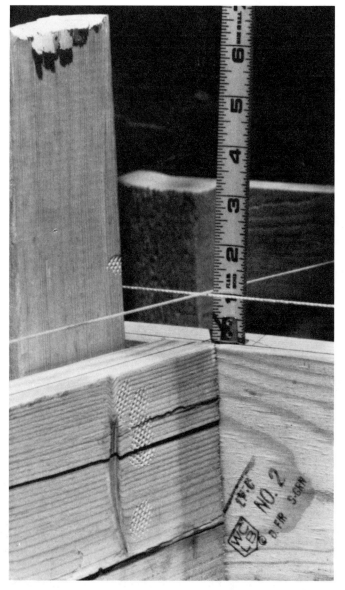

Photo 6-6. Layout line being used as reference to level top of form.

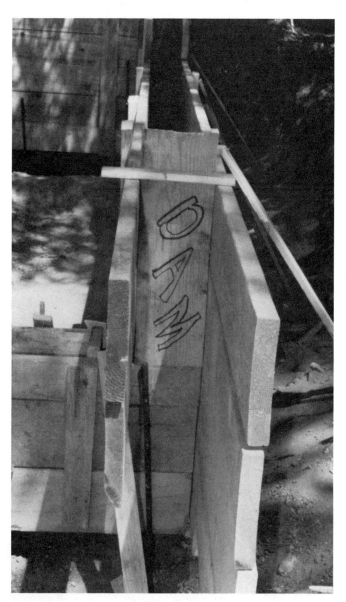

Photo 6-7. Dam being used to step foundation wall. Note how forms (floor joists) are not cut but extend past dam.

Step 3B
Nail on the Exterior Form Boards

Margin of Error: ⅛ to ¼ inch off level.

Most Common Mistakes: Not using straight stock for top boards; not leaving space for form ties; not aligning inside edge of form board with layout line.

Diagrams: Figures 6-12, 6-13.

Photograph: Photo 6-7.

Now it is time to start nailing on the exterior form boards. Usually these are the same boards you plan to use for the floor joists.

Use duplex (double-headed form nails) to nail through the stakes into the form boards so the nails can be easily pulled out when the forms are to be stripped. The metal stakes are predrilled so that you will be able to drive the nails through them. Hammer the nails through the stake while holding the sledge on the interior side of the form board for support. Take care not to step on the edge of the trench.

As you put this first top form board in place, take great care that it is exactly level. Since the concrete wall will be poured to the top of this board, the level of the foundation wall will depend on the level of this board. You can use a long 8-foot level, a builder's level or transit, or use your layout line as a level reference and check the level every 4 feet or so along the top of the board. *Important: Be sure the top board is a good straight board so that the top of the forms will be level.* Remember that the width of the bottom form board will need to be chosen so that the footing comes out the proper thickness. (Sometimes form boards become off-level or out of line, after they have been accurately erected, due to the wet boards warping as they dry or the stakes sinking into the ground.)

Do not line up any splices over the form boards in suc-

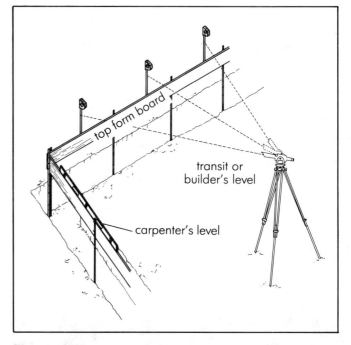

Figure 6-12. Using a builder's level or transit to check level of top form board. A carpenter's level can also be used, but it is not as accurate.

cessive courses, but rather stagger them so as not to create a hinge effect. Nail cleats over the splices. If there are steps in the foundation to reduce the use of concrete, these boards do not have to be cut at the steps. These full-length boards may be needed later. The boards can simply overlap and the dams can be placed between the 2 boards. (See Photo 6-7.)

A space must also be provided between each layer of form boards so that the form ties can be placed in. Use the shank of a nail to gap the forms between each layer of boards. Complete all the outside form boards, using the spacer, and then go on to the next part of Step 3.

Figure 6-13.

Step 3C
Plumb the Exterior Forms

Margin of Error: ¼ to ½ inch off true plumb; ⅛ to ⅜ inch off alignment with layout lines.

Most Common Mistake: Forms off plumb.

Diagram: Figure 6-14.

Photographs: Photos 6-8, 6-9.

If your stakes were properly placed, the forms should be pretty well lined up directly underneath the layout lines. The *interior* edge of the exterior forms is directly beneath the layout line. Drive your kickers into the ground (6 to 12 inches) at an angle and begin driving 2 nails in the kicker where it intersects the top of the form. Then, using a plumb bob or a level, align the *interior* edge of the form directly underneath the layout lines and drive in the nails the rest of the way. Place these kickers every 4 to 6 feet. It is usually best to cut their tops off flush with the tops of the forms to make levelling the concrete easier. Flat or round metal stakes can also be used for kickers. Check the forms with your level to see if, after their inside edges are aligned directly below the layout line, they are also plumb. The form can be within ¼ to ½ inch plumb—but if it is off by more than this you will need to remove the stakes and start again. The most important thing is that the inside edge of this form be directly below your layout line. Remember, this line marks the outside edge of your foundation wall.

Important: After all the exterior forms are erected, aligned and plumbed, check all your dimensions and check for squareness by checking the diagonals. All measurements should be

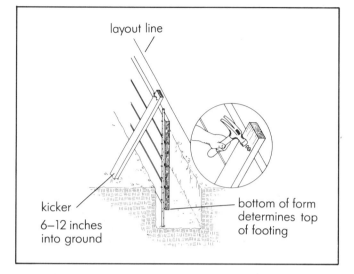

Figure 6-14. Be sure the form is directly below layout line before nailing kicker to top of form.

within ¼ to ½ inch. Your diagonals can be off as much as 1 inch every 50 feet of diagonal. Also place some extra bracing at the corners, as these are often weak areas that burst during the pour.

Photo 6-8. Using plumb bob to align inside edge of form directly below layout line. A level could also be used.

Photo 6-9. Cutting kickers.

Step 3D
Locate and Place the Interior Form Stakes

Margin of Error: ¼ inch off exact placement.

Most Common Mistake: Stakes not set in proper place.

Photograph: Photo 6-10.

Locating the interior vertical stakes is rather simple. You can use a spacer block as shown, locating an interior stake across from each exterior stake. This assures you that after the forms have been completely constructed, the open space between them will be the exact thickness of the foundation wall. You could also locate the corner stakes, as you did the exterior stakes, run a line between them, and locate the rest of the stakes along the line. If the size of the foundation wall changes, such as in switching from a one-story section to a two-story section (from a 6-inch to an 8-inch foundation wall), simply change the spacer to change the location of the interior stakes. The exterior stakes will always be on line, as the outside edge of the foundation wall is always straight.

Step 3E
Nail on the Interior Form Boards

Margin of Error: ⅛ to ¼ inch off level.

Most Common Mistakes: Not using straight stock for top boards; not leaving space for form ties; not aligning inside edge of form board with layout line.

Diagrams: Figures 6-15, 6-16.

Photograph: Photo 6-11.

Starting from the top and using a form nail as a spacer between each course of boards, nail on the interior form boards. Again, be sure to use good straight pieces for the top boards so the forms will be level. With these boards, be sure that they are not only level, but also at the same height as the exterior form boards. Remember, the width of the bottom board needs to be chosen so that the footing is the proper depth, give or take 1 to 1½ inches. As with the exterior forms, provide extra bracing at the inside corners. After you have completed all the interior forms, you are ready to place your wedge ties and rebar. The wedge ties will automatically set the interior forms the exact distance away from the exterior forms. If the exterior forms were aligned and plumb, then the wedges will pull the interior forms into alignment. No kickers are set for the interior forms until after the wedge ties are in place.

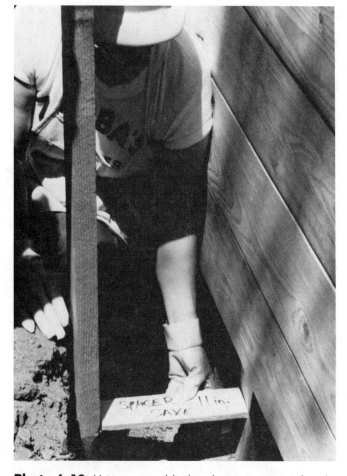

Photo 6-10. Using spacer block to locate interior stakes. In this example an 8-inch foundation wall is being built with 1½ inch thick form boards.

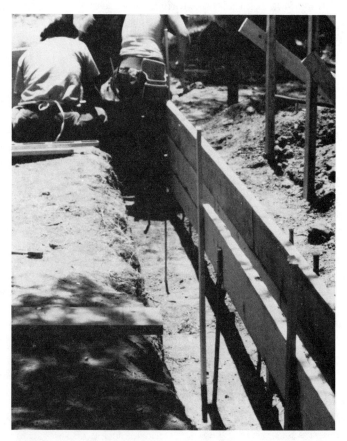

Photo 6-11. Top interior form being installed.

Figure 6-15. Using level to set interior form to the same height as the exterior form boards.

Figure 6-16. Bracing at corners. Top view shows bracing at inside and outside corners, and cleats.

Step 4
Place the Ties

Most Common Mistakes: Insufficient ties; forgetting to put in wedges; wedge ties in upside down.

Diagram: Figure 6-17.

There are several different varieties of form ties. The ones we will be showing are wedge ties and they are recommended. They not only hold the 2 sets of forms together until the concrete sets, but also automatically set the proper spacing between the interior and exterior forms so the foundation wall will be the proper width. Ties are available in different sizes for different wall widths. Six-inch and 8-inch ties are the most common, though larger and smaller ones are available. (*Note:* Sometimes in high walls, the ties are put in *as* the rebar is placed. See "Step 5.")

After the concrete has hardened, the ties will be stuck in the concrete forever, only the little wedges are recyclable. (Also note that many ties are concaved. Always point the open side up so that it can fill with concrete; otherwise you may leave a hole in the concrete.) Ties go between each course of boards and are usually staggered between courses and spaced every 32 inches. On higher walls there will be a great pressure on the bottom of the forms due to the heavy load of concrete. In these cases the spacing between the ties is reduced to handle the extra load. If you are not sure of the spacing for your wall, ask someone who knows. A busted form is a mess.

After you have placed the ties, hammer in their wedges till the form boards are tight against the prongs. Do not forget to put in the wedges on *both* sides of the ties. The flat side of the tie goes against the form, *not* the angled side.

After all the tie wedges are hammered in, our interior forms are aligned, spaced and plumb. Now nail on kickers for the interior forms directly across from the exterior kickers.

Figure 6-17. Wedge ties. Wedges are placed with straight, not angled, sides against the forms.

Figure 6-18. Supporting rebar inside of forms.

Step 5
Place the Rebar

Most Common Mistakes: Improper placing of rebar; rebar not well supported; rebar touching form or ground.

Diagram: Figure 6-18.

Photographs: Photos 6-12, 6-13.

Rebar (reinforcing bar) is used to strengthen the concrete by giving it greater bending strength. It helps the pour resist cracking and holds it together in the event of an earthquake or other movement. Most poured concrete foundations will require some rebar. Its location is shown in the rebar schedule of the plans (see "Plan Reading" at the beginning of this

Photo 6-12. Rebar, wire and ties.

chapter). In earthquake areas there can be quite a bit of rebar, as much as 1 bar every 2 feet vertically and horizontally, and sometimes more. Here are a few things to note about rebar:

☐ The number rebar always refers to the number of eighths of an inch diameter; i.e., #4 rebar equals 4/8 inch or ½ inch.

☐ When joining 2 lengths of rebar together, overlap the pieces 40 times their diameter; i.e., to overlap ½ inch rebar, the formula is ½ inch × 40 = 20 inches.

☐ No rebar can touch any form or dirt; it will be exposed after the pour and may cause the rebar to rust into the wall. No rebar can be within 3 inches of any earth or 1½ inches of any air.

☐ When oiling the forms (explained later in this chapter), be careful not to get any oil on the rebar, as oily metal will not adhere well to the concrete.

☐ Rebar is bent to extend around the corners 18 to 24 inches and also to join interior solid foundation walls with exterior walls.

You are now ready to place the rebar. I highly advise renting a rebar cutter that cuts and bends rebar; it will make the process much easier. The rebar can be supported in various ways as shown in the diagram. Note that in some cases the rebar is placed at the same time as the ties. If more than 2 levels of rebar are to be used or if you foresee any problems in threading the rebar through the ties, then I advise placing the rebar as you set the ties. Insert the lower level of rebar and then the ties, then rebar, then ties, till finished. Tie all rebar together wherever it overlaps with baling wire.

Photo 6-13. Using a rebar cutter and bender (a common rental tool).

Step 6
Provide for Negative Spaces and Step Dams

Margin of Error: ¼ inch off proper size and placement.

Most Common Mistake: Leaving out needed negative spaces.

Diagrams: Figures 6-19, 6-20, 6-21, 6-22.

After the rebar is all in place, build all needed dams at steps and provide any needed negative spaces. Negative spaces (holes or indentations left in the concrete) may be needed for any of the following:

☐ Pipes, sewer, underground electricity, etc.

☐ Girder into wall

☐ Access doors or vent space

Often your plans will not show the locations of all these and you will have to make job site decisions. Refer to *Floor Framing,* Chapter 9, "Step 7," for a discussion on how joist-girder connections may affect a foundation's negative spaces. (Negative spaces for girders should be ¼ inch wider and deeper than the girders.)

Figure 6-19. Dams and rebars at steps. Note: form boards can be left uncut. First step must be at least 15½ inches to avoid having any cripple studs less than 14 inches high.

Figure 6-21. Plug being used for negative space for utility or water. Coat with newspaper so plug will not stick to concrete.

Figure 6-20. Negative space for girder when joists sit on top of girders.

Figure 6-22. Form for access door.

Step 7
Set the Anchor Bolts

Most Common Mistakes: Anchor bolts set too deep; no anchor bolt within 12 inches of end of sill board.

Photograph: Photo 6-14.

Before the pour, all anchor bolts must be set. A jig (a 2×4 with a hole drilled in it to support the anchor bolt) can be used, or the bolts can be set in the fresh concrete and will support themselves until the concrete hardens. The anchor bolts are used to fasten the sill plates (2×6s that lie flat on the foundation) to the concrete foundation. Here are some things to know about anchor bolts:

□ They are usually ½ inch in diameter and 10 inches long; in earthquake areas a ⅝ inch diameter and 18-inch length are recommended.

□ Code usually requires them every 6 feet; in earthquake areas every 3 to 4 feet is recommended.

□ Code requires that at least 7 inches of the bolt be embedded in the pour.

Set the bolts in so they will be in the center of the sill plate. This may not always be the same as the center of the foundation wall. You could have an 8-inch wall and a 6-inch sill plate. The sill will be set flush to the outside edge of the foundation wall. For the bolts to be in the center of the 6-inch sill they will need to be 3 inches in from the edge, not in the center (4 inches from edge) of the wall. Do not keep the bolts exactly on line, but offset them about ¾ inch so as not to split the sill plate along the grain.

There must be a bolt within 12 inches of the end of any sill plate, so be sure you know where 2 pieces of sill stock will butt together along the wall. Also be sure there is a bolt within 12 inches of all corners (end of sills). Every piece of sill must have at least 2 bolts.

Step 8
Oil the Bottoms of the Forms and Stakes

Most Common Mistake: Getting oil on rebar.

Diagram: Figure 6-23.

After everything is ready for the pour, it is usually best to oil certain pieces so they will not stick to the concrete when it is time to remove them. I advise spraying or wiping old motor oil on the vertical stakes where they will be embedded in the footings and on the bottom of the lowest form boards, as they have a tendency to get embedded in the concrete as well. Some builders spray the entire interior of the forms, but I have never really found that necessary. You will need to scrape clean the form boards after they are removed and before they are cut. In very dry areas, you may also want to wet with water the inside of the form boards and the dirt so they do not draw the water from the concrete too quickly.

Figure 6-23. Oiling bottom of vertical stakes where they are embedded into concrete footing.

Photo 6-14. Anchor bolt jig to suspend bolt in form.

Step 9
Cleaning Out the Trench

Before the pour, be sure that the trench is clear of any debris. Any organic debris, such as limbs, mud clods, leaves, etc., will decay and leave a hole in the concrete. Be careful not to brush against any poison oak roots as you do this: an entire class of our students once got poison oak that way. Cut a piece of the root and smell it; poison oak roots smell foul.

Step 10
Calling for Code Inspection

Before the pour, most inspection bureaus will want to check your rebar, the depth of the footing trenches and the quality of the final earth bed. They will not, however, be inspecting for the quality and completeness of the forms. The following checklist will assist you in being sure you are ready for the pour. If possible, I advise having a professional inspect before you pour. It is very hard to un-pour concrete.

Checklist Before the Pour

☐ Are all forms stout and properly braced?

☐ Are all dams in place?

☐ Are all ties and their wedges in?

☐ Is the first step at least 17 inches high so no cripple wall stud will be less than 14 inches?

☐ Are vertical stakes and bottom of forms oiled?

☐ Is all rebar properly overlapped, wired together, bent around corners and the proper distance from the form or earth?

☐ Are all negative spaces provided for: girder pockets, electricity, sewer, access door, water, etc.?

☐ Is there an anchor bolt every 6 feet (3 feet in earthquake areas) and within 12 inches of the end of any sill board?

☐ Are anchor bolts the proper height above the foundation wall (2½ to 3 inches)?

☐ Are all forms level, square and the proper dimensions?

☐ Are extra ties and bracing provided at high walls (over 4 feet)?

☐ Do any bridges need to be built over the forms so you will not be stepping on them?

☐ Are pier holes dug?

After the forms have been built and everything checked for the pour, you are now ready to place the concrete. This is one of the most exciting and tiring days of the entire project. Be ready for it: psychically, mentally and physically. Be sure you are well prepared and rehearsed before the concrete trucks arrive. They create a lot of frantic energy at the site with all the noise they make. They also allow you only so much time; after that there is a charge of $30 to $70 per hour or any fraction thereof. Stay calm during the pour and move carefully, even if it means paying for overtime; it is better to do that than make a mistake, cause an accident or spend a generally frantic day.

About Concrete Companies, Pumpers and Booms

Unless there is no concrete delivery possible, I highly recommend against mixing your own concrete; it is not worth the effort and in the end can cost more than having it delivered. In most areas concrete companies can deliver to the site. They mix the concrete at their yards and keep it ready till it is delivered to your site. They may help you figure out how much you will need, or you will have to calculate your needs in cubic yards. Don't forget to figure for your pier footings. They deliver in a timed progression of trucks until your order is filled.

If you are new at this, you may ask them to spread the deliveries out, giving you a longer time between trucks than usual. Also they may have 5½- or 6½-bag mixes. This designates the number of bags of concrete in each cubic yard (concrete is always measured in cubic yards). Unless recommended otherwise, I would go with the cheaper 5½-bag mix. You will have to pay for all the concrete you order, even if you ordered too much. You can have some step pads or well house slabs ready in case there is an excess of concrete.

If the concrete trucks can get uphill and within a certain distance (about 25 feet) of all parts of the pour, no boom or pumper will be needed; the trucks can use their chutes. If only a small portion of the pour is outside of the reach of the trucks' chutes, you can finish it off with wheelbarrows. However, if your site does not allow for this, a boom pumper or standard pumper should be called in. These machines pump the concrete, both vertically and horizontally, and can place concrete a great distance from the concrete truck. If you plan to use one of these pumpers, let the concrete company know which type. The pumpers require a special concrete mix that is more liquid than most since it must pass through the hoses.

The boom truck is more expensive to hire than the standard hose pump, but it may actually be cheaper in the long run. A standard pumper needs a 6½-bag mix, which is more expensive than the boom truck's 5½-bag mix; so, after a certain number of yards of concrete, the boom is cheaper. Also the boom is many times easier to handle. The extremely heavy hose filled with fresh concrete is held by a tall, hydraulically controlled boom which is controlled by the driver. One other person at the spout can control the pour of the concrete. The standard pumper takes one person at the spout and 4 to 7 more to move the heavy hose around. My recommendation, therefore, is to use the boom when possible. Also, be sure everyone who handles the concrete wears thick rubber gloves to protect their skin.

Worksheet
Steps 1 through 10

ESTIMATED TIME

_____

_____

_____

_____

CREW:

_____ Phone _____

_____ Phone _____

_____ Phone _____

_____ Phone _____

_____ Phone _____

_____ Phone _____

MATERIALS NEEDED

Rebar, baling wire, anchor bolts, floor joists, stakes, kickers, wedge ties.

ESTIMATING MATERIALS

_____ feet of REBAR (#4)

_____ coils of BALING WIRE

_____ ANCHOR BOLTS

$2 \times$ _____ FLOOR JOIST _____ feet long = Quantity

_____

Additional material for forms _____

_____ precut stakes or _____ feet of 1×4 =

No. _____ stakes No. _____ kickers

_____ linear ft. of forms ÷ _____ ft. of spacing

between = No. _____ wedges

COST COMPARISON

REBAR:

_____ Store:

$ _____ per M = $ _____ total

_____ Store:

$ _____ per M = $ _____ total

_____ Store:

$ _____ per M = $ _____ total

FORMS:

$ _____ per M = $ _____ total

_____ Store:

$ _____ per M = $ _____ total

_____ Store:

$ _____ per M = $ _____ total

PEOPLE TO CONTACT

Concrete Supplier _____

Phone _____ Work Date _____

Concrete Pumper (if needed) _____

Phone _____ Work Date _____

Plumber _____

Phone _____ Work Date _____

Electrician _____

Phone _____ Work Date _____

Heating and Air
Conditioning _____

Phone _____ Work Date _____

Solar Panel Installer _____

Phone _____ Work Date _____

Gas _____

Phone _____ Work Date _____

Daily Checklist
Steps 1 through 10

CREW:

_____ Phone_____

_____ Phone_____

_____ Phone_____

_____ Phone_____

_____ Phone_____

_____ Phone_____

_____ Phone_____

TOOLS:

☐ sledge hammer

☐ framing hammer

☐ levelling device

☐ transit

☐ builder's level

☐ hydro level

☐ water level

☐ steel tape

☐ saw horses

☐ combination square

☐ safety goggles

☐ nail-pulling tools

☐ nail belt

☐ large crayon

☐ pencil

☐ carpenter's level

☐ extension cords

☐ plug junction boxes

☐ saw blades

RENTAL ITEMS:

☐ transit

☐ backhoe

☐ electric shovel

☐ rebar bender and cutter

DESIGN REVIEW: Review your decision for the location of access doors and other negative spaces. Also be sure the final height of the foundation wall is certain.

MATERIALS:

_____ feet of rebar

_____ quantity of anchor bolts

_____ coils of baling wire

_____ quantity of floor joists

_____ quantity of stakes

_____ quantity of kickers

_____ lbs. of duplex nails

_____ negative space materials

_____ lumber for cleats, miscellaneous needs

_____ no. of wedges

INSPECTIONS NEEDED:

Inspector _____

Phone _____

Time and Date of Inspection _____

WEATHER FORECAST:

For Week _____

For Day _____

What You'll Need
Steps 11 to 17

TIME   TO POUR, SCREED, SET ANCHOR BOLTS, PULL STAKES AND SET FORMS: 24 to 48 person-hours per 120 feet of foundation wall 3 feet high, with standard pumper. 10 to 20 person-hours per 130 feet of foundation wall 3 feet high, with boom pumper. (It will take much longer if you are mixing your own concrete.)

PEOPLE   This varies, depending on different factors about the pour. You need to carefully evaluate how many people will be needed and be sure that you have enough. Too few people can result in added expenses for delaying the concrete truck or, worse yet, allowing areas of the foundation to harden too soon.

If you are using chutes or a pumper, fewer people are needed than if you are using the pumper with the long hoses that lay on the ground. WITH CHUTES OR BOOM: 2 people to manage chute or boom. WITH HOSE PUMPER: 4 to 6 people to manage the hose.

In addition to this you will need: 1 person to run the vibrator (if you are using one), 1 to 2 people to screed the concrete, 1 person to set the anchor bolts and keep the concrete from trapping the form boards.

TOOLS   Screeds, floats, vibrator (if needed), framing hammer, tape, nails, shovels, rubber gloves, water hose, power saw, brush or insecticide spray can for oiling and watering, oil, sledge hammer, wrench for anchor bolt nuts, level, torpedo level, levelling device (transit, builder's level or water level), wheelbarrow, crow and pry bars, wire brush to clean anchor bolt threads, stake puller, pencil, nail belt, safety goggles, extension cords, plug junction boxes, saw blades.

RENTAL ITEM: Transit.

MATERIALS   The materials you will need are concrete, anchor bolts and pier blocks (if needed).

Contact concrete and pumper companies to determine size of aggregate and number of bags of cement in the mix.

In our example, we will be placing precast concrete pier blocks, with redwood sills embedded in the top of the pier. You can also build your own forms and pour these yourself, though this is more time consuming. On these blocks we will place 4-×-4 posts to support the girders. (See Figure 6-24.)

Another possibility is to use concrete block piers to support the girders. This method is often used on the East Coast. In this case you must adjust the depth of your footing hole so that the top of the piers will come out at the proper height. Each hole must be individually adjusted because you are working with 8-inch intervals for the blocks (4-inch blocks can be used at the top). Don't forget the small sill plate when figuring the height. A termite guard may be needed, a thin piece of metal on the pier, to prevent termites from tunneling into the wooden girder through the hollow cell of the block. (See Figure 6-25.)

Figure 6-24. Precast concrete pier block and two ways of attaching joist to girder.

Figure 6-25. Concrete block pier.

Figure 6-26. Precast concrete pier block with metal fastener.

Pier blocks with metal fasteners are sometimes used. They provide a greater bond between the pier and the wooden post, but are also somewhat more difficult to work with. You need to be more exact when you set them; the post must fit directly between the metal prongs. (See Figure 6-26.)

ESTIMATING MATERIALS NEEDED

CONCRETE: Concrete for foundation walls is always rather hard to estimate. Many concrete companies will do it for you if you give them the details of the project. The problem is, if you buy too little, you will need to call for a partial load, which will cost almost as much as a full load. If you order too much, you will have to pay for it; concrete companies will not take it back. It is best to order a little extra and have forms ready for something else, such as a door stoop, deck piers, etc., where any extra can be used.

To estimate, you will need to measure the widths and heights of the forms and trenches, and then calculate how much concrete measured in cubic yards they will hold. You can only get so exact in this. Then figure out how much the pier footings will use and add these together and order the concrete.

INFORMATION For the most part, the information in this section of the chapter is all you will need to successfully place your concrete, set the anchor bolts and strip the forms. If there is any section that is not clear to you, be sure that you talk to a professional or get clarity in some manner before you pour. Afterwards, it is too late.

INSPECTIONS NEEDED In most areas you will need an inspection before you pour, sometimes both from the government agency and any subdivision regulatory agency.

Do not pour if heavy rain is possible before the concrete has set. Hard rain will wash the cement from the stone aggregate in the concrete. A light rain is OK. (You can cover the freshly poured concrete in rain, but it is generally difficult and dangerous to do a pour in the rain). If there is a chance of freezing weather, wait if you can; the water in the concrete must not freeze before it dries. If you cannot wait, ask the concrete company to add an anti-freeze to the mix. In hot, dry weather, either keep the pour damp for a day or ask about having a drying retardant added to the mix.

Reading the Plans

See "Reading the Plans" in the beginning of this chapter.

Safety and Awareness

SAFETY: Unlike form building, the pour is rather dangerous. There are a lot of people, activity, noise and a need to finish by a certain time. Who could write a better script for an accident? Be sure everyone understands what they are doing, that one person is in charge and that people consciously seek to remain calm and move slowly in an otherwise anxiety-prone setting. The people staffing the concrete hoses or chutes need to be very careful.

AWARENESS: You are seeking to bring the level of the concrete to the top of the form and no higher. Be sure all your dams and negative space inserts hold up under the pressure of the falling concrete. Be sure the rebar remains in its proper location, and that the anchor bolts are accurately set high enough and their threads kept clean of concrete. Be sure the forms are not upset during the pour by knocking them, standing on them, letting the falling concrete pour against them, etc. Make sure the pour ends up as you planned it.

Overview of the Procedure

PART TWO: THE POUR

Step 11: Place the concrete — first pass
Step 12: Place the concrete — second pass
Step 13: Screed the concrete
Step 14: Place the interior pier blocks (if any)
Step 14A: Dig the holes
Step 14B: Reset the layout lines

Step 14C: Pour the footings
Step 14D: Place the interior piers
Step 15: Pull the vertical stakes
Step 16: Strip the forms
Step 17: Keep the foundation damp

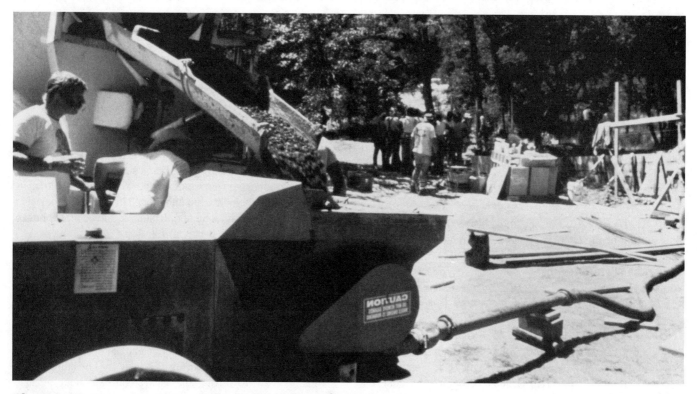

Photo 6-15. Concrete truck dumping concrete into standard pumper.

Step 11
Place the Concrete—First Pass

Most Common Mistake: Letting concrete beat against form and push form off.

Diagrams: Figures 6-27, 6-28, 6-29.

Photographs: Photos 6-15, 6-16, 6-17, 6-18, 6-19, 6-20.

After you have decided whether to use the chutes, boom pumper or standard pumper, check to be sure you have all the help, time and tools you will need. Go over the duties with your crew and be sure that one person will take charge and be in control during the pour. Lack of leadership at this point can cause problems. Many builders lightly spray the interior of the forms and the footing trenches with water before the pour. This is especially advised in very dry climates, as the dry wood and earth can draw the moisture out of the concrete too soon, causing it to be too brittle.

Next, begin to place the concrete (place, not pour, is the trade word, just in case you want to sound like a pro). Usually it is best for the first pass to complete the footing and go 6 inches into the forms. Return for the second and final passes *before* the first has set up. This process of 2 or 3 passes takes some of the pressure off the fresh concrete and prevents it from oozing around the bottom of the forms and embedding the form boards. On high walls, 3 passes are recommended. Remember, avoid pouring fresh concrete on top of set concrete. This will set up a "cold joint" which will be a weak spot. If you cannot finish the pour in one process, rough up the edges and place pieces of rebar in the first part of the pour before it dries.

As you pour the concrete be sure that the fresh concrete does not beat against the side of the forms. As much as possible pour straight down. A piece of plywood can be used for a splash. The pressure of the concrete beating against the sides can push the forms off plumb.

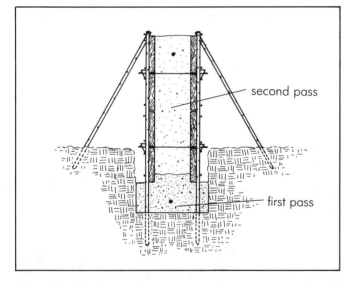

Figure 6-27. Placing the concrete in two passes. Avoid "cold joints."

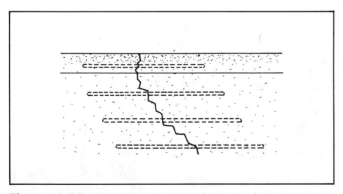

Figure 6-28. Using rebar on irregular joint when connecting a concrete pour to one which has already hardened.

Figure 6-29. Plywood splash being used to prevent concrete from battering form boards.

Photo 6-16. Holding heavy hose of standard pumper. The hose is hard to hold as it has a surging action.

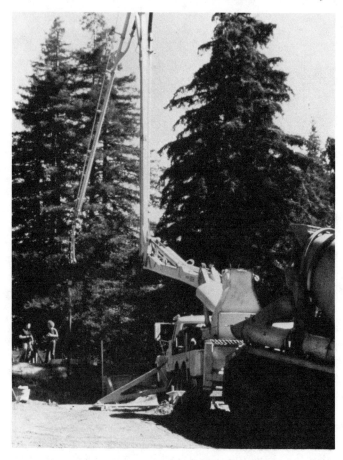

Photo 6-17. The boom pumper with suspended hose.

Photo 6-18. One person directing hose of boom pumper.

Photo 6-19. Concrete truck with chutes. This is easiest and cheapest if the chutes can reach all areas of the pour.

Photo 6-20. Pouring concrete straight down.

Photo 6-21. Using vibrator to settle concrete.

Step 12
Place the Concrete—Second Pass

Margin of Error: No concrete over top of form boards after screeding; ⅛ inch lower.

Most Common Mistake: Concrete poured too high or too low.

Photograph: Photo 6-21.

After your first pass, begin the second pass. At this stage you may want to use an electric concrete vibrator. This assures that the concrete is completely settled and there are no holes or any honeycombing effect. One person follows directly behind whomever is pouring the concrete and sticks the vibrator completely in and then quickly pulls it back out. Do not leave the vibrator in too long or it will cause the concrete to push out around the bottoms of the forms. Should any concrete creep up outside the bottom form boards and embed them, push the concrete away while it is still fresh or it will entrap the bottom form board. If you are not using a vibrator, you can use a piece of rebar and plunge it up and down, and beat on the sides of the forms with a small hand sledge to be sure that the concrete has settled properly.

As you pour, bring the concrete to the top of the form and ½ inch higher. Another person should be working behind you screeding the concrete and being sure the anchor bolts and negative spaces are in properly.

Note: Sometimes, as the concrete is compacted by the vibrator, you may have to add more to bring the concrete to the top of the form again.

Photo 6-22. Using 1 × 4 as screed board. 1 × 4 is being moved in short strokes perpendicular to the forms.

Step 13
Screed the Concrete

Margin of Error: Flush with top of forms.

Most Common Mistake: Concrete too high.

Photograph: Photo 6-22.

A common screed is a 1×4 or 2×4 used on edge and moved back and forth across the width of the foundation wall to level out the pour. Small hand concrete floats can be used also. Be sure this is done well and especially that there are no high spots that will later have to be chiseled down. Check that all anchor bolts are in, that they are plumb and that no concrete is in their threads. Screed around anchor bolts as you go along. If you don't have pier blocks to place, your next step will be to pull the vertical stakes that are sticking into the concrete footings. We will discuss that in "Step 15." "Step 14" will discuss the placement of pier blocks for interior girders.

Step 14
Place the Interior Pier Blocks (If Any)

Pier blocks are used to support any girders required in the floor frame. Girders are used for additional support of floor joists spanning from foundation wall to foundation wall. This step will be broken into sub-steps A through D.

Step 14A
Dig the Holes

Most Common Mistake: Pier holes off line.

Be sure that the holes are on line, the proper dimension and depth (deep enough for the entire footing to be below the frostline) and in good stable soil. Before pouring any concrete, be sure the hole is free of any debris.

Step 14B
Reset the Layout Lines

Margin of Error: ¼ inch.

Most Common Mistake: Inaccurate lines.

Diagram: Figure 6-30.

Photograph: Photo 6-23.

If the holes are dug and ready, reset the layout lines for the interior pier blocks. These lines can be running on either side of the blocks or in the center of the block; it does not matter as long as you know what part of the pier it designates and you place the pier accordingly. An easier way is to run new lines connected to the inside of the interior form boards. Keep these lines close to the ground and this will make locating your blocks much easier. Tie a little piece of string on the line to mark the exact center of the block. Hang a plumb bob from that string to locate where the center of the pier block should be placed.

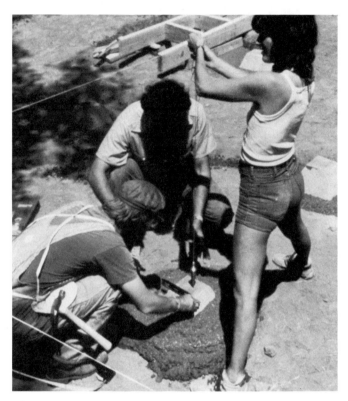

Photo 6-23. Using plumb bob and layout line to locate piers.

Step 14C
Pour the Footings

Diagram: Figure 6-31.

If possible, pour the footings before the concrete trucks leave, rather than having to mix your own concrete or having to call them back with a partial load. Pour the footing the proper thickness and screed it on the top so that it is relatively level. The only time this footing pour must be very level is when you are using concrete blocks. If this is the case, it is best to set up level lines so that you can measure down from them to be sure the top of the footing is where you want it to be. A water level, transit or builder's level will work well here.

Step 14D
Place the Interior Piers

Margin of Error: ⅛ inch off level; ¼ to ½ inch off proper location.

Most Common Mistakes: Pier block off level, or off line; piers not sunk deep enough.

Photograph: Photo 6-24.

While the footing concrete is still wet, press a pier block into it until about half of the block is embedded in the fresh concrete. Then using a small torpedo level, level the top of the block in both directions and diagonally. Continue using this method until all pier blocks have been placed.

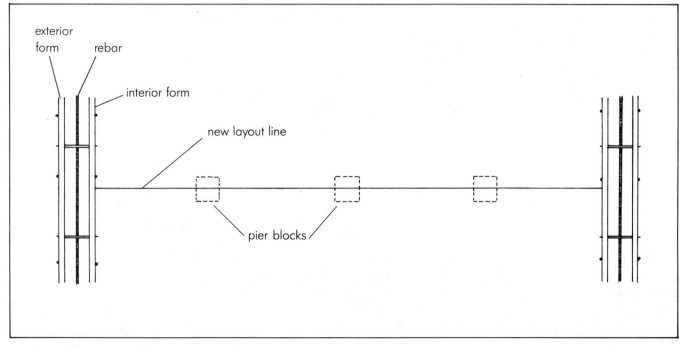

Figure 6-30. Attaching new pier layout line to inside of interior form board (top view). Note that the line demarcates the center of the piers in this example.

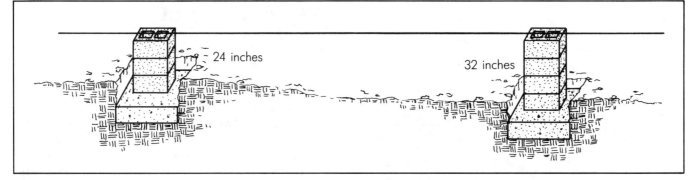

Figure 6-31. Using concrete blocks as piers. Note that the top of the footing must be located an even multiple of 8 inches below the bottom of the girder.

Photo 6-24. Using torpedo level to level pier block.

Figure 6-32. Pulling out a wooden vertical stake. Note the hole drilled for crowbar leverage.

Photo 6-25. Foundation immediately after the pour. Note: pier blocks in place.

Step 15
Pull the Vertical Stakes

Most Common Mistake: Allowing the concrete to become too hard.

Diagram: Figure 6-32.

Photograph: Photo 6-25.

Before the concrete has entirely set up, you need to pull out all the vertical stakes that are stuck into the concrete footing. Don't pull these too early, as they are still serving to hold the forms suspended over the footing trench, but if you wait too long you will not be able to pull the stakes loose from the concrete footings. It is hard to say exactly how long after the pour to wait before pulling the vertical stakes. It depends on shading conditions, humidity, temperature, dryness of the ground, mix of the concrete, etc. We have had to pull stakes one hour after the pour on a hot, dry California day and could pull them the next day on a wet, humid North Carolina day. Use your judgement. Usually, pull the stakes when you can press hard into the concrete with a hard object and make an indentation, but you cannot really penetrate the concrete. Test the stakes; when you feel you can wait no longer, start to pull. Sometimes you will have to come back after dinner or work at night under the lights to pull them at the right time, but don't let them get stuck. We still have $100 worth of metal stakes sticking in a foundation in the Sierra foothills. We waited too long. If you are using the round metal stakes, you can rent a special stake puller for these.

Figure 6-33. Stripping form using hammer (or crow or pry bar).

Step 16
Strip the Forms

Most Common Mistake: Straining your back.

Diagram: Figure 6-33.

Photograph: Photo 6-26.

Usually the forms can be stripped the next day. This is a rather simple process unless some of the bottom form boards have gotten embedded in the concrete. Simply remove all the wedges from the ties, and remove all cleats, stakes and kickers. Then, using a large crow or dry bar or a pick-ax, start to peel the boards off. Clean these boards by scraping them with a shovel and stack them neatly to be used as floor joists.

Step 17
Keeping the Foundation Damp

Though many builders ignore this step, it is usually advisable to keep the pour damp for 1 to 3 days. This allows the concrete to cure gradually and makes for a stronger pour. Often, if it cures too quickly, it can be very brittle. Sometimes chemicals (pozolith) are added to the concrete to slow the process. There are a number of ways of keeping the concrete damp. If possible, you can spray it with water every few hours or drape damp burlap bags over it. Some builders just strip the interior forms, leaving the exterior forms on for a few days; the concrete will stay damp under the forms. You are probably creating no great threat to the house if you skip this process, but, if possible, it is better to include it.

Special Situations

Foundation Drain
(Figures 6-34, 6-35, Photo 6-27)

Many areas of the country either require or recommend foundation drains. These drain pipes keep ground water from flowing into the crawlspace or basement or from undermining the footing. Consult with your local builders or inspection office to see if they are needed in your area.

Basically, they are perforated plastic pipes, about 3 to 4 inches in diameter, that are placed at the same level as or directly on top of the footing. Gravel is placed above and below them to keep dirt from clogging the holes. Tar paper is often placed above the gravel before the dirt is backfilled to further keep the sill from filling the holes.

If at all possible, place the pipes above the footings. If you place them at the same level, you will have to build a wider footing trench and form on one side of the footing wall. Check to be sure which is recommended before proceeding. If you are using the type of pipe that is only perforated for half the diameter of the pipe, point the holes down towards the ground, not up!

Photo 6-26. Prying bottom form board loose that has gotten embedded in footing concrete.

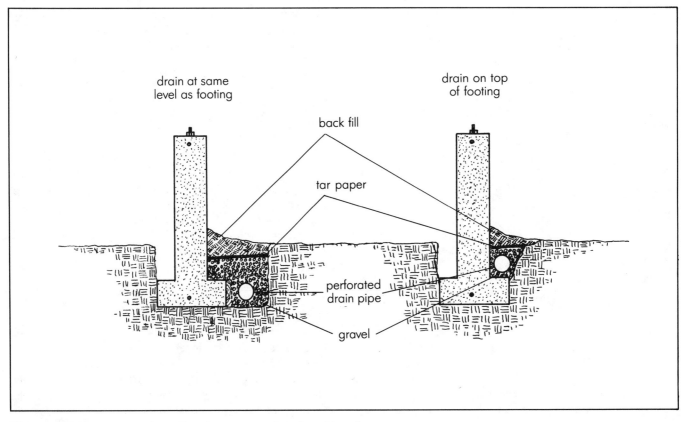

Figure 6-34. Two ways of installing drain pipe or tile at foundation footings.

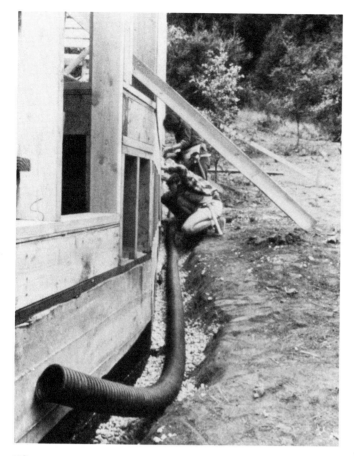

Photo 6-27. Drain pipe going in.

footing form

Figure 6-35. Footing form used in larger footing trench when placing drain pipe at same level as footing.

Photo 6-28. Air pockets left by insufficient packing or vibrating.

Figure 6-36. Sill anchor (not recommended).

Special Situations

Sill Anchors
(Figure 6-36)

Some builders use sill anchors instead of anchor bolts. It is tempting, since they make the application of the sill plates quicker and easier; you do not have to drill any holes. I would recommend against these, however, as they do not have the ability to pull any irregularities out of the sill plate board stock as the permanently set anchor bolts do.

Wet Sills

See wet sills in Chapter 7, *Sill Plates,* p. 157.

Air Pockets
(Photo 6-28)

Sometimes, due to insufficient vibrating, air pockets will be visible after the forms are removed. Unless this is severe, it will not affect the quality of the foundation. Simply take some mortar and fill in the spaces.

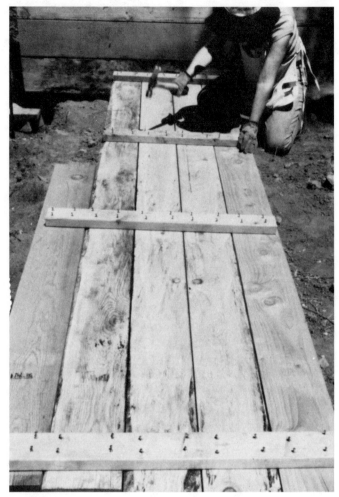

Photo 6-29. Building forms on a steep slope.

Building Forms by a High Bank
(Photo 6-29)

Sometimes if you are building the forms in front of a steep bank you may not be able to get a hammer between the bank and the outside of the form boards. In this case, the forms are built on the ground first and then lifted into place, levelled and plumbed.

Worksheet
Steps 11 through 17

ESTIMATED TIME

_____

_____

_____

_____

CREW

Skilled Leader

_____

_____

Unskilled

_____

_____

_____

_____

For Hose Pumper (Additional)

_____

_____

MATERIALS NEEDED

Concrete, anchor bolts, pier blocks (if needed).

ESTIMATING MATERIALS

Number of cubic yards in foundation walls

and wall footings _____

Number of cubic yards for pier footings _____

Yards of concrete _____

Number of anchor bolts _____

Number of pier blocks _____

COST COMPARISON

_____ Pumper Company:

$ _____ per hour; $ _____ per day

_____ Pumper Company:

$ _____ per hour; $ _____ per day

_____ Pumper Company:

$ _____ per hour; $ _____ per day

_____ Concrete Company:

$ _____ per yard; $ _____ per hr. overtime for truck

_____ Concrete Company:

$ _____ per yard; $ _____ per hr. overtime for truck

_____ Concrete Company:

$ _____ per yard; $ _____ per hr. overtime for truck

Daily Checklist
Steps 11 through 17

CREW:

_____ Phone _____

_____ Phone _____

_____ Phone _____

_____ Phone _____

_____ Phone _____

_____ Phone _____

_____ Phone _____

TOOLS:

☐ stake puller   ☐ sledge hammer

☐ vibrator   ☐ wrench

☐ floats   ☐ torpedo level

☐ brush   ☐ level

☐ spray can   ☐ levelling device

☐ oil   ☐ transit

☐ sledge   ☐ builder's level

☐ wheelbarrow   ☐ water level

☐ rubber gloves   ☐ crow and pry bars

☐ screeds   ☐ wire brush

☐ framing hammer   ☐ pencil

☐ tape   ☐ nail belt

☐ nails   ☐ safety goggles

☐ shovels   ☐ extension cords

☐ rubber gloves   ☐ plug junction boxes

☐ water hose   ☐ saw blades

☐ power saw

RENTAL ITEMS:

☐ transit

MATERIALS:

_____ concrete

_____ anchor bolts

_____ pier blocks

INSPECTIONS NEEDED:

Government Inspector _____

Phone _____

Time and Date of Inspection _____

Subdivision Inspector _____

Phone _____

Time and Date of Inspection _____

WEATHER FORECAST:

For Week _____

For Day _____

7 Sill Plates

Figure 7-1. An overview and a closeup of sill plates. Note that the sill plate is always flush with the outside (exterior) edge of the foundation wall.

What You'll Be Doing, What to Expect

SILL PLATE INSTALLATION is easy and enjoyable. There is little physical strain or effort. Your emphasis is on accuracy and correcting discrepancies in the foundation wall. It is just a matter of attaching the sills (see Figure 7-1) on the foundation wall so that they are square, the proper dimensions and, most important, level.

As in many areas of construction, there are several approaches to sill plate installation. I have chosen the one I feel is best for the novice builder. It involves a process of checking the squareness of the foundation before installing the sills. Although it is a little more time-consuming than other approaches, it assures you that the sill plates will be true and square even if the foundation is not. This is very important because the floor frame and the rest of the house will be built on these sills, and if they are off square it can cause problems further down the line. (See Photo 7-1.)

Jargon

ANCHOR BOLT. Bolt embedded in the concrete foundation that holds the sill plate (and thereby the house) to the foundation.

PRESSURE-TREATED OR TREATED LUMBER. Wood that has been thoroughly penetrated with a decay and termite preventative chemical. The chemical is inserted under pressure and replaces the natural moisture in the wood.

SHIM. A thin wedge of wood, metal, or a piece of plywood used for levelling or plumbing wood members.

SILL PLATE. Horizontal framing member that rests on top of the foundation wall and is bolted to the foundation. Usually a 2×6, pressure-treated or redwood, lying flat.

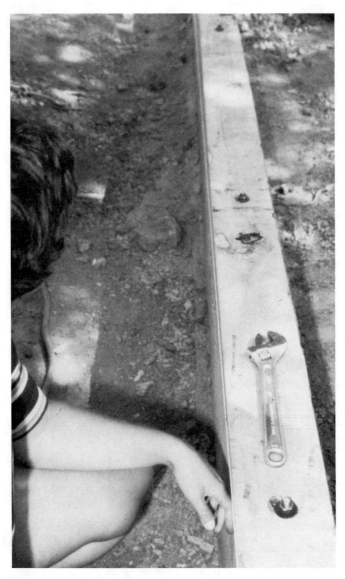

Photo 7-1. A sill plate installed on top of a foundation wall.

Purposes of Sill Plates

1) To attach the wooden house to the concrete foundation
2) To level the top of the foundation wall
3) To keep the framing lumber out of contact with the concrete, where it could rot

Design Decisions   None.

What You'll Need

TIME   10 to 20 person-hours per 120 linear feet of foundation wall.

PEOPLE   1 Minimum (skilled); 2 Optimum (1 skilled, 1 unskilled); 4 Maximum (2 teams of 2).

TOOLS   Framing hammer, power saw, level, carpenter's level, chalkline, string, 100-foot tape, 25-foot tape, combination square, wrench, pencil, nail belt, safety goggles, drill, bits, extension cords, plug junction boxes, saw blades, shims, chisels, charges and nails for nail gun (if needed).

RENTAL ITEMS: Transit, concrete nail gun (if needed).

MATERIALS   Usually only two types of materials are used for sill plates: foundation grade redwood and pressure-treated stock. Most codes will require one of these two. (Occasionally codes allow an untreated softwood to be used.) Often the stock sold for sill plates is very low quality; the sill is not in a structural position and cannot fail. Your greater concern is rotting, which is why a rot-resistant material is required. Be careful in buying your stock; badly bowed boards simply will not work. Knots in the boards are OK.

Pressure-treated lumber is usually a little cheaper than the redwood. If the pressure treatment has thoroughly penetrated the thickness of the stock, it should work as well as the foundation grade redwood. Also check to be sure it is as straight as the redwood. Often it is not. Of late, the foundation grade redwood, which is fairly inexpensive, has been such straight stock that we have been using it for deck planks.

ESTIMATING MATERIALS NEEDED

Since there must be an anchor bolt within 12 inches of the end of any piece or splice of sill stock, the length of the pieces needs to be coordinated with the placement of the anchor bolts. See *Poured Concrete Foundations,* "Step 7."

INFORMATION   This chapter should get you through without any other needed info.

PEOPLE TO CONTACT   None.

INSPECTIONS NEEDED   None.

Reading the Plans   None.

Safety and Awareness

SAFETY: This process of construction is rather safe, but as always never lose respect for power tools. If you are using the concrete nail gun (in order to apply vertical plates at steps in the foundation), be sure you understand its operation. Always use safety goggles and turn your head away when you fire. This is one of the most dangerous construction tools I know.

AWARENESS: When applying the sill plates, you are seeking exactness in level, squareness and dimension. Do not assume the foundations are true in any of these. Work out any foundation discrepancies with the sill plates.

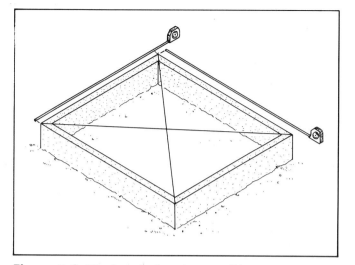

Figure 7-2. Checking the foundation wall for squareness and the proper dimensions before installing the sill plates.

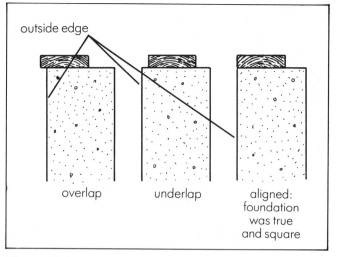

Figure 7-3. Three possibilities of sill plate alignment with the outside edge of the foundation wall.

Overview of the Procedure

Step 1: Check the squareness of the foundation wall
Step 2: Select the stock
Step 3: Measure the sill plates
Step 4: Establish inside corners of sill plates
Step 5: Snap chalklines for inside edges of sill plates
Step 6: Mark and drill anchor bolt holes
Step 7: Install and level sill plates

Step 1
Check the Squareness of the Foundation Wall

Margin of Error: ½ inch off square or off dimension.

Most Common Mistake: Allowing too great a margin of error.

Diagrams: Figures 7-2, 7-3.

Before installing the sill plates, check the squareness and dimensions of the foundation wall. Refer back to the plans to be sure you have the required dimensions. No matter how accurate you are, there will always be some error; it is the nature of the tools and materials you are using. Installing the sill plates precisely will allow you to make up for most minor discrepancies created at the foundation stage.

During this step, determine any errors in the foundation wall. This will give you a sense of how much adjustment will be needed in the sill plate stage. Even if the foundation wall is not exactly true and square, install the sill plates so that *they* are. This may mean that the outside edge of the sill plates will not align exactly with the outside edge of the foundation wall.

If the difference between the outside edge of the foundation wall and the outside edge of the sill plate is too great (over 1 to 1½ inches), only allow about a 1-inch difference and build the sill plates out of square. You may be able to adjust a little more in the floor framing stage.

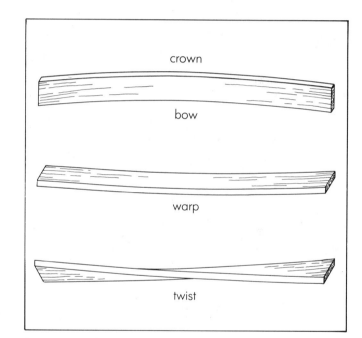

Figure 7-4. Examples of irregularities in lumber. Be careful of sill stock that is badly bowed.

Step 2
Select the Stock

Margin of Error: Bows — ½ to ¾ inches out of true.

Most Common Mistake: Bowed stock.

Diagram: Figure 7-4.

Photograph: Photo 7-2.

It is important that the stock be good straight pieces. All pieces will be somewhat bowed; it is the nature of wood. A small bow can be pulled or pushed out. Do not use badly bowed pieces. Warps in the boards are OK; they will flatten out once the weight of the house is placed on them.

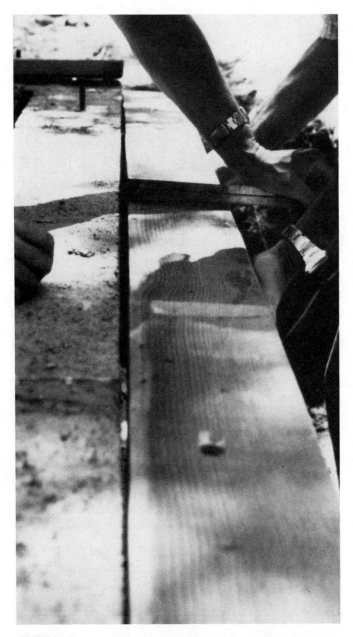

Photo 7-2. Using the foundation wall as a straight edge to test for straightness of the sill plate. A ½ to ¾-inch bow over a 12 to 14-foot board is allowable.

Step 3
Measure the Sill Plates

Margin of Error: ¼ inch off measurement.

Most Common Mistake: Inaccurate measurements.

Photograph: Photo 7-3.

After you have selected your stock, it is time to measure and cut. This is relatively simple and straightforward. The only thing to remember is that there must be an anchor bolt within 12 inches of the end of any sill plate and sill plates cannot butt together over any opening in the foundation wall, such as a vent opening or an access door.

Step 4
Establish Inside Corners of Sill Plates

Margin of Error: Exact.

Most Common Mistake: Not being exact.

Diagram: Figure 7-5.

After you have figured how far off the foundation wall is, mark these discrepancies on the top of the foundation wall indicating whether the true outside corner is farther in or farther out from the actual one.

Now using the exact outside corners as references, mark the corresponding inside corners of the sills on the foundation wall. To do this, you must know the exact width of the sill stock. In our example we are using 2×6 sills, so we will use 5½ inches as the exact width measurement. Do this at all corners of the foundation. Be sure you are marking for the inside, not the outside corners of the sill plates.

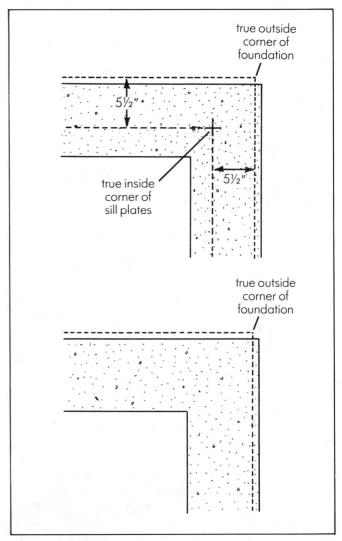

Figure 7-5. Locating the true inside and outside corners of the foundation wall.

Photo 7-3. Measuring for sill plates. Remember that anchor bolts are needed 12 inches from the end of the wall and 12 inches from where the sill ends come together along the wall.

Step 5
Snap Chalklines for Inside Edges of Sill Plates

Margin of Error: Exact.

Most Common Mistake: None.

Diagram: Figure 7-6.

After you have determined the exact inside corners of the sill plates, snap chalklines between these points. You will then have an outline on the top of the foundation wall of the exact inside edges of the sill plates. Once this is finished, check the dimensions and squareness of these lines to see if they are accurate.

Step 6
Mark and Drill Anchor Bolt Holes

Margin of Error: ¼ inch of exact location of bolts.

Most Common Mistake: Not drilling holes larger than anchor bolts.

Diagrams: Figures 7-7, 7-8.

Photographs: Photos 7-4, 7-5.

Figure 7-6. The dotted lines (chalklines) represent the inside edges of the sill plates.

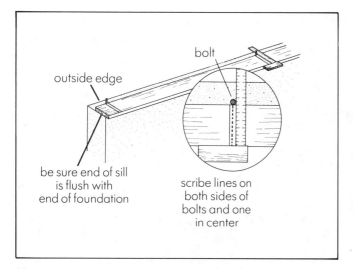

Figure 7-7. Marking the sill plates for anchor bolt holes.

Figure 7-8. Locating the anchor bolt holes on the sill plates.

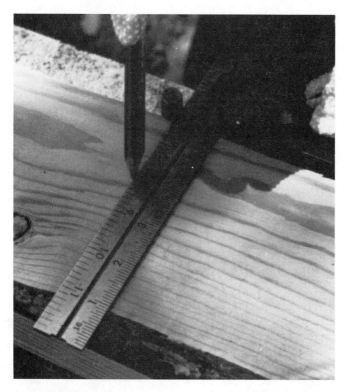

Photo 7-4. Marking an anchor bolt location on the sill plate.

Now place the sill pieces you have cut on top of the foundation wall. They should be placed on the inside of the bolts, aligning the ends into position. Press the sill plates against the inside of the anchor bolts and scribe lines on the sill, marking both sides of each bolt.

Draw a third line on the sill plate exactly between these first two lines. This new line, in the middle of the first two, marks where the center of the anchor bolt will be. Now you must determine where on this centerline to drill the hole. To do this, measure from the center of the anchor bolt to the line that you snapped marking the inside edge of the sill plate. Then transfer this measurement along the scribed bolt centerline from the inside edge of the sill plate.

After locating the marks, drill the anchor bolt holes. It is wise to use a drill bit that is ⅛ to ¼ inch larger in diameter than the anchor bolt itself to allow for final adjustment. Be sure that you drill a straight hole. You are now ready to install the sill plates.

Photo 7-5. Drilling holes for the anchor bolts. These holes should be ⅛ to ¼ inch larger in diameter than the bolts.

Step 7
Install and Level Sill Plates

Margin of Error: ⅛ to ¼ inch off level. ⅛ to ¼ inch off proper alignment with chalklines.

Most Common Mistake: Sill plates off level.

Diagram: Figure 7-9.

Photographs: Photos 7-6, 7-7, 7-8, 7-9.

Now simply place the sill plates over the bolts and check to see if the inside edges of the sills are aligned with the chalklines on top of the foundation wall. Also check to see if the inside corners are aligned with their marks. If the board is at all bowed (which most probably it will be), you may need to push or pull the sill while tightening the bolt.

note how sill plates meet at corners

Figure 7-9. Using a transit to check the level of the sill plates.

Photo 7-6. Pushing the crown out of a sill plate. Note that a plumb bob is being used to align the outside edge of the sill directly below the layout line.

Photo 7-7. Using levels to level the sill plates.

Photo 7-8. Wooden shims are being used to level the sill plate where the foundation wall was poured off level. Wooden shims may not be allowed by all codes.

Photo 7-9. Sill plates are finally being secured after all the levelling and alignment adjustments have been made. Note the string along the edge to test for straightness.

Figure 7-10. Termite guard.

Before you tighten the nuts permanently, partially tighten them and check the sill to see if it is level. This is a very important process. The entire house will be resting on these sills and if they are not level, it will throw off the floors and walls. You can check the level by placing a 4-foot, or preferably an 8-foot, level on top of the sill. A more exacting process, and one that I would recommend, is using a transit or builder's level and shooting the level every 3 or 4 feet along the sill.

If the sill is too low in areas, it can be shimmed. If you plan to use wood shims, I would suggest plywood shims as opposed to the standard cedar shims. Plywood shims will not compress under the weight. You can also pack the low areas with mortar; in some counties this may be required by code.

If the sill plate is too high, the high areas of the concrete will need to be chipped away. If a knee wall (cripple wall) is to go above the high area, you can install the sill as is and adjust the heights of the cripple studs to make the top of the knee wall level. (See next chapter, *Knee Walls.*)

After the adjustments are made to level the sill plates, tighten the bolts using a large washer underneath each bolt. Using your chalkline, be sure the plates are properly aligned as you tighten the bolts.

You are now finished with this stage; unless the foundation was aligned badly or the wood stock was of poor quality, it should have gone relatively smoothly and prepared you for the somewhat more difficult stage of knee walls and floor framing. You may want to check the square and dimensions of the finished sill plates to see how accurate you have been. Keep your standards high and at the same time use your margins of error to keep the work flowing at a good pace.

Special Situations

Termite Guards
Diagram: Figure 7-10.

In areas where there is a high risk of ground termite infestation, a termite guard is advised. It is especially suggested in areas where you are using concrete block foundations because the termites can tunnel through the hollow cells of the blocks. It also stops them from building mud tunnels on the inside of the foundation walls and finding their way into the wood. When in doubt, use it; it's cheap and quick, and may save a lot of problems down the way. It also keeps the wooden sill plate out of contact with the concrete, which can draw the moisture out of the wood.

Sill Insulation (Sill Sealer)
Photograph: Photo 7-10.

In colder climates or in houses where the underfloor areas are to be used as part of the heating ventilation system, or for storage or as a basement, a sill sealer or sill insulation is recommended. This prevents air from flowing between the sill plate and the foundation wall. Sill insulation can be bought in 6-inch wide by 1-inch thick fiberglass rolls, similar to stan-

Photo 7-10. Sill insulation is being applied before the sill plates are installed.

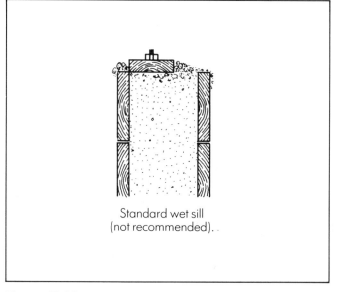

Figure 7-11. Two types of wet sills.

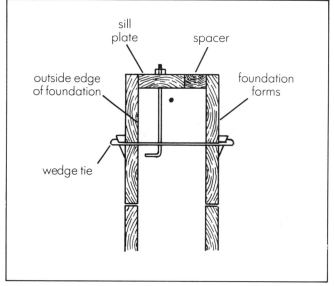

Figure 7-12. An alternate wet sill.

dard insulation. It is applied between the sill and the foundation wall or between the sill and the termite guard (if you are using a termite guard).

Wet Sills
Diagrams: Figures 7-11, 7-12.

Some builders use a "wet sill." This is basically a sill plate that is installed into the fresh concrete and levelled before the concrete dries. The anchor bolts are inserted into the sill and then the sill and bolts are set into the freshly poured concrete. This has a serious drawback. Since the anchor bolts

are not strongly anchored into hardened concrete as in the standard procedure, you cannot use them to pull out any bow or warp in the sill plate. It is a quicker way of applying the sill, and is therefore popular with many builders, but it is not advised for high quality construction.

An alternate process of using a wet sill may work to pull out any bows or warps. As shown in Figure 7-12, the foundation forms are built 1½ inches higher than the actual pour. The sill plate and anchor bolts are set into forms and the concrete is poured. Spacers are used if the foundation wall is wider than the sill plates. The straight foundation forms can then be used to pull out any warps or bows.

Photo 7-11. Sill anchors are being nailed to the sills. Use these only if the sill stock is very straight.

Photo 7-12. Using a concrete nailing gun to secure vertical sill plates. Be careful, the gun can be dangerous.

Figure 7-13. A sill plate on a slab foundation.

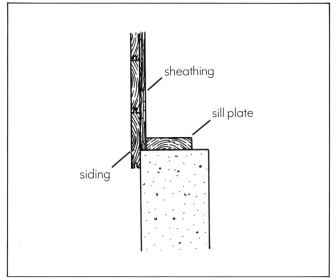

Figure 7-14. A sill plate kicked back to allow the siding to hide the sheathing when viewed from underneath (not recommended).

Sill Anchors
Photograph: Photo 7-11.

Sill anchors are sometimes used instead of anchor bolts. These are easier and quicker to put on because neither drilling nor measuring for anchor bolt holes is required. They are not advised either, because they do not assist in pulling out any bows or warps as do the anchor bolts.

Sill Plates on Concrete Slabs
Diagram: Figure 7-13.

Sill plates are installed in basically the same way on slabs as on concrete walls or concrete block foundations. Find the exact inside corners, pop lines and apply the sills. Usually these sills, which are often pressure treated or redwood, are 2×4s (unless you are building a 2×6 wall) and serve as the bottom (sole) plate of the wall. Often the entire wall is built using the predrilled sill as the bottom plate, and the wall is lifted and bolted to the slab.

Sill Plates Around Openings and at Steps
Photograph: Photo 7-12.

At steps and around the vertical walls of openings, sills are often required. Use the same material as the standard sill. A concrete nailing gun can be used to secure these to the foundation wall. Be very careful when using the concrete gun; it is dangerous.

Offset Sill Plates
Diagram: Figure 7-14.

When using a sheathing material below the siding, some builders kick the sill back towards the interior the thickness of the sheathing. The siding then overlaps the gap between the sill and the foundation wall. The only advantage here is that it hides the exposed end of the sheathing from view if you are looking from underneath.

Worksheet

ESTIMATED TIME

_____

_____

_____

_____

CREW

Skilled

_____ Phone _____

_____ Phone _____

_____ Phone _____

Unskilled

_____ Phone _____

_____ Phone _____

_____ Phone _____

_____ Phone _____

_____ Phone _____

MATERIALS NEEDED

Lumber for sill plates.

ESTIMATING MATERIALS

2×_____ SILL STOCK:

_____ pieces _____ feet long

_____ pieces _____ feet long

COST COMPARISON

_____ Store:

Cost per M foundation grade redwood $ _____

Cost per M pressure-treated stock $ _____

_____ Store:

Cost per M foundation grade redwood $ _____

Cost per M pressure-treated stock $ _____

_____ Store:

Cost per M foundation grade redwood $ _____

Cost per M pressure-treated stock $ _____

Daily Checklist

CREW:

_____ Phone _____

_____ Phone_____

_____ Phone _____

_____ Phone_____

_____ Phone_____

_____ Phone _____

MATERIALS:

_____ sill stock

_____ insulation (if needed)

_____ termite guard (if needed)

WEATHER FORECAST:

For week _____

For day _____

TOOLS:

☐ framing hammer

☐ power saw

☐ level

☐ carpenter's level

☐ chalkline

☐ string

☐ 100-foot tape

☐ 25-foot tape

☐ combination square

☐ wrench

☐ pencil

☐ nail belt

☐ safety goggles

☐ drill

☐ bits

☐ extension cords

☐ plug junction boxes

☐ saw blades

☐ shims

☐ chisels

RENTAL ITEMS:

☐ transit

☐ concrete nail gun

8 *Knee Walls*

Photo 8-1. Knee walls partially erected.

KNEE (CRIPPLE) WALLS are wooden extensions of concrete foundations. They are used on sloping sites to avoid the time and expense of building high concrete foundation walls. The foundation walls are stepped and then extended with wooden foundation walls. Not all of you will need to use these, especially if you are building on relatively level ground or if you are using a concrete or concrete block basement. If that is the case, this chapter can be skipped over, unless you care to read it for your own general information. If you do have a sloping site that requires a continuous concrete perimeter foundation, using knee walls at the lower areas is highly recommended.

What You'll Be Doing, What to Expect

If you do have a sloping site that requires a continuous concrete perimeter foundation, the use of knee walls at the lower areas is highly recommended. (See Figure 8-1, Photo 8-1.)

Since building knee walls is very similar to building standard stud walls, I advise reading the *Wall Framing* chapter before beginning knee wall construction. Although this part of construction is not difficult (you are working close to the ground with short walls), it is very important that the walls are built very level. Knee walls are an extension of the foun-

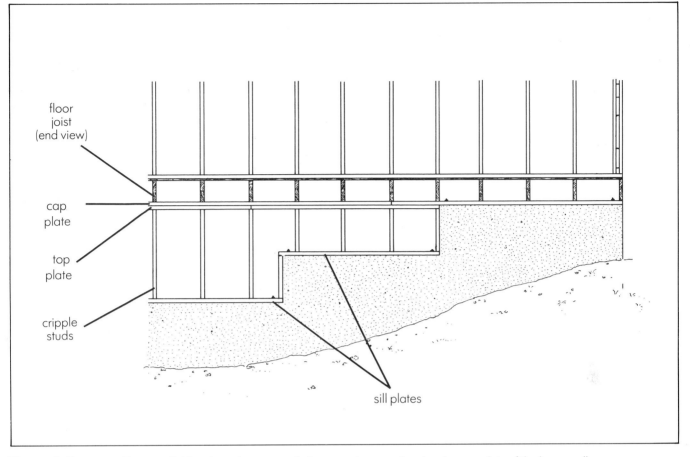

Figure 8-1. A typical knee wall. Note how the upper sill plate is at the same level as the cap plate of the knee wall.

dation on which the house will be built. Go slowly—be accurate.

In the event of an earthquake, knee walls can fail. Check with your local codes and take this fact into consideration, even if knee walls are allowed. At minimum, be sure to use a plywood sheathing skin.

Jargon

BOTTOM PLATE (SOLE PLATE). Horizontal base member of the wall partition.

FACE NAIL. To nail perpendicular to the finished face.

KNEE WALL OR CRIPPLE WALL. Wood wall extension of the concrete foundation; most often used in stepped foundations on sloping sites.

LAYOUT. Method of marking the location of a series of framing members on a sill, band, plate, girder or ridge.

ON CENTER. A term to indicate the spacing of framing members by using the measurement from the center of one member to the center of the succeeding one.

PLUMB. Exactly perpendicular or vertical.

STUDS. One of a series of vertical wood structural members in a wall or partition.

TOENAIL. Driving a nail at an angle.

TOP PLATE. Horizontal top member placed on the wall and supported by the studs.

Purposes of the Knee Wall

1) To extend the concrete foundation wall with a wooden wall (thereby avoiding the use of the more expensive concrete).
2) To create a level building surface on a sloping site.

Design Decisions

Consider carefully the location of the access door(s) for your crawlspace. The plumbing code often requires that the access door be within 15 feet of any drain cleanout plug. Check this out with your local authority. If it is difficult to place the door near the cleanout plug(s), the plug can poke through the house to the outside or a trap door can be built through the floor from the inside.

You must also consider if you are ever going to use this crawlspace for anything else: a half basement, storage, a full basement, etc. See if this affects any of your decisions. You can, for instance, add some rough window or door openings at this stage and cover over them until you build the basement. If you plan to use the crawlspace for storage, you may want to enlarge the access doors for wheelbarrows, lawnmowers, etc.

What You'll Need

TIME   8 to 16 person-hours per 30 linear feet of wall 3 feet high.

PEOPLE   1 Minimum (skilled); 3 Optimum (1 skilled, 2 unskilled); 6 Maximum (2 teams of three).

TOOLS   Framing hammer, nail belt, tape, pencil, combination square, power saw, carpenter's level, builder's level (optional), extension cords, plug junction box, saw blades, nail-pulling tools.

RENTAL ITEMS: Transit, com-a-long.

MATERIALS   The wood used is common framing grade lumber, either 2×4s or 2×6s. The only exception is the bottom plate of the knee wall, which is the sill plate. It will be either foundation grade redwood or pressure-treated lumber (see *Sill Plates*). All nails nailed into the sill plate to hold the bottoms of the knee wall studs must be hot-dipped galvanized, non-rusting nails. The top and cap plates are also framing grade lumber.

ESTIMATING MATERIALS NEEDED

Estimating the materials will take a little calculating, since many different length boards will be needed for the varying stud heights. Try to calculate what length board will create the least wastage.

INFORMATION   For a better understanding of this procedure, it is essential that you go over the *Wall Framing* chapter, especially for door and window openings. Check your local codes for any mandatory specifications on knee walls in your area. Other than this, you should be able to make it through without problems.

PEOPLE TO CONTACT   None.

INSPECTIONS NEEDED   None.

Reading the Plans

If your plans are well detailed (and few really are), all the information you will need to know about the knee (cripple) walls will be in the plans. This will include: where they are to be used, the size, length and spacing of the studs, location of crawlspace vents, size and location of access doors, etc. Often the plan will not provide all this information, especially if the plans have not been designed for a specific site. In this case, you will have to provide the knee walls wherever you decided to step the foundation walls. The depth and location

of these steps is what determines the location and height of the knee walls.

Be sure you check with your local permit office as to the required size and spacing of the studs. If the knee wall is over 4 feet high, it is considered a separate story; you may be required to use larger (2×6s) studs or closer stud spacings. The code also says that no knee wall stud can be less than 14 inches in height. This must be taken into consideration as you step your foundation.

Don't forget to use a double, not single, top plate on your knee walls. I once used a single plate on a house we built in California and the inspector made me jack the 2200-square-foot house up, cut 1½ inches out of the top of the studs and insert another plate. It was 2 days' work for 5 people. We found out later we could have corrected the problem by simply nailing a 2×6 on the side of the studs.

Safety and Awareness

SAFETY: No special considerations other than usual care, especially with power tools.

AWARENESS: Mainly you want to be sure that the wall is level, as this is an extension of the foundation walls on which the entire house will be built. Also be sure the walls are plumb.

Overview of the Procedure

Step 1: Lay out the studs
Step 2: Determine the heights of the studs
Step 3: Toenail the studs to the sills
Step 4: Face nail first top plate to studs
Step 5: Nail second top plate (cap plate) to first top plate
Step 6: Plumb corners and walls, and brace
Step 7: Check knee walls

Step 1
Lay Out the Studs

Margin of Error: ¼ inch during the layout.

Most Common Mistake: Placing stud on wrong side of layout mark.

Diagrams: Figures 8-2, 8-3, 8-4, 8-5.

Photograph: Photo 8-2.

At this point your sill plates should be level and fastened to the foundation wall. Before beginning with the knee walls, check to be sure the sills are level and in their proper place, as described in the *Sill Plates* chapter. If the sill plates are level and accurate, you are now ready to do the layout for the location of the cripple studs on the sill plate.

As in all standard construction, the framing members will be on 12-, 16- or 24-inch centers so that 4-×-8-foot panels of drywall, plywood and paneling can be used and they will always break on the center of a framing member. In all layouts, the first stud is set 15¼ inches on center rather than 16 inches, so that the edge of the first panel will fall at the edge of the framing member rather than at the center. After this first layout mark, use a 16-inch layout for the rest.

After you have completed the layout on the sill plates, choose a good, straight piece of stock that will be your top plate for the knee wall. Place it against the marked sill and transfer these marks to the top plate. While you are doing this, be sure that the top plate is properly aligned with the end of the wall and that any break in the top plate falls in the center of a stud.

After the top plate is marked, you are ready to cut the cripple studs. Corners and doors are done as shown in the *Wall Framing* chapter.

16" 16" 16" 16" 15¼"

There will be no knee walls or cripple studs on this step. Marks here are for layout only.

Figure 8-2. Laying out studs on the knee walls.

Photo 8-2. Using a level string line and plumb bob to locate the layout marks for studs on each step of the foundation.

16"   16"   15¼" ¾"

47¼" to center

48" to edge

plywood
to edge
of stud

plywood
to center
of stud

Figure 8-3. Dimensions are from center to center of studs. First sheet of plywood comes to edge, not center, of first stud. This accounts for the "lost" ¾ inch.

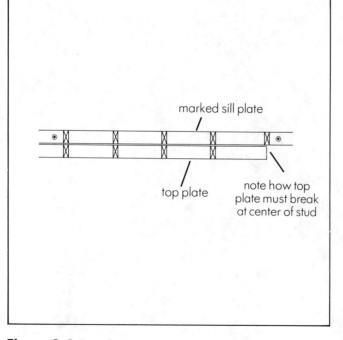

marked sill plate

top plate

note how top
plate must break
at center of stud

Figure 8-4. Transferring layout marks from the sill plate to the top plate of the knee wall.

cap plate

4' minimum between
splices in plates

top
plate

top plate splices
must occur in center
of stud

Figure 8-5. A finished knee wall showing plate splices.

Photo 8-3. Using a level string to determine the height of the knee wall studs.

Step 2
Determine the Heights of the Studs

Margin of Error: Within ⅛ inch of proper height.

Most Common Mistakes: Not figuring for second top plate (cap plate); not allowing for irregularities in level of foundation wall.

Diagrams: Figures 8-6, 8-7, 8-8.

Photograph: Photo 8-3.

Be very accurate in determining and cutting the heights of the knee wall studs. The level of the top of the foundation wall will be determined at this stage. If the concrete wall is off level at any spot and the discrepancy has not been properly adjusted with the sill plate, you can make adjustments now by adjusting the height of each knee wall stud.

If the concrete foundation wall is perfectly level or if all discrepancies have been adjusted by shimming the sill plates, all the studs can be cut the same height in any one section (or step) of the knee wall. When you determine the stud heights, remember that the *second* top plate (the cap plate), not the first, will be at the same level as the sill plates at the highest

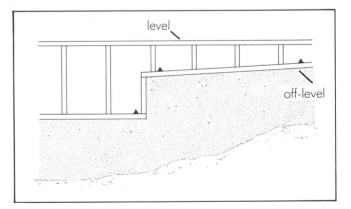

Figure 8-6. Knee wall studs are cut at varying lengths to correct an off-level foundation wall.

part of the foundation wall (where no knee walls are to be built).

To determine these stud heights, run a string, level with the bottom edge of the top plate, and measure from there to sill plates, as in Figure 8-7. A transit or builder's level can also be used.

After you have determined the height and number of studs, proceed to cut. Note that in some areas the minimum height allowed for knee wall studs is 14 inches.

Figure 8-7. Determining the heights of the cripple studs.

Figure 8-8. Using a transit to determine the heights of the cripple studs.

Step 3
Toenail the Studs to the Sills

Margin of Error: ⅛ inch on line with mark.

Most Common Mistake: Nailing to wrong side of layout mark.

Diagram: Figure 8-9.

Photograph: Photo 8-4.

Now toenail the studs to the sill plates at the proper marks as shown. Use 8d hot-dipped galvanized nails, two on each side of the stud. Be sure the stud is on the proper side of the mark. The "X"s make this easy. You may want to start the nails in the studs before you place the studs on the sill. You can also use a block of wood, cut to the exact size of the space in between the studs (use 14½ for 16-inch layouts), to help hold the stud in place as you nail. Be careful to have fairly straight studs, as bowed studs will create irregular surfaces for future siding application.

Figure 8-9. Nailing studs to the sill.

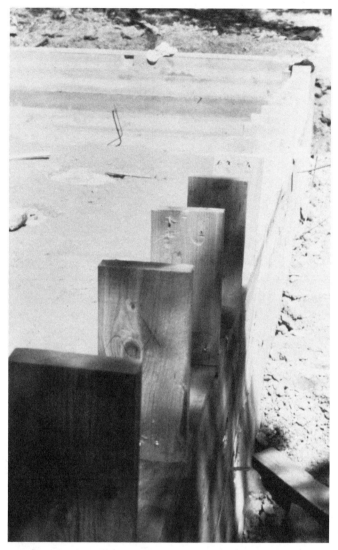

Photo 8-4. Knee wall studs nailed to sill plates.

Photo 8-5. Checking the level of the knee wall with a transit after the first top plate has been nailed to the studs.

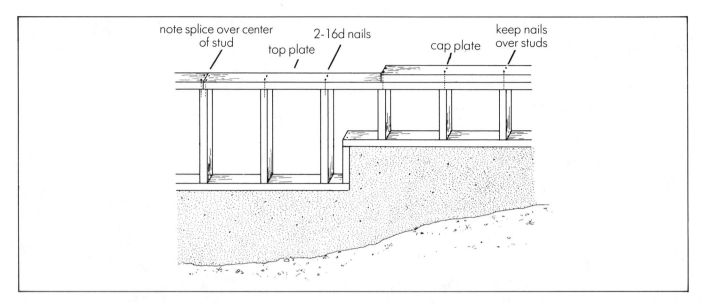

Figure 8-10. Nailing the top and cap plates to the cripple studs.

Figure 8-11. Bracing the knee wall plumb in all directions.

Step 4
Face Nail First Top Plate to Studs

Margin of Error: ⅛ inch on line with layout mark.

Most Common Mistakes: Using crooked plate stock; not nailing on layout mark.

Photograph: Photo 8-5.

Now nail the top plate over the studs. Using two 16d standard nails, face nail through the top plate into each stud. Be sure that splices in the top plate break in the center of a stud. The top plate should be of good straight stock or the wall will be crooked.

At this point, you should check the level of the wall. You can use a level or a transit to do this. If the level is off, determine why, and make the proper corrections. *It is important that the top of the wall be level within ⅛ to ¼ inch.*

Step 5
Nail Second Top Plate (Cap Plate) to First Top Plate

Margin of Error: Aligned with first top plate within ⅛ inch.

Most Common Mistakes: Using crooked stock; not nailing both plates flush to each other.

Diagram: Figure 8-10.

As you nail on the second top plate, also called the cap plate, be sure again you are using good straight stock, or the top of the foundation knee wall will be crooked. It is advisable that you nail the second top plate on with two 16d CC sinkers, directly over each stud. Keeping the nails over each stud will keep them out of the way of drill bits should you later run your plumbing or electricity through the top plates. Any splice in the cap plates must be at least 4 feet away from any splice in the top plate.

Figure 8-12. Two ways of checking the completed knee wall for level.

Step 6
Plumb Corners and Walls, and Brace

Margin of Error: Within ⅛ to ¼ inch off plumb.

Most Common Mistake: Off plumb.

Diagram: Figure 8-11.

Using a transit, level, or plumb bob, plumb the corners, which in turn should automatically plumb most of the studs. If the corners are plumb but some of the studs are not, brace till they are plumb. After the wall is plumbed, temporarily brace it by nailing boards diagonally across the studs to hold the wall in place as the floors and walls are being built.

Step 7
Check Knee Walls

Margin of Error: ⅛ to ¼ inch of level.

Most Common Mistake: Off level.

Diagram: Figure 8-12.

Before going on to the next step of floor framing, check to be sure that the knee wall is the proper dimension, square, level and plumb. This is very important as the floor frame will be built on top of the knee wall and it needs to be accurate. Take your time here and get it correct. It will save you hours down the line trying to adjust for sloppy work.

Worksheet

ESTIMATED TIME

_____

_____

_____

_____

CREW

Skilled

_____ Phone _____

_____ Phone _____

_____ Phone _____

Unskilled

_____ Phone _____

_____ Phone _____

_____ Phone _____

_____ Phone _____

_____ Phone _____

MATERIALS NEEDED

2×4s or 2×6s, lumber for plates, nails (8d hot-dipped galvanized and 16d CC sinkers).

ESTIMATING MATERIALS

STUDS:

2 × _____ BOARD _____ feet long: Quantity ____

2 × _____ BOARD _____ feet long: Quantity ____

2 × _____ BOARD _____ feet long: Quantity ____

PLATES:

2 × _____ BOARD _____ feet long: Quantity ____

2 × _____ BOARD _____ feet long: Quantity ____

NAILS:

_____ lbs. 8d galvanized

_____ lbs. 16d CC sinkers

COST COMPARISON

_____ Store:

$ _____ per M = $ _____ total

_____ Store:

$ _____ per M = $ _____ total

_____ Store:

$ _____ per M = $ _____ total

Daily Checklist

CREW:

_____Phone _____

_____Phone _____

_____Phone _____

_____Phone _____

_____Phone _____

_____Phone _____

TOOLS:

☐ framing hammer

☐ nail belt

☐ tape

☐ pencil

☐ combination square

☐ power saw

☐ carpenter's level

☐ builder's level (optional)

☐ extension cords

☐ plug junction box

☐ saw blades

☐ nail-pulling tools

RENTAL ITEMS:

☐ transit (optional)

☐ com-a-long

MATERIALS:

_____ feet of framing stock

_____ lbs. of 16d CC sinkers

_____ lbs. of 8d hot-dipped galvanized nails (for toenailing into sill plate)

DESIGN REVIEW: The location of the access door for the crawlspace will be finalized at this stage. Decide how you will use the space, whether to add windows, how big the doors need to be, etc. Be sure you're in compliance with plumbing codes concerning drain clean-out plugs.

WEATHER FORECAST:

For week _____

For day _____

9 Floor Framing

Photo 9-1. Floor joists are completed here and the subflooring is being applied.

What You'll Be Doing, What to Expect

FLOOR FRAMING (Photo 9-1) is the simplest of all framing processes and serves as an excellent introduction to carpentry. It is also a very exciting time of building, because the work goes very quickly and the house starts to take shape. Except for the joists becoming off level or out of line (discussed later), there are few mistakes. Don't be deceived by this stage of construction, however; almost no other stage will progress quite this rapidly.

This chapter will deal with the construction of a typical floor frame in a house that has a continuous concrete wall foundation (Figure 9-1) around the exterior of the home and a pier foundation (Figure 9-2) to support the girders on the interior of the home. By using this example, you will learn to construct a floor frame for both continuous wall foundations and pier foundations. Some houses may have all continuous wall foundations, both exterior and interior, others may use all pier foundations.

The example given here is fairly straightforward: a typical joist system, using girders and piers; an opening; and a load-bearing wall running parallel to the joist system. Your floor frame may not be that simple, so I have included other details of floor framing toward the end of the chapter.

Keep the high standards of quality you have set for yourself as you frame. (See Figure 9-3.) Make good tight-fitting cuts—it will increase the strength of your floor frame and help you practice good carpentry techniques. Remember, however, that a house is not a piece of custom furniture; make the demands on your work reasonable. Enjoy yourself!

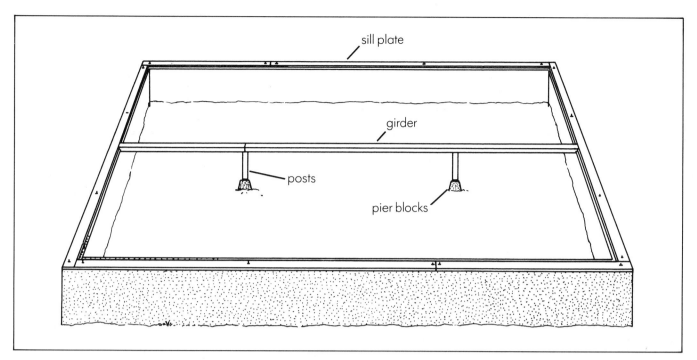

Figure 9-1. A concrete continuous-wall foundation with a girder supported by posts to reduce the span of the joists.

Figure 9-2. A pier foundation using girders to support the joists. The joists can either sit on top of the girders or be hung from them as shown.

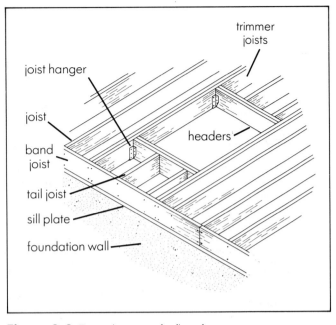

Figure 9-3. Typical pieces of a floor frame.

Jargon

BLOCKING OR BRIDGING. Metal straps, diagonally nailed 1×4s, or pieces of joist stock nailed between joists used to stiffen and add rigidity to the floor frame and decrease lateral movement.

CANTILEVER. A structural member that is supported at one end only and supports a projected load.

GIRDER. A large beam used to support a portion of the joist system, which serves to decrease the span of the joists. They are usually nominal 4- or 6-inch-thick stock or built up from 2 pieces of 3-inch-wide stock and are spaced from 4 to 14 feet apart.

JOIST. A parallel floor framing member used to support the floor. Usually it is a nominal 2-inch-thick board (2×6, 2×8, 2×10, 2×12, 2×14) on 12-, 16- or 24-inch centers.

JOIST HANGER. A metal fastener used to fasten the joists to the girders (they are required in earthquake areas).

JOIST HEADER. A piece of stock, the same size as the joists, that runs perpendicular to, and at the same level as, the joists, at the ends of the joists. It serves to keep the joists plumb and erect.

JOIST LAYOUT. Marking the locations of the joists on the sill plate, header or girder.

LOLLY COLUMN. A round metal support post, often used to support girders in the basement.

O.C.—ON CENTER. The distance from the center of one piece of framing member to the center of the adjacent member.

POST OR COLUMN. A vertical support used to support the girders or beams. They are made of concrete blocks, wood or metal.

R.O.—ROUGH OPENING. The opening in the floor, wall or roof frame for a window, door, stairway, chimney, etc.

Figure 9-4. Transfer of weight through the floor frame to the earth bed.

SCAB. A scrap piece of wood used to join other pieces of wood together.

T & G—TONGUE AND GROOVE. A joint made by cutting a groove in one board and mating tongue in the other.

TAIL JOIST. A relatively short joist used around openings or girders supported by a header at one end and a foundation wall or girder at the other.

THREADED NAIL. An annular ringed or barbed nail used for greater holding power.

TRIMMERS. Double or single joists around openings that run parallel with the common joists and along the edges of the openings.

Purposes of the Floor Frame

1) Transfers the weight of people, furniture, materials, etc., from the subfloor, to the floor framing, to the foundation wall, to the footing and finally to the earth bed. (See Figure 9-4.)
2) With the subfloor, it serves as a building platform for the walls of the house (hence the name, platform building).

Design Decisions

In floor framing, perhaps more than in any other framing process in the house, there is a large variety of choices. Aside from the standard joist system, there are two other floor framing systems currently in use: the floor truss system and the girder system. Both of these are briefly discussed at the end of the chapter under "Special Situations."

Even in conventional joist systems there are choices to be made. In one floor system you could, for instance, choose between 2×12s on 12-inch centers, or 2×10s on 16-inch centers or 2×8s on 12-inch centers. Or you could add an extra girder, thereby decreasing the span of the joists, and switch to yet another size and spacing of the floor joists. Whoever drew up your plans may or may not have had a good reason for choosing the system they did. You may want to rethink the decision and, if possible, discuss it with a professional.

I always like to be sure that the floors are a little over built. It's nice to be able to jump on a floor and have the house feel solid. When the kids run through the living room you don't want the cups to rattle in the kitchen cabinets. To build a solid floor, add an extra girder or increase the required size of the joist or decrease the required spacing. It costs a little more, but it makes for a stouter house.

What You'll Need

TIME 32 to 60 person-hours per 1,000 square feet of frame.

PEOPLE 2 Minimum (1 skilled, 1 unskilled); 3 Optimum (1 skilled, 2 unskilled); 5 Maximum (2 skilled, 3 unskilled).

TOOLS Framing hammers, combination square, hand saw, power saw, saw blades, saw horses, pencil, steel tape, nail belt, sledge hammer, safety goggles, nail-pulling tools, transit or hydro level, chalkline, 4-foot level, extension cords, junction box, framing square.

MATERIALS Almost all framing is done with Number 2 or better framing grade material of the local evergreen (Douglas fir, southern yellow pine, spruce, ponderosa pine, etc.). Lumber is graded according to the number and size of the knots as well as the general quality of the stock. Number 1 grade stock is used in structural situations where there is a tremendous stress factor, which is usually indicated on the plans by an architect or engineer. In non-structural situations a Number 3 or utility grade stock is sometimes used. Unless you indicate otherwise, the suppliers will always deliver the Number 2 or better framing stock when you order nominal 2-inch material. (Number 2 grade lumber or better indicates 60% is Number 2 grade and 40% is Number 1 grade.)

KILN DRIED OR WET LUMBER

Wood is made up of the same main ingredients as commercial plastics: lignin and cellulose. Lignin is an adhesive which gives strength and rigidity to the wood; cellulose is nature's own strong material. It is made up of long chains running the length of the tree, which accounts for wood splitting along its grain. The moisture in the wood is not held within these molecules so much as between them. When evaporation occurs, this moisture is lost and the molecules pull closer to each other, which is why wood shrinks much more along its width (laterally) than its length (longitudinally).

In choosing your floor frame material, you must make the major decision to use either wet or kiln dried materials. Wet lumber may well be in the forest a few weeks before you get it and will go through its drying process after it has been installed in your house. This causes certain problems. Kiln dried stock, on the other hand, has been dried in a heated kiln and a high percentage of the moisture content has been driven out of the material, both from within the cells and between the cells. The wood is therefore preshrunk before it is installed. Until the last ten or fifteen years only kiln dried materials were used. When we switched to using mostly wet framing lumber, the quality of houses went down.

Wet lumber has two advantages:

1) it is cheaper by 20 to 30% than kiln dried, and

2) it does not split as readily.

Kiln dried, on the other hand, has many advantages:

1) Because it is dry and preshrunk *before* it is installed, it will not shrink and twist after installation. Because of this your trim work will not be pulled off, your doors and windows are less likely to stick, and your nails will hold much better, thereby making a stronger house. Your finishing work will also be easier, since the boards have not warped and twisted.

2) Dry lumber is more resistant to fungus, mold and insects.

3) Dry lumber is lighter and easier to carry and handle.

4) Wet lumber, with a higher sap content, gums up saw blades more quickly.

5) Kiln dried stock, though graded as framing grade, is often higher quality than the same grade wet lumber.

6) Nails lose three-fourths their holding power when driven into wet lumber; as the lumber shrinks away from the nail, the friction between the wood and the nail is reduced. There is also a deterioration of moist wood due to the formation of iron oxides on a nail in the presence of wood acids.

If dry lumber is not available or you cannot afford the added expense, you may offset the disadvantages of wet lumber by doing two things.

First, use threaded nails throughout the house. The Virginia Polytechnic Institute found that a house built with threaded nails and green lumber could withstand four times the load as a house built with green lumber and plain shank nails. This is also an excellent reason to use threaded nails in earthquake areas. These are sometimes difficult to find but keep looking; they add only about $40 to the cost of the house.

The second thing you can do if you are using green lumber is to close the house in and allow it to season for 6 months to a year so that it will dry before you put on the finishing material. For many owner builders, it's about a year between these two stages anyway. If you did the finishing work before the wood dried, the finishing boards would be pulled off as the wood shrank.

Though it costs a little more ($400 to $600 per 2000-

square-foot home), I advise using kiln dried lumber for the entire frame.

How to check for moisture content. To determine the moisture content of your lumber, pick 6 random pieces. Cut out a 1-inch slice across the entire width and at least 1 foot from the end. Trim these samples so that they measure 6 inches in width and place them in a warm dry place for 48 hours. The 6-inch dimension is then measured to determine the shrinkage. If it shrinks over ¼ inch in the 6-inch dimension, it is not satisfactory for framing. If it shrinks over ⅛ inch, it is not satisfactory for interior trim or finish.

ESTIMATING MATERIALS NEEDED

JOIST STOCK: Figure joist needs by calculating on center measurements and the length the joist needs to be to span the supports. Include band joist and material for blocking, if necessary.

GIRDER STOCK: Figure how many pieces are needed and lengths so girders break over centers of posts.

POSTS: Order enough length of post stock to span piers to girders.

NAILS: 15 pounds of 16d CC sinkers per 1500-square-foot house.

METAL FASTENERS AND FASTENER NAILS: Figure the number needed.

INFORMATION This chapter deals with the most common floor frame situations. If your plans call for any unusual situations, contact a professional for further information. Some situations can be worked out by novices using common sense. Just be sure that your solution will work, pass codes and is the easiest.

All lumber used as joists, girders, posts and other load-bearing pieces, and all plywood used as subflooring, must be graded and show the grading mark. Often recycled or rough cut lumber with no marks will be allowed if inspectors think it is high quality. Other times they will require a lumber grader, structural engineer or architect to grade it. Check first. Blocking can be ungraded stock.

Check the local codes for specifications on joist and girder spans, and the sizes of framing materials, required in the course of the framing process in your area.

PEOPLE TO CONTACT If underfloor utilities need to be inspected before the subfloor is placed and you do not plan to do the work yourself, contact subcontractors: electrician, plumber, solar panel installer, and gas, heating and air conditioning services.

INSPECTIONS NEEDED None.

Reading the Plans

Most plans (Figure 9-5) will tell you everything you need to know about the floor framing system. All of the following should be included:

A) Type (species) of wood; e.g., df (Douglas fir), syp (southern yellow pine), etc.
B) Size, location and spacing of the: posts or columns, joists, girders or beams
C) Direction of both the joists and girders
D) Manner in which the joists connect to the girders, see "Step 7"
E) Location of any load-bearing interior walls that run parallel to the joists, see "Step 6"
F) Location of any toilet drains, see "Step 6"
G) Size (rough opening) and location of any openings in the floor for stairs, crawlspace access, chimneys, etc.

Aside from the above, the following specialized information may also be included:

H) Any cantilevering situations, see "Special Situations"
I) Any changes in floor levels
J) Any special structural situations needed to carry certain loads
K) Any special metal fasteners needed in earthquake areas, see "Step 4"
L) Any special details needed to connect floor frame into a slab floor
M) Location, size and spacing of any large beams to be used as exposed timbers (in the second or third floor frame)
N) Type of blocking or bridging, see "Step 8"
O) Clearance from soil to girders and joists

Safety and Awareness

SAFETY: As always, be careful when using the power tools; also, be careful walking on the joists—be sure they are stable; many accidents happen when people fall through the joists.

AWARENESS: Be sure your layout is accurate and the joist placed to the proper side of the layout mark. Be sure joists are installed crown up and their tops are flush with the top of the band and the girder. Use straight girders.

Overview of the Procedure

Step 1: Check the level, squareness and dimensions of the sill plates
Step 2: Erect the posts
Step 3: Erect the girders
Step 4: Erect the band
Step 5: Lay out the joists on the band and the girders
Step 6: Layout for special situations
Step 7: Install the joists
Step 8: Install the bridging or blocking
Step 9: Check the system

typical joist spacing — 16 inches o.c.

foundation wall

typical joist 2″×8″

4×6 girder

girder spacing 6′3″ o.c.

typical pier

typical pier

one story footing thickness

two story footing thickness

double joists under load bearing partitions — see detail

LEGEND

A size of joist
B size of girder
C size of post
D floor opening
E subfloor
F location of double joist
G location of blocking
H joist spacing
I girder spacing

E ⅝″ t&g plywood subfloor

load bearing wall system

finished floor surface

foundation wall

redwood mud sill

A 2×8 joist typ.

B 4×6 girder typ.

G 2×8 blocking 8′ o.c.

ledger for deck

footing

C 4×4 post typical, except where girders meet, then 4×6 nec.

pier typ.

ground level

FLOOR FRAMING SECTION

Figure 9-5. Foundation plan.

Figure 9-6. (A) Joists on top of the girder (the top of the sill is level with the top of the girder). (B) Joists hung from the girder (the top of the sill is flush with the bottom of the girder).

Step 1
Check the Level, Squareness and Dimensions of the Sill Plates

Margin of Error: For level—⅛ inch (shim or notch to correct). For dimensions—¼ inch (adjust floor frame). For squareness—¼ inch (adjust floor frame).

Most Common Mistake: Allowing too great a margin of error.

Diagram: Figure 9-6.

Before beginning the floor frame, use a transit (a water or hydro level will work) to check the heights of your sill plates. (See *Sill Plate* chapter, "Step 7.") The height of the joists and girders is determined by the level of the top of the sill plates. The joists will rest on the top of the sill plates. The top of the girders will be level with either the top of the sills or the top of the joists, depending on whether the joists sit on top of the girders or are hung from the girders. Because of this, it is wise to check the sill plate levels every 6 to 8 feet to see how you are doing.

Mark any areas that are off level. The joists and girders in these areas can be shimmed or notched to bring the entire floor frame to level. If the sill plates and foundation walls are off dimension or not square, you can build the floor frame true and square, even though it will underlap or overlap the sill plates, to correct this error. Be sure you check it carefully; it will make many of the procedures down the road much easier.

NOTE: You may want to backfill around the foundation at this time to make working on the floor frame easier.

Step 2
Erect the Posts

Margin of Error: In straight line—¼ inch. Tops of posts level—⅛ inch.

Most Common Mistakes: Post tops not level; posts not centered under girder.

Diagrams: Figures 9-7, 9-8, 9-9, 9-10, 9-11.

Photographs: Photos 9-2, 9-3.

There are four possible posts to use: concrete block, brick, metal or wood (either solid or built-up). The wood posts are the most common and easiest to use, except where there is a basement, in which case round, metal lolly columns are the most common. Bricks and concrete blocks are more difficult to use because their level cannot be adjusted as easily as that of wooden posts, which can be cut, and metal posts, which screw out to any height. When using concrete blocks or bricks as posts, the height of the footings must be accurately set so that when using 4-inch-thick bricks or 8-inch-tall blocks, their tops can come out at level heights. See *Poured Concrete Foundation,* "Step 14C." In our example we will focus on wooden posts; they are the simplest and the quickest.

Figure 9-7. Common foundation posts are being used to support girders.

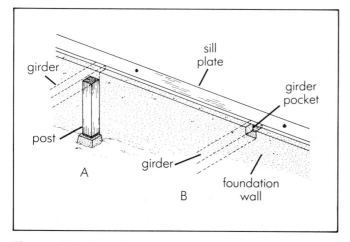

Figure 9-8. (A) Girder supported by a post at the foundation wall. (B) Girder supported by a girder pocket provided in the foundation wall.

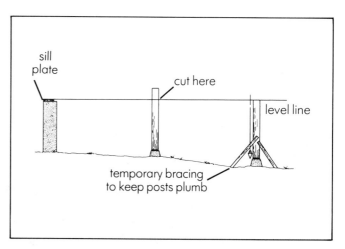

Figure 9-9. A string is being run at the top of the posts, the same height as the bottom of the girder. (In this example, the joist will be hung from girders with metal joist hangers.)

Figure 9-10. Using a string to align the posts with the center of girder. (In this example, joists will sit on top of the girder.)

Figure 9-11. Using a properly set level line and a tape measure to determine the height of the posts.

Usually 4-×-4 or 4-×-6 posts are used. All posts must be as wide as the girder and a 4×6 is often required where girder stock is joined over a post. As described earlier, the pier blocks for the wooden piers should already be set in their concrete footings and properly aligned. Proper negative spaces should have been left to receive the girders both in the continuous foundation wall and any cripple or knee walls. (See *Poured Concrete Foundations*, "Step 14" and "Step 6.") If a negative space is missing, you will need to set another post up against the foundation wall to support the end of the girder. If all the pier blocks are properly placed and all the

negative spaces are there, check to be sure the surfaces where the girders are to be set (top of posts and girder pockets) are perfectly flat so the girders will not be resting on any high spots.

Remember: the height of the posts will depend on the manner in which the joists are connected to the girder—they can be either on top of the girder or hung from the girder.

You are now ready to cut the posts. The best way to do this is to use a transit or hydro level and locate and place 2 nails on each foundation wall, where the girders will rest, at the level of the bottom of the girder (which is the level of the

Photo 9-2. Posts are being nailed to metal fasteners embedded in the concrete pier blocks. Metal post caps are also being used here to attach girders to posts (recommended in earthquake areas).

top of the posts). Run a taut line between these 2 nails. Next, temporarily set the posts on their pier blocks. Be sure they are plumb and that the top of the pier block is clean of all debris. Mark the posts where they cross the string. Remove the posts and cut them at that mark; nail them to the pier block or metal fastener; and brace them plumb. They should now all be cut at exactly the same height, allowing the girder to sit level on them.

When installing the posts, it is more important that they sit directly underneath the girders than that they all be directly in the center of the pier block. As you install them, use a straight string to line them up directly underneath the girder that will be placed on top. Remember: where two pieces of girder stock meet over a post use a 4-×-6 post. Check girder stock lengths at this time to determine where to place these 4×6s.

Another way you can cut the posts is to measure down from the level string (set by your transit) to the pier block, record the exact dimension and cut the posts the corresponding height. This is somewhat quicker and can be just as accurate if you take your time. A water or hydro level can also be used. No matter which method you choose, be sure that you make a good flat cut at either end of the pier, providing a good bearing surface. Some builders also seal each end of the post with a wood preservative. It couldn't hurt!

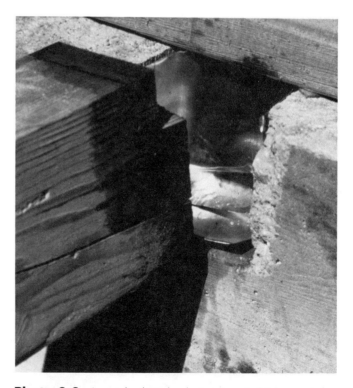

Photo 9-3. A notched girder being inserted into a girder pocket of a foundation wall. Note the use of metal flashing to keep the wooden girder from touching concrete.

Figure 9-12. A girder built from individual 2-inch pieces of stock nailed together. Note how the splices are staggered.

Figure 9-13. Girders are being inserted into the knee wall (A) or the foundation wall (B).

Step 3
Erect the Girders

Margin of Error: Off level ¼ inch.

Most Common Mistakes: Using badly bowed stock; not using a 4-×-6 post under splice in girder.

Diagrams: Figures 9-12, 9-13, 9-14, 9-15, 9-16, 9-17, 9-18.

Photographs: Photos 9-4, 9-5, 9-6.

As with posts, there are several ways you can go in your choice of girders: solid timbers, built-up wooden girders, steel beams or glulams. Each has its advantages and disadvantages. Metal beams will be able to span the greatest distances and may be the best choice when few or no piers or interior supports are called for, as in a basement. Also they can span greater distances with smaller beam sizes, thereby creating greater headroom in the basement or crawlspace. A 6-inch-high steel beam may support the same load as an 8-inch or 10-inch-high wooden beam. Being metal, they are more expensive than wood and harder to work with. They are seldom used unless the design calls for it.

Wooden beams are most common and the cheapest and easiest to use. Often solid pieces are badly bowed and can create a rise in the floor unless the crowns are pulled down. If you can find good, straight large timber girder stock (4×6, 4×8, 6×6, etc.), use it; you will save time by not having to build up the girders. Check the price of manufactured glulam beams—beams created from individual 2-inch-thick material glued and laminated together. You may want to consider using them for girder stock; they are often very straight with few crowns or warps.

On the East coast where there are fewer large trees, and therefore fewer large timbers, girders are usually built up from nominal 2-inch stock, nailed together well to act as one

Photo 9-4. Metal I-beams and metal columns in the basement are used as girders to support the first-floor joists.

Photo 9-5. Built-up girders on concrete block piers. Note the sill plate and metal termite guard on top of the piers. Note also that the splice in the girder occurs over the piers.

Figure 9-14. Using a rope twister to draw the crowned girder down to the post. Twisting the board shortens the rope and draws down the girder.

Figure 9-15. A metal girder post fastener. These are used in earthquake areas and to keep crowned girders down on posts. These are also used to join splices where 2 pieces of solid girder stock meet.

piece. Because of the opposing grain patterns created when using different pieces of stock, the built-up girder is actually stronger than the one large, solid piece of girder stock. You can often work the bows and crowns out of the built-up girders by nailing boards together in such a way that their bows point in opposite directions.

After you have decided what type of girder you plan to use, build or cut them in such a way that any splices in the solid girder (and if required, joints in a built-up girder) occur over a post or column. With built-up girders nail the individual boards together according to code requirements.

Where the girders meet the concrete wall foundation, you

should shim on both sides as well as underneath the girder. (The negative space left should be larger and deeper than the girder.) This helps to avoid rot. Cedar shims are OK on the sides, but underneath the girder, where a great amount of weight will be bearing, you should use plywood or even metal shims. In some cases, metal plates which extend 2 inches on either side of the girder are inserted in the fresh concrete. NOTE: In concrete block foundations, fill the cells of the blocks directly below the girders with concrete for greater bearing strength. Where the girder intersects the wooden knee wall, a special pocket is built as shown in the diagram.

If the tops of the posts are all level to each other, and the

Photo 9-6. A house during the floor frame stages. Here the posts and girders are erected and the joists are about to be installed.

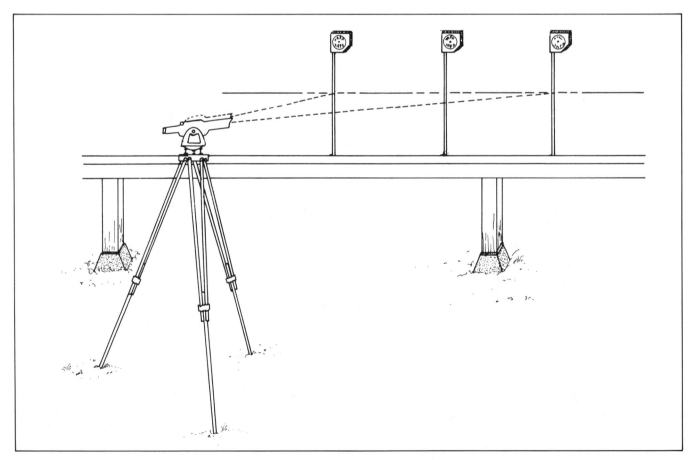

Figure 9-16. Using a transit to check the level of the girder.

Figure 9-17. Using a level or level line and measuring tape to determine the level of the girder.

Figure 9-18. Using a power saw to remove the crown from the girder.

girder is not resting on the posts but a little above them, your girder is bowed. Rather than shim it, thereby trapping the bow, you should work on pushing the crown down so that the girder rests on the top of the post. This can be done by having someone stand on it while you nail it to a metal or plywood plate that fastens the post to the girder. If this does not work you can use a rope and crank it down as shown in the diagram. If you are still unable to bring down the crown, do not shim, but allow the girder to float above the post in the hope that in time the crown will settle out. Check it at later stages of building.

After the girder is in place, it is a good idea to check along the length of the girder to be sure that it is level. If it is not level, it will throw all the joists off level, and thereby that entire floor area off. You can check the level by using your transit or using nails at each end of the girder with a string attached at level points of the nail. Then note the distance from the string to the top of the girder. An 8-foot level, placed directly on top of the girder, can also be used.

If there is a bad bow in the girder, you can either choose not to use it at all or to cut out the high section of the crown. You can also notch the girders or joists where they rest on the girder. No matter what you choose to do, be sure that your girders are true and level or that the girder or joist is notched or shimmed for the high and low spots so that *the tops of the floor joists are level.*

Where individual pieces of solid girder stock come together, they should meet over a 4-×-6 post and be joined by 24-inch-long scabs on both sides (2 inches thick and the same width as the girders) or by metal plates.

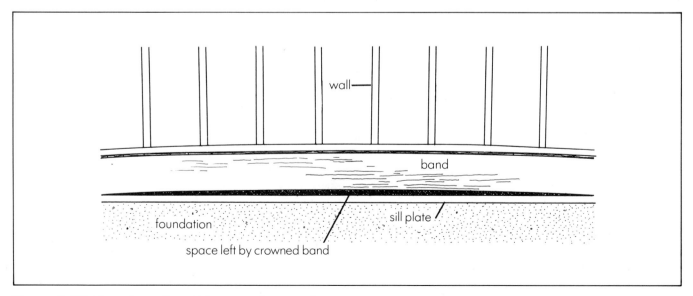

Figure 9-19. How a bowed band joist can push up a wall.

Figure 9-20. The outside edge of the band is flush with the outside edge of the sill plate.

Figure 9-21. A scab is being used to join a splice in the header joist.

Figure 9-22. Using metal fasteners to attach joists to girders and sill plates.

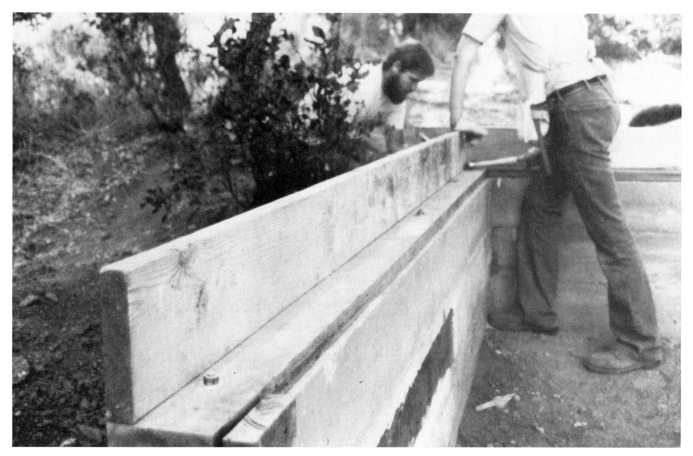

Photo 9-7. A band being installed flush with the outside of the sill plate.

Step 4
Erect the Band

Margin of Error: Off level ¼ inch. Flush with sill — ⅛ inch, unless adjustment is needed to make frame square or proper dimension.

Most Common Mistakes: Using bowed stock; building band off square or with improper dimensions.

Diagrams: Figures 9-19, 9-20, 9-21, 9-22, 9-23.

Photograph: Photo 9-7.

After the girders are all in place, erect the band. The band is made up of the pieces running perpendicular to the joists (called the header joists) and the first and last joists. The band encircles the joist system and is made from the same size stock as the joist material. Choose good straight pieces of stock so that they do not rise above the sill plates. They need to sit flat on the sill so as not to push up the wall. Nail these pieces into the sill plates with 10d nails, every 16 inches. Unless you need to make adjustment for mistakes in the sills or foundation, the outside edge of the band should be flush with the outside edge of the sill plates. Splices that occur in the header joists can either meet in the center of a joist or be joined by a scab.

Where the first and last joists meet the header joists, face nail these together. Check your diagonals and your mea-

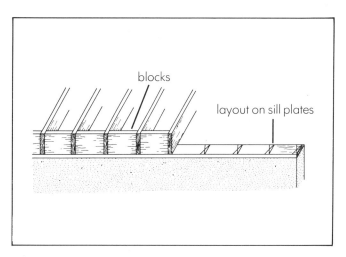

Figure 9-23. Using blocks instead of a band.

surements after the band is completed to see how true your floor system is. You may also want to test the band joist with a string to see if it is straight.

In some areas, where there are earthquakes or hurricanes or tornadoes, metal fasteners are used to further attach the band to the sills. Some builders do not use headers; they use blocks at the end of the joists instead. I like the header method better, but either will pass code. When using the blocks, the joist layout is done on the sill plates rather than the headers.

This edge falls at outside edge
of 1st joist, not in the center

48"   96"

³⁄₄" ³⁄₄"

15¼" 16" 16" 16" 16" 16" 16"

joist

Figure 9-24. How 16-inch on center joists accommodate 48-inch or 96-inch panels. The bubble shows how 2 panels meet over a joist. The distance from the outside edge of the 1st joist to the center of the 4th joist is 48 inches, and to the center of the 7th joist, 96 inches.

Step 5
Lay Out the Joists on the Band and the Girders

Margin of Error: Exact.

Most Common Mistakes: Not starting with 15¼ inches (or 11¼ inches or 23¼ inches) layout; placing "X" on wrong side of line; using framing square to do layout.

Diagrams: Figures 9-24, 9-25, 9-26, 9-27.

You are now ready to do your first layout. You will do similar layouts for wall framing and roof framing. Laying out framing members is simply marking where the individual members of a series will be placed and nailed. In this case we will be marking the location of the joists where they are nailed to the girder and the band.

Before beginning the layout, study your plans well. You may want to build a plan table to support your plans. Note the direction the joists will run and how they will be attached at the girder. Also note the location of any load-bearing partitions running parallel to the floor joists, openings, load-bearing columns or posts, or toilet drains. These will be dealt with in the next step. The most common spacing for floor joists is 16 inches on center but 12-inch and 24-inch centers are also used. All these distances are used to accommodate the 4-×-8-foot plywood subfloor panels and provide a nailing surface where 2 panels meet. In our example, we will use the 16-inch O.C. (on center) measurement.

The band and girders are marked with straight lines made with a combination square and an "X" marked on one side of the line to show the position of the actual joist. These lines will mark the edge of the joists, not the center. Use a thick-leaded carpenter's pencil.

It does not really matter on which end of the building you begin your layout, unless there is already a foundation cripple or knee wall in place. In that case, begin the floor frame layout at the same end where you began your cripple wall layout. Your wall and roof rafter layout will also begin from this end. This enables all your cripple studs, floor joists, wall studs and rafters to line up directly over one another (assuming they have the same on center distance). This provides greater strength, but more important, allows open straight channels through which to run any heating or cooling duct-work or large plumbing waste pipes.

To begin the layout, hook the tape at the end of the header joist and measure out 15¼ inches (23¼ inches for 24-inch O.C. layouts, 11¼ inches for 12-inch O.C. layouts). Drive a nail at this point and draw a line on the band at this spot. Hook your tape on this nail and mark the header every 16 inches from this point. Your "X"s (joists) will fall to the right (see diagram) of these marks.

The reason 15¼ inches, not 16 inches, is used as your first measurement is so that your first piece of plywood will come to the outside edge of your first joist, not to the center of it. All pieces, except the first and last, need to fall on the center of the joists to provide a nailing surface for the adjoining piece of plywood. The first and last pieces do not have adjoining pieces of plywood on one side. By reducing your first measurement by ¾ inch, half the thickness of a joist (1½ inches), you shift the first piece of plywood from the center of the first joist to the outside edge of it.

Figure 9-25. Laying out joists on the band.

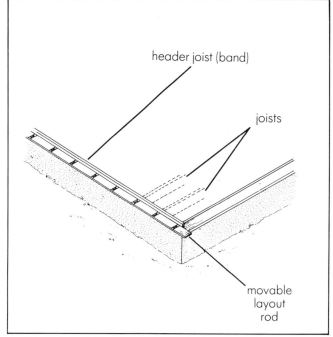

Figure 9-26. Using a layout rod to mark joist locations on the band.

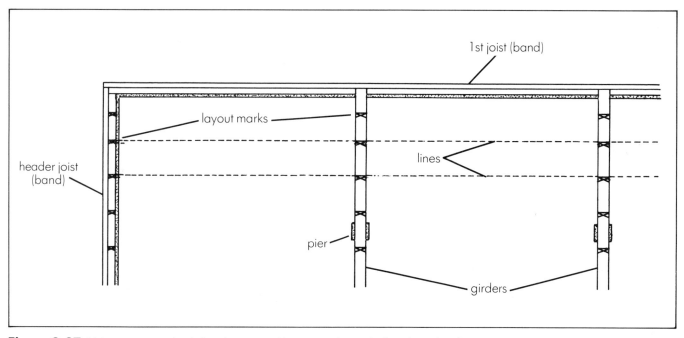

Figure 9-27. Using strings to check the alignment of layout marks on the bands and girders.

Some builders mark a layout rod with the proper measurements and use that at the band and girders. Other builders lay out the bands before they are nailed to the sill plates. Continue laying out the band at 16-inch intervals down the entire length. The distance between the last two joists may not be exactly 16 inches. This is OK, as long as it is not greater than 16 inches O.C. Be sure you always make your "X"s on the proper side of the line. It is a common mistake, even among professionals, to place the "X" on the wrong side of the line.

After you have laid out the first band, repeat this process on the girders and the band on the opposite side. Once I have marked the band and girders, I usually run a straight chalkline from band to band to see if all the marks line up with each other.

After you have laid out all the common 16-inch O.C. joists, you are now ready to mark for any load-bearing partitions, openings in the floor, toilet and bathtub drains, large ductwork or other special situations.

Figure 9-28. Some common floor frame situations: (A) Spaced double joists for a load-bearing interior wall directly above. The spacing allows for pipes and wires to run into the wall. (B) Typical floor opening. (C) Double joists (no spacing) for an interior load-bearing wall above. (D) Bathtub, shower or toilet drain. Note how the joist is broken by headers. (E) Bathtub, shower or toilet drain. Note how the joist has been moved.

Step 6
Layout for Special Situations

Margin of Error: Within ¼ inch of proper placement.

Most Common Mistake: Forgetting to allow for special situations.

Diagrams: Figures 9-28, 9-29, 9-30, 9-31, 9-32, 9-33.

Photograph: Photo 9-8.

Refer back to your plans and see if there are any details in the plan that may need special attention during layout. I will deal with a few of the common situations here and a few not so common ones, such as cantilevering, toward the end of the chapter.

Openings in the Floor Frame

Sometimes an opening is called for in the floor frame. Usually these are for chimneys, stairs, and access doors into the crawlspace. The plans should give you the location in the floor frame and the size of the rough opening. As with the window and door openings in the wall frame, the size of the opening will be listed as the "rough opening" or R.O. This represents the dimensions from the inside of one trimmer to

Figure 9-29. Typical opening in floor.

the inside of the other and from the inside edge of one header to the inside edge of the other. A trimmer is a double or single joist at the edge of an opening that runs parallel with the common joists.

The width of the opening will determine how many common joists must be cut. This will then determine how much

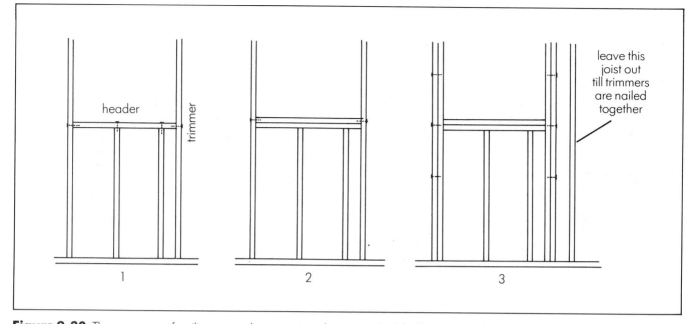

Figure 9-30. The sequence of nailing around an opening when using doubled headers and trimmers.

Figure 9-31. A load-bearing wall running perpendicular to the joist system. No special framing is needed.

Figure 9-32. A load-bearing wall running parallel to the joist system. Note the double joists separated by blocks to allow pipes and wires to pass into the wall.

weight will be carried by the headers and trimmers. The more common joists that are cut, the more weight they will carry. Usually the trimmers and headers are doubled when the opening is over 4 feet wide. If the opening is over 6 feet wide, special metal hangers are needed to attach the headers to the trimmers. If the tail joists are over 12 feet long, joist hangers are used to attach them to the headers. Note that the tail joists are placed along the original 16-inch O.C. marks to assure a continuous layout that will provide the center of a joist at each splice in the plywood subfloor.

The trimmers and headers are nailed together in a certain sequence so that there is never a need to nail through a doubled piece of stock. Note the diagram for the sequence.

Load-Bearing Interior Walls

Load-bearing walls are interior stud walls that carry a load. Non-load-bearing partition walls only section off a space; there is no load or weight placed on them. Typical loads on walls are from second-floor joists, or rafters or roof truss systems. When these walls are running perpendicular to the floor joists, nothing special is needed, because their weight is distributed evenly over several floor framing members which, in turn, carry the weight over to the foundation. If, however, these walls are running parallel to the floor joists and are falling between the joists, the weight being carried by the wall can be great enough to cause the plywood subfloor to bend and even fail. Because of this, codes require that a

Photo 9-8. An opening in the second-floor floor frame for stairs. Note the double headers, double trimmers and metal hangers supporting the headers and tail joists.

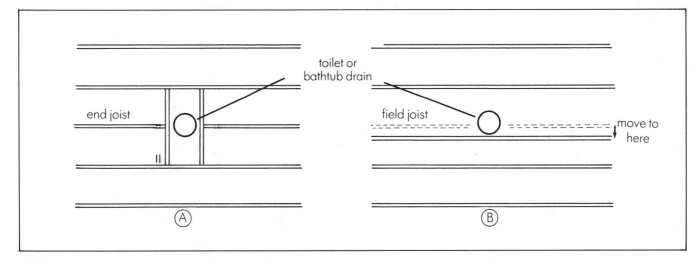

Figure 9-33. Providing for a bathtub or toilet drains. (A) Box for end joists. (B) Field joists can be moved a few inches.

double joist be placed below all load-bearing walls that run parallel to the joists. Often these joists are separated by 2-×-4 blocks placed every 4 feet. This allows any ductwork, plumbing or electrical wires to pass into the wall from below. If a 6-inch-diameter drain pipe is located in the wall, it will be made of 2×6s, not 2×4s, and the joists can be separated by 2-×-6 blocks.

Sometimes one of the wall-supporting joists needs to occur at the same spot as a common joist, in which case a joist is saved. Often they fall between the common joists, and the common joists will be located only a few inches away from the double joists. If this is the case, you may leave out the close common joists if: 1) the distance between joists does not exceed code regulations, and 2) the joist being eliminated is not an "end joist," a joist that is needed to support the splice between two pieces of plywood subfloor, but a "field joist," one where no splice occurs. Measurements can determine this, since the joist at every 4-foot interval will be an end joist.

Toilet and Bathtub Drains

Toilet and bathtub drains occur on the floors within rooms, whereas other plumbing drains are located within the wall cavities. Because of this, their locations have to be anticipated during the floor framing stage so that there is not a joist directly below the drain. If a joist is scheduled to fall directly below the drain, you can either box around it or move the joists a little bit to avoid the drain. If the joist is one that occurs at the splice of two pieces of plywood subflooring (end joist), it cannot be moved. You will either have to box around it or relocate the drain.

Large Ductwork

Sometimes ductwork for furnaces or air conditioning or fan-assisted passive solar circulation systems is too large to fit between the standard joist spacing. In these cases, openings have to be provided to allow for the ductwork.

Step 7
Install the Joists

Margin of Error: Height of crown—½ inch. Proper location—¼ inch.

Most Common Mistakes: Not turning crown up; placing joist on wrong side of line.

Diagrams: Figures 9-34, 9-35.

Photographs: Photos 9-9, 9-10, 9-11, 9-12, 9-13.

There are different ways to join the joists to the girders. Four ways were discussed in the "Design Decisions" section of Chapter 6, *Poured Concrete Foundations*. You should have already decided which method you will use and the proper negative spaces for girder pockets should have been allowed for when pouring the foundation.

The layout having been completed, you now measure and cut the joists. If everything is true and straight, you can just measure at a few spots and cut all your joists; if it isn't, and it rarely is, it may be best to measure for each joist, record the measurements and then cut all the joists.

When installing the joists it is very important to check each joist to locate the crown of the bow. Almost every joist will have one no matter how slight. Always point this crown UP as it will settle down during construction. If there are any large knots on the edge of the boards, place them on the top; it is stronger than having them on the bottom.

Try to cut the boards to fit as tightly as possible. Even though the common margin of error in framing is ¼ inch, the tighter the floor frame fits, the stronger and more rigid it will be. Nail the joists to the header joists with 3 or 4 16d nails. These nails, like all framing nails, should be no closer to each other than half their length and no closer to the edge than a

Figure 9-34. Point crown up. Note: knot is up.

quarter of their length. When nailing at the header joists, be sure joists are installed plumb. If you are using joist hangers, special short nails are available to attach the hanger to the joists.

As you nail the joists in place, be sure that they are being nailed on the proper side of the layout line. Placing them on the wrong side is a common mistake in building. It is a good idea to run your tape out every few joists to be sure there is a center of a joist at every 4-foot interval. When nailing the joists to the header joists and girders, see that they are flush along their top edges. If they are low, shim using cedar shims; if they are too high, notch the joists so they will sit lower.

Continue down the frame until all the joists are installed and openings are completed.

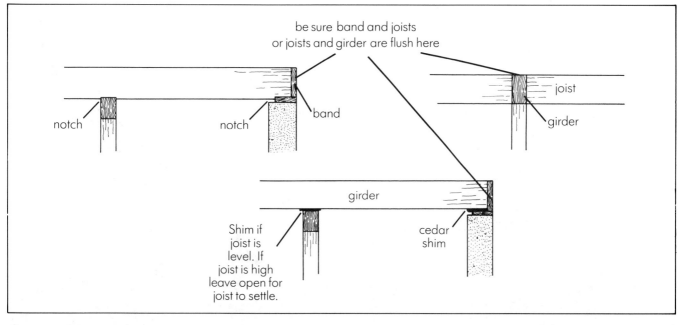

Figure 9-35. Use notches and shims to be sure the girders are level and the tops of joists are flush with the tops of bands and girders.

Photo 9-9. Joists are on top of the girders and joined by scabs. Note a scab is used where 2 band joists are spliced.

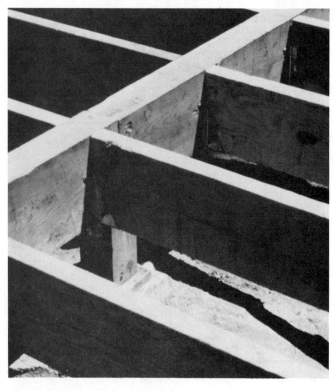

Photo 9-10. Joists are hung from the girders with metal joist hangers.

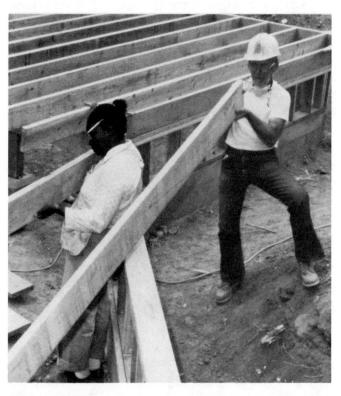

Photo 9-11. Eyeing the joist to locate the crown. Point the crown up.

Photo 9-12. The joists are being nailed to the band. Be sure that the joists and band are flush.

Photo 9-13. Floor framing in progress.

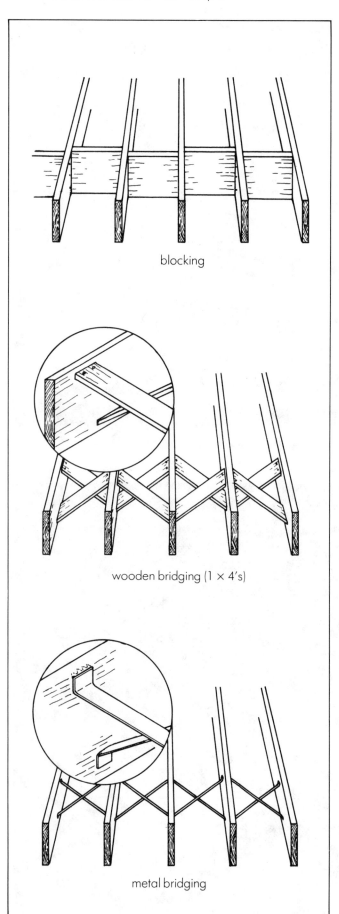

blocking

wooden bridging (1 × 4's)

metal bridging

Figure 9-36. Three types of blocking or bridging.

Step 8
Install Bridging or Blocking

Margin of Error: Solid blocking—exact. Bridging—¼ inch.

Most Common Mistake: Cutting blocking too long or too short.

Diagrams: Figures 9-36, 9-37, 9-38, 9-39.

Photographs: Photos 9-14, 9-15, 9-16.

Most floor frames and most codes require blocking or bridging to be installed in the frame. Blocking or bridging is the placing of metal straps, diagonally nailed 1×4s or pieces of joist stock between the joists to provide greater rigidity and strength to the floor, to prevent the joists from twisting and to transfer the weight from one joist to another.

The metal strap method is rather new and seems quick and easy to apply, but I do not know if it adds as much rigidity and strength as the other systems do. The solid blocking method, using pieces of joist stock, has been the most prevalent in recent years, almost totally replacing the older system of bridging with 1×4s diagonally nailed between the joists. It has replaced it probably because it is quicker, not particularly because it is better. After years of using the solid blocking system, I am leaning more and more towards the 1×4 bridging system. It offers several advantages that the solid blocking system does not.

1) Solid blocking tends to keep bows in place rather than allowing them to settle. Diagonally placed wooden bridging is nailed only at the top in the beginning and late in construction it is nailed along the bottom, giving the bows in the joists time to settle down.

Photo 9-14. Measuring at the end of joists for blocking that will be in the middle. This ensures that the joists will be parallel and straight.

Photo 9-15. Blocking is staggered to allow for face-nailing through the joists into the blocks. Here joists are supported (hung) by girders at both ends.

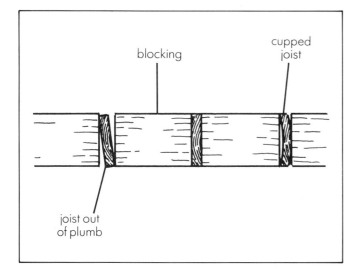

Figure 9-37. Blocking throwing the floor frame out of line because of cupped or out of plumb joists.

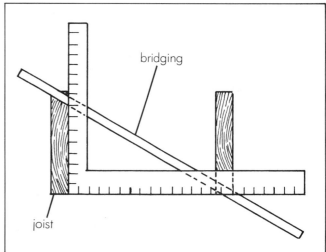

Figure 9-38. Use a framing square to determine the length and angle to cut bridging pieces.

2) When using the solid blocking, if you cut the blocks too long or too short, they will push or pull the joists system out of line. Even if they are cut perfectly, or bought from the lumber yard precut, a cup or twist in the joists will not allow the block to sit flat against the joists, and it will throw things off.

3) The diagonal bridging is easier to run pipes and wires through.

In any of the systems, blocking or bridging is usually spaced every 8 feet or in the center of the span, e.g., a 14-foot span would have blocking 7 feet in. Measure the proper distance from each end of the floor frame, pop a line across the top of the joists with a chalkline, and begin installing either the blocking or the bridging. (Some builders install the solid blocking as they place each joist; this avoids having to nail in the small areas between the joists.)

Figure 9-39. Jig to cut bridging.

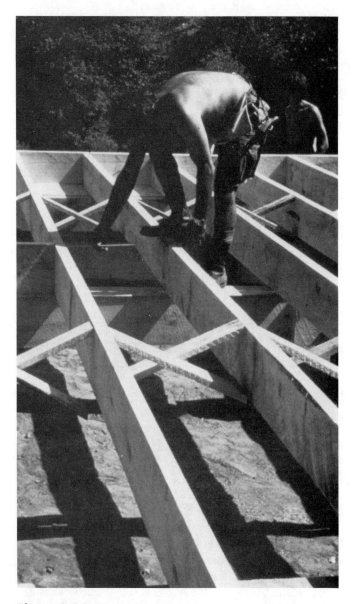

Photo 9-16. The bridging (1×4s) is in place. Only the top is nailed; the bottom is nailed after the house is completed, to allow the crowns in the joists to settle.

Solid Blocking

When using solid blocking, stagger the blocks on opposite sides of the center chalkline so they can be face nailed on both sides (see photo). Be sure the tops are flush with the tops of the joists. In the case of second- and third-floor frames, where sheetrock ceilings will be applied to the bottom of the joists, be sure the blocks are flush with the bottom of the joists as well. When measuring the space between the joists for the size of block to be placed, measure at the end of the joists where the joists are nailed to the band rather than where the blocking is to be installed; there may be a warp in the joist that could throw the measurement off. Be sure the joists are straight and in line as you block.

Bridging

When bridging, be sure that the 2 pieces do not touch or they will cause the floor to squeak when it is walked on. The top of bridging should be about ⅜ inch *below* the top of the joists and the bottom of the bridging should be the same distance *above* the bottom of the joists. The top of the bridging is always directly on line with the top of the adjacent piece of bridging located in the adjoining space. Nail only the top of the bridging; the bottom will be nailed later when the joists settle.

You may want to nail a 1-×-6 board across the tops of the joists as you nail the bridging. This will keep the joists in their proper place until the subflooring is installed. The bridging, unlike the solid blocking, will not hold them in place.

When cutting bridging, you can figure out the length and the angles of the cuts by using a framing square. It is worthwhile to build a small cutting jig to enable you to cut many pieces at once.

Step 9
Check the System

Margin of Error: ¼ inch.

After the floor frame is complete, check for the following before going on to the subfloor:

- ☐ Dimensions

- ☐ Squareness (check diagonals)

- ☐ All joists parallel and on proper mark

- ☐ All crowns up

- ☐ Joists flush with girders and headers

- ☐ Proper rough openings/squareness

- ☐ Center of joist every 4 feet

- ☐ All joists properly nailed

note some codes
call for inverted
joist hanger

common
joist

cantilevered joist

2X

X

Figure 9-40. Cantilevered joists running the same direction as common joists.

Special Situations

Cantilevering

Diagrams: Figures 9-40, 9-41, 9-42.

Cantilevering is used as a design effect both for porches and decks as well as for projections from the building itself. They overhang the foundation wall and are suspended without any vertical support posts. Where part of a room is being suspended, you may have to get this okayed by the building code office; some building codes read that there must be a foundation system (usually a solid wall foundation) under all exterior walls.

If you plan to cantilever a deck, remember you will be exposing your floor joist system to the weather. This exposure could cause rot which, in time, could travel into the house and cause structural damage to the joist system. You can switch to a rot-resistant wood for these joists (redwood, cedar, pressure treated), which will be more expensive than common joist material. Since joist lumber is also weaker, it will have to be either larger or more closely spaced than the

other joists. If you plan to expose your common framing lumber, at least treat the lumber to help prevent rot. You may want to consider avoiding cantilevering altogether and just build a standard deck with vertical supports.

Should you decide to use a cantilevered system, it will make a difference whether the cantilevered joists are running parallel or perpendicular to the common joist system. If they are parallel, you simply run the joists out past the foundation wall. If your cantilevered joists are to run perpendicular to the common joists, you have to double up a common joist and tie the cantilevered joists into this double joist. There is always a 1 to 2 relationship between the length of the total joist and the distance it can be cantilevered past the foundation wall (it can be cantilevered ⅓ the length of the joist). There is also a code limit to how long a joist any size can be cantilevered which must be taken into consideration as well.

If you are cantilevering for a deck, you will need to notch the cantilevered section 2 inches to allow the deck boards to sit below the level of the inside floor. This further reduces the strength of the joist.

Figure 9-41. Cantilevering when the deck runs perpendicular to the regular joist.

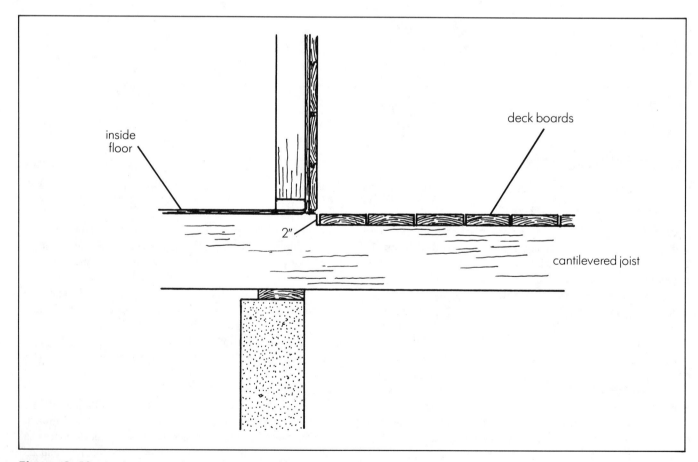

Figure 9-42. Notching a cantilevered joist to keep the deck slightly lower than inside floor level.

Figure 9-43. Changing the height of the joists to accommodate tiles being set on top of reinforced concrete.

Photo 9-17. A girder system using 4-inch-thick girders on 4-foot centers. A thicker subflooring, either 1⅛-inch plywood or 2-inch tongue and groove boards, is used. Note that underfloor utilities are already installed (optional in most areas).

Photo 9-18. Floor trusses being installed. They are lightweight, but can span greater distances than common floor joists.

Figure 9-44. Manner in which the tops of walls are fastened to floor joists above and below.

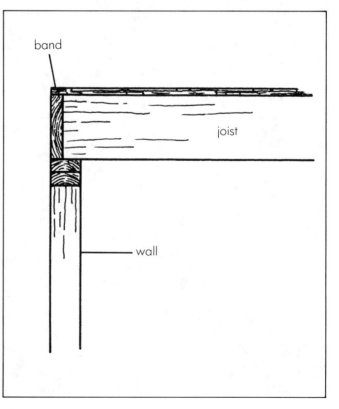

Figure 9-45. First-floor wall frame supporting second-floor joists.

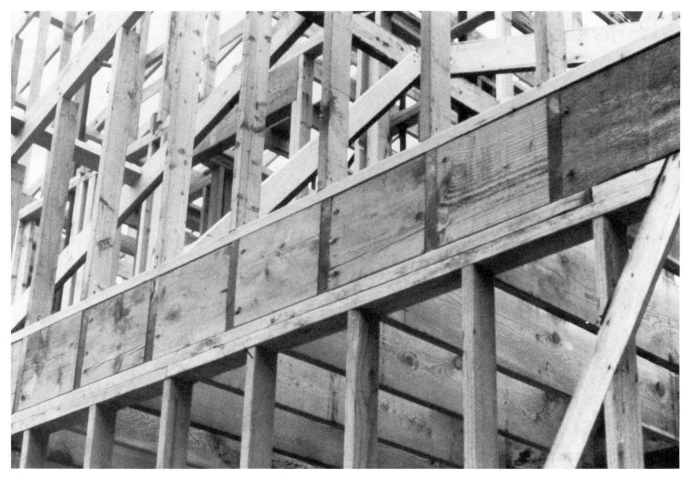

Photo 9-19. Second-floor joists resting on the walls. Note that blocks are used at the end of the joists instead of a solid band.

Tile Floors

Diagram: Figure 9-43.

Sometimes in entrance halls and bathrooms, where tile on top of reinforced concrete is to be used as a flooring, you will need to lower the floor frame to accommodate the difference in height of this type of flooring. You will need to use either smaller joists or 4-inch stock or doubled joists to provide for this. If you are using standard thickness tile with mastic (adhesive) and no concrete base, usually no special adaptations are needed.

Girder System

Photograph: Photo 9-17.

Some builders choose to use a floor frame system made up entirely of 4-inch girders (usually 4×6s or 4×8s). This system requires girders every 4 feet supported by the standard posts; there are no joists. Because of the 4-foot span of the girders, you will need to use a thicker subfloor. 2-4-1 plywood (a 1⅛-inch-thick plywood) or 2-inch tongue and groove boards (2×6s or 2×8s) are used as subflooring. From what I know, this system is comparable in price and time to the standard floor frame system. You may want to ask a local builder who uses this system what they think. Some builders have switched to it.

Floor Trusses

Photograph: Photo 9-18.

As with roof framing, you can purchase pre-made trusses to be used as floor framing. These are made up of 2-inch material and plywood specially designed and built to be able to span long distances with lightweight materials. They seem to work pretty well. (See Photo 9-18.)

Second-Floor Joists

Diagrams: Figures 9-44, 9-45.

Photograph: Photo 9-19.

Floor framing for the second floor is almost identical to that of the first floor. Instead of bearing on foundation walls and girders, the joists bear on exterior and interior walls. The layout is done on the top of the wall's top plates and the band is nailed flush to the outside edge of the wall. Note the way parallel first-floor walls connect to second-floor joists.

Many designers or owner builders use large attractive timbers for second-floor joists and expose them to the downstairs. Usually 2-inch tongue and groove boards are used as a second-floor subfloor (and even as the finished floor). These make an attractive first-floor ceiling. Be aware when doing this that the noise transmission between floors is high.

Worksheet

ESTIMATED TIME

_____

_____

_____

_____

CREW

Skilled or Semi-Skilled

_____ Phone _____

_____ Phone _____

_____ Phone _____

Unskilled

_____ Phone _____

_____ Phone _____

_____ Phone _____

_____ Phone _____

_____ Phone _____

MATERIALS NEEDED

Joist stock, girder stock, posts and nails

ESTIMATING MATERIALS

_____ × _____ JOISTS _____ feet long: Quantity _____

Linear feet of HEADERS and BAND _____

Linear feet needed for BLOCKING _____

Quantity _____ of TAIL JOISTS at _____ feet long

_____ × _____ GIRDERS _____ feet long: Quantity _____

_____ × _____ POSTS _____ feet long: Quantity _____

_____ lbs. of 16d FRAMING NAILS (100 lbs. to frame a 1500 sq. ft. house.)

COST COMPARISON

_____ Store:

$ _____ per M = $ _____ total

_____ Store:

$ _____ per M = $ _____ total

_____ Store:

$ _____ per M = $ _____ total

_____ Store:

$ _____ per M = $ _____ total

PEOPLE TO CONTACT

If underfloor utilities need to be inspected before the subfloor goes on, you may want to contact any required subcontractors if you do not plan to do the work yourself.

Roofer _____

Phone _____ Work Date _____

Roofing materials supplier _____

Phone _____ Work Date _____

Sheet metal person _____

Phone _____ Work Date _____

Plumber _____

Phone _____ Work Date _____

Solar panel installer _____

Phone _____ Work Date _____

Daily Checklist

CREW:

_____ Phone _____

_____ Phone _____

_____ Phone _____

_____ Phone _____

_____ Phone _____

_____ Phone _____

TOOLS:

☐ framing hammers

☐ combination square

☐ hand saw

☐ power saw

☐ saw blades

☐ saw horses

☐ pencil

☐ steel tape

☐ nail belt

☐ sledge hammer

☐ safety goggles

☐ nail-pulling tools

☐ transit or hydro level

☐ chalkline

☐ 4-foot level

☐ extension cords

☐ junction box

☐ framing square

MATERIALS:

_____ joists

_____ joist stock for band, blocking, etc.

_____ 16d CC sinkers

_____ metal fasteners

_____ metal fastener nails

_____ bridging material

_____ bridging nails

DESIGN REVIEW: Just review to see if your planned joist installation system is the easiest and cheapest method. Would an added girder greatly increase the rigidity of the floor?

WEATHER FORECAST:

For week _____

For day _____

10 Subflooring

Photo 10-1. House with plywood subflooring being applied.

What You'll Be Doing, What to Expect

SUBFLOORING IS A SKIN or surface that covers the open floor joists. There are several different options in your choice of materials: plywood, 2-inch-thick (nominal) tongue and groove boards, particle board and 1-inch-thick (nominal) regular cut boards. This phase of construction is one of the simplest. It involves nailing and/or gluing the subflooring to the joists; an easy process with few possible mistakes. Though it can become monotonous, the work goes quickly. Since it is work that requires only one real skill, nailing, and little information, it is a good place to use your free or inexperienced help. Kids do well at this task. (See Photo 10-1.)

You will be working in a bending position for long periods of time so you may feel a strain. Finding the most comfortable positions to facilitate the flow of work can make a great difference in both the ease and speed of the work. As in other phases that require fastening large surfaces, like wall and roof sheathing, I would highly recommend using a pneumatic nailer (Photo 10-2). This tool, run by an air-compressor, can cut your application time by as much as 50 to 75% and is great when you are working with only 1 or 2 people. You can even rent a moving nailer mounted on wheels that you push while walking along, squeezing the trigger to drive the nails.

In this chapter we will introduce different types of subflooring and discuss plywood subflooring in detail.

Jargon

SUBFLOORING. Boards or panels that are installed over the floor joists and over which a finished floor will be applied.

SUBFLOORING NAILS. A deformed or annular shank nail (8d) that has a much greater holding power than a regular nail. These help prevent the floor from squeaking.

SUBFLOOR-UNDERLAYMENT. A plywood or particle board panel that is used both as the subfloor and underlayment.

TONGUE AND GROOVE (T & G). Boards that are cut in such a manner that their sides (and sometimes their ends) have a tongue or protruding strip on one side and a groove or continuous indentation on the other side.

2-4-1 PLYWOOD. A 1⅛-inch-thick plywood that can be used for subflooring when your supports are up to 48 inches on center.

UNDERFLOOR UTILITIES. All the different utilities that have wires, pipes, ducts, etc., that are installed below the subfloor in the crawlspace or basement. These include electrical and plumbing systems, heating and air conditioning, gas lines, solar pipes or ductwork.

UNDERLAYMENT. Sheets or particle board or plywood laid on top of the subfloor to provide a smoother surface for some finished flooring. This surface is applied after the house is built but before the finished floor is laid.

Purposes of the Subfloor

1) Provides a base for the application of the finished flooring
2) Adds rigidity to the floor frame
3) Provides a platform or surface on which the carpenters can lay out and construct the rest of the framing

Design Decisions

Here are the different types of subflooring materials available:

PLYWOOD (Figure 10-1). Plywood, either tongue and groove or butt edge, is the most common form of subflooring and perhaps the best. It goes on quickly and easily and adds a tremendous amount of rigidity to the floor frame. This is especially important in earthquake areas. Usually a ⅝-inch or ¾-inch CD exterior glue plywood is used. Exterior glue plywood is plywood that can get somewhat wet during construction, but cannot stay wet for long periods of time as can exterior plywood used for siding. Exterior glue plywood is also called exterior/interior plywood as it can be exposed during construction, but after construction it will be in the interior of the home.

Exterior glue plywood has knotholes on both surfaces. This is of little consequence since it will be covered by a finished floor. If, however, your finished flooring will be a thin linoleum that could press into these knotholes, a plug and

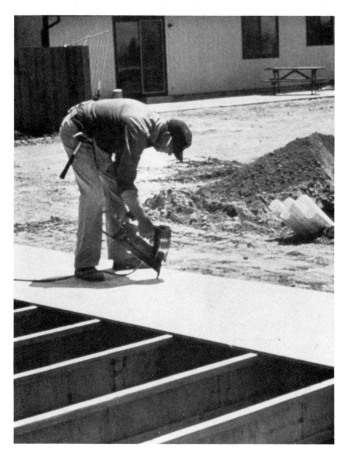

Photo 10-2. Using compressed-air nailing gun to apply subfloor.

Figure 10-1. Plywood subflooring. Note that the splices are staggered.

Figure 10-2. Particle board subflooring.

Figure 10-3. 2-4-1 plywood (1⅛ inch thick).

touch sanded (P & TS) grade is required, where the holes have been filled and sanded. (An underlayment grade can also be used.)

PARTICLE BOARD (Figure 10-2). This material is similar to plywood, but instead of being sheets laminated (glued) together, it is made of wood chips or particles and glue poured to form a sheet. This material is somewhat less expensive than plywood and is therefore becoming popular.

It does, however, have some drawbacks. The glue composition gives off a formaldehyde fume or gas, and if it gets wet, and stays wet (if a pipe were to burst while you were on vacation, for instance), it can totally dissolve. Some builders use it in bathrooms; if it only gets damp or a little wet it will hold up better than plywood, which can delaminate. It is also harder to nail through than plywood.

2-4-1 PLYWOOD (Figure 10-3). This is a 1⅛-inch-thick plywood that is used in the girder floor frame system (discussed in Chapter 9, *Floor Framing,* "Step 7") where the supports are 48 inches on center. This or a nominal 2-inch tongue and groove board is your only choice when framing members are on this great span.

NOMINAL 2-INCH TONGUE AND GROOVE BOARDS (Photo 10-3). Tongue and groove boards, either 2×6s or 2×8s, are sometimes used as subflooring. Like 2-4-1, they can span up

to 48 inches on center supports. Especially when used on framing members 16 or 24 inches on center, this material makes for a very stout floor.

When you are using large floor frame members for the second floor that will be exposed from the first floor below, and the subfloor will also be exposed from underneath, tongue and groove boards are often used. They look better from below than plywood, and sometimes you can even sand, stain and varnish the upper surface to make it into a finished floor as well. Be aware, however, that this type of system affords little sound control between floors.

Tongue and groove boards take a good bit more time to apply than does a plywood subfloor. The difference is applying many individual boards compared to large panels. You will need to check locally for the difference in the cost of the two systems for material and labor (if you are paying for labor). If you plan to expose one or both of the surfaces, buy "dry" lumber to avoid cracks caused by shrinkage.

NOMINAL 1-INCH COMMON BOARDS (Figure 10-4). Before the advent of plywood, this was the most common subflooring material. It consists of common 1×6 or 1×8 boards with regular surfaces and no tongue and groove, applied diagonally across the floor frame at a 45° angle for greater strength. This type of subflooring is much slower to apply and not nearly as strong as plywood; it is not recommended.

Photo 10-3. Tongue and groove 2×6 subflooring being applied. Large second-floor floor joists and the subflooring will be exposed from below.

What You'll Need

TIME   24 to 40 person-hours per 1000 square feet.

PEOPLE   2 Minimum (1 skilled, 1 unskilled); 3 Optimum (1 skilled, 2 unskilled); 6 Maximum (2 teams of 3 each).

TOOLS   Framing hammer, chalkline, power saw, hand saw, pneumatic nailer (optional), pencil, nail belt, tape measure, framing square, caulking gun, sledge hammer or maul, nail-pulling tools, saw blades, extension cords, plug junction box.

RENTAL ITEMS: Air compressor, nailing gun.

MATERIALS   With plywood subfloors I would use a tongue and groove plywood, at least ⅝ inch or thicker. A ¾-inch board makes for a stouter floor and is recommended. Use a CDX exterior glue plywood. In areas where the finished flooring will be a thin vinyl or linoleum or where the plywood subfloor will be the finished floor (e.g., laundry-room, workshop, unfinished areas, etc.), use an underlayment grade, plug and touch sanded (P & TS). Be sure when you buy the panels that they are all the same size. Some

Figure 10-4. Nominal 1-inch (¾-inch) boards applied diagonally as subflooring.

manufacturers make them 48 inches wide, others 47½ inches wide. *You cannot mix the two; they all have to be the same size!*

Buy a high-quality subflooring adhesive and 8d subflooring nails. This should eliminate all squeaks.

ESTIMATING MATERIALS NEEDED

PLYWOOD: To estimate plywood divide the number of square feet of floor by 32 square feet (4-×-8-foot plywood sheet) and add 15% for waste.

ADHESIVE: Refer to the manufacturer's suggested use.

NAILS: Two pounds per sheet (CC sinkers 8d or threaded subflooring nails).

INFORMATION This chapter will deal in detail with applying plywood subfloors. For applying 1-inch common boards, consult some of the older housebuilding books written when this type of subflooring was prevalent. For more information on applying T & G boards, see section on 2-×-6-foot T & G in Chapter 14, *Roof Sheathing*, p. 327.

Be sure you meet all the specifications of your local codes for subflooring, e.g., plywood for subflooring must be graded, it must be the required thickness, etc.

PEOPLE TO CONTACT If in your area underfloor utilities need to be inspected, you may need to contact the plumber, electrician, solar installer and someone to install the sheet metal for the heating and air-conditioning.

INSPECTIONS NEEDED In many areas, especially those covered by the Uniform Building Code, you may need to get an underfloor utilities inspection before the subfloor is applied but after the floor framing is built. This means the following must be installed below floor level: water supply lines, both hot and cold water pipes, air conditioning and heating ductwork, waste-water pipes, electrical wires and gas lines. The inspector will want to inspect these before the subflooring is applied. If, however, you have a high crawl-space, the inspector may waive the inspection until after the frame is built. Getting a waiver, if you can, is usually an easier way to go.

Reading the Plans

Most plans will clearly state the thickness and type of sub-flooring to be used. Often they will not tell you whether it is tongue and groove or regular plywood. Tongue and groove is always recommended. You may decide to increase the thickness of the plywood called for in the plans in order to provide a stouter floor. Note that the plywood always is applied with its long (8-foot) dimension running perpendicular to the floor joists.

Your plans should show you any areas on the second or third floor where an open-beam floor system will be used, exposing the floor joists to the floor below. In these areas you may want to use 2-inch tongue and groove subflooring. Be sure there are no plumbing fixtures in these areas that need their drain or supply pipes protruding through the floor or they will be exposed from below.

Safety and Awareness

SAFETY: Be very careful with the pneumatic nailer.

Be careful not to fall between the floor joists, especially by stepping on an unnailed sheet of plywood that is hanging over a joist. This is a common accident.

Beware of back strain from bending over all day.

AWARENESS: Plywood always runs with its long dimension perpendicular to the joists. End edges must meet on the center of a joist. Stagger the splices in the panels. Best looking side faces up. Use glue and threaded nails.

Overview of the Procedure

Step 1: Check floor frame
Step 2: Spread the glue
Step 3: Lay the first course
Step 4: Lay the remaining sheets

Step 1
Check the Floor Frame

Margin of Error: Floor joist must be installed so that ends of plywood subfloor panels are at least within ¼ inch of center of joist.

Most Common Mistake: Joist not properly aligned.

Figure 10-5. 2-×-4 nailer used to provide nailing surface where joists are off line.

Photo 10-4. Using a caulking gun to spread on subfloor adhesive.

Diagram: Figure 10-5.

Before starting on the subfloor, look over your floor joists. Do this both visually and with a tape measure. Walk along the system and sight down the joists. You should be able to tell if they are all running parallel. If you have accidentally placed one on the wrong side of the layout mark, you should be able to spot it with this check.

Starting at the end where your joist layout began (you will begin laying the plywood panels from this end), take a steel tape and measure from the outside edge of the first floor joist (where the first panel will start) to see if there is a center of a joist at every 4-foot interval. You have about a ¼-inch margin of error here. If there is not a center of a joist, determine why, and correct the situation. If only one or two joists are off, it is best to move them into place, or you can add a nailing surface by solidly nailing a 2×4 to the joist to catch the plywood edge.

Once you are sure there will be a center of a joist to catch the ends of the panels, you can begin to install the subfloor. If you are fairly certain that it will not rain before the house is weather tight, you can even install a floor insulation at this time. If there is a good chance of rain, wait until the roofing is on to protect the insulation.

Step 2
Spread the Glue

Margin of Error: Spread it wide, but don't be sloppy.

Most Common Mistake: Using wrong glue.

Photograph: Photo 10-4.

Many builders do not use subflooring glue; they just nail down the subfloor. Using glue, however, not only eliminates squeaks but also adds a tremendous amount of strength to the floor system as it ties it all together into one continuous piece. If you are planning to use wet lumber, instead of kiln-dried, this is even more important. As the lumber dries and shrinks, the nails can loosen up to half their holding power, causing the floor to squeak and lose strength. The use of glue is inexpensive and easy and I highly recommend it.

Be sure you are using subflooring adhesive. A novice builder I know used panel adhesive, which does not have as much bonding effect. The subfloor "pops" as it is walked on due to the sticking and then releasing of this less effective glue.

Spread approximately a ¼-inch-wide bead of glue over all the joists and headers that this first panel will cover. Use a

Figure 10-6. Correcting for an off-square floor frame.

nice even bead. Just spread the glue over enough area to apply 1 panel at a time, until you feel you have the subfloor installation system down fast enough to spread the glue for 2 panels at once. Remember to disengage the caulking gun and stick a 16d nail in the open end each time you finish using it, to stop the cartridge from leaking.

Step 3
Lay the First Course

Margin of Error: Must have at least a ½-inch bearing on joist at end of panel.

Most Common Mistakes: Pointing wrong side up; not applying exactly perpendicular to the joists; not facing the tongue towards the outside.

Diagrams: Figures 10-6, 10-7, 10-8.

After the glue is spread, you are ready to apply the first course. As you apply the first row, it is more important that it be applied exactly perpendicular to the floor frame than that it be aligned exactly along the edge of the band. If your floor frame was accurately installed, both these conditions, good alignment and panels running exactly perpendicular, should exist. If it is off, align the panel perpendicular with the joists and, if need be, cut a small piece of subflooring to fill in the gap left by improper alignment. You may want to pop some chalklines that run perpendicular to the joists to assist you in laying the panels if the floor frame is not running true.

Be sure that you are pointing the good (smooth) side of the plywood towards the sky and the bad side towards the ground. The tongue edge should face the outside of the house as you apply, not the inside. You will need to pound on the edges of the plywood in order to get the tongue and grooves to interlock and it is always best to be pounding on the groove edge.

After the first panel is laid into place, use your chalkline and pop lines across the panels directly above the center of the joists. Use threaded 8d nails, nailing every 12 inches in the field and every 6 inches along the edge. Nail while the glue is still wet. Do not nail a few nails to hold the sheet in place and then return later to complete the nailing process. Nail it well at this time so that the panel presses against the joists and spreads the glue.

Some joists, you'll find, are simple field joists; no edge of any plywood sheet will break on them. Other joists will be used to support the ends of the panels. Since the joints are staggered in adjacent courses, one course's field joists may be the adjacent course's end joists. It is best to leave all end joists unnailed until the adjacent course has been installed, in case you need to push an end joist forward or backward a little to align its center with the end of the plywood panel.

Now continue to lay the rest of the course you have been working on. It is usually best to lay one entire course at a time, though this is not mandatory. As you lay the remaining sheets in each course, be sure their inside edges are in a straight line (a string stretched taut helps here) and be sure the ends of the panels fit tightly.

nail on this line

Figure 10-7. Popping a chalkline to mark the center of a joist on a plywood subfloor panel.

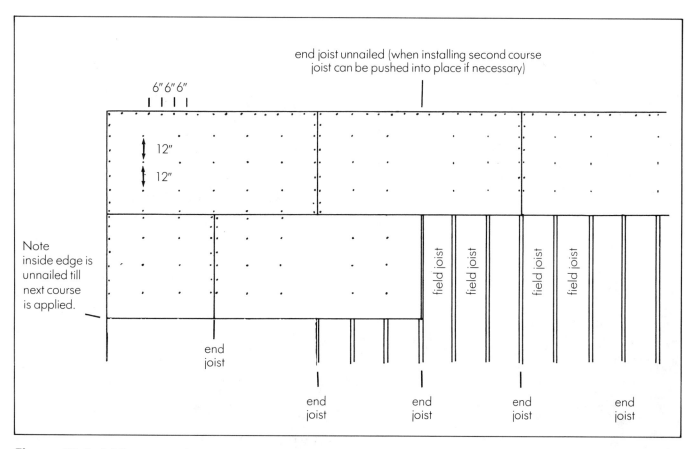

end joist unnailed (when installing second course
joist can be pushed into place if necessary)

6" 6" 6"

12"

12"

Note
inside edge is
unnailed till
next course
is applied.

field joist

field joist

field joist

field joist

end
joist

end
joist

end
joist

end
joist

end
joist

Figure 10-8. Subflooring application showing the nailing pattern. Note that the staggered splices and end joists are left unnailed until the adjacent course is laid.

Photo 10-5. Laying remaining sheets. Note the plywood has been cut for underfloor utilities. (Not required in many areas.)

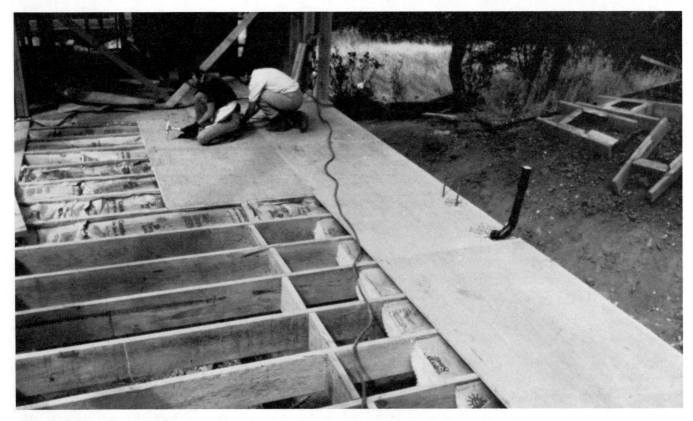

Photo 10-6. Subfloor further along.

Photo 10-7. Using sledge and block of wood to tightly join T&G plywood.

Step 4
Lay the Remaining Sheets

Margin of Error: Snug fits between panels at all edges (except where spacing is recommended for possible swelling); edges of sheets aligned in a straight line — ¹⁄₁₆ inch.

Most Common Mistakes: Sheets not fitting together well or properly aligned; not staggering the joints during the application.

Photographs: Photos 10-5, 10-6, 10-7, 10-8, 10-9.

You are now ready to lay your next course. The ends and the edges of the panels should ordinarily fit tightly, but there is an exception to this. In many areas of the country it is recommended that you leave a ¹⁄₁₆-inch gap between the ends of the panels and a ⅛-inch gap at their edges. This is to ensure that should the panels get soaked during construction and swell, they will not buckle. If you will be able to close up the house (put roof and walls on it) before the subfloor gets soaked, such as in areas of the West where there are long, dry building seasons, or if you are willing to cover the subfloor with plastic in case of rain, the gap can be eliminated.

In order to get the tongue and grooves to interlock (assuming you are using T & G, not butt-end plywood), you will often have to force the tongue into the groove. Use a sledge hammer and a block of wood to prevent dinging the edge of the plywood. Sometimes this will take a little effort, but the sheets must fit snugly. The sheets are often manufactured to have a small surface gap even when the tongue has bottomed out in the groove. Don't bust a gut trying to close that gap; when you can feel the tongue hit bottom, stop hammering.

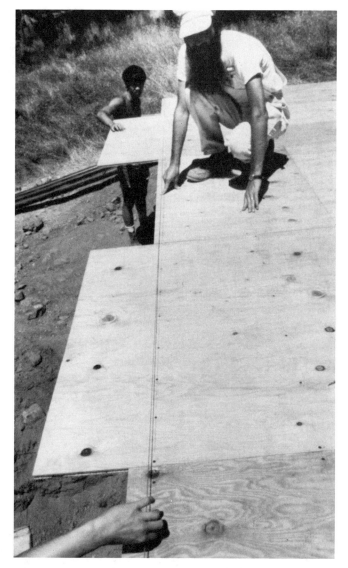

Photo 10-8. Marking "wild ends" of subfloor before cutting in place.

As you get to the end of the floor frame, the last sheet can either extend out to be cut after it is nailed or be cut before it is installed. Don't forget to apply the glue before nailing and be sure the good side is pointing up. As you start the second course, begin with a half (4-foot-long) sheet. If you begin every other course with a half sheet, this will automatically stagger your joints throughout the system. Continue applying the rest of the sheets in the manner described. If your last course will not take a full sheet, you will have to rip sheets to fit.

Photo 10-9. Finished subfloor.

Photo 10-10. Second-floor subfloor applied with area cut for stair entrance.

Figure 10-9. Notching subfloor to fit around underfloor utilities.

Special Situations

Subfloor Application and Underfloor Utilities

Diagram: Figure 10-9.

Photograph: Photo 10-10.

In some areas of the country, especially areas of the West, the building codes will require that you install all underfloor utilities *before* the subfloor is installed. This is to allow the inspectors to inspect the systems without having to crawl underneath the building. If this applies in your area but you have a high crawlspace that is easily accessible, often the inspector will waive this rule and allow you to erect the shell and later install the underfloor utilities. I think it is best to get the waiver if possible; installing the underfloor utilities before the subfloor has a few drawbacks:

1) You have to decide the exact location of your plumbing fixtures when only the joist are in place, and fix them in place;
2) Your subflooring is harder to apply when notches and holes will need to be cut to allow for the pipes to poke through;
3) The bottom plates of your walls will need to be notched to allow for these pipes;
4) You have to do your rough plumbing piecemeal; some at this stage, and the above floor part at a later stage.

Worksheet

ESTIMATED TIME

_____

_____

_____

_____

CREW

Skilled or Semi-Skilled

_____ Phone _____

_____ Phone _____

_____ Phone _____

Unskilled

_____ Phone _____

_____ Phone _____

_____ Phone _____

_____ Phone _____

MATERIALS NEEDED

Plywood, subflooring adhesive, nails.

ESTIMATING MATERIALS

PLYWOOD:

No. of sq. ft. of floor _____ divided by 32 sq. ft.
(4-×-8 plywood sheet) + 15% waste

= _____ sheets

ADHESIVE:

One tube covers _____ sq. ft. of subflooring

Total no. of tubes needed _____

NAILS:

_____ pounds cover _____ sq. ft.

Total no. of lbs. needed _____

COST COMPARISON

_____ Store:

$ _____ per sheet = $ _____ total

_____ Store:

$ _____ per sheet = $ _____ total

_____ Store:

$ _____ per sheet = $ _____ total

_____ Store:

$ _____ per sheet = $ _____ total

PEOPLE TO CONTACT

If underfloor utilities need to be inspected, do any of the
following need to be contacted about doing their work?

Electrician _____

Phone _____ Work Date _____

Plumber _____

Phone _____ Work Date _____

Sheet metal installer (Heating and Air Conditioning)

Phone _____ Work Date _____

Solar installer (for any pipes or panels or hybrid passive
solar ductwork) _____

Phone _____ Work Date _____

Do any suppliers need to make deliveries before beginning?

☐ YES   ☐ NO

If YES, Who _____

Delivery date _____ Time _____

Inspector (if needed) _____ Phone _____

Daily Checklist

CREW:

_____ phone _____

_____ phone _____

_____ phone _____

_____ phone _____

_____ phone _____

TOOLS:

- ☐ framing hammer
- ☐ chalkline
- ☐ power saw
- ☐ hand saw
- ☐ pneumatic nailer (optional)
- ☐ pencil
- ☐ nail belt
- ☐ tape measure
- ☐ framing square
- ☐ caulking gun
- ☐ sledge hammer or maul
- ☐ nail-pulling tools
- ☐ saw blades
- ☐ extension cords
- ☐ plug junction box

RENTAL ITEMS:

- ☐ air compressor
- ☐ nailing gun

MATERIALS:

_____ sheets of PLYWOOD

_____ cartridges of SUBFLOORING ADHESIVE

_____ lbs. of SUBFLOORING NAILS

DESIGN REVIEW:

Type of subflooring to be used _____

_____

Where to use plug and touch sanded plywood _____

_____

Do builders in your area leave gaps between panels to avoid buckling?

☐ YES   ☐ NO

If YES, how much?

_____ at end _____ at edges

Thickness of plywood subflooring _____

Nailing pattern (refer to code book)

_____ " in the field _____ " at edges

Tongue and groove plywood or regular edge _____

INSPECTIONS NEEDED:

Underfloor utilities inspection needed?

☐ YES   ☐ NO

Waiver OK'd by _____

Inspector's Name _____

Phone _____

Time and Date of Inspection _____

WEATHER FORECAST:

For Week _____

For Day _____

If heavy rain is expected cover the subflooring with polyethylene, both the sheets that have been applied and those stacked and waiting to go on. This will prevent expansion and warping. On windy days be careful while lifting panels.

Wall Framing

Photo 11-1. House with first-floor walls in place.

What You'll Be Doing, What to Expect

WALL FRAMING (Photo 11-1) is a very exciting process in housebuilding. In a very short time, the form and skeleton of the house begin to take shape. Each day the house becomes more of a reality as its outline takes form against the sky and the trees. It is a process to be savored and enjoyed.

Though simpler than doing a complex roof, wall framing (Figure 11-1) is somewhat more difficult than floor framing, but floor framing has prepared you well for this experience. Since most of the framing pieces are 2×4s and 2×6s, there are few physical demands and little strain during this process. You will, however, need to be absolutely clear on the size and location of all your wall openings for doors and windows. This means that a lot of very crucial decisions are being finalized; decisions that will make a great impact on the way it feels to live in the house. Study well the information in "Special Situations" at the end of this chapter to acquaint yourself with all the variables in wall framing.

Jargon

BOTTOM OR SOLE PLATE.   A horizontal base member to which the bottoms of the studs are nailed.

CAP PLATE (DOUBLE TOP PLATE OR DOUBLER).   The second and uppermost horizontal member that is nailed to the top plate.

CRIPPLE STUDS (CRIPPLES).   The shorter studs that are nailed below the window sills or sometimes above the headers.

HEADERS.   Horizontal wood framing members that support and carry the load over a window or door opening in the wall frame. Usually 4×4s to 4×12s are used.

JAMBS.   Vertical posts or pieces of a door or window frame.

PARTITION CHANNEL.   A pattern of studs built into a wall to receive an intersecting interior wall at a 90° angle.

SILL (ROUGH SILL).   The lowest horizontal member of a window opening in the wall, usually a 2×4 or 2×6 lying flat.

STUD.   One of a series of wooden wall framing members, either 2×4s or 2×6s.

Figure 11-1. The components of a wall frame.

TOP PLATE.   A horizontal member to which the tops of the studs are nailed.

TRIMMER STUD (SHOULDER STUD OR JACK STUD).   The vertical wall framing member that supports the header and adds strength to the side of the opening.

Purposes of Wall Framing

1) Supports the load of the roof and carries this load to the floor frame, the foundation, and ultimately, the ground
2) Encloses the house and provides a framework on which to hang interior and exterior skins, doors and windows
3) Creates hollow cavities in which to place plumbing and an electrical system and insulation

Design Decisions

In the design classes at the Center, I have often said that a house that turns out looking exactly like its blueprints is a house whose design stopped growing during its most fertile growth period: the construction period. Many things become clear during this stage. The platform is complete and the actual location and sizes of the windows, doors and interior partition walls can now be evaluated.

Most builders build true to the blueprints, seldom making changes during this incredibly creative period. They are being paid to build it exactly as the plans read. But now is the best time for you to consider making changes. Will the view be better if a window is enlarged or moved? Will the room feel more intimate if a planned window is deleted; will the room feel safer if a door is moved? Locate the interior partitions on the floor and get a sense of the size of the room, now that you can visualize it. Stand where the wall is to be built and ask: Is this where I want this wall to be? Visit houses with rooms that have different height walls and ceilings. A wall 9 to 11 feet high gives the room a greater sense of space without much energy loss. The house will never be more pliable than at this stage; give it a chance to grow and expand on its original design.

If you are designing and building a passive solar house (in all but the most moderate climate I would advise building no other type of house) you may want to make a final check on your south-facing solar gain windows. This can be done with a "Solar Site Selector." This instrument (Photo 11-2) can give you a reading on how much sunlight will be entering the solar windows at different times of the day, at different times of the year. You may find that by moving an opening slightly to the left or right or up and down you can increase the amount of sunlight entering the house. If there are windows that are expected to admit sunlight during certain parts of the day for lighting purposes, e.g., sunlight in the morning in the kitchen, sunlight in the afternoon in the workshop, etc., you can observe the path of the sun to be sure it will indeed come through the openings. Remember to account for changes in the sun's height in the sky at different times of the year.

Photo 11-2. Using a site selector to check solar gain through windows on the southern wall.

Even after a wall is up, it is not too late to change it if it doesn't feel right. Granted, this will be harder to do; you will never want to re-do *any* of your work, especially when you are on a tight schedule. There were many times when I sensed that the decisions I made on window, door or interior wall placement did not work after I had erected them, but I did not want to go back and change them. Later, after the house was completed, I wished I had taken the 4 extra hours or even a full day to get it like I really wanted it. What are a few extra days of work, when you may have to live with the decisions for many years?

You may want to allot yourself a certain amount of time at the outset, say 20 working days, for re-doing any areas of the house you do not feel comfortable with after they are done. The house may take 20 days longer to finish (a small percentage of the overall time), but it will be what you really want, and isn't that what building your own home is all about?

I did a lot of design changing on the last house we built. The carpenters often threw their hands, and sometimes their hammers, up in exasperation at the idea of having to re-do their work. In the end I was glad I fought for the changes. The house pleases me and there are few compromises.

If you plan to change the location of an interior load-bearing wall, be sure any needed underfloor supports (double joists, girders, piers, etc.) are provided.

2x4s or 2x6s?

If you are planning to build a standard stud house, as opposed to a post and beam house, a dome, etc., one major decision you will have to make is whether the exterior walls should be constructed of 2×4s or 2×6s. (Sometimes the code will require the use of 2×6s in the first floor of a three-story structure, for instance.) More and more houses are

being built with 2-×-6 walls because they have the ability to hold more insulation (6 inches instead of 4 inches), reducing heat loss and, consequently, energy bills. Some builders are using 2-×-4 walls with an added layer of styrofoam insulation on the outside surface of the studs to increase the energy efficiency of the home (see Chapter 12, *Wall Sheathing*, p. 265).

The 2-×-6 wall increases your energy efficiency and gives the house a sense of greater strength since the walls are thicker. Also, their wider cavities make plumbing and electrical systems easier to install. Except for moderate climates where 2×4s are sufficient, we are encouraging our students to use 2×6 walls; we expect energy rates to continue to rise. Most window manufacturers now make windows to fit 2×6 walls, though the windows will cost more due to their wider jambs. Ask the energy-minded builders in your area what they recommend. Situations in wall framing having to do with 2-×-6 walls will appear at the end of the chapter under "Special Situations."

After you have made your design decisions, check and then *recheck* the sizes of all the openings (rough openings). Often builders build these openings to the wrong specs and it is not till much later, during the window and door installation stage, that they discover the error. Then it is much harder to repair. As you lay out the wall, go slowly and double and triple check your work; it will save many hassles later. Unless you are building very complex walls with many angles or slopes, wall framing is challenging but not too difficult once you get the hang of it.

What You'll Need

TIME   8 to 16 person-hours per 30 linear feet of wall 8 feet tall

PEOPLE   2 Minimum (1 skilled, 1 unskilled); 3 Optimum (2 skilled, 1 semi-skilled); 6 Maximum (2 teams of 3 each).

TOOLS   Framing hammer, tape, sledge hammer, string, chalkline, power saw, hand saw, pencil, nail belt, combination square, framing square, plumb bob, 4- or 8-foot level, nail-pulling tool, com-a-long (hand winch), architect's rule, extension cords, plug junction boxes, saw blades.

RENTAL ITEMS: Ladders or scaffolding (if you are working on high walls); com-a-long (hand winch) to straighten walls after they are up. (They cost $30 to $40.)

MATERIALS   You will need to choose whether to use standard "wet" lumber or kiln-dried lumber. Kiln-dried lumber (Photo 11-3) is somewhat more expensive and a little harder to nail. It does, however, have several advantages that I believe make it worth the added money and energy. This has all been discussed in Chapter 9, *Floor Framing*, under "Materials."

You will, of course, need standard studs. For conventional building, with interior skins made of 8-foot panels of drywall or paneling, the stud length is commonly 92¼ inches, not 96.

The reason for this, as shown in Figure 11-2, is that to determine the length of wall studs in a typical 8-foot wall, you must allow 1½ inches for the bottom plate, 1½ inches for the top plate and 1½ inches for the cap plate. Since the ceiling board rests on the wall boards, ¾ inch, including a margin of error of ¼ inch, is added to the wall height to accommodate an 8-foot board. If from the top of the cap plate to the lower edge of the bottom plate it's 96¾ inches and you subtract the 4½-inch allowance for plates, the stud becomes 92¼ inches.

If you are not planning to use standard 8-foot panels, you can order different length studs in increments of 2 feet beginning at 6 feet. If your wall is 12 feet high or over, consider building 2 walls. For instance, with a 12-foot wall, you can build a lower 8-foot wall supporting a higher 4-foot wall. (See Photo 11-4. Note that the cap plate of the lower wall is the bottom plate of the upper wall.) It is difficult to locate true, straight studs (Photo 11-5) over 12 feet long; the 2-wall process eliminates the need for this.

Photo 11-3. Kiln-dried studs.

You will also need plate stock. These are long 2×4s (or 2×6s, if you are building a 2-×-6 wall) that will be used for bottom plates, top plates, and cap plates. These need to be true, straight boards as long as possible (12-foot boards will do, 14- or 16-foot are better, if you can find them). They must be straight, or the walls will be crooked.

You will need header stock which can be built up from 2-inch material or in many areas can be ordered in one solid piece, 3½ inches wide.

You will need nails, 8d, 10d and 16d CC sinkers (cement-coated sinkers). Steer clear of box nails or vinyl-coated nails. Box nails have thinner shafts than common nails, and vinyl-coated nails do not have the holding power of CC sinkers. In earthquake, tornado or hurricane areas, metal fasteners may be required or advised. If you are using wet lumber you may want to consider framing with threaded nails for added holding power.

ESTIMATING MATERIALS NEEDED

STUDS: Figure the number of studs needed per linear feet of wall using 12-, 16- or 24-inch centers. Add studs for the corners, king studs, trimmers, partition channel assembly, sills, cripples and blocking. Add 15% for waste.

PLATES: Use 10-foot, 12-foot or 14-foot lengths as needed to cover linear feet of wall. Add 15% for waste.

HEADERS: Exact linear feet needed. Remember, headers are 3 inches longer than rough opening widths.

NAILS: 1 pound of 16d sinkers per linear foot of wall, and ¼ pound of 8d sinkers per linear foot of wall.

INFORMATION   This chapter deals with standard stud construction for both 2-×-4 and 2-×-6 walls. In most houses that are stud constructed, this will be all that is needed. If you have some tricky or very complex wall-framing situations, you may want to consult with a local builder before beginning. Be sure you check all the door and window rough-opening sizes with your manufacturer's catalogue.

Photo 11-4. A 12-foot-high wall erected with a standard 8-foot-high frame plus a 4-foot-high frame.

PEOPLE TO CONTACT   If you have made any *major* changes from your original set of plans, contact the inspection office to notify the governing bodies and get their OK. Minor changes such as changing the size or location of doors or windows often do not need to be approved.

INSPECTIONS NEEDED   Usually no inspections are needed before or during this stage of construction, unless you have made major changes.

Figure 11-3. Plans.

NOTES

- All plan dimensions are to face of stud unless indicated otherwise
- Headers 4'-8" no. 2 grade unless otherwise indicated
- Walls 2×6s @ 16" o.c. stud grade wood
- Wood windows, fixed glass unless shown otherwise prefabricated in field

SMITH WINDOW COMPANY

WINDOW SCHEDULE

No.	Model No.	Rough Opening Ht.	Rough Opening Width	Remarks
1		3'-0-⅜"	3'-0½-"	
2		3'-0-⅜"	1'-6½-"	
3		3'-0-⅜"	1'-6½-"	
4		3'-0-⅜"	1'-6½-"	
5		3'-0-⅜"	1'-6½-"	
6		3'-0-⅜"	3'-0½-"	
7		3'-0-⅜"	1'-6½-"	Above clo. see plan
8		1'-0-⅜"	3'-0½-"	
9		1'-0-⅜"	3'-0½-"	
10		3'-0-⅜"	3'-0½-"	
11		3'-0-⅜"	2'-6½-"	
12		3'-0-⅜"	7'-0½-"	Dbl. gl. plate glass
13		3'-0-⅜"	2'-6½-"	
14		4'-0-⅜"	3'-6½-"	
15		4'-0-⅜"	3'-6½-"	
16		4'-0-⅜"	3'-6½-"	
17		4'-0-⅜"	4'-0½-"	
18		4'-0-⅜"	4'-0½-"	
19		3'-0-⅜"	2'-0½-"	
20		3'-0-⅜"	2'-0½-"	

F

DOOR SCHEDULE

No.	Size	Type	Remark
101	3⁰×6⁸	French door	Impact resist. C-typ.
102	3⁰×6⁸	French door	
103	1⁴×6⁸	H.C. wood	
104	4⁰×6⁸ (two)	Fr. sliding drs.	H.C.
105	2⁰×6⁸ (two)	French doors pr.	
106	2⁰×6⁸	French doors pr.	
107	2⁴×6⁸	H.C. wood	
108	2⁴×6⁸	H.C. wood	
109	2⁰×__	Wood	Cut to fit under sec.
110	3⁰×6⁸	French door	
111	2⁴×6⁸	H.C. wood	
112	2⁴×6⁸ (two)	French door	
113	2⁴×6⁸ (two)	French doors pr.	

G

WALL FRAMING SECTION

LEGEND

A height of wall	**D** inside wall covering
B fireblocking	**E** exterior wall covering
C size & spacing of studs	**F** window rough openings
	G door rough openings

Reading the Plans

Your plans carry a tremendous amount of information about wall framing. (Figure 11-3.) They must be accurate and complete in regard to this information, unless you plan to be making many of the decisions at the job site. In this case many details can remain vague until you are ready to finalize them. The following is a review of details that will be listed in your plans.

2×4 OR 2×6: Your plans should call out which walls are 2×4s and which walls are 2×6s. The exterior walls may be 2×6s to provide added depth for insulation. The first floor of a three-story building may be 2×6s for greater structural strength. Some interior walls may be 2×6s to allow for plumbing pipes of larger diameter.

HEIGHT OF WALLS: Usually the elevations will note the heights of your walls.

LOCATION OF INTERIOR PARTITION WALLS: Be careful in this area; this is where many plan drawers make mistakes. The dimensions are often wrong, and the total of the distances called out does not equal the total in reality. Many times this mistake doesn't come to light until after you have erected the walls; the 3-foot-wide closet can only be 1 foot wide. Check all room/closet dimensions and total them up now. Take into account the width of each wall, i.e., the width of the studs (3½ inches or 5½ inches) and the wall coverings (½ to 1 inch).

This part of the plans will also tell you where to locate, in any wall, the partition channels for tying intersecting walls together at a 90° angle. Be aware of where the dimension given on the plans refers to, the middle of the partition wall or to one of its edges; a lot of mistakes are created in this area.

LOCATION OF DOORS AND WINDOWS: Your plans will show the placement of all the doors and windows. Often the exact measurements are not given; many times the location of a window is indicated by a measurement to the center line of the window. You may have to determine the exact measurements by measuring on the plan with an architect's rule and converting these measurements into dimensions on the proper scale. Remember, you can reconsider these locations at this time.

SIZES OF DOORS AND WINDOWS AND ROUGH OPENINGS: Your plans usually contain a separate door and window schedule with measurements for each door and window. See "Ordering Windows," in Chapter 17, *Windows,* p. 421. The schedule matches each number with a corresponding door or window size, or a manufacturer's model number. The rough opening sizes for the manufacturer's model numbers are listed in the window or door catalogue. The width is always given first, the height of the rough opening second. For windows and sliding doors you must know the manufacturer, the exact model and the corresponding rough openings.

For most common doors, both interior and exterior, the

Figure 11-2. Determining the length of the common stud.

Figure 11-4. Example of from where a rough opening is measured.

plans will give only the width of the door; the height is often not mentioned because the height of common doors is 6 feet 8 inches. The width can range from 12 to 48 inches. These measurements are for the doors themselves, their rough openings are larger.

The width of a door's rough opening is the width of the actual door plus 2 inches. These 2 inches account for a ¾-inch finished jamb board on each side plus ½-inch adjustment room.

The height of the rough opening is the height of the door (6 feet 8 inches or 80 inches) plus a ¾-inch top jamb.

Door measurements are often written on the door schedule in 4 digits, e.g., 2068. This means the door itself is 2 feet, no inches, by 6 feet 8 inches, *not* 20 inches by 68 inches.

nailing surfaces
for interior wall covering

nailing surfaces
for interior wall covering

Swedish or Hollywood corner
(not recommended)

standard corner
(recommended)

Figure 11-5. Two types of framing corner units.

Example of a typical window rough opening situation (Figure 11-4). Your manufacturer's catalogue calls for a window rough opening that is 3 feet 4½ inches × 5 feet 2¼ inches. Remember that the width comes first and the height next. The width measurement is between the inside edges of the trimmers. The height measurement is from the top of the rough sill to the bottom of the header. In this particular example, the bottom of the window is called out in the plans to occur 14 inches above the subfloor.

SIZE OF FIXED WINDOWS: Fixed windows (ones that don't open) are considered straightforward and often are not keyed to a catalogue or schedule for size. The dimensions of the actual glass of fixed windows are often called out on the plans. Your rough openings are usually these measurements plus 2 inches added to the height and width to allow for the window jambs on all 4 sides (¾ inch thick) and a margin of error (½ inch).

SPECIAL SITUATIONS: Your plans should also indicate, and often detail, any special situations in regard to wall framing. Some of these possible situations may include: load-bearing posts or beams, specially sized headers, fireblocking or other blocking needs, special support for wall-hung toilets or sinks, let-in bracing, chimney and hearth framing, arches, framing for cabinets or ductwork, etc.

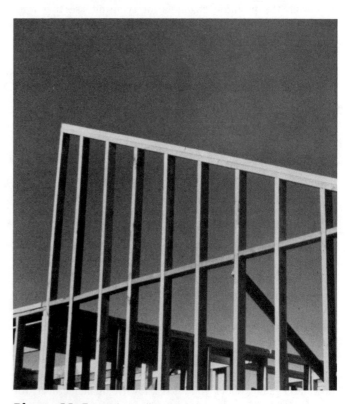

Photo 11-5. High wall using long studs. (The horizontal blocks are therefore fireblocking.)

Parts of a Wall

Before beginning the actual construction of a typical wall, I thought it might be best to review in detail the parts of a wall and how they are built. Not only will it assist you in learning the jargon better but it should de-mystify many things about wall framing itself.

CORNERS (Figure 11-5): Outside corners of the exterior wall frame are usually done in one of two methods. As shown in the figure the section is either made of 3 or 4 studs (or 3 studs with some blocks). This is not so much for strength as to provide a nailing surface for the interior wall covering. Blocks are used for center spacers rather than a full stud because the blocks help prevent decay should any moisture get into this area. Usually the entire corner section is assembled, and installed into the wall as it is being built on the floor.

PARTITION CHANNELS (Photo 11-6, Figures 11-6, 11-7): Where interior partitions intersect outside walls, good anchorage is required. Nailing surfaces must also be provided for the interior wallboard on both sides of the partition, as well as on the exterior wall. The figures show 2 typical partition channels. The channel shown in Figure 11-6 is the most common and recommended, even though it will require a few more studs. These channels are preassembled and placed in the wall as the wall is nailed together. The same channels are used at the intersections of interior walls.

DOORS AND WINDOWS (Figure 11-8, Photo 11-6): Probably the most complex part of a wall frame is framing the door and window openings. Actually this is not very difficult at all. You are simply making a hole in the rough frame to hold the finished window or door frame. As you can see, the typical rough opening is made of the following pieces: king studs, trimmers, headers, sills, and cripples.

TRIMMERS: The trimmers in Figure 11-8 are the most typical, though some builders choose to cut through their trimmers and insert the rough sill as shown in Photo 11-6. This tends to hold the sill tightly in place, but it can weaken the wall when the trimmer shrinks or if the cuts are not tight.

To determine the height of a trimmer, determine the distance from the bottom of the header to the top edge of the bottom plate. Trimmers for standard doors and windows in standard 8-foot walls are 81 inches high. This allows the proper height for the opening when using a 4-×-12 header (11¼ inches deep) with a standard 92¼-inch stud (92¼ − 11¼ = 81 inches). Note: on occasion, when dealing with very wide openings such as garage doors, trimmers are doubled or even tripled.

SILLS: Some builders use double rough sills because they will tend to stay straighter as the wood shrinks; the single sills may twist and pull the interior trim off alignment. In some areas if the rough opening is over a certain width, usually 4 to 6 feet, a double sill may be required by code. The

Figure 11-6. A partition channel.

Figure 11-7. A partition channel.

length of the sill usually equals the width of the rough opening.

HEADERS: Headers can either be a solid piece of header stock (3½ inches thick, usually used in the West Coast areas), or a built-up header of 2 pieces of nominal 2-inch materials, or a trussed header.

Photo 11-6. The trimmers are cut and the rough sill is inserted.

king studs

header

trimmers
(shoulder studs)

rough sill

(double sill
optional)

cripples

Figure 11-8. A typical window rough opening.

Types. Solid headers are most often seen on the West Coast (due to the availability of larger trees and therefore larger lumber stock). Header stock comes in heights from nominal lengths of 4 to 14 inches and is 3½ inches wide to match the width of a stud wall. They save the time needed to build headers out of pieces of lumber. They do warp and twist as they dry, however, more so than built-up headers.

The built-up header is another type commonly used. It consists of two pieces of nominal stock, sandwiched by pieces of ½-inch plywood (sometimes ⅜-inch plywood is used) to provide a header that is 3½ inches thick, the same as the stud wall itself. These pieces are nailed with 16d nails every 16 inches O.C. along each edge from both sides of the header.

Trussed headers (manufactured headers) are used where there is an unusually heavy load or where the span is unusually wide. These headers need to be designed by an architect or engineer and detailed in the plans.

Sizes. The length of the header is always the width of the rough opening plus 3 inches, assuming you are using single trimmers. The size of a header is determined by the width of the opening (this will affect the amount of load carried by the header) and whether the header will be supporting a floor above it or just a ceiling and roof. All exterior walls require full-size headers even if the wall is not a load-bearing wall (e.g., a gable wall). Interior walls will be discussed below. Local building codes usually have requirements for the sizes

HEADER SPANS

size of header	supporting one floor, ceiling, roof	supporting only ceiling and roof
2 × 4	3 feet, 0 inches	3 feet, 6 inches
2 × 6	5 feet, 0 inches	6 feet, 0 inches
2 × 8	7 feet, 0 inches	8 feet, 0 inches
2 × 10	8 feet, 0 inches	10 feet, 0 inches
2 × 12	9 feet, 0 inches	12 feet, 0 inches

the headers need to be. Above is a table that shows normal requirements.

Often, however, nominal 12-inch (11¼-inch) headers are used throughout for all window and door openings no matter what their width and loading. This is done for several reasons. First, in using nominal 12-inch-wide headers you can be sure they'll be sufficient to span almost any size opening in a typical single-family dwelling (except perhaps for the garage opening). Second, by using the nominal 12-inch header tight up against the bottom of the top plate, there is no need for bothersome cripples to be installed above the header. Thirdly, the industry has worked it out so that using a nominal 12-inch-wide header leaves just enough room to install a pre-hung standard size door. Finally, using nominal 12-inch-wide headers for all openings automatically sets the tops of all doors and windows at the same level, giving the house a more symmetrical look. There is one drawback however, 12-inch solid headers tend to crack and warp more than smaller headers, throwing your trim off. Filling the entire space with wood, where there could have been insulation, also increases your energy use.

CRIPPLES: Cripples are provided above the headers (unless nominal 12-inch-wide headers are used) and below the rough sills. These cripples need to continue the 12-, 16- or 24-inch layout pattern of the standard studs in order to support the top plate and/or rough sill, and to provide a nailing surface should 2 pieces of plywood or wallboard join in the area of an opening. Cripples are cut and measured to fill the space from the bottom of the rough sill to the top of the bottom plate and from the top of the header to the bottom of the top plate. There needs to be a cripple at either end of the rough sill to support the sill at the ends. You can draw a diagram and work out these measurements once you know your rough opening sizes and their locations in the wall.

Safety and Awareness

SAFETY: Standard precautions should be taken with your power saw. Watch that the wall does not fall off the platform when you lift it into place. Be careful on ladders while nailing on the cap plate (second top plate).

AWARENESS: Check, check and triple check your rough opening sizes. Be sure stud faces are flush with plate surfaces and headers are flush with stud surfaces. Use good plate stock and your straightest studs around doors and windows.

Overview of the Procedure

Step 1: Check the plans carefully

Step 2: Chalk walls on the subfloor

Step 3: Cut the bottom and top plates

Step 4: Lay out the wall

Step 5: Cut or build studs, headers, trimmer-king stud combinations, rough sills, corners, partition channels and cripples

Step 6: Nail the wall together

Step 7: Temporarily square and brace the wall

Step 8: Lift the wall into place and nail it to the floor

Step 9: Brace and plumb the wall

Step 10: Nail on the cap plates

Step 1
Check the Plans Carefully

Most Common Mistake: Misreading rough opening dimensions.

Photograph: Photo 11-7.

Before beginning construction of each wall, check the plans for the following:

1) Check the R.O. sizes to make sure they're right. Is the window and door schedule accurate? (See "Reading the Plans.")

2) Check opening locations, especially for solar gain, view, etc. Note how location is called out (e.g., is measurement to center or edge of opening?).

3) Check location of 6-inch-diameter plumbing pipes to see if any 2-×-6 interior walls are needed. (See "Reading the Plans.")

4) Check to see if room dimensions on plans will work out in reality.

5) Are wall heights properly called out?

Once all your decisions are finalized, the rough opening measurements thoroughly checked and the solar gain verified, you are ready to chalk the location of the walls on the subfloor. During framing, keep the plans on a table, near to where you are working, and check them at each step.

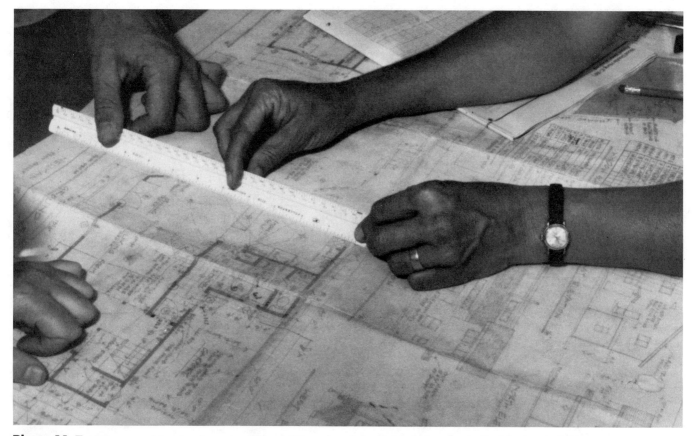

Photo 11-7. Using an architect's rule to check plans. Often plan dimensions are incorrect; check before building.

Step 2
Chalk Walls on the Subfloor

Margin of Error: ¼ inch off proper location.

Most Common Mistakes: Locating the walls in inaccurate locations; not checking all dimensions after all walls are chalked.

Diagram: Figure 11-9.

Photograph: Photo 11-8.

It is recommended that you locate and mark all the walls, both interior and exterior, on the subfloor with chalklines before you begin the actual wall construction. Many professional builders do this, and I highly recommend it for the novice builder. It gives you a chance to really see where the walls will be erected. All the measurements can be checked at this time to be sure they match the plan dimensions. You will get a better feel of the size of the rooms you have designed and can decide if they still feel right to you.

Another important reason for chalking the exterior walls is to make sure they are erected straight. If you use the edge of the floor platform as a guide, and align the outside edge of the bottom plate with the edge of the platform, the wall can come out crooked if the platform is crooked or bowed. By using a chalkline, you can be sure the wall is straight even if the platform is off.

To set your chalklines for your exterior walls (do these first), measure in at each end of the wall 3½ inches (5½ inches if you are using 2-×-6 walls), make a mark, and pop the chalkline between these 2 marks. If the walls are over 20 feet long, I recommend that you make a mark midway as well. Have a person at each end of the wall and a third at the center, pressing the line to the floor. The middle person then pops the chalkline by picking it up and releasing it first on one side of the center and then on the other.

Once all the exterior walls are chalked, do the interior partition walls. To locate the partitions, measure in from the outside edge of the platform the distance indicated on the plans. Be clear as to which point on the walls the dimensions are measured for, the inside edge, the outside edge or the middle of the wall. There is usually a small arrowhead at the end of the line on the plan, which calls out the dimensions by pointing to an edge or the middle of the wall. Measure in from the platform edge to each end of the wall, make marks and pop a line between these marks. Then locate the other edge of the wall 3½ inches from this line (5½ inches if using 2-×-6 walls), and pop another line. These 2 lines will mark where the 2 edges of the bottom plate will rest. Check the chalklines by measuring from another point of reference, i.e., the other end of the house, to be sure everything is working out. If you used, for instance, the north edge of the platform to locate a wall running east to west, measure again from the south edge of the platform to ensure the proper dimensions.

Once you have chalked all the walls, check and recheck their locations; make sure all the dimensions are working out according to plan. Re-evaluate your design decisions if necessary. *Now* you can start constructing the walls.

The choice of which wall to build first is not a random one. The main consideration in choosing the order in which the walls are built is the availability of open platform space; you need to leave space to build the last walls on the platform, after the first walls are raised. The exterior walls are usually built before the interior partitions. Some builders do not even build the non-load-bearing interior partitions until the house is dried in. If you have a large fiberglass tub/shower enclosure or any other large object that can not pass through door openings, you need to set that in its proper room before building walls around it. I once forgot about this in a house I was building and had to tear out part of a wall to install the tub enclosure.

In any case, consider the sequence of building the walls and remember to leave room on the platform to build all the walls. Usually the longest exterior walls are built and set into place; then the shorter exterior walls are completed in descending order, the shortest being built last; and finally the interior walls are finished, again in descending order.

Some builders erect 2 parallel walls 2 inches farther apart than called for. (The walls hang over the edge of the platform slightly.) These walls are then temporarily nailed and braced. This allows more working room to place the walls that fit in between. Once the in-between walls are built and permanently set, the 2 outer, parallel walls are moved into their proper places and nailed to the subfloor.

Step 3
Cut the Bottom and Top Plates

Margin of Error: ¼ inch off proper measurement.

Most Common Mistakes: Not using very straight stock; not cutting top plate so it breaks at the center of a stud.

Diagrams: Figures 11-10, 11-11.

Photographs: Photos 11-9, 11-10.

Having chosen the order or sequence of building your walls, you are now ready to build your first wall. All walls are built horizontally on the platform and then lifted into place. The first step is to cut the bottom plate and top plate (but not your cap plate, the uppermost of the 2 top plates). After these are cut you will lay out the wall on these plates by spreading them the appropriate distance apart and placing the adjoining pieces between them. Everything is then nailed together and the wall is lifted into place. All of this will be discussed in the remainder of this chapter.

In cutting your plates, you need to use very straight stock. If your plates aren't straight, your wall won't be either. Order good straight plate stock 12 to 14 feet long. Usually if it is longer than this it will have some warp or bow. Ask your lumber yard; they might have some straight 16- or 18-footers. Check each piece to be *sure* it is relatively straight.

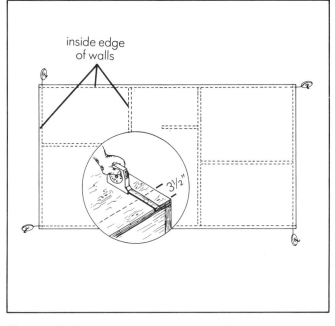

Figure 11-9. Walls being chalked on subfloors.

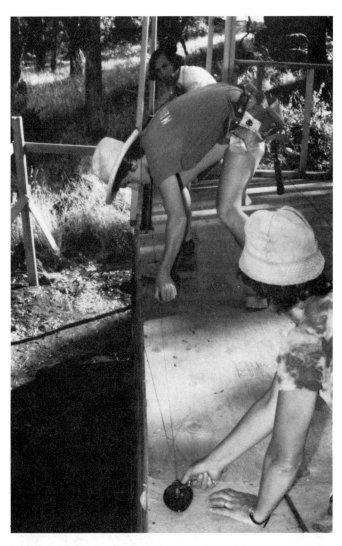

Photo 11-8. Snapping a line on the subfloor to mark the inside edge of a wall's bottom plate.

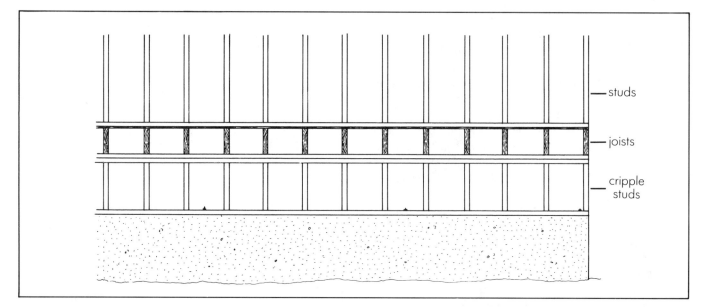

Figure 11-10. Lining up studs, joists and cripple studs. This allows for easy passage of the plumbing, electrical, and heating systems.

Figure 11-11. The bottom and top plate lengths are usually equal to the length of the wall, less the width of a bottom plate (3½ inches).

Photo 11-9. Top plates meeting over a stud. (Cap plates can meet anywhere, but must be at least 4 feet from any splice in the top plate.)

Photo 11-10. Top and bottom plates being marked along edges.

This can be done by using a taut piece of string on the plate to spot any curve along its length, or by setting the plate on its edge on the subflooring and looking for any gaps created by a bow. A plate that is bowed out of true by ½ inch or less is acceptable since no board is totally true.

Since the walls are generally longer than 14 feet, you will need to use several pieces of plate stock to make up the entire plate. There are a few rules when doing this.

1) Avoid very short pieces, under 6 feet.

2) Two separate plate pieces can join anywhere in the bottom plate.

3) The splices in the bottom plate stock, however, must allow at least 4 feet between any splice in the top plate.

4) Any splice in the top plate stock must break in the center of a stud, not in between studs, to ensure the strength of the plate.

5) Splices in the cap plate can occur between studs but must be at least 4 feet from any splice in the top plate.

You can begin piecing together the entire bottom plate, but the top plate is added as you go along. In this way you will know where your studs are located before cutting the top plate stock and can plan it so it breaks at the center of a stud. Generally, the total length of each plate equals the total length of the wall less 3½ inches (5½ inches for 2-×-6 walls), the allowance for overlapping 2 walls where they meet. When the end of a wall goes to the end of the platform on one side, its other end stops short of the platform edge on the other side and is overlapped by the intersecting wall, which extends to the edge of the platform.

Cut and piece together the entire bottom plate, cutting and placing the top plate for the first section only. Don't worry about any door openings in the bottom plate at this time. As you progress in the layout, the top plate will be added as you reach the end of each section. Cut each section of top plate so that it breaks in the center of a stud. (Be careful to be at least 4 feet from any splice in the bottom plate.) Repeat this process until you reach the end.

Another option is to figure out where the studs will be located (the center of a stud will be at every 4- and 8-foot interval to join plywood and drywall boards) and cut all the top plates at once so the splices always fall on the center of a stud. Lay the top and bottom plates together, joining them with a few double-headed nails or clamps, and do the layout on both plates at the same time. Now the top and bottom plates are totally ready to go. I prefer this method because it allows for a continuous flow of work from the beginning of the layout to the end.

Step 4
Lay Out the Wall

Margin of Error: Exact.

Most Common Mistakes: Not dropping ¾ inch for first layout mark; inaccurate measurements; not using straight plates; not breaking top plate at center of stud; not following a continuous unbroken 16-inch (or 12-inch or 24-inch) layout; using framing square for layout.

Diagrams: Figures 11-12, 11-13, 11-14.

Photograph: Photo 11-11.

As with the floor frame layout, the wall frame layout is a process by which you mark the exact locations of the studs, cripples, king studs, trimmers, corners and partition channels on both the bottom plates and the top plates. It is the most crucial part of wall construction, and the one where most of the mistakes are made—so *go slowly* and do good, accurate work.

Lay the plates out on the floor on edge (the 1½-inch side); you will be marking this side. The ends must be exactly flush. Then, join the top and bottom plates together with double-headed nails or clamps so they do not move apart during the layout. You can nail them to the floor temporarily to stabilize them. You will be marking both plates at the same time and the plates need to be in exact position, right next to each other, so the marks will correspond precisely once they are separated.

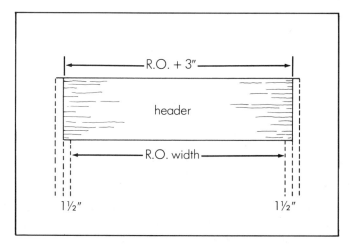

Figure 11-12. The length of a header is equal to the width of the R.O. + 3 inches.

Figure 11-13. A layout pattern stick for a 24-inch door (26-inch-wide rough opening).

Figure 11-14. Partition channel.

Photo 11-11. Laying out a wall on plates. (It's best to use only one tape to make measurements accurate.)

Here are the symbols you will be using for the different pieces.

> X = Standard stud
>
> T = Trimmer
>
> C = Cripples above doors or windows and below windows
>
> K = King stud

There are several different sequences for doing the layout. I have chosen what I think is the most effective one to teach here. First, decide on which end of the wall to begin the layout. This may or may not be optional. If you are using a knee or cripple wall, you need to begin the wall layout from the same end of the building where the knee wall layout began. In this way, the studs in the knee wall will line up exactly with the studs in the wall above it. This is important when you apply the siding and sheathing.

If there are no knee walls, and the floor joists run perpendicular to the wall you're making, you may want to line the studs up directly over the floor joists. (This assumes that the on-center layout for the joists is the same as that for the studs.) This is of value if you plan to run any ductwork for your heating or cooling systems from under the floor up into the walls. It leaves a continuous unobstructed channel in which to run the ductwork. It also makes running any plumbing pipes or electrical wires easier.

After you have determined from which end you plan to begin, you are ready to start the layout. Let's assume you are using a 16-inch on center stud placement. Measure in from the end of the plates, assuming they are flush with the edge of the floor, 15¼ inches. (The reason for this is explained in Chapter 9, *Floor Framing*, "Step 5".) Using a sharp carpenter's pencil, make a clear mark and drive a nail at this point. Hook the end of steel tape over it (a 16- to 25-foot tape is recommended) and run the tape along the plates. Make a *clear* mark at every 16-inch interval, until you have marked the entire length of the plates. You may need to stop to cut and add new top plate sections if you have not already done so.

You now have marks at every 16-inch interval. Not all of these will be full studs, however. In the door and window openings they will be cripples (except for doors with 12-inch-wide headers, where the cripples are eliminated altogether). After marking one plate, draw a line across both the plates at each mark, but do not mark the line with an "X" yet (indicating stud); you can't be sure which marks will indicate full studs and which cripples yet. (See Figure 11-1.) At the end of the wall where you began the layout, mark the 3 full studs that will make up the corner section, where an end extends to the edge of the platform. The opposite end, which is set in from the edge of the platform, will have only 1 full stud.

Now you are ready to locate the door and window openings and the partition channels. In our example (Figure 11-3), there is a window with a rough opening of 3 feet 4½ inches wide × 5 feet 2¼ inches high. The center of the window is 64 inches from the end of the wall, it has a full 12-inch header above it, and the cripples below are whatever length needed to fill the space from the bottom of the sill to the top of the bottom plate. There is also a door opening for a 3-foot door, so the door itself is 3068 or 3 feet wide by 6 feet 8 inches high. The door's R.O. will therefore be 3 feet 2 inches wide × 6 feet 10 inches high. The center of the door opening is 12 feet from the end of the wall.

To locate the trimmers and king studs for the window, hook your tape at the end of the plates and put a mark at 64 inches, the center of the window. This represents the center of a 3 foot 4½ inch opening, so measure on each side of this mark ½ this distance or 20¼ inches. These 2 marks represent the inside edge of the trimmers. There will be 2 studs, the trimmer and the king studs, *to the outside* of each of these marks. Mark a "T" for trimmer and a "K" for the adjoining king stud. Now mark all the studs between the 2 trimmers with "C" for cripples. The door marking process is just the same, but without the cripples below the sill, though there may be cripples above the headers. Repeat the process for any doors or windows. Check your measurement once or twice, or better yet, have someone else check your work and tell them to look for any mistakes.

Many professional builders use jigs and patterns to make their work go easier. You can make patterns like these for your wall construction and layout, and it will make your work easier, quicker and more accurate. Make a pattern stick for your door layout as shown here. Use a good straight 1×4 for your pattern stick. You can make a pattern for all the common-width doors that you will be using. The pattern shows the centerline, the location of the trimmers and king studs for each width door. Then you can just mark the centerline on your plate and match this with the centerline of your pattern for the door width called for and draw on your plates the locations of the trimmers and king studs. Similar patterns can also be made for the locations of the kings and trimmers for common windows.

At this time check your openings to make sure they all have nailing surfaces for the trim. (See "Special Situations— Providing Nailing Surfaces for Trim.") Mark for any interior partitions. Make sure to place the center of the partition channel where the center of the wall will be. You can ascertain this location by measuring the chalklines on the floor or referring to your plans.

Photo 11-12. Cutting many studs to length in one cut. Standard-length studs in 8-foot walls need no cutting.

Photo 11-13. Eyeing for straightness of studs. The straightest studs are used for headers and trimmers.

Photo 11-14. Cutting a one-piece header, a 4×6 (3½ inches × 5½ inches), is shown. Often 4×12s (3½ inches × 11¼ inches) are used for all headers.

Photo 11-15. Nailing the corner assembly together.

Step 5
Cut or Build Studs, Headers, Trimmer-King Stud Combinations, Rough Sills, Corners, Partition Channels and Cripples

Margin of Error: ⅛ inch for measurement; ⅛ inch joined flush.

Most Common Mistakes: Boards cut to wrong size; using warped or bowed pieces around openings.

Photographs: Photos 11-12, 11-13, 11-14, 11-15, 11-16.

You are now ready to cut all the different components that will make up the wall. Collect all the full studs you will need. In a typical non-custom home you will be using standard-size studs that are 92¼ inches long (see "Materials" for explanation). If you are using another stud length or if you did not order the standard-length stud, you have to cut the studs you will need for the wall. You can cut several studs at a time for greater speed and accuracy. Use the straightest ones around your openings, for trimmers and king studs. This is very important; it makes nailing the final trim to these studs much easier.

HEADERS

If you are using solid 3½-inch-thick headers, you will simply need to cut them to the proper size, the width of the rough opening plus 3 inches. If you are using a typical hand power saw, you will need to make 2 cuts, one from each side, as the blade will not cut 3½ inches deep. Be sure not to leave much of a burr or it will throw your measurement off. If you are building headers, be sure they are nailed with all edges flush.

TRIMMER-KING STUD COMBINATIONS

Use the straightest studs you can find when building trimmer-king stud combinations. Be more concerned about a bow than a warp, because a warp can be nailed out. The king is a full-size stud. The trimmer is cut to whatever length is needed to support the header. In our example, we have a standard wall height, 96¾ inches from the subfloor to top of the cap plate, and a 6 foot 10 inch rough opening height (81 inches) for the door and for the window. The trimmer length, therefore, is 81 inches. This is a standard trimmer height in stud construction if your headers are 11¼ inches wide. Nail the trimmer to the king studs using 16d CC sinkers driven at a slight angle every 16 inches, alternating edges of the studs. Be sure that the king and trimmer are flush all along their edges and at each end. (See "Special Situations: Providing Nailing Surfaces for Trim" at the end of this chapter.)

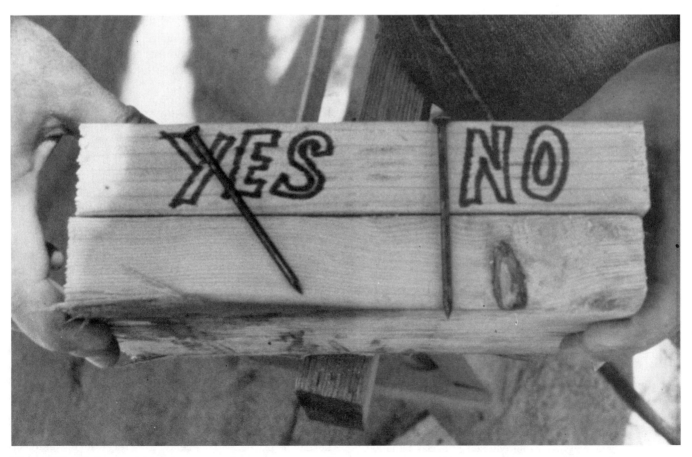

Photo 11-16. Driving 16d nails at an angle.

Photo 11-17. Separating the plates and placing wall pieces between plates. Note the underfloor utilities in the foreground.

ROUGH SILLS

Rough sills are cut the width of the rough opening unless you plan to break the trimmers for the sills (see "Parts of a Wall: Trimmers"). In this case the sills are cut the width of the rough opening plus 3 inches (1½ inches for each trimmer). If you are using a double sill, cut 2 pieces the same size.

CORNERS

Prepare the corners for the wall by nailing full-length studs together (unless you are using blocking as a filler). Nail these together with 16d CC sinkers every 16 inches (some codes allow every 30 inches). They must be flush on all surfaces. (See "Parts of a Wall: Corners," p. 229.)

PARTITION CHANNELS

Partition channels are made from full-length studs nailed together. All surfaces must be flush. (See "Parts of a Wall: Partition Channels," p. 229.)

CRIPPLES

Where there are cripples above and below openings, they will need to be calculated and cut to length. Be sure there is one for each 16-inch layout mark. There needs to be one on each end of the sill also, to support it (unless the sill penetrates the trimmers). In our example (Figure 11-3), the cripples below the window sills are 28½ inches long. This is a good place to save lumber by using your short scrap pieces of wood. Bracing may be required; see "Special Situations: Bracing."

Step 6
Nail the Wall Together

Margin of Error: Exactly flush where pieces come together.

Most Common Mistakes: Insufficient nailing; studs not nailed flush with plates; headers not nailed flush with king studs; putting the partition channel in backwards.

Photographs: Photos 11-17, 11-18, 11-19, 11-20.

It is relatively simple to nail the wall together *if* your layout marks are accurate and your pieces are the proper size. Plan to build the wall as close to its final location as possible to avoid having to transport it too far. Start by separating the 2 plates a little more than a stud's length apart and placing the different pieces—the partition channels, full studs, corners, etc.—in position. Sometimes you need to nail a plate to the floor or brace it against something to prevent the wall from moving while you are nailing it together. Two people can nail, one at the top plate and one at the bottom plate, in unison, to prevent the wall from jumping around. This can be tricky, though.

Drive 2 nails (16d CC sinkers) through each plate at the ends into every stud. This applies to *each* stud in the corner assemblies, partition channels and trimmer-king stud combinations. Drive 2 nails into each cripple through the sill and plates. Nail the headers in place. Be sure, as you nail, all adjoining pieces have their edges flush with each other; no stud should protrude from the plates nor a header from the king studs. This can cause problems further down the line. Remember too that there is only *one* way the partition channel can be placed: with its center stud receiving the intersecting wall.

Photo 11-18. Nailing the wall together.

Photo 11-19. Nailing in cripples at the end of a rough sill.

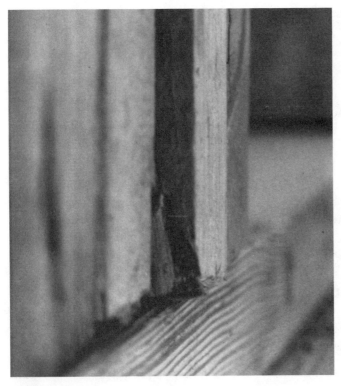

Photo 11-20. A stud not nailed flush with the plate.

Step 7
Temporarily Square and Brace the Wall

Margin of Error: Square within ½-inch measurement of diagonals.

Photographs: Photos 11-21, 11-22, 11-23.

Once the wall is nailed together, it is advised that you temporarily square the wall and brace it. This makes lifting easier and provides the wall with some rigidity during moving. To square the wall, stretch a tape measure across diagonally, adjusting the wall until they are equal. Then nail a 1×4 or 1×6 diagonally across the outside surface of the wall to hold it square. The brace should extend from plate to plate. Check to see if each opening is the proper dimensions and if it is square at this time; they are a lot harder to fix when the wall is up.

Photo 11-21. Squaring a wall by checking for equal diagonals.

Photo 11-22. Let-in bracing notched at the top and cap plates. Note the cripples above the header at the left.

Photo 11-23. Let-in bracing installed before the wall is in place.

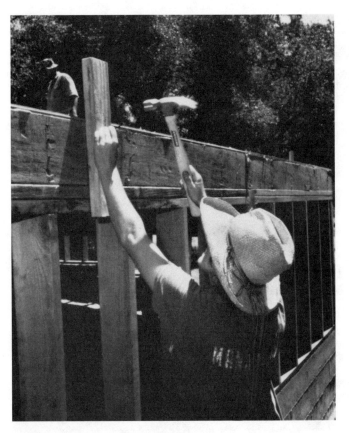

Photo 11-24. Blocks installed on the outside to keep the wall from slipping off the platform.

Step 8
Lift the Wall into Place and Nail It to the Floor

Margin of Error: Exact alignment with chalkline.

Most Common Mistakes: Wall falling off platform; plate not nailed flush to chalkline; not enough people to lift the wall; nailing the bottom plate in doorways.

Photographs: Photos 11-24, 11-25, 11-26.

The wall can now be raised and set into its proper place. One person for every 10 to 12 feet of wall is necessary to stabilize the wall and make lifting and carrying easier. When the wall is in position, start at one end and drive 1 16d CC sinker through the bottom plate into the subfloor about every 16 inches. If possible, drive the nails into the band joist or any joists below the subfloor. Be sure the inside edge of the bottom plate is aligned exactly with the chalkline. Do not nail the bottom plate at any of the door openings; the plate in these areas will be cut out later. You may want to nail some blocks to the outside edge into the rim joist to stop the wall from slipping off the platform. I once dropped a 22-foot wall off a second story. Fortunately no one was down below. Often a good sledge hammer (the "gentle persuader") comes in handy here to tap the wall into alignment with the chalk-

Photo 11-25. Lifting the wall into place.

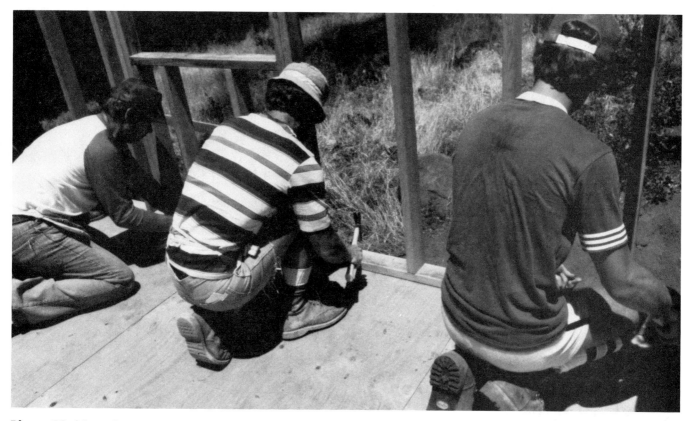

Photo 11-26. Nailing the bottom plate to the subflooring and joists.

Photo 11-27. Plumbing a wall with a brace nailed to a cleat on the floor. Note the level being used at the wall.

Photo 11-28. Using a block and string to test the straightness of the cap plate.

Figure 11-15. Using an 8-foot level with spacers or a plumb bob to plumb the wall.

Figure 11-16. Using blocks and string to check straightness of the top plate.

Figure 11-17. How cap plates interlock at corners.

Figure 11-18. Note the location of the center stud.

lines. Always start nailing at one end and work your way to the other. If you have 2 people, 1 at each end, nailing towards the middle, you may trap a bow in the middle that you will never get out.

Step 9
Brace and Plumb the Wall

Margin of Error: Exactly plumb.

Most Common Mistakes: Using an inaccurate level; using a 4-foot level on an 8-foot-high wall; not nailing braces securely.

Diagrams: Figures 11-15, 11-16, 11-17, 11-18, 11-19.

Photographs: Photos 11-27, 11-28.

The wall, now nailed to the floor, will need to be braced and plumbed in all four directions. This is a rather simple task but a very important one. Do not rush through this stage. A few extra minutes will save you hours down the road.

The wall is braced by running diagonal 2-×-4 braces from the top of the wall to the floor where they are nailed to a temporary cleat. Erect a brace every 10 to 12 feet and secure it well. Drive double-headed nails through the brace into the cleats and the tops of the studs. The 2 ends of the wall can be braced with braces running to the outside edge of the building.

It is best to use an 8-foot level with spacers at each end to ride over the irregularities in the stud. A 4-foot level cannot do this and is, therefore, not advised. If you do not have a long level, a plumb bob can be used with equal accuracy.

Work your way down the wall, placing a brace every 10 to

12 feet. To allow for more building space on the platform, you can brace to the outside. Once you have finished, check the top plate for straightness before nailing on the cap plate. You can do this by running a string along the top plate over two 1-inch spacer blocks at either end of the top plate. By measuring the distance from the string to the top plate all along the wall, you can determine how straight it is. Where it is bowed in or out, use your braces and push or pull against the wall to try to straighten it. When it is as close to straight as you can get it and still plumb, nail a brace at the point where the bow was to hold it straight. If you have used good straight plate stock, this should not be very hard to do. If you haven't, you will have to do the best you can; it will probably never be completely straight.

After the wall is plumbed in this direction, check the plumb in the other direction by placing the level on the flat (3½-inch) side of each stud. Rather than adjusting for each stud, try to define a pattern in the wall as a whole, and ascertain where the top of the wall needs to be pushed to your right or your left. In these areas you will have to push against the top or hit the end of the wall with a sledge.

A trick that I have found to work very well is to use a com-a-long or hand winch to slowly crank the wall back into position. This ingenious tool is very useful where a slow, steady, yet powerful force needs to be applied. Attach the com-a-long to the bottom of the wall and the cable end of the winch to the top of the wall at the opposite end. Then slowly draw in the cable until the wall is plumb in this direction. Nail some diagonal braces temporarily across the inside surface of the wall and release the com-a-long. The braces will hold the wall in place until the siding and sheathing are on. Keep checking the wall until you are sure it is plumb in all four directions and the top plate is straight.

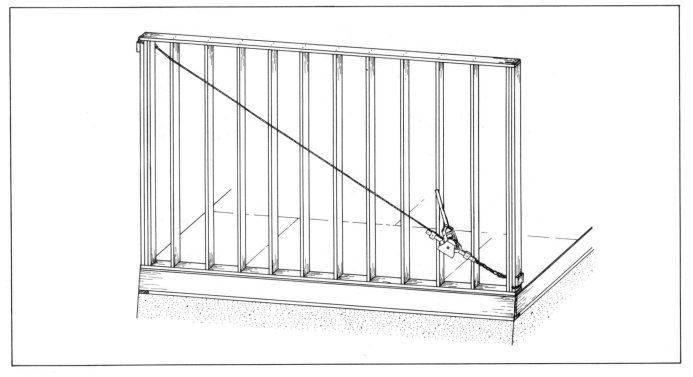

Figure 11-19. Using com-a-long to plumb a wall.

Photo 11-29. Nailing on the cap plate after the top plate is straightened.

Step 10
Nail on the Cap Plates

Margin of Error: Exactly flush with top plate.

Most Common Mistakes: Bowed stock; nails not over studs; falling off the wall; splinters in your rear end.

Photographs: Photos 11-29, 11-30, 11-31.

Steps 1 to 9 are repeated for each wall. When all the walls are up and well braced, you are ready to nail on the cap plates. This is done in a way that it interlocks, and thus strengthens, the intersecting walls. The cap plates lap each other at the corners, and intersect where interior walls meet exterior walls.

Use good, straight stock for these plates. Secure the 2 plates together with two 16d CC sinkers over each stud. By placing the nails over the studs, they will never be in the way of drill bits when you have to drill holes for plumbing and electricity later. Be sure that the edges are flush with the edges of the top plate, and that the cap plates fit tightly to make a strong interlocking joint.

Photo 11-30. A partition wall cap plate intersecting an exterior wall cap plate.

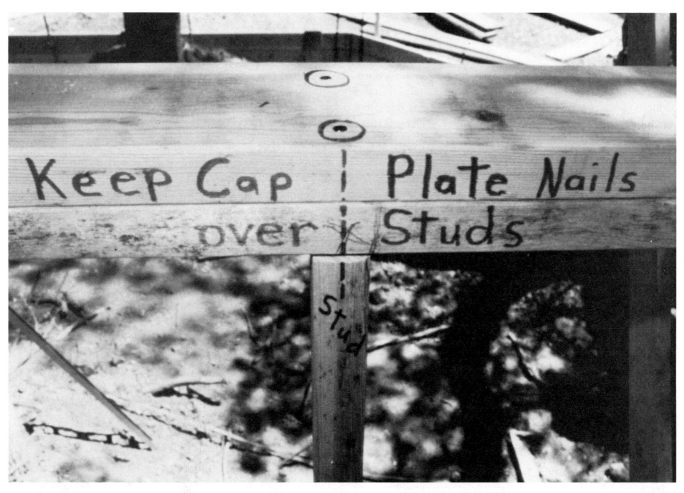

Photo 11-31. Aligning the cap plate nails over the studs to keep them out of the way when drilling holes for the plumbing and electricity.

Figure 11-20. Headers for 2-×-6 walls.

Figure 11-21. A partition channel for a 2-×-4 wall intersecting a 2-×-6 wall.

Special Situations

Unlike floor framing, which is usually fairly straightforward, wall framing and roof framing can have many variables. In this section, I will discuss some of the most common ones, but even this will not be a complete study of the subject. If there are any other situations that you are confronted with, refer to another resource—a builder, book or class that may help you.

2-x-6 Framing
(Figures 11-20, 11-21)

As mentioned earlier in the chapter, there are reasons that make using a 2-×-6 exterior wall frame desirable. In addition to energy benefits, the thicker wall panel provides for a quieter house and gives the house a greater sense of strength. In many areas of the country, a state energy-efficiency tax credit (as well as the existing federal credit) may allow you to deduct from your taxes the difference in cost between building a 2-×-4 wall and a 2-×-6 wall. There will be some added expense for using larger wood studs and switching to 6 inches of insulation (but this may still be cost effective—see *Wall Sheathing,* Chapter 12, "Design Decisions"), and door and window frames will also have to be extended for the thicker wall cavity (most companies do this for a small price increase). There can be some savings, however, if you can switch from a 16-inch center required for 2-×-4 framing to a 24-inch center for 2-×-6 framing. Be careful though, an increased span can require you to go from an interior drywall covering of ½ inch to ⅝ inch. This will definitely cost more.

Should you decide to go with a 2-×-6 wall frame (or if you happen to have an interior 2-×-6 wall to accommodate large plumbing pipes), there are a few things you will need to know. For the most part, 2-×-6 framing is the same as framing a 2-×-4 wall with slight adaptations for partition channels, corner assemblies and headers.

Partition channels: Partition channels for a 2-×-4 wall are built with the 2 side pieces from 2-×-6 stock and the center piece is a 2×4. If the intersecting wall is a 2×6, the center piece is also a 2×6.

Corner assemblies: Remember that the corner assemblies of a wall need to provide both interior and exterior nailing surfaces for the interior and exterior wall coverings. If we only used three 2×6s nailed together, as we do in 2-×-4 framing, the corner assembly's total thickness would only be 4½ inches. This is not enough for the 5½-inch intersecting wall used in 2-×-6 framing. To provide the needed nailing surfaces, 2-×-6 corners are built with two 2-×-6 side pieces sandwiching a 2×4. This gives the corner a total width of 6½ inches (1½ inches for each side, 3½ inches for the center 2×4), and allows for a 1-inch nailing surface on the inside.

Headers: Headers must also be adjusted for the thicker wall panels. They will still need to be the code required depth, but their construction will change for the thicker wall.

Post and Beam Construction
(Photos 11-32, 11-33, Figures 11-22, 11-23)

Earlier in the book, I discussed post and beam construction (see Chapter 2, *Types of Construction*). Even if you are not planning to build a post and beam home, you may want to use some large exposed timbers in a few places for aesthetic

Figure 11-22. Posts and beams being used to support the second-floor frame.

metal strap used to tie plates together where they were broken by post

load-bearing ridge beam

post carries load to foundation

roof beams or rafters

small blocks to provide solid bearing under post

post

Figure 11-23. Using a post to support a load-bearing ridge beam.

Photo 11-32. Post and beam construction. The load is carried by vertical posts and horizontal beams.

Photo 11-33. A post installed in stud wall to support a roof ridge beam. Note the metal strap used to join plates where they are broken by posts.

1 × 4

notch for brace

Figure 11-24. Let-in bracing.

purposes and to give the house a greater "sense of strength." Some special structural situations, such as a low sloping roof or large open areas, may also call for some post and beam framing to support the loads.

Post and beam construction is very common in a house that calls for an "open plan" design with large rooms and few interior partitions. The large post can be partially buried in the wall, leaving it partly projecting into the interior. The horizontal large beams can be partially or totally exposed. If your design is like this for the first floor, the load of the second floor frame can be carried by a post and beam situation as shown in the diagram. Another common situation where post and beam construction can be used to carry the load is in a low sloping roof panel where the ridge board has become a load-bearing beam.

In both the above situations, special foundation piers may be needed directly below the posts to help carry the load to the ground. If a vertical post must penetrate the top and cap plates, a flat metal strap is often required to join the two sections of plates together.

Walls over Standard Height

In almost all building there will be walls that are taller than the standard stud length. These can be dealt with in one of two ways. Either long studs can be purchased so that the taller walls can be built with single-length studs, or the walls can be built in 2 sections.

If walls are 10 to 12 feet high and you have access to good straight studs of that length, it is usually easier to build the wall from single-length studs. Often the code may require some horizontal fireblocks for safety and strength. If these are angled walls running from a high point to a low point, the upper end of the stud will have to be cut at an angle. The ends of the top and cap plates of the sloping walls will also be cut at an angle and will not fit as neatly with intersecting walls.

If walls are over 12 feet high, straight studs are hard to find and you may want to consider using 2 walls, a standard height wall and a smaller wall on top of this one. Build the lower wall first, but leave off the cap plate as this will be the upper wall's bottom plate. Brace and plumb the lower wall. Construct the upper wall with its bottom plate, a top plate and a cap plate. Lift it on top of the lower wall and nail through its bottom plate into the lower wall's top plate. Then brace and plumb this wall.

Bracing
(Figure 11-24, Photos 11-34, 11-35)

For rigidity and strength (so the wall frame does not collapse like an accordion) some type of bracing is needed for the walls. You won't need bracing if you are using plywood sheathing, plywood siding of intermediate density, fiberboard, or individual board sheathing applied at a diagonal. (See *Wall Sheathing*, Chapter 12.) If you are not using one of these types of sheathing, you probably will need wall bracing. There are two common types of wall bracing, metal straps and let-in bracing.

Metal bracing is relatively new on the market and may not pass all codes for bracing. It is quick and easy to apply and it

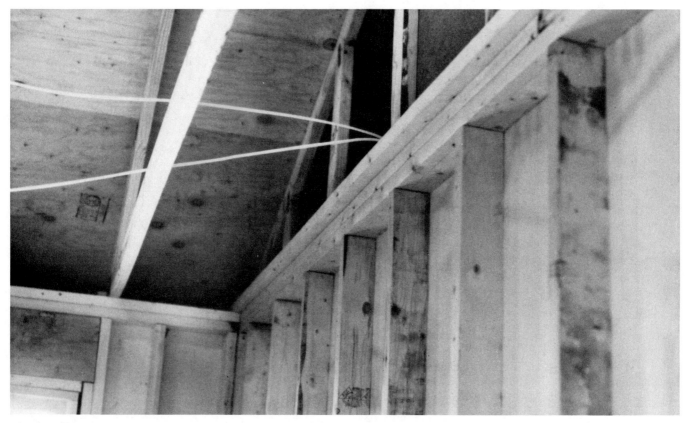

Photo 11-34. Metal diagonal bracing.

Photo 11-35. Metal bracing notched into studs.

only requires that you cut a small notch in each stud and plate. I am not sure of its strength as compared to let-in bracing. You may want to check the codes and ask builders about its strength before using it.

Let-in bracing is a process of cutting notches in the studs and plates and inserting a 1-×-4 brace diagonally. You nail it to each stud with two 8d nails. Each brace should start at a top corner and head down at a 45° angle. If a door or window opening is in the way, it is better to increase the angle rather than break the brace into pieces.

To install, temporarily tack the brace across the studs and plates at the best possible angle and draw lines for notches across the studs and plates on both sides of the brace. Remove the brace and set your saw cut for a depth of ¾ inch (the thickness of the nominal 1-inch brace). Cut on both lines and make an extra cut in the middle. Do this at each stud and plate. Using a chisel remove the wood to a depth of ¾ inch between the cuts. Make good cuts so the brace will be snug. After all notches are complete, cut the brace the proper length and with the proper angles at each end, and insert it into the notches. Nail at each stud and plate with two 8d nails. You can use glue for added strength.

Nailing Surfaces for Ceiling Boards
(Photo 11-36, Figure 11-25)

After you have finished your wall framing for each floor, walk from room to room and think about ceiling boards. Imagine how the ceiling boards will run and be sure there is a nailing surface at each edge. Along the edges where ceiling

Photo 11-36. A board nailed to the top of a wall to provide a nailing surface for the ceiling drywall.

boards will run parallel to the ceiling joists or the second-floor framing, special blocking will be needed. Refer to your plans to pre-visualize what floor and ceiling framing will go in on the second floor.

Wall Running Parallel to Floor Frame or Floor Above
(Figure 11-26)

If a first-floor interior partition wall is running perpendicular to the floor joists of the second floor, you can toenail the cap plate into the floor joist where the wall crosses the joists. This will help stabilize the wall. If, however, the first-floor wall is running parallel to the second-floor joists, you will either have to arrange special joists on either side of the wall or block every 4 feet between 2 standard joists to provide a nailing surface to stabilize the wall.

Fireblocking
(Photo 11-37)

In the past, fireblocking (blocks placed horizontally between the studs) was used to prevent fires from spreading inside a wall cavity and creating a chimney effect in the space between the studs. Now we fill this cavity with insulation that is fireproof, and use fire resistant drywall gypsum board as an interior wall covering. Top and cap plates also prevent fires from spreading from floor to floor. Because of this, fireblocking is often not used. Consult your local codes to see if it is still required. Some areas require it if the wall is over 10 feet high for strength as well as fire protection. If it is not required, omit it.

Figure 11-25. Using nailing blocks to nail the edges of ceiling boards.

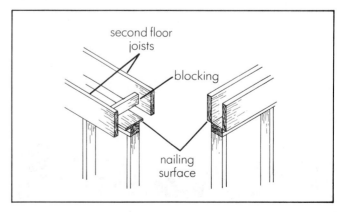

Figure 11-26. Two framing methods for second-floor joists to stabilize a first-floor wall that is running parallel to the joists.

Photo 11-37. Installing fireblocking on a 2-×-6 wall.

Figure 11-27. Framing for pocket door. Note the total opening must be twice the size of the actual door opening.

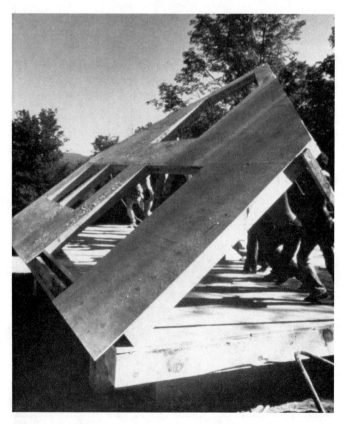

Photo 11-38. Sheathing a wall before the erection (courtesy of Heartwood Owner Builder School).

Sheathing or Siding the Walls Before Erection
(Photo 11-38)

Some builders sheath or side their walls while they are still on the platform and then lift them into place. I would not recommend this for the novice builder; it allows for less adjustment for mistakes or inaccuracies. It also takes more people to lift and move the wall. If you plan to go this route, check with a local builder as to things you should be aware of before you try it, e.g., that the floor is level, without irregularities; that studs are plumb after wall is lifted; that sheathing protrudes below the sill plate, etc.

Pocket Doors
(Figure 11-27)

Pocket doors are doors that slide and disappear into a wall. They create a pleasing effect and save space since no floor space is required for their swing. If you plan to use a pocket door, you can buy pocket door frames in different sizes from your lumber company. They are common and easy to install. Remember that the rough opening for a pocket door will need to be at least twice the size of the door itself, one space for the door passage and another for an empty pocket for the door to slide into. Always use good quality rollers with pocket doors so they will slide easily.

Wall Sinks, Tubs, Toilets, Toilet Paper Holders
(Figure 11-28)

Sometimes special pieces are inserted between studs for the following fixtures: wall sinks, built-in tubs, wall mounted toilets (details for these mounts are described in the manufac-

Figure 11-28. The backing for wall mounted fixtures or toilet paper holders.

turer's spec book), toilet paper holders, toothbrush holders, paper towel holders, etc. If you think back on all the times you searched a sheetrock wall for a solid framing member to hang something on, you may want to walk the house and anticipate this by adding an occasional interior horizontal framing mount. Be sure to mark where you have placed all backings so you can locate them after the sheetrock is up.

Figure 11-29. Notching or drilling for previously set under-floor utilities.

Building Walls Around Rough Plumbing Stub Outs
(Figure 11-29)

As mentioned in Chapter 10, *Subflooring,* "Special Situations," some codes require that the underfloor utilities be placed in before the subflooring is installed and the walls built. If this is the case in your area, and you can't get the variance, you will need to drill or notch all your bottom plates to allow for the plumbing pipes. If I need to drill or notch the plates, I do it after the wall is built, but before it is erected.

Nailing Surfaces for Vertical Siding
(Figure 11-30)

If you are using individual board vertical siding (such as cedar T & G or board and batten) and especially if there is no plywood sheathing, you will need to provide some horizontal nailing pieces between the studs so the boards can be nailed along their lengths. A piece every 30 inches is recommended. These pieces can be 2×4s installed flat, rather than crosswise, like fireblocking. In this way you can run batt (rolled fiberglass) insulation directly over them rather than having to cut the insulation at each block. These nailing pieces also make installing your plumbing and electricity easier.

Figure 11-30. Nailing blocks for vertical siding.

Figure 11-31. Rafters directly over studs on 24-inch centers.

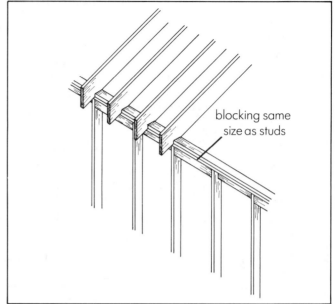

Figure 11-32. Alternate method of blocking when rafters fall between 24-inch o.c. studs.

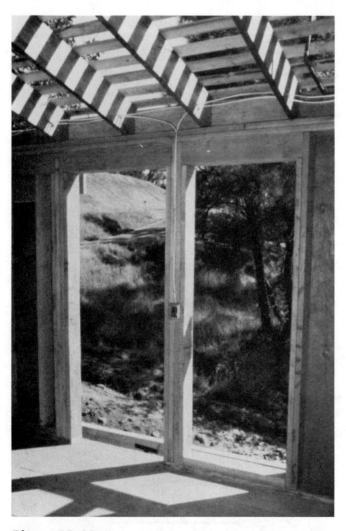

Photo 11-39. The window and door are built so close together here that trimming will be difficult. No channels are provided to run the wires through so the studs are notched.

An Alternative to Placing Rafters Directly over Studs on 24-Inch Centers
(Figures 11-31, 11-32)

If you are using 24-inch centers for your wall studs, most codes require that the rafters be placed on 24-inch centers and fall directly over the studs. If they occurred between studs, the top (and cap) plates would be too weak to support the weight. If you don't want to match all the rafters and studs, you can place blocks at the very top of the studs, touching the bottom of the top plate. These blocks are installed on edge and alternate flush with the inside and exterior edges of the studs. The blocks are made from the same stock as the wall studs, 2×4s for a 2-×-4 wall, 2×6s for a 2-×-6 wall.

Providing Nailing Surfaces for Trim
(Photo 11-39)

As you build the walls, be sure that there will always be enough space and solid nailing for any window or door trim. This is especially important in walls that have a door right near one end of the wall. If it is built too close to the intersecting wall there will be no room for trim unless you are using a very thin trim. Adding an extra stud to the outside of the king stud can prevent problems. Trim can also be a problem when windows are built right next to each other or by a door. In this case they can share a common king stud if your trim will be working out OK. Be thinking "trim" as you take a look at all the openings.

Figure 11-33. Framing for large ducts.

Ductwork

(Figure 11-33)

Most ducts are made to fit between 16-inch center studs. If one of your ducts will not fit, use the method shown in the diagram to accommodate the duct.

Metal Fasteners

In earthquake, hurricane or tornado areas, you may want (or you may be required) to use metal fasteners. It adds strength for holding the house together should any unusual forces be applied. In a catastrophe it could make a difference, and they are easy and inexpensive to install. Special fastener nails are provided with the fasteners.

Soundwall

Noise has a greater impact on our living space than most of us realize. My whole body relaxes when our washing machine finally cuts off. Fortunately our 11 year old took up the clarinet, but it could have been the drums. We lose a lot of peace of mind and sense of privacy due to unwanted noise. Walls (as well as floors and ceilings) can be constructed to minimize this. You can use a sound deadening board, which is easy and inexpensive to install, underneath the wall covering. Also you can use 2-×-6 plates with offset 2-×-4 studs on 12-inch centers to help reduce the passage of the sound waves from room to room (remember to use ⅝-inch drywalls, not ½-inch drywalls, on 24-inch centers). Willis Wagner's *Modern Carpentry* (Goodheart and Wilcox, publisher, 1973) has an excellent chapter on sound control.

Closet and alcove framing

You may want to consider using 2 × 2s, 2 × 3s or 2 × 4s flat to frame closets and alcoves. This will allow more interior space and less space required for the wall panel. For plates you can rip 2 × 4s into 2 × 2 plates. Check with your codes first.

Continuous headers

If your code will allow it, you may want to consider using a continuous header in the wall. It makes wall construction quicker and easier than the usual individual headers IF the wall has a lot of openings. It also allows you to easily change your mind about your door and window decisions. On one house I changed my mind so many times, I though about leaving a map of all the covered up windows and door openings for the buyers in case they ever wanted to add them back in.

Worksheet

ESTIMATED TIME

_____

_____

_____

CREW

Skilled or Semi-Skilled

_____ Phone _____

_____ Phone _____

_____ Phone _____

Unskilled

_____ Phone _____

_____ Phone _____

_____ Phone _____

_____ Phone _____

_____ Phone _____

MATERIALS NEEDED

Lumber, nails, metal fasteners (optional).

ESTIMATING MATERIALS

Number of STUDS needed _____ × _____ ft. long

= _____ total linear feet

PLATE STOCK:

Linear feet of total walls (interior and exterior) _____

Double this (top and cap plates) + 15% waste _____

HEADER STOCK:

Exact linear feet needed. Remember, headers are 3 inches longer than RO widths.

NAILS:

_____ lbs. of 16d per 1000 sq. ft. = _____ lbs.

_____ lbs. 8d per 1000 sq. ft. = _____ lbs.

(Usually 100-150 lbs. of 16d per 2000-sq.-ft. home)

METAL FASTENERS: No. _____

COST COMPARISON

_____ Store:

$ _____ per M board feet 2×4 (or 2×6) = $ _____

_____ Store:

$ _____ per M board feet 2×4 (or 2×6) = $ _____

_____ Store:

$ _____ per M board feet 2×4 (or 2×6) = $ _____

PEOPLE TO CONTACT

If you have made any major changes, contact inspection office.

Name _____ Phone _____

Changes approved _____ Date _____

You may want to contact the following people to let them know their work may soon be coming up, if you are planning to contract it out:

Plumber _____

Phone _____ Work Date _____

Electrician _____

Phone _____ Work Date _____

Solar Panel Installer _____

Phone _____ Work Date _____

Roofer _____

Phone _____ Work Date _____

Insulation Contractor _____

Phone _____ Work Date _____

Window Supplier _____

Phone _____ Work Date _____

Door Supplier _____

Phone _____ Work Date _____

Roofing Supplier _____

Phone _____ Work Date _____

Siding Supplier _____

Phone _____ Work Date _____

Skylight Supplier _____

Phone _____ Work Date _____

Daily Checklist

CREW:

_____Phone _____

_____Phone _____

_____Phone _____

_____Phone _____

_____Phone _____

TOOLS:

☐ framing hammer

☐ tape

☐ sledge hammer

☐ string

☐ chalkline

☐ power saw

☐ hand saw

☐ pencil

☐ nail belt

☐ combination square

☐ framing square

☐ plumb bob

☐ 4- or 8-foot level

☐ nail-pulling tool

☐ com-a-long (hand winch)

☐ architect's rule

☐ extension cords

☐ plug junction boxes

☐ saw blades

RENTAL ITEMS:

☐ Ladders or scaffolding may be needed if you are working on high walls.

☐ A com-a-long or hand winch may be used to straighten the walls after they are up. (These can be purchased for $30-40.)

MATERIALS:

_____ studs

_____ ft. header stock

_____ lbs. 16d CC sinkers

_____ lbs. 8d CC sinkers

_____ metal fasteners (optional)

DESIGN REVIEW:

Be sure that all your window and door location and sizes have been reconsidered before beginning this stage of construction.

1. Be sure each choice is a definite "Yes, that is exactly how I want it to be."

2. Take out your solar site selector (if you have access to one) and be sure any windows or glass doors that are supposed to allow sunlight in for solar or design reasons will function properly.

3. Decide on a window manufacturer and obtain their rough opening sizes before beginning. Any effort you put in improving your design at this stage will pay off a hundredfold later.

INSPECTIONS NEEDED:

Usually no inspections will be needed before or during this stage of construction.

WEATHER FORECAST:

For Week _____

For Day _____

12 Wall Sheathing

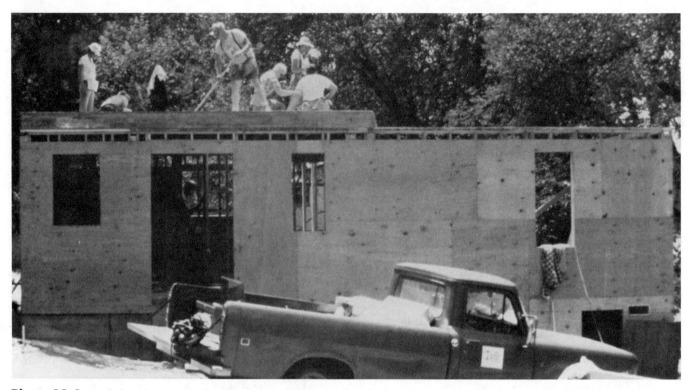

Photo 12-1. Wall sheathing applied to a building. Usually the sheathing is applied after the first and second floors are framed. This sheathing was applied early to accommodate the needs of a summer program class.

What You'll Be Doing, What to Expect

WALL SHEATHING consists of boards or panels that cover the wall frame like a skin. They not only provide rigidity and strength, but may also provide a nailing surface for the exterior siding. Sheathing also minimizes air and moisture leakage through the wall panels and adds an element of stoutness to the wall.

Most codes do not require that the walls be sheathed. Generally wall bracing (see Chapter 11, *Wall Framing*, "Special Situations: Bracing," p. 253) is allowed. Even in many earthquake areas it is not required, though I would highly recommend using plywood sheathing in such areas; it is your house's main protection in the event of a major earthquake. Though not required, many builders use sheathing for the advantages it provides.

The different materials used in sheathing include plywood sheathing, plywood siding, three types of fiberboard, rigid insulation and individual nominal 1-inch boards. There is a complete discussion comparing these different types of sheathing materials later in the chapter.

Wall sheathing, like subflooring and roof sheathing, is a simple, but very monotonous, procedure in housebuilding. Since it will later be covered by the finished exterior siding (unless you are using plywood siding for sheathing), looks, accuracy and the quality of your cuts and fits are not important. You can pay minimal attention and still do a good job. There are few mistakes to make and it goes quickly. Physically, it is a little strenuous since you will be lifting and holding large plywood panels and doing a lot of nailing. It is somewhat easier if you are using fiberboard panels, individual board sheathing, or rigid insulation. If you have a high wall, it is even more physically demanding and you may want to consider using scaffolding.

Keep in mind that this is a rather formative stage that the house is going through. It is similar to entering puberty; kind of awkward and lanky. You are not really sure what the final product will look like. All the rough openings are gaping holes and the material itself is rather unattractive. You may think: "I've created a monster." Indeed, you may have, but this is

wall sheathing

Rafters installed after the wall sheathing. | Rafters installed before the wall sheathing.

Figure 12-1.

really not the stage to judge. It is the most unappealing stage the house goes through.

Wall sheathing can be applied before or after the roof framing, or before or after the roofing is applied. If the siding and sheathing must go between the rafters, the rafters must be put on before the sheathing (Figure 12-1). If there is a need to protect the building from the elements, the roofing can be applied before the sheathing. If you are building for an extended period, you should finish the sheathing and roofing as soon as possible. (Photo 12-1.)

Jargon

ANNULAR-GROOVED NAILS (THREADED NAILS). Nails with grooves on their shanks to provide greater holding power.
END-MATCHED BOARDS. Boards with a tongue or groove at the ends as well as along their sides or edges.
EXTERIOR GLUE PLYWOOD. Plywood that can get wet for a period during construction and not delaminate.
FIBERBOARD. A sheet or panel made of wood fiber impregnated with a waterproofing chemical.
NAIL BASE. A board or panel that can be used as a nailing surface for attaching exterior siding.
SHEATHING. A covering, structural or non-structural, consisting of panels or boards and attached to the exterior of the studs or rafters.
SHIPLAPPED. Panels of boards that have been rabbeted to form a lap joint between adjacent pieces.
TEXTURE 1-11 (T-ONE ELEVEN). A plywood exterior siding that serves as the finished exterior siding and sheathing at the same time.
TONGUE AND GROOVE (T&G). Boards or panels with a tongue protrusion along one edge and a groove indentation along the other.

Purposes of Wall Sheathing

1) To provide rigidity and strength to the wall frame
2) To provide a nailing base for the exterior siding
3) To reduce air and moisture leakage

Design Decisions

A decision as to which material you will use for sheathing needs to be made at this point. Here is a review of the different types of sheathing available.

CD EXTERIOR GLUE PLYWOOD: Since its introduction into the construction industry, plywood has become the most common type of sheathing. It is also by far the strongest material. Usually a CD (refers to quality of ply) exterior glue plywood is used. It can get wet during construction and still not become delaminated, and since it will be covered by the exterior siding, a CD quality surface is all that is needed. Though it is a little costlier than some of the other materials, it takes little time or effort to install. Code requirements in most areas are as follows:

Thickness of Plywood	Inches on center for studs	Direction to studs
5/16 inch	16 inch	perpendicular or parallel
3/8 inch	16 inch	parallel only
3/8 inch	24 inch	perpendicular only
1/2 inch	24 inch	perpendicular or parallel

Most builders use ⅜-inch or ½-inch panels. I recommend the ⅜-inch-thick panels, as the added thickness of the ½-inch does not really add greater strength. The strength is more a function of the nailing and fastening process. As the chart shows, it is not as strong if it is applied horizontally because a

Photo 12-2. Black fiberboard is often used for wall sheathing. It has few structural qualities but reduces air and water infiltration.

great part of its 8-foot edge is left unnailed. This can be somewhat compensated for by placing blocking between the studs in order to provide a nailing surface for this edge. In areas where hurricanes or earthquakes are a problem, the sheathing is glued as well as nailed.

SHIPLAPPED EXTERIOR PLYWOOD SIDING: This is an exterior grade plywood that can withstand constant exposure to the weather. The final exterior ply of the plywood is of a higher grade fir or redwood that is meant to be exposed and serve as the finished exterior skin. No siding will be placed on top of it. It is applied similar to CD plywood sheathing with a few differences (see Chapter 16, *Siding,* "Plywood," p. 393). It is shiplapped to provide a better seal against water that will be running directly on the panels.

Most codes require that it be at least ⅜ inch thick, as there will be no sheathing underneath it. No additional wall bracing is required. Both ½-inch and ⅝-inch thicknesses are common. Most codes require that one ⅜ inch thick has at least 3 plys and can span 16 inches on center studs. Those ½ inch thick must have at least 4 plys and span 24 inches on center.

Shiplapped siding is becoming one of the most common types of siding used in the country. The advantages are that it is quick and easy to install. It does not, however, provide for a very stout wall, and the final finished plys have been known to bubble and delaminate. In material cost it tends to be rather expensive (though its labor application cost is rather low). If you purchase the lower-priced panel, it can have as many as 12 to 24 plugs in the finished surface, and unless you plan to paint over them it looks terrible. The better quality

panels without plugs are very expensive. Some panels require an additional sealant every few years, further increasing the cost.

FIBERBOARD (Photo 12-2): Fiberboard is a wood fiber impregnated with a waterproofing chemical. One side usually has a black tar-like surface and the other is brown. It has little structural strength and can easily be broken over your knee. Fiberboard sheathing is also called insulating board, but this is very deceiving as it has little insulating value. It is often used in homes that do not need sheathing for rigidity and structural purposes but need an air and moisture preventative and in some cases a nailing surface.

Fiberboard comes in three types: regular density, intermediate density and nailing-base density. Regular density is manufactured in both ½-inch and ²⁵⁄₃₂-inch thicknesses and comes in footage of 2×8, 4×8 and 4×9. Corner bracing is usually required on all fiberboard sheathing applied horizontally as well as on the ½-inch board regular density applied vertically. Corner bracing is described in Chapter 11, *Wall Framing,* "Special Situations: Bracing" (p. 253). Also ½-inch plywood sheets can be applied at all corners of the house. The space between these sheets is then filled in with fiberboard. Nailing of regular density is usually every 3 inches along the edges and every 6 inches in the intermediate framing members. A 1½-inch galvanized roofing nail is used for ½-inch thickness and a 1¾-inch for ²⁵⁄₃₂-inch thickness. Most manufacturers recommend leaving a ⅛-inch spacing between sheets.

Intermediate-density and nail-base sheathing are denser

Photo 12-3. Diagonally applied ¾-inch boards are seldom used since the arrival of plywood.

than the regular-density material and have more structural strength. The nail-base sheathing can be used when directly applying shingles to the wall using annular grooved nails. They are manufactured only in a ½-inch thickness and in panel footage of 4×8 and 4×9. These are usually installed vertically and require no corner bracing. The same nailing pattern and size apply for ½-inch-thick panels.

This type of sheathing will work OK in areas where no great shearing strength (ability to resist racking) is needed. As mentioned earlier, plywood sheathing or siding is recommended in earthquake, tornado, hurricane or high wind areas. Plywood sheathing, at a small increase in labor and cost, will generally make for a stronger house and stouter wall panel than fiberboard sheathing. It is worth considering no matter what your situation is.

INDIVIDUAL BOARD SHEATHING (Photo 12-3):   Before the advent of plywood, individual boards, nominally 1 inch thick and from 6 to 12 inches wide, were used for sheathing. They were butt end boards (with no tongue and groove or shiplap that ended over a stud), and were generally applied at a 45° angle for greater strength. Occasionally they were applied horizontally, in which case corner bracing was needed (diagonally, no additional corner bracing was needed). Boards with a 15% moisture content or less, usually a lower quality Number 2 or Number 3 common grade softwood, were used to reduce shrinkage and gaps between the boards. Three 8d nails were used at each stud for fasteners. Unless for some reason you have a cheap or free supply of 1-inch boards, I do not recommend using this type of sheathing. It does not provide the shearing strength of plywood and is labor and

cost intensive. It can, however, be used as a nail base for siding.

RIGID INSULATION (Photos 12-4, 12-5):   In the last few years, with the increased awareness of energy consumption in homes, builders have begun applying rigid insulation to the exterior edge of the studs and then applying siding over this. If a house needs greater strength, and rigid insulation affords almost none, plywood can be applied under the insulation. Both ½-inch and ¾-inch-thick panels of differing sizes are available with tongue and groove edges. The application, with flat-headed fasteners, is rather quick. It is good in colder climates as well as in very hot areas. Before making a decision, calculate the cost of adding this insulation and compare it to the cost of increasing your wall panels from 2×4s to 2×6s. If there's not much difference, I would recommend using the 2×6s. (You would seldom need a combination of 2×6s *and* rigid insulation sheathing.) The 2×6 provides a quieter, stouter wall panel while saving energy as well. When calculating the cost, add in the projected savings in energy to see what your pay-back period would be. Remember, your state and federal energy tax credit may apply.

GYPSUM BOARD SHEATHING: In some areas, where there is a threat of brush fires or other exterior fires, or where buildings are built very close to each other, the local codes may require that gypsum board (drywall) be applied on the exterior of the studs under the siding. This is to insure that, should the siding catch fire, the fire will not travel into the structural frame of the house. Check your local codes if you think this might apply.

Photo 12-4. Styrofoam wall sheathing comes in tongue and groove sheets.

Photo 12-5. Thin foil-faced boards are often placed behind brick. The boards offer little in the way of insulation but do help keep some heat out in summer.

What You'll Need

TIME   The time needed will depend on the complexity and height of the building as well as the number of window and door openings in the wall. All the nailing takes most of the time, and the times listed can be reduced if you are using a pneumatic nailer. 5 to 10 person-hours per 320 square feet (ten 4-×-8 panels).

PEOPLE   2 Minimum (both unskilled); 3 Optimum (2 nailers, 1 cutter, all unskilled); 6 Maximum (2 teams of 3, all unskilled).

TOOLS   Framing hammer, nail belt, chalkline, level, plumb bob, caulk gun (optional), power saw, pneumatic nailer (optional) pencil, tape measure, saw horses, framing square, nail-pulling tool, hammer tacker or staple gun, staples.

RENTAL ITEMS   Air compressor, scaffolding, nailing gun and ladders.

MATERIALS   You will be using ⅜- to ½-inch-thick plywood panels (⁵⁄₁₆ inch is often allowed but seldom actually used) in 4-×-8 or 4-×-9 sheets. CDX exterior glue plywood is used. Calculate how many sheets you will need to cover the house with a 10 to 20% waste factor. Do not use tongue and groove plywood; it is much harder to apply. Use 8d nails (CC sinkers) for fasteners and subflooring glue in heavy earthquake or hurricane areas. You will also need sheathing or builder's paper. This is either 15-pound felt or brown builder's paper.

ESTIMATING MATERIALS NEEDED

PLYWOOD: Determine the linear square feet of wall to be covered, divide by 32 square feet and add 10% for waste.

NAILS: 2 pounds of 8d CC sinkers per sheet of plywood.

SUBFLOORING GLUE: According to manufacturer's instructions.

BUILDER'S PAPER or 15-POUND FELT: According to number of square feet needed.

INFORMATION   This chapter will deal in detail with applying plywood sheathing. If you are using a plywood siding for sheathing as well, read this chapter and the section on plywood siding in Chapter 16, *Siding* (p.393). If you are using fiberboard sheathing or individual boards, refer to the section in this chapter comparing materials. If you are using rigid insulation, follow the manufacturer's instructions.

PEOPLE TO CONTACT   Unless you plan to do these things yourself, you will soon be needing the roofer, plumber and electrician. Contact them now. Suppliers will also be needed soon. Contact suppliers for siding, roofing, exterior doors and windows.

INSPECTIONS NEEDED   Most areas require an inspection of your sheathing-nailing pattern before it is covered by the sheathing paper and siding. Call the inspectors before the paper is applied and after the sheathing is up.

Reading the Plans

Usually your plans will clearly call for the needed sheathing. Generally you can find it on the elevations or cross sections. Sometimes no sheathing is called for and only diagonal bracing is indicated. You may want to consider adding plywood sheathing anyway. Some designers call out the minimal sheathing required (⁵⁄₁₆ inch); most builders upgrade this to ⅜ inch or ½ inch. If plywood siding is to be used without sheathing, its thickness (½ inch or ⅝ inch), the type of wood used (redwood or fir), its quality and its style will be called out in the elevations.

Safety and Awareness

SAFETY: Be very careful handling sheets on windy days, they can act as a sail. Be careful on ladders and scaffolding when handling the sheets, they are heavy and awkward. So that the power saw does not bind when cutting the panels, support the plywood properly.

AWARENESS: Be sure the sheets are plumb as they are applied and that they meet on a stud. Check that rough openings are the correct dimensions and square before beginning. In tall homes, stagger the end splices of the sheets. Be sure to overlap the crack between the top of the foundation wall and the bottom edge of the sill plate by at least 1 inch.

Overview of the Procedure

Step 1: Recheck the rough frame openings
Step 2: Apply the first panel
Step 3: Apply the remaining panels, cutting out doors and windows
Step 4: Apply the sheathing paper

Step 1
Recheck the Rough Frame Openings

Margin of Error: ⅛ inch off dimension; ⅛ inch off square in measurement of diagonal.

Most Common Mistake: Reading the window or door sizes incorrectly.

Before beginning to sheath any wall, check each rough opening size to be sure it is correct. Recheck to see if each opening is square or rectangular, either by using your framing

horizontal
joints

plywood breaking
on center of stud

plywood overlapping on to foundation

Figure 12-2. Pieces of siding are cut for use in the knee wall areas to keep the horizontal joints straight.

square or by measuring the diagonals of the openings (if it is a rectangle or square the diagonals will be equal). If you want to move or change an opening, it will never be easier than now.

Step 2
Apply the First Panel

Margin of Error: Exactly plumb.

Most Common Mistake: Not plumb.

Diagram: Figure 12-2.

Photographs: Photos 12-6, 12-7, 12-8.

You are now ready to apply your first sheet. You can begin on whatever wall of the house you want. Begin at the end of the wall, where you began your layout.

If you are using finished plywood siding (Texture 1-11) other factors must be considered. The sheathing will also be your finished siding, so you must accommodate for appearance. If the wall length is not exactly in 4-foot intervals, a

piece of siding will need to be ripped to finish out the wall. Decide on which end of the wall it will be least noticed and apply the ripped end there. The wall may be too high for one 8- or 9-foot-long panel to span. Decide where you would like the splice to be, low or high on the wall.

If there is a stepped wood knee wall in the foundation, and you are using plywood siding, begin at the lowest part of the wall and cut the lower panels. This will allow all the splices to line up across the wall.

After determining where to begin, check to see if there is a center of a stud at every 4-foot interval and that your corner stud assembly is plumb. (The first sheet should be applied plumb even if the corner stud is not exactly plumb.) Apply the first piece. It is important that this piece be very plumb (vertical); if it is out of plumb, all the others that follow will be out of plumb.

Usually the sheets stretch from 1 inch below the top of the foundation wall to the top of the cap plate. If the rafters have already been applied, the sheathing can come to the bottom of the rafters. Most often the sheets are applied vertically, though they can be applied horizontally with no wall bracing needed. Vertical application, however, is stronger.

Photo 12-6. Check to be sure walls are plumb in all directions before applying the wall sheathing or siding.

Photo 12-7. Be sure that the first course of sheathing you apply is level and plumb.

As you start to nail, start at one side of the sheet and work towards the other. If 2 people start at each side and work towards the center, it may create a bubble in the board. Use 8dCCsinkers or 8d annular groove nails every 6 inches around the edges and every 12 inches on the intermediate studs. It is easiest to pop a chalkline on the plywood to locate the center of each stud to make nailing easier. Apply a ¼-inch-wide bead of subflooring glue at this time if you are planning to use any.

Step 3
Apply the Remaining Panels, Cutting Out Doors and Windows

Margin of Error: Exactly plumb; within ½ inch to edge of opening, but do not extend sheathing into opening.

Most Common Mistakes: Extending sheathing into opening; inadequate nailing.

Diagram: Figure 12-3.

Photographs: Photos 12-9, 12-10.

After the first sheet is plumbed and nailed into place, continue with the rest of the sheets. Some builders leave a ¹/₁₆-inch gap at the ends of the panels and a ⅛-inch gap at the edges to avoid bubbles in the panels caused by expansion due to moisture rain. Unless you are planning to leave the sheathing uncovered for a long period of time (several months), I do not think it is really needed. Water runs more quickly off the walls than the subflooring or roof sheathing and is not as great a

Photo 12-8. Using a chalkline to locate the studs for nailing.

Figure 12-3. Plywood siding is cut between the rafters where siding will not be concealed by the soffit.

problem. Making sure the sheets are still plumb, nail flat against the studs. Try to use sheets as large as possible.

Openings for doors and windows can be handled in one of two ways. Some builders nail the sheathing on, covering over all the rough openings. Then from the inside, holes are drilled at the corners of each opening, and the sheathing covering the opening is cut out from the inside with a reciprocating saw. Chalklines representing the opening can also be popped on the outside of the sheathing and the sheathing cut out with a power saw. As in cutting any wood with a power saw, set the depth of your cut to penetrate about ¼ inch deeper than the wood.

I think an easier way is to temporarily tack the sheathing in place with 2 or 3 nails, press it tightly up against the studs and have someone mark the outline of the opening on the sheet from the inside. Then take the sheathing down, cut out the excess for the opening and permanently nail the piece into place. No matter what technique you use, be sure the sheathing does not overlap into the rough opening; this will reduce the size of the rough opening and the window or door will not fit unless it is later cut away.

Photo 12-9. Usually the wall sheathing is held or tacked temporarily in place and the openings are marked on the plywood from the interior. The sheet is then removed and the opening cut out.

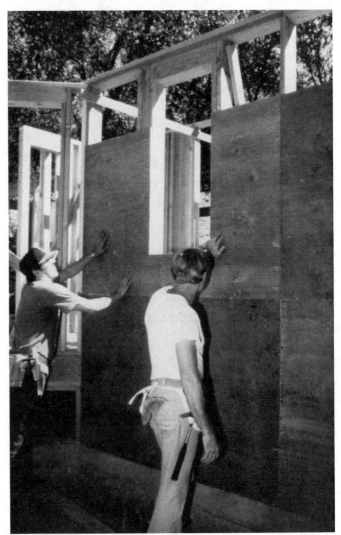

Photo 12-10. Nailing sheathing on the wall after the window opening has been cut out. Wall sheathing can be applied either vertically or horizontally.

Photo 12-11. Sheathing or plywood siding can be attached to the wall framing before it is lifted into place. This is not recommended for the first-time builder, since making adjustments for mistakes is easier when the sheathing is applied after the wall is up and plumb.

Continue with the rest of the sheets until the wall is entirely covered and then go on to another wall. If there is not a stud or cripple at the edge of each sheet, add an extra one. All edges of the plywood must fall on the center of a full stud or cripple.

Remember, as you apply the sheets, that the bottom plates in the door openings will be cut out (you can cut them now) and you should not cover this section of bottom plate with sheathing.

If the siding will run between the rafters, thereby exposing the overhangs of the rafters, the sheathing must also run between the rafters. Blocks will be needed between the rafters and flush with the outside edge of the cap plate to act as a nailing surface for the sheathing and siding. For more about these blocks see Chapter 13, *Roof Framing,* "Step 8."

Step 4
Apply the Sheathing Paper

Margin of Error: Just keep it flat.

Most Common Mistake: Not overlapping top piece over bottom piece.

Photograph: Photo 12-11.

Usually a sheathing paper is applied between the sheathing and the finished siding. If you are using Texture 1-11 plywood siding, this paper is applied directly over the studs. The purpose of the paper is to help prevent moisture and air leakage into the wall cavity and is essential in most good construction. The paper must be able to breathe to allow moisture to escape from the wall in the form of vapor, not water. The paper must have a perm rating of at least 6 (6 perms of water vapor can pass through it).

Generally a builder's paper or 15-pound felt is used. Builder's paper is 2 pieces of brown paper sandwiching a moisture-proof (but breathing) layer. Begin the paper at the bottom of the wall, letting each sheet overlap the one below it for a shingle effect. Tack it flat with a nailing gun or better yet a hammer tacker. The tacker is much easier to use and may be worth renting if one is not otherwise available to you. Overlap the paper 4 inches along the edges and 6 inches at the ends. Overlap the corners 6 inches and into the wall openings 2 to 3 inches.

Worksheet

ESTIMATED TIME

_____

_____

_____

CREW

Skilled

_____ Phone _____

_____ Phone _____

Unskilled

_____ Phone _____

_____ Phone _____

_____ Phone _____

_____ Phone _____

MATERIALS NEEDED

Plywood, nails, glue, sheathing paper.

ESTIMATING MATERIALS

PLYWOOD SHEETS:

Number of square feet of wall area _____

divided by 32 (4-×-8 plywood sheet, use 36 if

using 4-×-9 sheets) = _____

+ 10-20% waste _____ = _____ sheets

NAILS:

_____ pounds cover _____ sq. ft.

Total number of lbs. needed _____

ADHESIVE (optional):

One cartridge covers _____ sq. ft.

Total number of cartridges needed _____

SHEATHING PAPER or 15-LB. FELT:

One roll covers _____ sq. ft.

Total rolls needed _____

COST COMPARISON

_____ Store:

$ _____ per sheet = $ _____ total

_____ Store:

$ _____ per sheet = $ _____ total

_____ Store:

$ _____ per sheet = $ _____ total

_____ Store:

$ _____ per sheet = $ _____ total

PEOPLE TO CONTACT

You will soon be needing the roofer, plumbers and electricians, unless you are doing this yourself:

Electrician _____

Phone _____ Work Date _____

Plumber _____

Phone _____ Work Date _____

Roofer _____

SUPPLIERS:

Siding _____

Phone _____ Work Date _____

Roofing _____

Phone _____ Work Date _____

Doors (exterior) _____

Phone _____ Work Date _____

Windows _____

Phone _____ Work Date _____

Do any suppliers need to be called about daily deliveries?

☐ YES ☐ NO

If yes, who _____

Daily Checklist

CREW:

_____ Phone _____

_____ Phone _____

_____ Phone _____

_____ Phone _____

_____ Phone _____

TOOLS:

☐ framing hammer
☐ nail belt
☐ chalkline
☐ level
☐ plumb bob
☐ caulk gun (optional)
☐ power saw
☐ hand saw
☐ pencil
☐ tape measure
☐ saw horses
☐ framing square
☐ nail-pulling tool
☐ hammer, tacker or staple gun
☐ staples

RENTAL ITEMS:

☐ air compressor
☐ nailing gun
☐ scaffolding
☐ ladders

MATERIALS:

_____ sheets of plywood

_____ lbs. of nails

_____ cartridges of subflooring glue (optional)

_____ rolls of builder's paper or 15-lb. felt

DESIGN REVIEW:

Check all rough opening measurements and re-evaluate all your design decisions regarding their size and location. After the sheathing is applied, they are much harder to change.

INSPECTIONS NEEDED

Most areas require an inspection of your sheathing-nailing pattern before it is covered by the sheathing paper and siding. Call the inspector before the paper is applied and after the sheathing is up.

Inspection called for _____

Time of inspection _____

Person contacted _____

WEATHER FORECAST:

For Week _____

For Day _____

13 Roof Framing

Photo 13-1. A house with all the rafters in place. The lower story rafters are cut at the wall line to accommodate a veranda roof that will be added later. Note that the lookouts off the front of the building are ready to receive the rake rafter.

What You'll Be Doing, What to Expect

THIS CHAPTER WILL deal with four different aspects of residential roof construction. The first section of the chapter will discuss various roof styles: flat, shed, gable, gambrel, and mansard. The second part will discuss the three main approaches to roof framing: site-built with standard materials, trusses, and large beam construction. The third part will deal with the actual step-by-step construction of a standard roof frame (simple gable roof). The last part of the chapter will deal with special situations in roof framing.

Roof framing can be anywhere from the simplest to one of the most complex types of framing; it depends on the complexity of the roof design. Complex roofs, with their many valleys, hips, ridges and intersections, can be a challenge even to a very experienced carpenter. Whereas simpler roofs, such as flat, gable or shed, can be easily mastered by the novice. My advice to you is, if you are building a complex roof frame (Photo 13-3), hire an experienced framer to serve as your consultant or perhaps even work with you at the job site. It is one of those areas of building your own home in which paid professional help may be a good investment. You can accept the challenge of framing a complex roof for yourself, but be sure you understand the scope of the challenge.

Roof framing (Photos 13-1, 13-2) involves installing the roof framing members, ceiling joists, dormers and openings. It is mentally demanding; it takes a certain amount of comprehension of simple mathematical relationships as well as the ability to visualize the framing components. Physically, it is also a very demanding process. The roof ridges and rafters, usually the largest structural members used in the home, must be raised to the highest, and therefore the most dangerous, position. If ever your bad back will go out (if it hasn't already during the concrete pour), now is the time.

Safety should always be uppermost in your mind. Even a small fall can be disastrous. I was recently contacted by a lawyer from San Francisco who was representing a carpenter who had fallen only 9 feet and was paralyzed for life. *Be careful on the roof!*

Photo 13-2. A house with the large ridge beam sitting on top of 2 support posts. The first 2 rafters are in place.

Photo 13-3. Complex roof framing like this may require professional assistance.

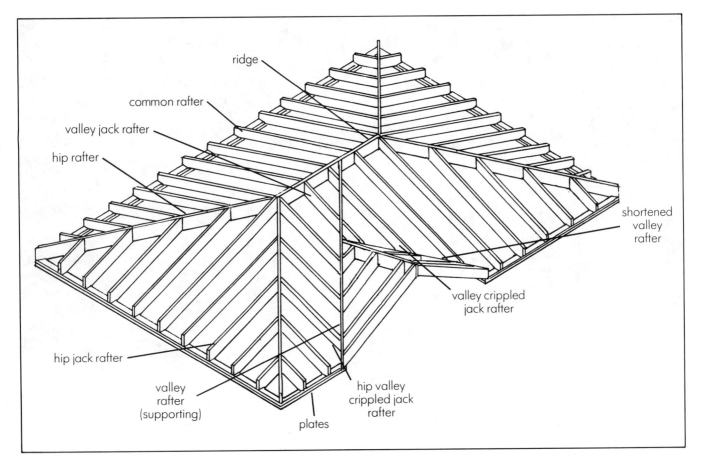

Figure 13-1. Names of roof framing components.

Jargon

Roof Framing

(Figure 13-1)

COMMON RAFTER. An individual sloping member of the roof frame. Usually it runs at a right angle from the exterior walls and rests on the ridge.

CRIPPLE JACK RAFTER OR CRIPPLE RAFTER. This rafter does not intersect the wall plate or the ridge. It is terminated at each end either by the hip or valley rafters. Both ends will be mitered where they intersect the valley or hip.

HIP JACK RAFTER. A rafter running from the wall plate to a hip, where it is cut at an angle.

HIP RAFTER. A rafter that runs diagonally (at a 45° angle) from the corner of 2 intersecting exterior walls to the ridge, to form the intersection of adjacent slopes of a hip roof.

HIP VALLEY CRIPPLE JACK RAFTER. A cripple jack rafter that runs from a hip to a valley.

RAKE RAFTER. The outermost rafter that runs parallel to the roof slope and forms the overhang between the roof and the wall at the gable end.

RIDGE. The highest horizontal running member of the roof frame; it aligns the rafters and supports them at their upper end.

SHORTENED VALLEY RAFTER. This rafter runs from the wall plate to the supporting valley rafter, where 2 sloping roof sections intersect and their ridges are at different elevations.

SUPPORTING VALLEY RAFTER. The longer rafter that runs from the wall plate to the ridge, in a "valley" or hollow of 2 intersecting, sloping roof surfaces, where the 2 ridges are at different elevations.

VALLEY CRIPPLE JACK RAFTER. A cripple jack rafter that runs from a valley to a valley.

VALLEY JACK RAFTER. A rafter that runs from the ridge to the valley rafter.

VALLEY RAFTER. A rafter running from the ridge to the wall plate in a "valley" or hollow of 2 intersecting, sloping roof surfaces, whose ridges intersect at the same elevation.

Rafters

(Figure 13-2)

BIRDSMOUTH. This is the cut near the lower edge of the rafter where the rafter sits on top of the wall plate. It is made up of 2 cuts: the vertical plumb cut and the horizontal seat cut.

PLUMB CUT OR RIDGE CUT. The cut of the rafter where it meets the ridge.

Figure 13-2. The parts of a rafter.

TAIL CUT OR OVERHANG CUT.   The cut at the lowest edge of the rafter.

TAIL OR OVERHANG.   The part of the rafter that extends past the exterior wall line.

Layout
(Figure 13-3)

In almost all layout principles, we are relating the cuts and dimensions of the rafters to 3 sides of a right triangle. Some common terms are as follows.

LINE LENGTH.   The hypotenuse of the triangle. The sloping distance measured along the top edge of the rafter, along the slope, from parallel lines drawn perpendicular from the rafter, at the centerline of the ridge, to the outside edge of the plate.

PITCH.   This term describes the incline of the roof as a ratio of the vertical rise to the total run of the entire roof. It is expressed as a fraction, e.g., a roof that rises 6 feet over a total wall span of 30 feet has a pitch of $6/30$ or $1/5$.

RISE.   The vertical side of the triangle. The altitude or total vertical distance the rafter rises as measured from the top of the wall plate to the top edge of the rafter.

RUN.   The horizontal side of the triangle. The total distance of the rafter as measured horizontally from the outside of the wall to the centerline of the ridge.

SLOPE OR THE CUT OF THE ROOF.   The incline of the roof as expressed in a ratio of its vertical rise to its horizontal run. The horizontal run is always expressed as 12 (for 12 inches) and the vertical rise varies. For example a roof that rises 3 inches for each horizontal 12 inches has a 3 in 12 slope.

SPAN.   The distance between the outside edges of 2 opposite walls.

Unit Measurements
(Figure 13-4)

UNIT LENGTH.   The measurement of the hypotenuse formed by a right triangle where one side is the unit rise and the other is the unit run.

UNIT RISE.   The vertical rise or distance the rafter extends in a vertical direction for every one foot it runs horizontally.

UNIT RUN.   Unit run is always one foot. This is the distance measured along the horizontal (level) plane.

Purposes of the Roof Frame

1) Protect the building from the weather
2) Provide the base onto which the roofing materials are applied
3) Contribute to the design of the home
4) Parking space for Santa's sleigh

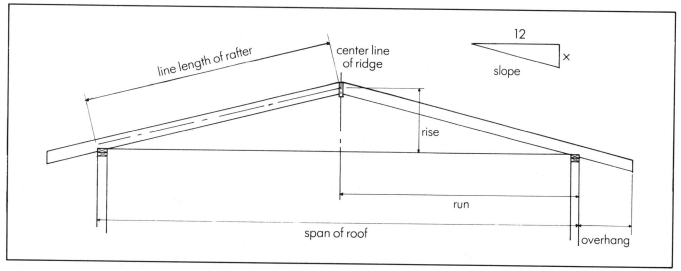

Figure 13-3. Terms used for a rafter layout.

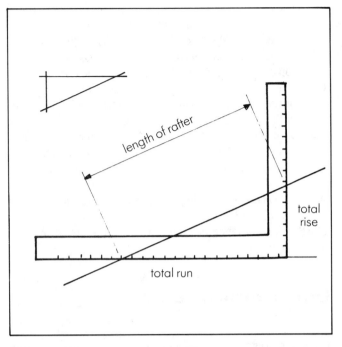

Figure 13-4. The length of a rafter as measured along its slope.

Design Decisions

In roof framing, perhaps more so than in any other part of housebuilding, there are many design decisions to make. These include two major decisions: the style of the roof and the type of members to be used; as well as minor decisions, including the type of fasteners used, the way in which the rafters intersect the ridge, etc.

Before you begin to order your materials, you will have to make several design decisions. Most of these may have been made during your initial design process and may be incorporated into your plans. Others may not have occurred to you until now. You may also want to reconsider any previously made design decisions to see if they are still in your best interest. The following sections will deal with three main areas: first, the style of the roof; second, the type of materials to be used; and third, we will consider some smaller design decisions that need to be clear at this stage. The list here is rather extensive, but it is important that you understand all the possible choices for each situation before you begin to build the roof frame. Otherwise your choices will be made for you, and they may or may not be the best ones.

Figure 13-5. A typical roof framing for flat roofs.

Photo 13-4. Shed roofs running in different directions.

Style of the Roof

There are many different styles or designs of roofs. Each one has advantages and disadvantages. Your choice here is very critical for two main reasons: design and cost.

Probably no other design decision that you make will have more impact on your total exterior design as the style roof you choose. It is the most visual exterior element of the house, and thereby the most important, as far as the design is concerned. The same exact house, fitted with different style roofs, will appear very different. As you drive around your neighborhood, visualize the houses with different roofs or just different size overhangs, and you will get a sense of the impact a roof has. Be sure you have accurately visualized your dream house with its roof in place. Do some drawings and then try on different "hats" to see how much each changes the character of the house. Put a hat on your own head to see how different it makes you look.

You will want to consider your roof as an umbrella for the home. It should not only protect the interior but the exterior walls as well. If the overhangs prevent rainwater from running down the exterior walls, your windows and doors will never leak, and your painting and siding will be easier to maintain. Aesthetically, broader overhangs often look better also.

The design of the roof will affect the cost of the roof in money, time and energy. The design of the roof will affect the amount of roofing materials needed, as will the slope of the roof, and may also affect the size and dimensions of the roof frame that is needed. It's true that simple roofs go up more quickly than complex roofs; but before you throw out your much-loved complex roof for the less-loved simple roof, determine how much more the desired roof will cost. It may be only several hundred dollars and may be well worth the money. It may cost several thousand dollars of an already stretched budget and cause you to consider some redesigning. Just be sure you are not making decisions, especially major ones, with incomplete data.

FLAT ROOF (Figure 13-5). A flat roof is perhaps the easiest, cheapest and quickest to build, but the hardest to seal. The roof rafters serve also as the ceiling joists and all needed insulation must be placed inside the rafter cavity, since there is no attic. As with all roof framing members, be sure flat roofs meet all local codes (e.g., snow can gather easily on these types of roofs).

Actually many flat roofs are not truly flat; they incorporate slight slopes to drain water. The flat roof will have to be sealed with a continuous membrane roofing material. Hot tar is the most common, and this usually must be professionally applied.

Overhangs are created by simply extending the roof rafters past the edge of the building, where the rafters are running perpendicular to these walls. When the rafters are running parallel to the walls, overhangs are created as shown in the diagram.

Photo 13-5. A simple off-center gable roof.

Photo 13-6. An off-center gable roof frame.

Photo 13-7. Two gable roofs on a multi-level house.

SHED ROOF (Photo 13-4). A shed roof is also very simple and quick to build. It spans 2 walls, one higher than the other. This type of roof has become very popular in modern architecture. Solar designers seem to have forgotten that other styles even exist. Unless you plan to drop a ceiling to form an attic, the insulation will go between the rafters (or on top of the exterior sheathing) and the rafters can serve as the ceiling joists as well. Since a shed roof is, in essence, half of a gable roof, the information in this chapter will enable you to build a shed roof.

GABLE ROOF (Photos 13-5, 13-6, 13-7). The gable roof is probably the most common roof style in the United States. It is formed by 2 roof planes meeting at a ridge. This ridge can either be centered over the house or offset to one side. Like the shed and flat roof, it is quick and simple to build. It can either be combined with an attic or the ceiling boards can be attached to the sloping rafters to create a cathedral ceiling. Usually ceiling joists or collar beams are used to take the stress off the rafters (the "A" splitting factor from the downward thrust of the roof), so the deletion of these must be considered from a structural standpoint. (See pp. 289–290, "Special Considerations: Ceiling Joists" and "Size, Spacing and Span" in this chapter.)

INTERSECTING GABLE ROOF (Photo 13-8). Though this roof can become complex, it is also rather attractive. It consists of several gables, each similar to the standard gable, intersecting and running in different directions.

THE HIP ROOF (Photo 13-9). In this type of roof, the ridge does not run the full length of the house; it stops short, and hip rafters extend diagonally from the end of the ridge to the corners of each wall. Though this roof can be difficult to build, a simple hip roof is well within the reach of a novice owner builder.

GAMBREL ROOF (Photo 13-10). The gambrel roof is very popular in many areas of the country. It consists of a top ridge with a slope being broken on each side by a second ridge, usually half way down the slope. The advantage of having this type roof is that it allows more head room upstairs and you can use your attic as a second floor.

MANSARD ROOF. This is a French style roof that is somewhat popular in this country as well. All 4 sides have a double slope; the lower slope is nearly vertical, while the upper slope is almost flat.

Types of Roof Construction

Most houses built today incorporate one of three different types of roof construction: standard materials, trusses or large beams. Each of these systems has its advantages and disadvantages, and your decision should be well considered. The decision between using either standard framing materials or trusses is mostly based on time, labor and money factors. Once installed, these two systems look the same. The decision to use large beams (e.g., exposing large beams to the interior) is usually a design decision made for aesthetic reasons.

Photo 13-8. An intersecting gable roof.

Photo 13-9. A hip roof. Note how the exterior wall facing us protrudes past the gabled-roof section.

Photo 13-10. Gambrel roofs, though more difficult to construct, offer beauty as well as greater head room on the top floor.

STANDARD MATERIALS. For many houses, the rafters, ridges, valley rafters, etc. are all constructed at the job site with standard framing lumber. This lumber can be as small as a 2×4 or as large as a 2×14. Until the introduction of trusses, all roofs were built this way, and many builders still prefer this way to using trusses.

Whereas trusses need to be ordered a few weeks ahead of time, site-constructed framing systems are built the day they are installed, allowing for last minute changes and avoiding mistakes made by the truss companies. Another advantage is that, if you are not paying for labor, site-built systems may be somewhat cheaper than trusses. You can also use larger materials in site-built framing than are used in trusses. Plus the quality of construction is controlled by the builder not the factory. This chapter will explain in detail how to build a roof frame using this method.

TRUSSES (Figure 13-6, Photos 13-11–13-14). Roof trusses are units which incorporate a series of structural members that are used to carry the load of both the roof and the ceiling to the outside walls. The structural members are usually 2×4s or 2×6s. Most trusses consist of a bottom chord, which also serves as the ceiling joist; a sloping member or top chord, which serves as the rafter; and diagonal connecting pieces, called webbing, that transfer the weight from one member to the next. These pieces are connected by metal truss connectors or plywood gusset plates, which are nailed

and glued. Often the bottom chord will have a slight camber or crown (about ½ inch over 24 feet) to compensate for the stress applied over the span. Most trusses are built in truss factories from engineering calculations. You may be able to build your own at the site, but check with the building inspector first.

Trusses are almost always used in tract development. Though the advantages are not as great in a single home project, trusses are becoming popular in this area as well. You order trusses from the factory to your individual specifications, and the factory then builds them for you and delivers them to the site. Usually the delivery is made with a special truck that can place the trusses on top of the walls. Trusses can be built for almost any roof, except for very complex designs. You must be sure to provide the truss factory with the proper information to build your trusses. I worked on a job where $1800 worth of trusses were built 1 inch too short. The moment of realization was not a pleasant one. The factory will want to know the span, the slope, the overhang, soffit details, etc. Just be sure you are having the correct trusses built.

There are several advantages to using trusses. Obviously there is a savings in time and labor, since much of the labor of roof framing is done by the factory. Once delivered, the roof framing erection process is much quicker. Trusses can often span greater distances than standard rafters, making load-bearing interior walls unnecessary. This, in turn, means you

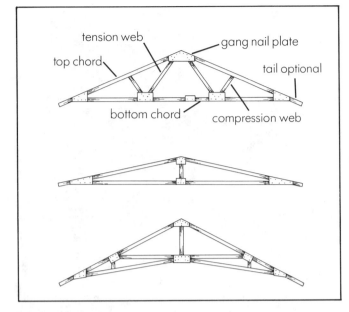

Figure 13-6. Three types of trusses.

can get the roof on faster, protecting the house from the weather, and then finish the interior walls. Trusses allow a greater freedom in design, since load-bearing walls are no longer necessary in certain locations. Be sure to inspect the trusses you have received from the factory to see that they have kept their standards of quality high. I have seen trusses with split, and even broken, members or with the fasteners hanging loose.

Trusses are rather easy to erect. They are usually delivered to the site and placed, point down, on the walls in the order they are to be installed. Usually 3 people are needed to handle the installation, and in the case of larger trusses 4 or more people may be needed. After the layout marks are drawn on the cap plates of each wall, the trusses are rolled into place. One person works at each wall while a person down below, using a long 2×4 or guide, holds the truss upright until it is secured. After it is nailed to the plate on both walls, a board is nailed across the sloping top chord to temporarily hold it plumb and in place. These temporary supports are removed when the sheathing is applied.

Photo 13-11. Trusses ready to be erected.

Photo 13-12. Trusses can be made for many different style roofs. Trusses for a mansard roof are shown here.

Photo 13-13. Using a long board to hold trusses in place until they are nailed and braced.

Photo 13-14. Trusses being delivered to the top plate of a garage. Most lumber companies use a truss truck which carries the trusses on a high rack for easy unloading. Trusses are then rolled off into place.

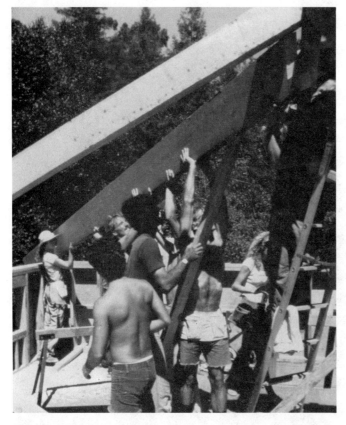

Photo 13-15. Large timber roof construction often requires several people or a crane. Be careful at this stage—accidents are not uncommon.

LARGE TIMBER ROOFS (Photos 13-15–13-18). Many houses use large beams for the roof frame. The beams are usually taken from 4-inch or 6-inch stock, 6 to 20 inches wide. Glulams (several boards laminated into a large beam) are often used. Sometimes these larger timbers are used because the loads applied to the roof (usually snow loads) are so great that the smaller, common framing lumber would not carry them. Other times large timbers are used just for the ridge beam because it has become a load-bearing ridge (see next section, "Ridge Beam or Board").

More commonly, however, these larger, more expensive beams are used in place of rafters because you are planning to expose them to the interior of the house and appearances are important. Visually, 4×8s on 4-foot centers are much more attractive than 2×10s on 16-inch centers. Usually 2-inch-thick decking is applied as the roof sheathing and this also is exposed to the interior. The insulation, usually rigid, is applied over the sheathing. If you are planning to use this type of roof construction, be sure you have compared the cost of it to that of the standard roof system with drywall ceilings. Often, with the more expensive large timbers, 2-inch decking, rigid insulation, etc., the roof can be quite costly. (A compromise would be to use a large ridge beam that is partially exposed to the interior; and standard rafters, with drywall attached directly to the interior of sloping rafters, creating a cathedral ceiling.)

For the most part, the principles used in building a roof frame with 2-inch materials are the same as in using 4-inch or 6-inch materials. All the cuts and layouts are the same, only

Photo 13-16. Large ridge beams and beams are being used instead of 2-inch rafters to create an exposed beam ceiling.

Photo 13-17. A crane is being used here to place large roof timbers. This might well be worth the $100 to $200 per day fee. It is safer, easier and quicker.

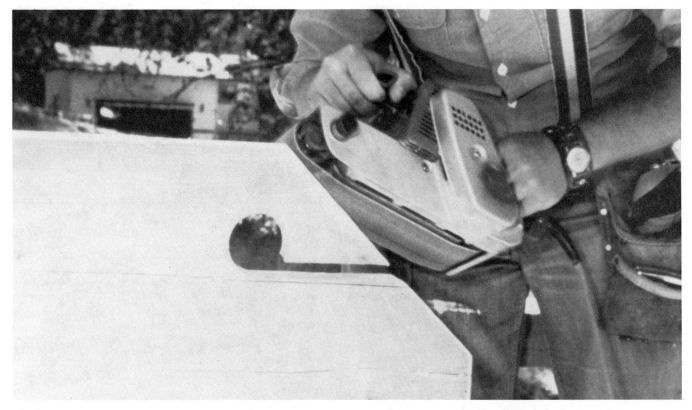

Photo 13-18. The ends of ridge beams and boards can be specially cut if they are going to be visible from the exterior.

the spacing is different. This chapter should give you all the needed information to build a large timber construction roof.

Aside from the aesthetic value of exposing the large timbers, the advantages are more subtle. They have to do with a sense of strength or the character of the home. Though it is subtle, its effect is profound. Modern houses are becoming lighter and lighter—small wall framing members, lightweight trusses in the roof, thin wallboards, hollow core doors, etc. In fact, stud construction was called "balloon construction" when it was first introduced. The old-time carpenters, who were used to post and beam construction, laughed and said the house would be so light that it would blow away like a balloon. The use of large framing timbers, especially when exposed in the walls and roof, lends the character and integrity that is missing in many modern houses. Solid doors, plaster walls, hardwood floors, tile, and good windows can also add to this. Visit, if you can, similar houses, one with large exposed framing members and the other without. See if for you the houses seem any different.

Aside from the expense of the large timber roof frame, the other great disadvantage is the availability of materials. On the West Coast, where there are still large trees (though they too are quickly diminishing), most lumber yards carry a large stock of timbers, of different lengths and dimensions. On the East Coast the selection is not so great. If they have to be specially ordered, there can be a time delay and greater expense, and the material shipped is often very wet, twisted and unattractive. As it starts to dry it twists and warps to a point that it is highly noticeable once the building is completed.

I have had more fights with my lumber suppliers over this than any other issue. I inform them that the timbers will be exposed to the interior and that I can use only the highest quality material. When it is delivered, before I allow it to be unloaded or pay the bill, I check it carefully for knots, straightness, delivery damage, checks, splits, twists, bad areas, etc., and, if I do not like it, I send it back (or use it at the gable where it will be covered). Be very clear with your supplier, especially if it is a special order, that it must look good enough to expose. If you are going to expose the overhang area to the outside, this must also look good. If possible, buy "dry" stock; it will not shrink and twist after it is installed.

Special Considerations

RIDGE BEAM OR BOARD (Photo 13-19). In most homes the ridges are not load bearing. They simply act to align and stabilize the top part of all the rafters. Though they are usually made of 2-inch-thick stock, the code will often allow 1-inch stock to be used, since they bear no load. In some cases, however, this ridge bears the load of the roof. It then becomes a ridge beam that must be calculated according to its span, loading, type of wood, etc. Usually the non-load-bearing ridge board becomes a load-bearing ridge beam when the slope is low (3 inches in 12 inches or less, for example), the span of the rafters is broad, or the loading, due to roofing materials, snow, etc., is great. Sometimes it may be a com-

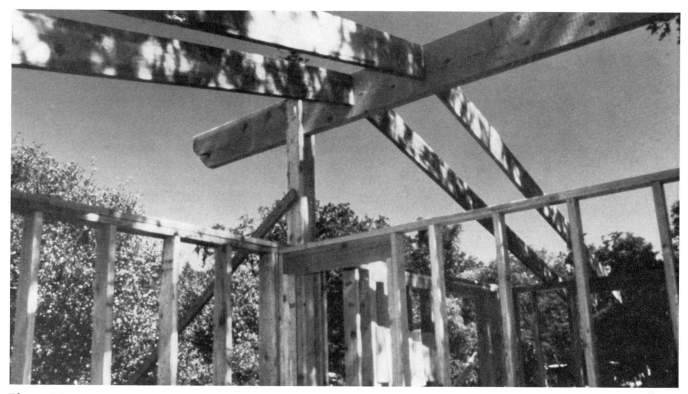

Photo 13-19. Roof rafters hung from a load-bearing ridge beam.

bination of these factors. (Often the hip and valleys will need to be sized accordingly as well.)

If you are using a large ridge beam with standard rafters, you may want to expose the ridge to the interior for aesthetic purposes. If you are using large timbers as rafters as well, you will definitely want to expose the entire roof frame. But if only the large ridge is being used, the standard rafters can either be set on top of the ridge or hung from the ridge.

OVERHANGS, SOFFITS AND FASCIAS (Photo 13-20, Figure 13-7). Before laying out and cutting your rafters, you need to determine the type of fascia and soffit you plan to use, as well as the size of the overhang. The soffit is the underside part of the overhang of the rafters. The fascia is the board(s) nailed to the outer edge of the rafters. As you can see in the diagrams and photo, the manner in which the soffit is to be built and the way in which the fascia is to be attached will have a bearing on the way in which the end of the rafter is cut. Also the method of installing the "rake" rafters must be determined before beginning (see "Step 6" of this chapter).

CEILING JOISTS. The size and location of the ceiling rafters, as well as the manner and frequency in which they are attached to the rafters, may affect your roof framing. You may, for instance, be able to avoid collar beams (see "Span" in this next section) if you are attaching ceiling joists to the rafters. The spacing of the ceiling joists also needs to be coordinated with the spacing of the rafters to allow some of the joists to be nailed to the rafters. For more on ceiling joists and their installation see "Special Situations: Ceiling Joists" in the back of this chapter.

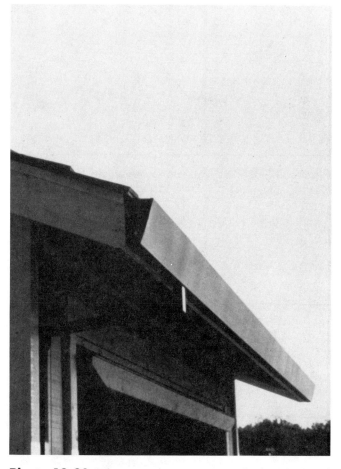

Photo 13-20. When a wide gutter is attached to the band rafter, no fascia board is needed.

Figure 13-7. Details of two possible types of fascia and soffit.

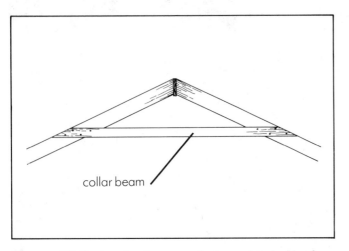

Figure 13-8. A collar beam or tie is used to hold rafters together and reduce the span of the rafters.

Figure 13-9. Using king and queen posts to reduce the span of the rafters.

SIZE, SPACING AND SPAN. The size, spacing and span of the roof rafters are all related to each other. And these are all related to the roof load (snow, wind, roofing materials, etc.). All these factors are coordinated so that certain size rafters, spanning certain distances, according to certain spacing will effectively carry a certain load. Usually there are a number of different combinations of these factors that will work for any one roof. Let's discuss each one of these factors now.

Size: Rafter sizes vary from 2×4s (rare) to 2×14s, with 2×10s and 2×12s being most common. If insulation is to be placed between the rafters, the rafters must be wide enough to provide for the thickness of the insulation. Other than this consideration, the size you use depends on what you will need to carry the weight over the span at that spacing. The larger sizes are a little more expensive, but tend to be better quality boards.

Spacing: As with all stud construction, rafters are usually spaced on 12-, 16- or 24-inch intervals, with 12 and 16 inches being most common. As with sizes, whatever will work is fine. You will want to be sure the spacing is coordinated with the ceiling joists, so that every second or third ceiling joist can be nailed to a rafter to help reduce the outward thrust of the rafters on the wall.

Span: (Photos 13-21, 13-22, Figures 13-8, 13-9.) Rafter span, the distance between supported points of the rafter, affects both size and spacing. There is an upper limit that standard materials can span. In order to reduce the total span of the rafters, different techniques are used: a modified post and beam situation is placed either in the attic area or in the interior; or a load-bearing wall is used to break the span.

Collar beams can also be used to reduce the span of the rafters. They are attached across opposing rafters to reduce the outward thrust of the roof load, which wants to split the "A" formed by the gable rafters. They also serve to reduce the distance between support points on the rafters.

King or queen posts, usually made up of 2×4s running

Photo 13-21. Post and beam construction like this can be used in the attic area to break the span of a rafter. Two pieces are used to create the rafter, which is less expensive than one large, long rafter.

Photo 13-22. Using bolts to attach a double collar beam where they will be exposed to the inside.

Figure 13-10. Vent space is shown above the blocking between the rafters at the wall.

Figure 13-11. Ventilation in attic areas. Vents at eaves create an air flow between the rafters into the insulated area.

from the rafters to the ceiling joists, can also be used to reduce the span and transfer some of the load of the rafters to the ceiling joists and then over to the wall.

VENTILATION (Figures 13-10, 13-11). If you plan to incorporate an attic into your house, it must be ventilated. This not only allows hot air to be ventilated out in the summer but also avoids dampening of the attic insulation in the winter. The dampening is caused by condensation in the air in the attic. At a certain temperature, called the dew point, all the water molecules in the air will liquefy into water. This temperature often occurs in the attic or wall section of the house. Ventilating the attic allows this moisture to constantly be dried. Vents are usually placed in the gable walls of the attic area and are often built into the roof itself. It may also be wise to allow air to the floor from the overhang by placing vents between the rafters at the wall plates, as shown. Check with builders in your area to see if these are needed.

If you are planning to place the insulation between the rafters and then install the ceiling directly to the bottom edge of the rafter to create a sloping ceiling, you may want to ventilate between the rafters as well. This will allow air into the insulated area to dry any moisture build-up. It lowers the insulating properties of the roof section by only a negligible amount. Allow air to flow from the eaves to the ridge between each set of rafters as shown.

Be sure that the blocking between the rafters does not block the air flow, either at the wall, the ridge, or along the span. If you plan on including vents, make sure that the roof insulation stops 1½ inch short of the ridge.

Building a Roof Frame With Standard Materials

What You'll Need

TIME   The time you will need to do a roof frame is hard to generalize; it really depends on the size, complexity and height of the roof. Also how much thinking time you will need is hard to judge. A simple gable roof for a 2000-square-foot house could be completed in 3 or 4 days by two novice builders. A complex roof frame, with intersecting gables, valleys, hips, etc., could take 5 to 10 days.

PEOPLE   2 Minimum (1 skilled, 1 unskilled); 3 to 4 Optimum (2 skilled, 1 to 2 unskilled); 3 to 4 Maximum (all skilled).

TOOLS   Framing hammer, level, tape, pencil, saw horses, combination square, framing square, stair gauges, safety goggles, nail-pulling tools, nail belt, extension cords, power saw, saw blades, hand saw.

RENTAL ITEMS: Scaffolding or ladders, safety harness.

MATERIALS   As mentioned early in the chapter, your roof frame can be trusses, large timbers or standard rafters. The rest of the chapter will deal with roof construction with standard materials. To do the roof frame you will be using

framing grade lumber, usually 2×10s or 2×12s. Aside from the rafter stock, you will need framing materials for the ridges, hips, and valleys (often one dimension wider than the rafters); blocking; bracing (temporary); band rafters and ceiling joists. Also you will need nails (8d and 16d) and any fasteners you plan to use.

ESTIMATING MATERIALS NEEDED

Since the rafter stock is usually rather expensive, you will want to order as close to what you really need as possible. Count all the rafters needed (don't forget the rake rafters and gable rafters). Order a few extra for blocking (use the worst pieces for this). Calculate the lengths of the hips, valleys and ridges, including the overhang lengths, and order these. Try to stay as close to the standardized 2-foot intervals in length as you can. It's a shame to have to order an 18-foot length for a 16-foot-2-inch rafter, but the scrap can be used for blocking. Order any ceiling joists at this time, too.

INFORMATION   This chapter should provide you with all the information you need to build a gable or shed roof. To build a complex roof may require added information. There are a few books available just on roof framing which may be available at a technical book store. I would advise you to consult with a good framer for complex roofs and even consider paying them to work with you.

If you are using large timber rafters instead of common framing materials, almost everything is the same as shown in this chapter, except that the stock is thicker and the spacing greater. You may want to buy a rafter table book for layout of the rafters. These books, which are readily available, supply layout information on common rafters, valleys, hips, etc.

PEOPLE TO CONTACT   If you do not intend to do the roof yourself or if you decide you need help, a roofer must be contacted at this time. Aside from the crew you will use, the roofing materials supplier and a plumber should be contacted. (A plumber is needed to install the vent pipes, that protrude through the roof, before the roof framing begins.)

INSPECTIONS NEEDED   The roof framing is inspected at a later date, during the general framing inspection, which occurs after the sheathing is installed. You may, however, want the inspector to inspect the frame as soon as you are finished, before you put on the roof sheathing. If there are any mistakes in the framing, it will be easier to repair before the sheathing is in place. (I once had a house totally enclosed, roofing—everything, when the inspector told me I needed a double ridge because of a loading factor.)

Reading the Plans

Most plans will give you the basic information about building the roof framing but often not many of the details. These are left for the builder to work out at the job site. So don't be surprised if you are standing around scratching your head for long periods of time. Many of the roof framing situations need to be worked out at the site, where it is easier to visualize

F cedar shingles over
15# bldg. paper over ⅝" plywd. over
2×10' rafters @ 16" o.c.

blocking

D 2" screen vent
continuous
centered in soffit
typ. @ eaves

G cedar shingles over building paper
over 1×4 wood boards,
typical @ all porch areas

4×6 beam

4×6 rafters (typ.)
48" o.c. (typ)

4×6
column

12
slope 3

insulation

½" gypsum

D ridge vent (contn.)

C 4×14 ridge beam
supported at each
end of 16'0" span
by 4×4 posts

A 12
3

slope (typ.)

LEGEND

A slope
B distance of overhangs
C ridge beam
D vents
E rise of rafter
F rafter size & spacing
G veranda roof detail
H soffit detail or
overhang cut detail

typ. wall

6'0"
B

D

typ. wall
system

nailing
ledger

top of ledger 12
3
top of
beam

finished floor

3'0" typ.

7'3"

8'10"

top of ridge

E 5'2"

bot. soffit

ROOFING SECTION

2×10 rafters
16" o.c.

nailed to
rafter

plywood
sheathing

12
3

2×
blocking

typ. wall

3×6 tail rafter
32" o.c.

t&g
sheathing

1×
starter

2× fascia

optional
shaping of
rafter tail

5'0"

H TAIL RAFTER
EAVE DETAIL

solid blocking (reduce
blkn.'s height or provide
openings @ 60" o.c.

plywood
sheathing

12
3

2×10 rafter—16" o.c.

ceiling

2×4 continuous

2×4 @ 24" o.c.

typ. wall

cedar shingles

1× = starter
board

2×10 fascia

trim

2" screened
vent

H EAVE DETAIL—soffit (boxed eave)

Figure 13-12. Plans.

Photo 13-23. The use of scaffolding during roof framing makes the work easier, quicker and safer.

and take measurements. The plans (Figure 13-12) should however include the following:

A) Slope
B) Size of rafters
C) Spacing of rafters
D) Length of overhang
E) Soffit detail for end cut of rafter
F) Location and size of ceiling joists
G) Size of ridge and any bearing beams
H) Location of any collar beam
I) Loading weights, including live and dead loads

Safety and Awareness

SAFETY: Roof framing is the most dangerous of all the building processes (except for estimating). There is little stable support while working in a high location. Also you are working with long, heavy framing members and the chances for a fall or dropping something on somebody is high. Move at a slow, safe speed and always be safety minded. Use scaffolding (Photo 13-23); it is your best insurance. Be careful where you are stepping and always be sure no one is standing below the work unless absolutely necessary.

Even with all this, there may be situations that just call for bravery (though not stupidity). I remember having to hold an 18-foot 4×8 in the air while sitting on top of a band rafter, looking 32 feet down, as we tried to nail it into the band.

Scaffolding was impossible, so we used a safety harness, which, fortunately, wasn't needed.

AWARENESS: Like all framing, roof framing is not highly exacting (¼ inch margin of error). The main thing to be aware of is that all the pieces fit into each other in the proper way. This can be demanding in complex roofs. Be sure to place the rafters on the correct layout marks, and that the end cuts at the overhangs are in a straight line.

Overview of the Procedure

Step 1: Select a pattern piece
Step 2: Lay out the pattern rafter
Step 2A: Do layout for the ridge cut
Step 2B: Do layout for the odd unit
Step 2C: Do layout for the full units
Step 2D: Do layout for the birdsmouth cut
Step 2E: Do layout for the overhang
Step 2F: Adjust for the ridge
Step 2G: Cut the pattern rafter
Step 3: Check the pattern rafter
Step 4: Lay out the top plates and ridge
Step 5: Install the first sets of rafters and the ridge
Step 6: Install rake or fly rafter
Step 7: Install the band rafter
Step 8: Install blocking (if needed)

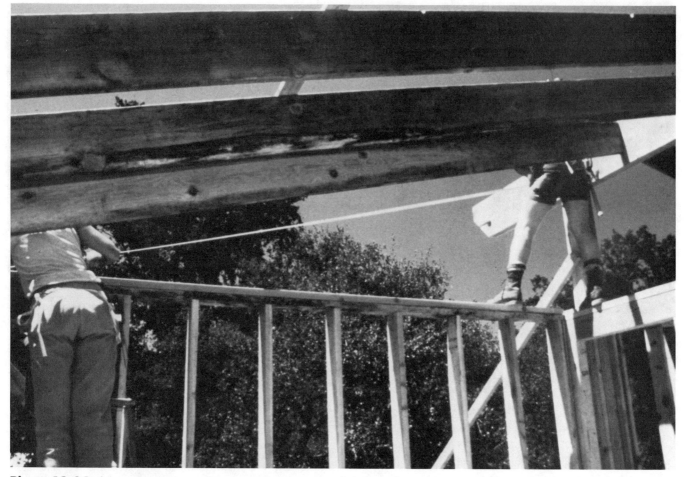

Photo 13-24. If the ridge or the walls are not straight or parallel, you will need to measure for each rafter instead of using a pattern rafter.

Step 1
Select a Pattern Piece

Margin of Error: ¼ inch off true over a 12-foot length.

Most Common Mistakes: Not using your best piece for the pattern; not allowing for deviations in the wall of ridge beam.

Photograph: Photo 13-24.

After digesting all the information in the beginning of this chapter (and I assume you have), and ordering all the proper materials, you are now ready for that glorious moment when you begin the roof framing—the most difficult of all framing. If you think you're not up to the task, step back and look at what you've already done. Then roll up your sleeves and go to work.

Most houses require a series of rafters that need to be cut equal lengths. In a gable (or shed) style roof, these rafters will be running from the ridge to the wall plates. When cutting a series of identical rafters, it is best to cut a pattern, test it and then use this pattern to mark the others. That is what we will be doing.

Before you begin (and this is crucial), you need to check the

walls to be sure that, indeed, all the rafters resting on them will need to be identical. If the tops of the walls where the rafters will rest are not parallel and straight, the distance from the ridge to the wall will vary along its length. If the walls cannot be straightened, and the variance is over ¼ inch, you may have to adjust your cuts as you go along to be sure that the rafters rest flat on the wall plates and tight against the ridge. Often walls can be forced out or pulled in to correct any problems.

If you have already installed a large load-bearing beam to serve as the ridge (see "Ridge Beam or Board" in the beginning of this chapter), you need to check this as well. Sometimes large timbers are warped, and the warps cannot be pulled out. This results in a ridge that does not run in a straight line, and, consequently, the distance from the ridge to the wall is not constant.

If at all possible, correct the warp in the beam. (You may have to winch it in place.) But if it cannot be corrected or if the walls are very crooked, you will need to make adjustments as you cut the rafters. This could involve measuring for each rafter, as shown in the photo. This is when you start realizing that there are no shortcuts: What you do at one stage of construction, affects what you do at later stages.

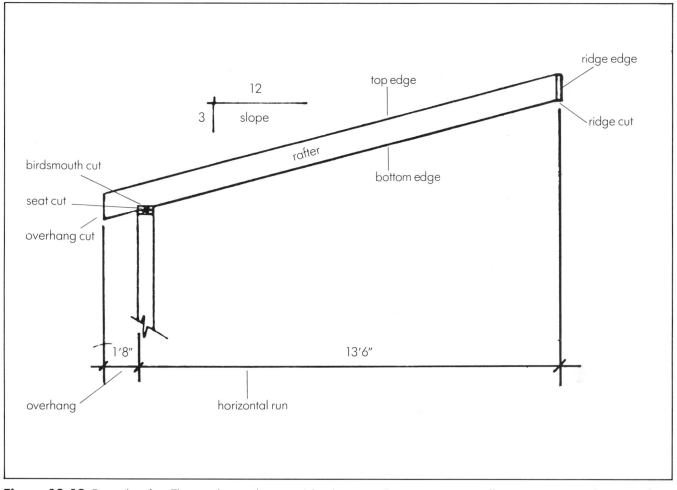

Figure 13-13. Example rafter. The run, the overhang and the slope are all necessary to step off a pattern piece to determine the ridge, birdsmouth and overhang cuts and their angles.

Step 2
Lay Out the Pattern Rafter

Margin of Error: Exact.

Most Common Mistake: Not laying out an accurate pattern.

Diagram: Figure 13-13.

Because of the length of this step, I have broken it into several sub-steps. In our example, which we will use in all the steps, the rafter will have a 13-foot-6-inch run (the horizontal distance from the outside edge of the wall to the centerline of the ridge), a 3 in 12 slope, and a 1-foot-8-inch overhang (the horizontal distance from the outside edge of the wall to the edge of the overhang cut). This is all you need to know to lay out the pattern, and your plans should contain all of this information.

Remember that the layout you are doing (the stepping off process), on the pattern piece is for the purpose of locating 3 cuts: the ridge cut, the birdsmouth cut and the overhang cut; and to determine their angles. This pattern will, in turn, be used to mark the cuts and angles on the rest of the rafters.

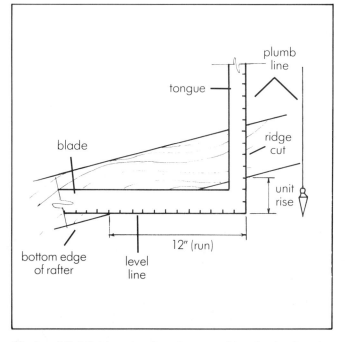

Figure 13-14. Note that the ridge cut will be plumb when the rafter is installed at its proper slope.

Photo 13-25. The square in place to mark off a rafter for a 3 in 12 slope roof. Note the unit rise, 3 inches, is set on the tongue (shorter arm) at the bottom edge of the board; and the unit run, 12 inches, is set on the blade (longer arm), also at the bottom edge of the board. Be sure you are using the numbers on the same side of the blade for both.

Step 2A
Do Layout for the Ridge Cut

Diagram: Figure 13-14.

Photograph: Photo 13-25.

After you have chosen your pattern piece, lay it flat between 2 saw horses. Even though you will be laying out the pattern in this position, you will still need to be able to visualize the rafter in place. Sometimes, if I get confused, I hold up the ridge end during the layout to visualize it.

Place the framing square on the pattern piece, as shown in the photo, with the shorter arm (the tongue) within an inch or two of the ridge end (the end that will eventually be against the ridge) of the rafter. Align the framing square so that the unit rise (3 in our example) is aligned with the bottom edge of the rafter on the tongue, and the unit run (always 12 inches) is aligned with the bottom edge of the rafter at the blade (the longer arm of the square).

Now draw a line along the outside edge of the tongue, close to the ridge end of the board. This will be the ridge or plumb cut. (Actually, we will be adjusting this cut later on to allow for half the thickness of the ridge board. See "Step 2F.")

Some builders do their alignment on the top edge of the rafter instead of the bottom; both will work. Be sure you are very accurate; use a sharp pencil, so you have thin precise marks. Use the numbers imprinted on the outside edge of the square, not those stamped on the inside. Patented clips, called stair gauges, are available that will maintain the square in position as you lay out the pattern.

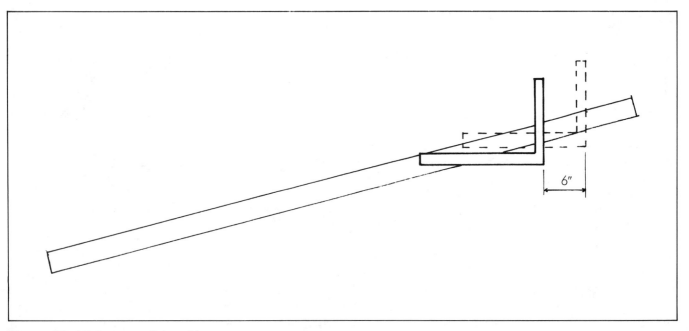

Figure 13-15. Stepping off the odd unit.

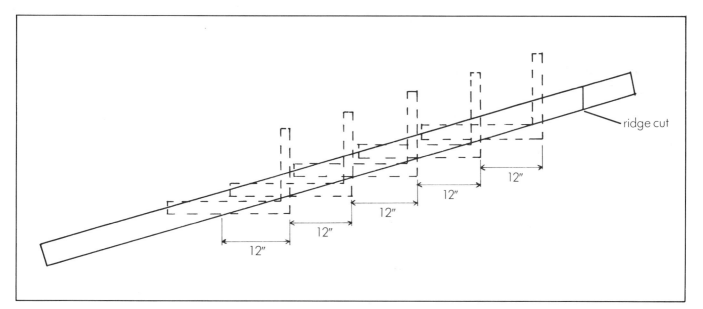

Figure 13-16. Stepping off full units.

Step 2B
Do Layout for the Odd Unit

Diagram: Figure 13-15.

After you have drawn the ridge cut, you are ready to step off the horizontal run, with a 3-inch rise for every 12 inches, in order to ascertain the next cut, the birdsmouth cut. First, you must measure the odd unit. This is a unit of measure on the horizontal run that is less than one foot along the horizontal. Since in our example, there are 13 feet 6 inches in the horizontal run, there is one odd unit measurement of 6 inches. Measure this odd unit (6 inches) along the blade (longer edge) of the square, which should still be in its original position on the stock. Mark the bottom edge of the stock at 6 inches. (Use a straight edge to transfer this point from the outside edge of the square to the board.) As always in the rafter layout, be precise.

You have now accounted for 6 inches of the 13 feet 6 inches that you must measure between the centerline of the ridge and the plumb cut of the birdsmouth (the horizontal run).

Step 2C
Do Layout for the Full Units

Diagram: Figure 13-16.

Photographs: Photos 13-26, 13-27.

Now begin to step off the full units (12-inch units). Slide the square along the stock until the 3-inch mark on the tongue of the square is on this 6-inch mark you have just made on the stock. Make another mark on the board where the 12-inch mark of the blade is crossing the bottom of the stock. Move

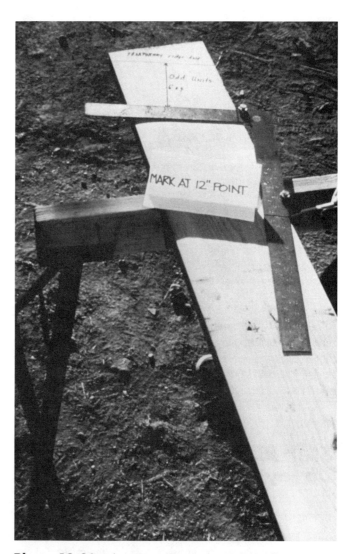

Photo 13-26. After the odd unit is marked off, move the square down the rafter to the odd unit mark and mark the rafter at the 12-inch mark on the blade.

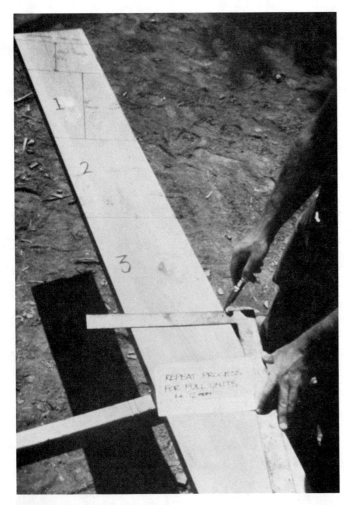

Photo 13-27. Stepping off the full units. Continue down the board, placing a mark along the blade at the 12-inch mark, and then transferring the unit rise mark on the tongue (the 3-inch mark) to this point.

your square down again, until the 3-inch mark on the tongue is aligned with this 12-inch mark. Make another mark here and you have just stepped off another 12 inches along the horizontal run, for a total of 2 feet 6 inches. Transfer the tongue to this mark and continue to do this for the rest of the full units in our example 13. The last 12-inch mark that you make will correspond with the building line (the exterior edge of the wall), since it is exactly 13 feet 6 inches along the horizontal run from the beginning point at the ridge. This point also corresponds with the plumb cut of the birdsmouth.

Step 2D
Do Layout for the Birdsmouth Cut

Photograph: Photo 13-28.

After laying out all the full and odd units, you are ready to do the layout for the birdsmouth cut—where the rafter will rest on the wall. The birdsmouth is actually made up of 2 cuts: the seat or level cut, which is the horizontal (level) cut where the

rafter rests on top of the wall providing a good nailing surface; and the plumb cut, where the rafter "hooks" the exterior edge of the wall, preventing the walls from pushing out.

The seat is usually 3½ inches (5½ inches, if it is resting on top of a 2-×-6 wall), and the plumb cut is whatever is created by the seat cut being 3½ inches. To form this cut, turn your framing square over and align one arm along the last full unit mark. (The unit mark should extend, as shown in the photo, across the entire width of the rafter.) With the 3½-inch mark on the other arm of the square crossing the bottom edge of the rafter, draw a line running perpendicular from the last full unit line, toward the ridge end, to the 3½-inch mark. This line represents the seat cut of the birdsmouth.

Step 2E
Do Layout for the Overhang

Photograph: Photo 13-29.

After the birdsmouth cut layout is completed, you are ready to do the layout for the overhang and the overhang cut. You will have to ascertain what cut you plan to use at the end (see p. 289, "Overhangs, Soffits and Fascias" at the beginning of this chapter). In our example, there is a 1-foot-8-inch overhang (measured along the horizontal run) and a plumb cut for the overhang cut.

To lay this out, place the square on the top edge of the rafter, instead of the bottom edge. Once again, adjust the square so that the tongue (which is towards the overhang) crosses the top of the rafter at 3 inches, and the blade (which is towards the ridge) crosses the top edge at 12 inches. Be exact. (Remember to use the numbers on the outer edge of the square.) As shown in the photo, starting at the plumb cut of the birdsmouth (or building line, or last full unit mark, they are all the same), measure the odd unit, in our example 8 inches, and mark at the tongue. Then, move the 12-inch mark on the blade to this mark and draw a line along the outer edge of the tongue. You have now moved 1 foot 8 inches along the horizontal to the overhang plumb cut. In just a few pages I will show you how to check your layout using a rafter table book or the tables imprinted on the square.

Step 2F
Adjust for the Ridge

Diagram: Figure 13-17.

Photographs: Photos 13-30, 13-31.

Before we start to cut our pattern rafter, we need to make an adjustment at the ridge. If you remember, all our measurements have originated at a point that corresponds with the centerline of the ridge board. Obviously, the rafter does not extend this far. The rafter begins short of the centerline by

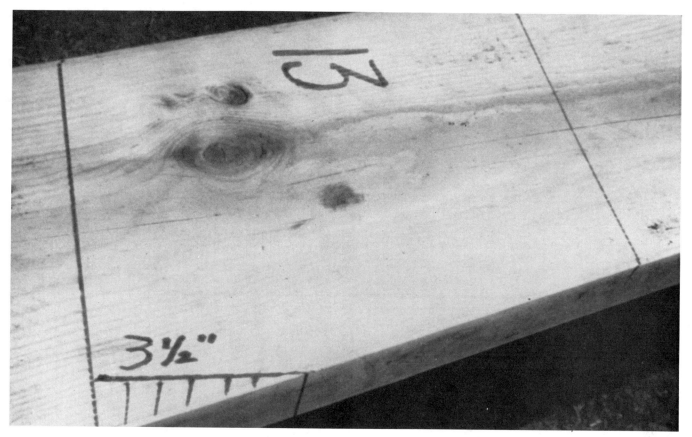

Photo 13-28. Rafter marked for the birdsmouth cut.

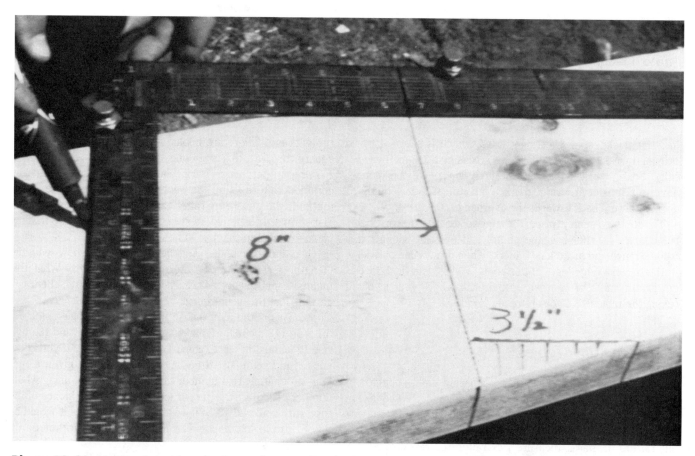

Photo 13-29. Marking the odd unit for the overhang cut (8 inches). Note that the square is now on the top edge of the rafter.

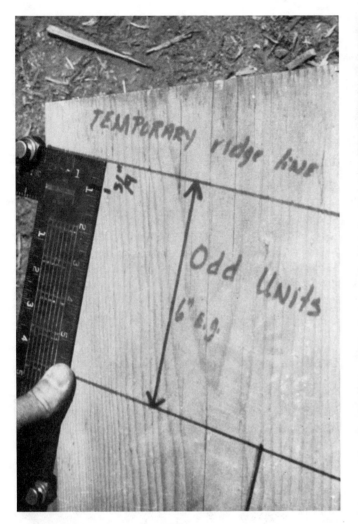

Photo 13-30. Marking the ¾-inch adjustment for the final ridge line.

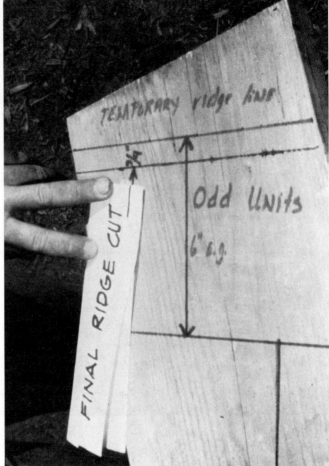

Photo 13-31. Adjusting for the ridge cut involves laying out a new ridge cut line that is ½ the thickness of the ridge (along a horizontal plane), towards the overhang. In this example the ridge is 1½ inches, so the cut is ¾ inch towards the overhang.

half the thickness of the ridge board, which is short of our original mark. (In our example, we are using a 1½-inch-wide ridge board, so half the distance is ¾ inch). We therefore have to bring our first ridge mark ¾ inch (measured along the horizontal run) back towards the overhang.

To do this, simply place the square against the original ridge mark as shown in the photo, and measure along the blade ¾ inch and make a new mark. Then draw a line parallel to the original ridge mark at this point. This is your final ridge cut layout line. Pat yourself on the back, check your layout (using the tables) and you are ready to cut.

Using the Rafter Tables

Your framing square is a rather amazing tool. Though it seems simple, it holds a wealth of knowledge; somewhat like the great pyramids of Egypt, where, behind a mass of stones, many answers to the universe lie. The framing square can lay out rafters or stairs; measure jack rafters or valley rafters; calculate board feet of lumber; shine your shoes and take out

the garbage. There are books written just on the use of the square, but alas, this is not one of them.

For our purposes, I will show you how to lay out the common rafters using the square. You can then use either method, the square or rafter tables, or the step-off method just shown. Most builders step off the rafter with the framing square, and then check it with the tables.

The square can be used because it will show you the "length of the common rafter, per foot of run." What this means is that for every 12 inches of horizontal run, there is a certain length measured along the slope, for a given roof slope. This is the hypotenuse formed by a triangle using the unit run (12 inches, in our example) as one side and the unit rise (3 inches, in our example) as the other side. If you know what this hypotenuse (the unit length) is for a given slope, you can multiply that number times the total run, using whole numbers and decimals (in our example, 13 feet 6 inches of the total run would be 13.5; if it were 8 feet 8 inches it would be 8.666, etc.). Use a pocket calculator for the arithmetic involved in this process.

The unit length measurement can be obtained from a rafter

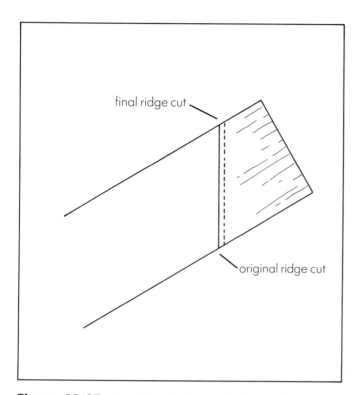

Figure 13-17. To adjust for ½ the thickness of the ridge board, the ridge cut is moved back from the original layout line, towards the overhang.

table book. In these books there are tables that give the unit lengths for all slopes and runs. These tables are also stamped on the blade of the square. Under the full inch numbers stamped on the blade are other series of numbers. The top series is unit length or, as written on the square, "length common rafter per foot run." One of these numbers times the total run would give you the total length along the slope from the building line (the outside edge of the wall) to the centerline of the rafter, as measured along its slope. Looking at the square under 3 inches (since we are using a 3 in 12 slope in our example), we find the number 12.37. Multiply this number times the total run, 13.5 (13 feet 6 inches), and get 13.5 × 12.37 = 166.995 inches (166.995/12), which in turn equals 13.91 feet or 13 feet 11 inches. This is the total length along the slope.

You can use this measurement to check your layout of the pattern. The distance on the pattern rafter from the overhang cut to the centerline of the ridge (the original, not final, ridge cut) should be the same as this measurement. If you are off more than ⅛ inch, check to see if you have measured wrong or stepped the rafter off incorrectly.

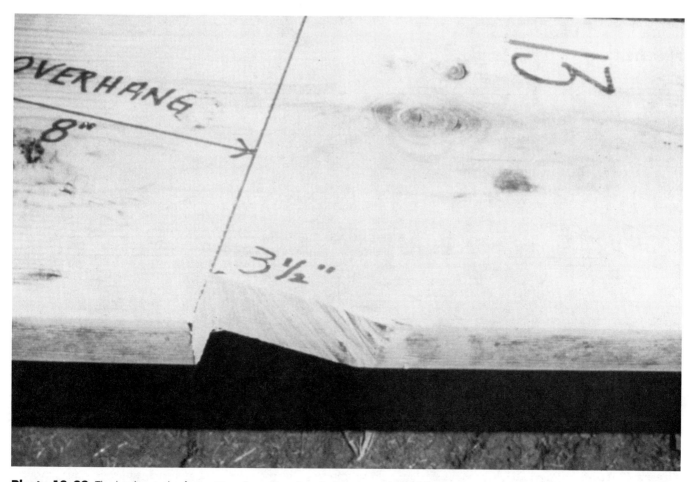

Photo 13-32. The birdsmouth after cutting. For a 2-×-6 wall, the cut would be 5½ inches.

Photo 13-33. Cutting the ridge cut.

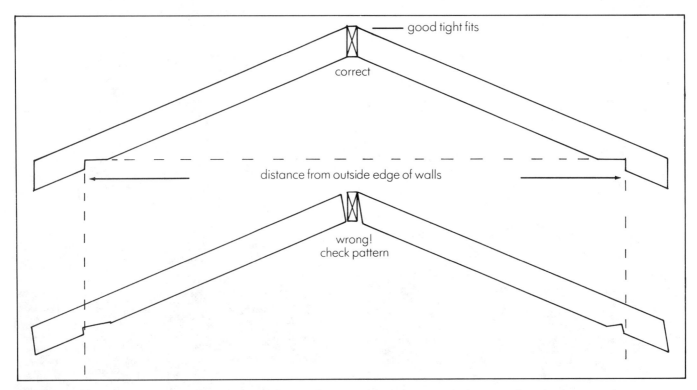

Figure 13-18. Place 2 pattern rafters on the subfloor, with a scrap block the same thickness as the ridge between them, to see how they fit.

Step 2G
Cut the Pattern Rafter

Photographs: Photos 13-32, 13-33.

If the calculated measurements are the same as those used for the cutting lines you made on the pattern, you can cut your pattern rafter. Do this very exactly because the other rafters will be cut from this pattern. Make your cuts at the ridge and overhang with a power saw, and at the birdsmouth, use a hand saw and power saw. You may want to let the overhang end of the rafter run "wild" and cut all the overhang cuts once the rafters are in place (see "Step 7").

Step 3
Check the Pattern Rafter

Diagram: Figure 13-18.

Aside from checking the pattern rafter with the tables, there is one last easy way of checking the rafter before you go and cut all that expensive stock. From the pattern rafter, cut one more rafter. Place these 2 rafters on a flat surface (preferably, on the subfloor) in opposing places, as if they were forming the gable roof. Place a scrap block the same thickness as the ridge between them and spread them out so that the distance between the plumb cuts of the birdsmouths equals the distance between the outside edges of the 2 walls (the roof span). When the rafters are spread like this, they should meet squarely and tightly at the mock ridge board, with no gaps between the rafters and the ridge pieces. If there are gaps, check to see where you are off before cutting more rafters.

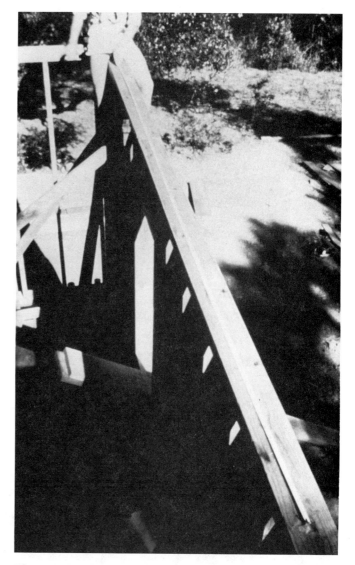

Photo 13-34. Lay out the rafter locations on both the ridge and the wall plates. Be careful of splinters and falling.

Step 4
Lay Out the Top Plates and Ridge

Margin of Error: ¼ inch off proper layout location.

Most Common Mistakes: Not allowing for the rake (fly) rafter; placing the "X" on the wrong side of the layout mark; not allowing for any openings; falling off the wall.

Photograph: Photo 13-34.

Once you have ascertained that you have cut an accurate pattern and that the walls (or ridge beams) are not out of alignment to the extent that special measurements are needed, you can begin to cut all the remaining identical rafters. Always use the original pattern piece as the pattern, or you will be compounding errors by switching patterns. You are now ready to place the layout marks on the walls and ridge board in the same way a layout was done for the walls and floors.

When you begin your layout be sure you have accounted for any rake (fly) rafters. Actually your layout should begin from the outer edge of this rafter. Since these rafters are not yet in place you will have to calculate their eventual location, and lay out the other rafters from there.

Usually builders straddle the wall and lay out the top plates from this position. The greatest drawback to this method, needless to say, is getting splinters in the worst places. You may want to use a ladder. Mark your layout on the cap plates on a 12-, 16- or 24-inch center (wider if you are using large timbers for rafters).

Now lay out the ridge board on saw horses. Any joints in the ridge (where 2 pieces of ridge stock come together) must occur at the centerline of a rafter. To do this, you will have to cut your ridge pieces as you lay them out to make them work.

You will also be laying out ceiling joists on the walls at this time, if you are using them. Install them before the rafters; they can be used as a platform in erecting the roof framing. If you are not using any ceiling joists, seriously consider using scaffolding. I would advise it.

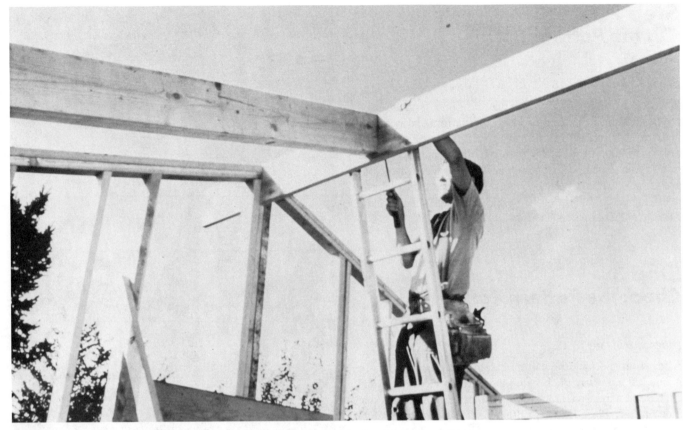

Photo 13-35. The ridge board is in place and permanently attached at the gable wall.

Photo 13-36. After the rafters are cut from the pattern, lean them against the wall near where they will be installed.

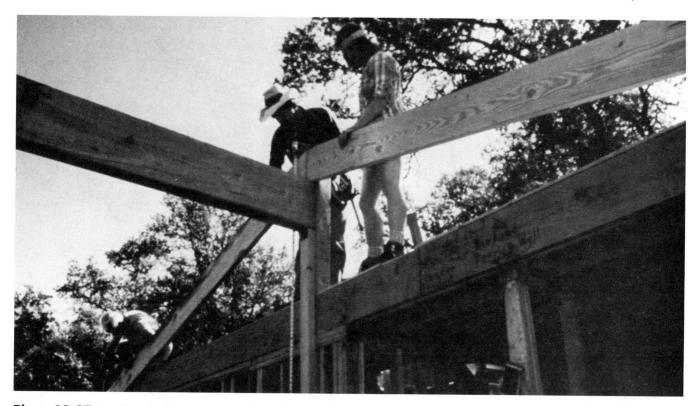

Photo 13-37. Installing the first set of rafters.

Step 5
Install the First Sets of Rafters and the Ridge

Margin of Error: ¼ inch.

Most Common Mistakes: Splice in ridge not occurring in the centerline of a rafter; placing the rafter on the wrong side of the layout mark; falling off the roof.

Diagram: Figure 13-19.

Photographs: Photos 13-35, 13-36, 13-37, 13-38, 13-39, 13-40, 13-41.

You are now ready to start erecting the rafters and ridge. In some buildings, the ridge will already be set permanently in place if the gable wall has been built (see photo). This makes things somewhat easier; the ridge is in place and stable. Often, however, gable walls (walls formed in the triangle created by the gables of the roof rafters) are not built until the roof rafters are in place. In this case, you will need to temporarily hold the ridge in place as you nail in the first few sets of rafters. If there are enough people around to help, they can just hold the ridge in its proper location. Or, you can build temporary supports for the ridge, as shown in the diagram, to hold it in place until the rafters can secure it.

After the ridge is secured, lean the rafters against the walls, each one near its layout mark. Starting at one gable end (use straight rafters at the gable), position one person at each wall and one person at the ridge. The workers at the wall should slide their rafters over the wall towards the ridge, and the worker at the ridge can hold these rafters against the ridge until the people at the wall toenail the rafters (use 10d) into the cap plates of the wall.

After the first 2 rafters are toenailed at the walls, the person at the ridge can nail them to the ridge board; one rafter can be face nailed (use 16d), but the other rafter will need to be toenailed (use 10d). As you install the rafters, alternate face nailing and toenailing the rafters, e.g., toenail the first one on the left hand side of the ridge, then the next one on the right hand side). Nail in every fourth set of rafters to stabilize the ridge before going back to fill in the other sets. Be sure, as with floor framing, that you install the rafters with the crown up so it will eventually settle down. Plumb and brace the assembly as you go; the ridge must remain straight.

If any metal fasteners are needed for hurricane, earthquake or other structural reasons, install these. In most cases they will be used where the rafters meet the wall and/or where the rafters meet the ridge, as shown in the photos. Check with your inspector to see if any metal fasteners are needed. In earthquake or hurricane areas, I would recommend them; they are inexpensive and quick to apply, but still offer protection in the event of a hurricane or earthquake.

If you are using a ridge beam instead of a ridge board, it will be permanently in place before you begin to install the rafters. This makes roof framing somewhat simpler. The beam rests on posts, usually built into the walls. These posts often require foundation piers directly below because they carry the weight of the roof. The rafters are either set on top of the ridge beam or hung from it.

Figure 13-19. Temporary braces can be built to support the ridge rafters.

Photo 13-38. Rafter-to-wall metal fasteners are not common, but they are a good idea in earthquake or hurricane areas.

Photo 13-39. Installing metal plates over the ridge to connect corresponding rafters in a set is not always required, but it is a good idea in earthquake country.

Photo 13-40. Nailing a load-bearing ridge beam to support posts. The 2×4s being nailed on either side of the beam are temporary supports that keep the beam from falling off the posts during construction. Ridge boards are much smaller in dimension than this ridge beam.

Photo 13-41. Installing rafters on top of a load-bearing beam.

Step 6
Install Rake or Fly Rafter

Margin of Error: ¼ inch.

Most Common Mistakes: Not providing adequate support; not installing rafters straight and aligned; falling off the roof.

Diagram: Figure 13-20.

Photographs: Photos 13-42, 13-43, 13-44, 13-45.

After all the common rafters are in place, you are now ready to install the rake or fly rafters. These rafters run parallel to the slope of the roof and create the overhang between the gable wall and the exterior edge of the roof (see diagram). There are several ways these cantilevered rafters can be supported, and you need to determine which method you are going to use before starting the roof framing.

One method for installing the rake rafters is as shown in the diagram and photo. This involves "lookouts" (usually the same dimension lumber as the rafters) being installed between the rake rafter and the last common rafter. As you can see there is no gable rafter and the gable wall serves as a fulcrum to support the weight of the rake rafters.

Another method involves installing the gable rafters, notching them, and then installing 2×4s flat running from the rake rafters to the rafter immediately inside the gable rafter.

The final method does not involve lookouts at all. In this case, the rake rafters are attached only at the ridge beam and the band rafter (see photo). You will need to be sure that the

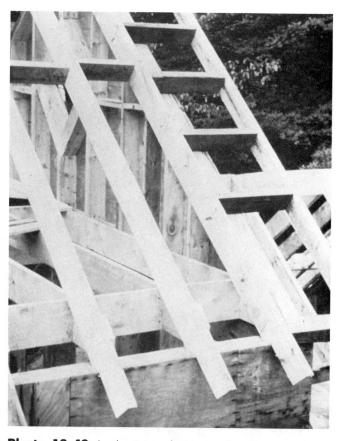

Photo 13-42. Lookouts are being used to support a suspended rake rafter. Note that there is no gable rafter used here (rafter at the gable wall).

Photo 13-43. These "lookouts" are supporting the rake rafter. Note how the gable rafter is notched and the "lookouts" are inserted.

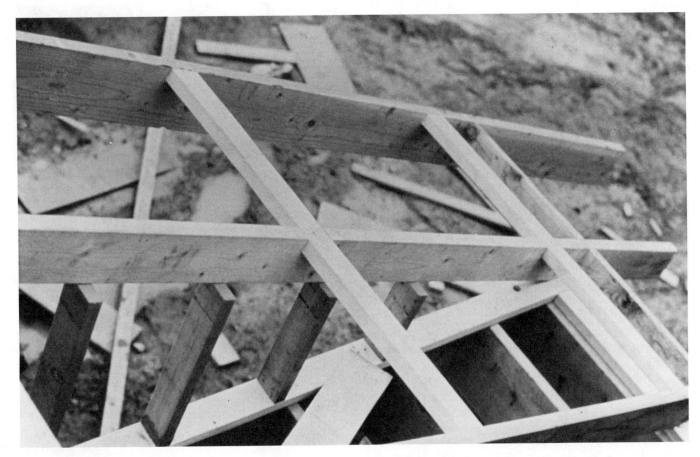

Photo 13-44. Attaching the rake rafter can be very dangerous. Do not take any chances.

Figure 13-20. Using lookouts to support the rake rafter. Note there is no gable rafter.

Photo 13-45. In large timber roof framing, often the rake rafter is one piece, attached at the large ridge beam and band rafter.

rake rafter is properly sized; there are no supports to break the span. This is the easiest process if you can build the rake with one piece of stock. You will also need to install the band rafter before the rake in this case, since the rake is attached to the band at one end.

No matter what process you use, choose good stock for the rake rafters. Be careful installing these rafters, for nowhere is roof framing more dangerous than when you are leaning over the side of the building to install the rake rafters. Be sure they are installed in a straight line parallel with the gable wall. Check for straightness with a string to be sure it is true. With the sky as a backdrop, any discrepancy or wave in the board will be easily noticed from below.

Step 7
Install the Band Rafter

Margin of Error: ¼ inch.

Most Common Mistakes: Band rafter not installed straight; falling off the roof.

Photographs: Photos 13-46, 13-47.

After all the common rafters are installed, you can apply the band rafter or fascia. You can do this before or after the rake rafters (see "Step 6") are installed. The band rafter or fascia is the board that is nailed to the end of the common rafters at the overhang cut. The size and details of installing this board will depend on your soffit design (see p. 289, "Special Considerations: Overhangs, Soffits and Fascias" at the beginning of this chapter). Depending on the design, you will either be

using a 2-inch board (band rafter) or a 1-inch trim board (fascia) or both. Usually if you are installing the 2-inch-thick band rafter, this will later be covered with a more attractive 1-inch fascia as trim. Often a high-quality 2-inch band rafter is installed, painted or stained and left as the finished fascia.

In our example, we will be installing a 2-inch band rafter. The overhang cut at the end of the rafter is a plumb cut and the band rafter will be installed in a plumb position. The most important thing to remember when installing this rafter (as with the rake rafter) is that it must be installed straight. Any wave in the rafter should be easily noticeable against the sky backdrop, when viewed from the ground. Getting the band rafter straight can be difficult. Often all the overhang cuts are not aligned (in fact I have seldom known them to be). This may be due to a sloppy cut, or a wall or ridge that's not straight.

I highly recommend allowing the overhang ends of the rafters to run wild and cutting the overhang cuts after all the rafters are in place. Whether you are going to cut them in place or check them after they are cut and installed, run a string along the upper edge of the common rafters to see if the ends are all on line (mark them if they are running wild). They need to be straight within ⅛ inch maximum; no waver should be detected. Be very exacting with your cuts here. One of the first things I always do, to check a builder's attention to detail, is to check the straightness of the band rafters.

Once the string is in place, make marks on the rafters where you plan to make the overhang cuts. It there is one rafter shorter than all the rest, all the rafters will need to be cut back to this rafter (you can shim this rafter if it will not be exposed from below). With the square, mark the new overhang cuts. Using the power saw, as shown, make accurate cuts along these marks.

Photo 13-46. The band rafter is applied only after you have checked to be sure that the overhang cuts of the rafters are all in a straight line. Be sure this board is put on straight and level.

Photo 13-47. Cutting the overhang cuts after the rafters are installed is often suggested or required, if they are not all aligned. Wear safety glasses to protect your eyes, unlike the photo.

This is one of the most difficult cuts to make in framing. You are holding the saw in an awkward position and there is sawdust flying in your eyes. If possible, try to climb on top of the rafters and cut in a downward direction. In any case, be sure you are in a secure position and make an *accurate* cut. If you are cutting from below, wear safety goggles and a hooded sweatshirt and gloves. There is nothing more uncomfortable than spending the rest of the day working with sawdust down your back from cuts you made early in the morning. The gloves and hooded sweatshirt will also come in handy when you start to install insulation; another enjoyable task.

Step 8
Install Blocking (If Needed)

Margin of Error: ¼ inch.

Most Common Mistakes: Omitting blocking where needed; totally blocking rafter space where air passages are needed for ventilation; cutting blocking too small, too long or crooked; falling off the roof.

Photographs: Photos 13-48, 13-49, 13-50, 13-51.

As in floor framing, blocking may be required in the roof framing. Blocking, which would occur at the wall line and every 8 feet along the length of the rafters, adds rigidity to the roof frame and keeps the rafters plumb. Check with your plans or local inspector to see if blocking is required.

Photo 13-48. If you need to ventilate an attic area, screen vents can be installed every few rafters.

Photo 13-49. Blocking is often installed every 8 feet. Note that the blocks are smaller than the rafters to allow for ventilation.

Photo 13-50. Installing blocking at the wall line is done either after all the rafters are in place or as they are installed. Note that the blocks are aligned with the outside edge of the wall and do not reach the top of the rafter, to allow for ventilation.

Photo 13-51. If rafters are resting on top of the ridge, instead of hung from it, you will need to install blocking at the ridge.

notch ceiling joist
here if needed

rafters

ceiling joists

metal straps
(in earthquake areas)

Figure 13-21. The relationship of ceiling joists to rafters.

Blocking is often installed at the building line (the outside edge of the wall) between the rafters. If a ventilation area is needed between the rafters (see, p. 293, "Special Considerations: Ventilation" at the beginning of this chapter), be sure that the blocks do not totally fill the rafter cavity; this will block ventilation. A 1½-inch gap at the top should be left for air flow. This gap will later be covered by a screen.

Install the blocks *flush with the outside edge of the wall*. If the interior wallboards are going to run up between the rafters on the inside (as in an exposed beam ceiling), you will need to provide a second nailing surface for the interior wall flush with the inside edge of the wall as well.

Blocks may be required along the length of the rafters as shown in the photo. Usually these are placed every 8 feet and, again, do not totally block the passage if air is to ventilate between the rafters. Stagger the blocks so they can always be face nailed, and be sure they are cut the proper size and straight so that they do not push the rafters out of alignment. Also check to see if the rafter is cupped or warped or twisted before installing the blocks. If any are, adjust the blocks to be sure the rafters stay on line.

Special Situations

Ceiling Joists
Diagrams: Figures 13-21, 13-22, 13-23, 13-24.

Many homes will require ceiling joists on which to hang the ceiling materials. If you are using a truss roof frame, the bottom chord of the truss will serve as the ceiling joists (see p. 283, "Design Decisions: Trusses" at the beginning of this chapter). If you are building the roof frame at the job site, you will need to cut and install your own ceiling joists. These ceiling joists are similar to the floor frame, but are lighter and have no band around the outside. They are usually 12 inches and 16 inches on center and are sized to carry a 20-pound dead or live load. Their size varies according to span, load and type of wood, but if you ever plan to use the attic as a living space or to store heavy objects, be sure to size the joists to handle these loads.

Ceiling joists can be supported in a number of ways. If the span is not too great or the loads are not too heavy, you can simply span the joists from wall to wall. If the span needs to

Figure 13-22. The ceiling joists are spanning from wall to wall. The ends have been cut so as not to protrude past the rafters.

Figure 13-23. Stub ceiling joists are being used here in a low-pitched roof. The rafters will be running perpendicular to the regular ceiling joists.

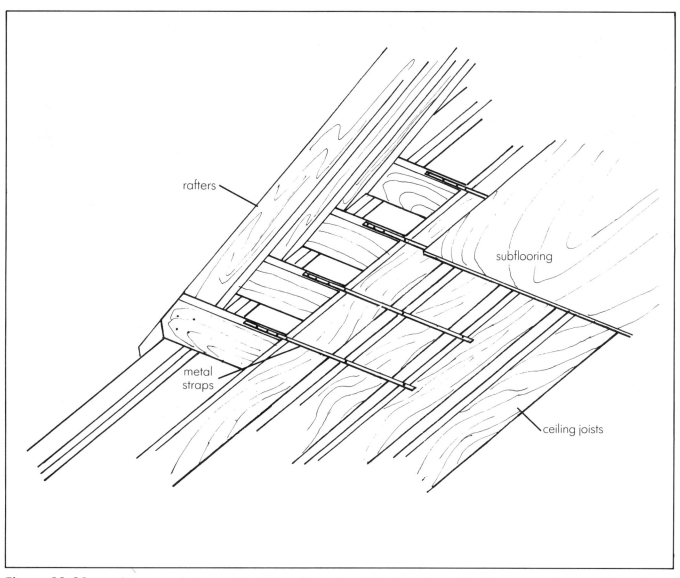

rafters

subflooring

metal
straps

ceiling joists

Figure 13-24. Metal straps are being used to tie the rafters to the subflooring when ceiling joists are running at a right angle to the rafters.

be broken by a support, you can build a post and beam into the building on which the joists can rest. Also you can hide this post and beam in the wall and ceiling, if this better suits your design. You can also use a "stongback," which is a beam in the attic fastened to the ceiling joists from above. This is often "retro-fitted" into existing ceilings that later have to be strengthened to carry a greater load.

Ceiling joists are usually cut to the slope of the roof where they intersect the rafters. These can often be rough cuts done with a hatchet, since they will be hidden in the attic. If you are using a very low sloped roof, you may need to use "stub ceiling joists" to replace the ceiling joists that are parallel and adjacent to the wall on which the rafters rest (see diagram). Otherwise the ceiling joist closest to the wall will be in the way of the rafters resting on the wall.

If the rafters run at right angles to the ceiling joists, stub joists and straps (metal) can be used to tie the rafters (and walls) to the attic floor diaphragm. These help to reduce the

pressure created by the rafters to split the walls apart.

If any walls on the story below the ceiling are running parallel to the ceiling joists, the tops of these walls can be stabilized by placing blocks between the ceiling joists flush with the bottom edge of the joists. The cap plate of the wall is then toenailed into these blocks. Some ceilings may also need to be blocked (or bridged) as in floor framing. Again this adds rigidity to the ceiling and keeps the joists straight. Ask the inspector if it's needed, or if you ever plan to carry much of a load on the joists, install these now.

When there are openings in the ceilings (fireplace, chimneys, stairs, skylight shafts, etc.), they are framed identical to floor frame openings. You may not be required to use double trimmer joists or headers, however, if the ceiling does not carry a large load. Remember that most codes require an access to the attic (often built into the closet ceiling). This access is at least 22 inches × 30 inches with a clear height of at least 30 inches in the attic.

Photo 13-52. To frame for a skylight is similar to framing an opening in a floor.

Figure 13-25. A skylight or chimney opening. The headers and trimmers are single or double, depending on the opening sizes and the roof loading factors.

Openings in the Roof Frame
Diagram: Figure 13-25.
Photograph: Photo 13-52.

Openings in the roof framing, created to allow for skylights or chimneys, are constructed in a similar way to those in the floor frame. If the opening can be formed within the normal span of 2 rafters, thereby eliminating the need to cut any rafters, only headers need to be added at the proper locations. Indeed, many skylight manufacturers do build their skylights to fit between the rafters. If a rafter needs to be cut, however, you may need to double the trimmer rafters and the headers, depending on the size of the opening and the load of the roof. The headers can be installed either plumb or square with the rafter, whichever way the design or manufacturer's requirements dictate.

As you create the opening, be sure that it is the proper rough opening as called for by the manufacturer's dimensions for that skylight. If you are building your own skylights, be sure that they match the rough opening you have provided in the roof framing. Check also the locations of these openings with respect to the fireplace chimney or the place you need light, to be sure they are properly located. You would not want to build a rock chimney and then find the opening was not aligned.

Never attach a masonry chimney to the frame. The chimney, due to its weight, will settle faster than the building, and if you attach the frame to it, it will pull the frame down. I saw this in an older house; the floor actually dipped at the hearth

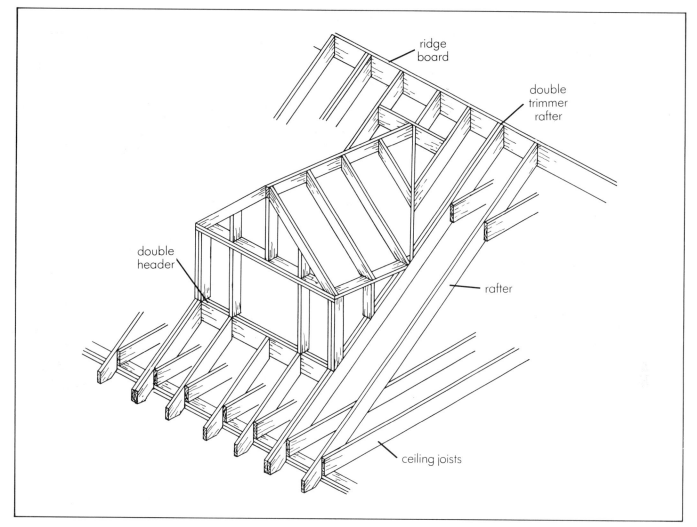

Figure 13-26. The framing of a roof dormer.

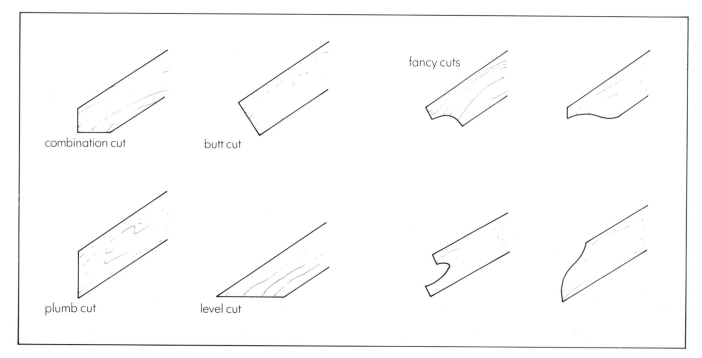

Figure 13-27. Different ways in which overhangs can be cut.

Photo 13-53. A Japanese tradition is to attach an evergreen twig to the top of the highest framing member as soon as it is erected and to celebrate. Not a bad idea to regain your perspective on how far you've come at this stage.

because they had attached the floor frame to the fireplace foundation. Leave at least a 1½-inch airspace between the frame and the chimney for fire safety (more, if required locally).

Dormers
Diagram: Figure 13-26.

A dormer is a framed part of the roof projecting from a sloping area of the roof, that contains a vertical window unit. They are often built into attic areas or upstairs rooms with sloping ceilings to allow for ventilation, light and more head room. They are also considered appealing from both the interior and exterior. An opening for a dormer is created in the same way as those for skylights or chimneys with the dormer framing built on top of the frame, as shown in the diagram. They can be built on either shed or gable roofs.

Fancy Cuts
Diagram: Figure 13-27.

Often fancy cuts are made on a ridge or at the end of the rafters when they are to be exposed to the exterior of the home. Your imagination is the limit. You would be surprised at what a difference these cuts make aesthetically, and they only take a few extra minutes per rafter. A little detailing like this really gives the house a lot of character. Be sure your design does not catch and hold water. If the rafters are exposed to the weather, use a weather-proof sealant on them.

Twig at the Top
Photograph: Photo 13-53.

The Japanese have a very nice custom. When the last roof framing member is in place, they attach the twig of an evergreen tree to the highest member and celebrate the completion of the frame of the house. I suggest you also build in ceremonial activities to your house construction. They allow you time to step back and get in touch with the beauty and joy of building your own house. It is also a chance to be thankful for the abundance that allows all this to happen.

Worksheet

ESTIMATED TIME

_____

_____

_____

_____

CREW

Skilled

_____ Phone _____

_____ Phone _____

_____ Phone _____

Unskilled

_____ Phone _____

_____ Phone _____

_____ Phone _____

_____ Phone _____

_____ Phone _____

COST COMPARISON

_____ Store:

$ _____ per 1000 board ft. rafter stock, $ _____ total

_____ Store:

$ _____ per 1000 board ft. rafter stock, $ _____ total

_____ Store:

$ _____ per 1000 board ft. rafter stock, $ _____ total

_____ Store:

$ _____ per 1000 board ft. rafter stock, $ _____ total

PEOPLE TO CONTACT

Roofer _____

Phone _____ Work Date _____

Roofing materials supplier _____

Phone _____ Work Date _____

Plumber _____

Phone _____ Work Date _____

MATERIALS NEEDED Rafter stock; framing materials for ridges, hips and valleys; blocking, bracing and band rafter material; ceiling joists and nails.

ESTIMATING MATERIALS

RAFTERS: Size: _____ Length: _____ Number: ____
(include blocking)

RIDGES: Size: _____ Length: _____ Number: _____

VALLEYS: Size: _____ Length: _____ Number: ____

HIPS: Size: _____ Length: _____ Number: _____

CEILING JOISTS: Size: _____ Length: _____

Number: _____

Daily Checklist

CREW:

_____ Phone _____

_____ Phone _____

_____ Phone _____

_____ Phone _____

TOOLS:

☐ framing hammer

☐ level

☐ tape

☐ pencil

☐ saw horses

☐ combination square

☐ framing square

☐ stair gauges

☐ safety goggles

☐ nail-pulling tools

☐ nail belt

☐ extension cords

☐ power saw

☐ saw blades

☐ hand saw

RENTAL ITEMS:

☐ ladders

☐ scaffolding

☐ safety harness

MATERIALS:

Rafter stock _____

Hips _____

Ridges _____

Valley _____

Blocking _____

Band rafters _____

Ceiling joists _____

Nails _____

Fasteners _____

DESIGN REVIEW:

Are you sure where you want that skylight?

INSPECTIONS NEEDED:

Inspector's name _____

Phone _____

Time and date of inspection _____

WEATHER FORECAST:

For week _____

For day _____

14 Roof Sheathing

Photo 14-1. Skip sheathing before the ends are cut.

What You'll Be Doing, What to Expect

ROOF SHEATHING is the skin or surface that covers the roof rafters. There are different choices in materials: plywood, 2-×-6 T&G boards, skip sheathing, 1-×-6 butt-end boards, etc. We will discuss each one of these and then, in detail, describe how to apply three of them: plywood sheets, skip sheathing and 2-×-6 T&G boards.

Like wall sheathing and subflooring, roof sheathing is rather straightforward and boring work to do. There are few opportunities for mistakes and since it will all be covered by the roofing material, appearance is not a concern. In some ways it is easier than wall sheathing, because you are nailing on a flat, near-horizontal surface, and the sheets do not have

to be supported while the first nails are being driven. There are also fewer openings to cut out. However, since you are working high on the roof, the materials have to be lifted up high and your pace is slower because of the increased danger.

Sheathing can become very tiring since there is a lot of repetitive nailing from a bending position. Stretch a few times each hour to relieve the pressure from your back. Knee pads are highly recommended. As with wall sheathing and subflooring, you may want to consider using a pneumatic nailer in these areas.

This stage goes quickly and easily. The view from your working position can often be restful. Though somewhat physically demanding, the mental demands are few and it may be a good time to use some of those inexperienced friends who promised to come help.

Jargon

EAVES. The part of the roof that extends beyond and over the walls of the building.

END MATCHED BOARDS. Boards with tongue and groove on their ends as well as their edges.

EXPOSED BEAM CEILING. A ceiling where the roof beams or rafters (usually 4 inches thick or more) are exposed to the living space below as a design effect.

ROOFING FELT. Asphalt impregnated paper used as a moisture barrier and added protection below the roofing.

ROOF LOAD. The weight or load on the roof from the combined weight of the sheathing, roofing materials, snow and wind.

ROOF SHEATHING. A structural covering consisting of boards or panels that are attached to the exterior surface of the rafters and on which the roofing is nailed.

SELECT DRY DECKING. Tongue and groove boards, 2×6s or 2×8s, used for roof sheathing, especially in areas where the sheathing will be exposed to the living surface below. It is select, meaning there are few knots; and dry, meaning it has a low moisture content, reducing shrinkage to a minimum.

SKIP SHEATHING OR SPACE SHEATHING. Butt-end boards, 1×4s or 1×3s, applied to the exterior surfaces of the rafters with a designated space between each board. Used for rigid roofing materials only (e.g., wood shakes, metal, tile, etc.).

SOFFIT. The underside area, where the roof projects to the outside of the walls of the building.

TONGUE AND GROOVE BOARDS. Boards that are cut in such a manner that they have a tongue or protruding section on one side and a groove or continuous indentation on the other side, and each panel locks into the one adjacent to it.

2-4-1 PLYWOOD. A 1½-inch-thick plywood that can be used for roof sheathing when the rafters are up to 48 inches on center.

UNDER LAYMENT. A layer of roofing felt below the roofing.

WEATHER EXPOSURE. The part or area of the shake or shingle that is exposed to the weather.

Purposes of the Roof Sheathing

1) Nailing surface for the roofing material
2) Adds strength and rigidity
3) Carries the roof load to the rafters

Design Decisions

Your choice of roof sheathing materials depends on a few different factors: roof loading, type of roofing, use of exposed ceilings, and spacing of the rafters. Read carefully the following section and narrow down your choices.

Factors to Consider in Selecting Sheathing Materials

ROOF LOADING: The roof load is the combined weight or load of the sheathing, roofing, snow and wind. The codes also factor in additional weight for people and materials on the roof during re-roofing. The heavier the roof load, the thicker or stronger the sheathing must be for any rafter span. In areas of high snow loads, both the thickness of the sheathing and the size of the rafters are increased. Check your local codes for the roof-load factor in your area to determine the sheathing thickness and the rafter size and spacing for your house.

TYPE OF ROOFING MATERIAL: (Photo 14-1.) Flexible or pliable roofing materials, such as asphalt shingles, rolled roofing, built-up hot tar roofing, etc., must have solid sheathing; they are too soft and pliable to span a gap. Rigid roofing materials, such as tile, wood shakes or shingles, metal, etc., can span a gap and skip sheathing (boards or slats with spacing between them) can be used. This type of sheathing is less expensive, and quicker and easier to install. In some areas, skip sheathing is required for wood shakes or shingles to provide adequate ventilation and reduce the risk of the shakes or shingles rotting.

EXPOSED BEAM CEILING: If you plan to expose your roof beams or roof framing structure to the interior of the room below, you will need a sheathing that will have at least one finished side, the side that will serve as the finished interior ceiling.

SPACING OF THE ROOF RAFTERS OR BEAMS: The greater the spacing between the roof supports, the stronger the sheathing will need to be in order to span the distances. Often, exposed beam ceilings are 4-inch-thick beams on 4- to 8-foot centers. Situations like this will demand the use of either 2-4-1 plywood or 2-inch T&G boards for roof sheathing.

In the following discussion on the different types of roof sheathing, decide which ones can be used in your specific situation, and which one of these is the best choice.

Types of Roof Sheathing

PLYWOOD SHEATHING: (Photo 14-2, Figure 14-1.) Unless wood shakes or shingles are used, plywood roof sheathing is most commonly used. It is relatively low in cost and it is quick and easy to apply. Usually an exterior glue plywood that is water resistant is used for protection during construction. Some builders even paint over exposed exterior edges, at the eaves, to prevent exposure to any wet weather. In homes where there are no exposed ceilings or rafter spacings over 48 inches, this is used.

The chart on page 327, from the 1976 Uniform Building Code, gives the regulated thickness of plywood, given the span, the use of blocking or not, and the load capacity ("total" is for both live and dead weight). Check with your local codes to see if these apply in your area. The Identification Index refers to the numbers stamped on each piece of plywood. The first number refers to the maximum rafter spacing; the second, the maximum joist spacing.

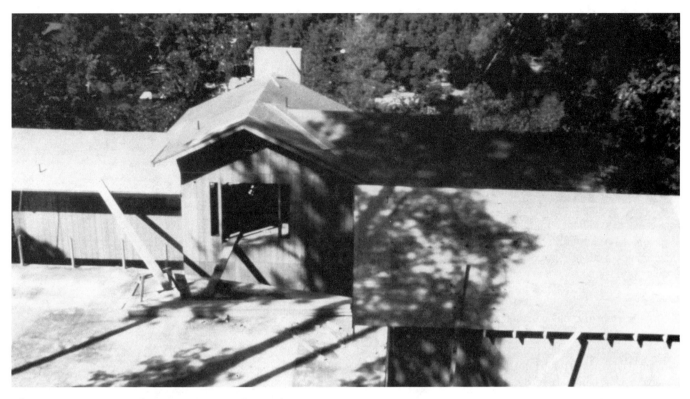

Photo 14-2. Plywood roof sheathing is most commonly used if you are not using a rigid roofing material. It is not only strong, but it is quick and easy to apply.

Photo 14-3. Individual 1-inch-thick boards are seldom used for sheathing since the introduction of the stronger plywood. (Photo courtesy of Heartwood Owner Builder School, Washington, Massachusetts.)

Photo 14-4. This is an insulated roof sheathing panel. It has a foam center with a particleboard exterior sheathing and a drywall interior siding. (Photo courtesy of Heartwood Owner Builder School, Washington, Massachusetts.)

Photo 14-5. A closeup of insulated roof sheathing.

Panel Identification Index	Plywood Thickness	Maximum Span (inches)		Load (lbs. per sq. ft.)	
		Edges Blocked	Unblocked	Live	Total
12/0	5/16	12	—	150	155
16/0	5/16, 3/8	16	—	75	95
20/0	5/16, 3/8	20	—	65	75
24/0	3/8, 1/2	24	16	50	65
30/12	5/8	30	26	50	70
32/16	1/2, 5/8	32	28	40	55
36/16	3/4	36	30	50	55
42/20	5/8, 3/4, 7/8	42	32	35	40
48/24	3/4, 7/8	48	36	35	40

Even in roofs with exposed beam ceilings, plywood can be used. 2-4-1 Plywood is a 1⅛-inch-thick plywood that can span roof beams with a 4- to 6-foot on center span (unless there are heavy snow loads or other loads). This material can be bought with one surface finished so that it looks OK from below. (I recently saw, in a student's home, where she had used a plywood siding, with a rough-sawn finished side, as roof sheathing exposed to the interior. I was pleasantly surprised by its attractive appearance, as I seldom like plywood ceilings.)

The minimum thickness plywood used for roof sheathing is $5/16$ inch. Usually, however, roof sheathing is between ⅜ inch and ¾ inch thick. The sheets are always applied perpendicular to the rafters and need to span at least 3 rafters for strength. This type of sheathing may be used with wooden shakes and shingles. In some areas the shakes or shingles are nailed directly to the plywood. In other areas, where greater ventilation is required, 1×2s are nailed to the sheathing with spaces between each slat, and the shakes or shingles are nailed to these.

2-INCH TONGUE AND GROOVE BOARDS: This type of siding is very popular in areas where there is an exposed beam ceiling. It is also used in flat or low-pitched roofs. It can span a 4- to 8-foot span, depending on the roof load, and has an appealing look when viewed from below. Selected for its few knots, it is called "Select Dry Pine Decking," as it is often of pine, and has a low moisture content to reduce shrinkage. Cedar, redwood and fir are also available. The most common size is 2×6 or 2×8, though 3×6 and 4×6 are also sometimes used. The 4×6 can span from 10 to 12 feet.

Usually this type of decking or sheathing is "V" grooved. This means that as the tongue and groove are fitted together, the edges on one surface meet at a V shape, rather than flush. This "V" groove helps hide the inevitable gaps that will form (even dry boards will eventually shrink). The groove is faced downward towards the living area, making a very attractive ceiling. Insulating is usually done by nailing rigid styrofoam sheets to the exterior side of the sheathing. Roofing is sometimes nailed through this insulation and into, but not totally penetrating, the decking. This is not always a satisfactory application, especially in high wind areas. In this case, another layer of plywood sheathing is nailed over the decking and the roofing is nailed to this. With wood shakes or shingles, slats are often nailed to the insulation to provide the proper ventilation and nailing strength.

This type of exposed beam ceiling can become expensive, for the following reasons: the high cost of the heavier roof timbers, the more expensive Select Dry Decking, the more expensive insulation (rigid insulation is more expensive than the same "R" factor in fiberglass insulation), the added labor to apply the individual boards and finally, the possible need for a second layer of sheathing. Before deciding whether it is worth the added expense or not, calculate the exact additional costs. Decisions made without complete data can be very dangerous in housebuilding.

SLATS OR SKIP SHEATHING: Skip sheathing (also called space sheathing) is used with various types of rigid roofing materials. These include wooden shakes and shingles, tile, metal roofs and slate. (Solid sheathing should be used in areas with blowing snow.) All of these materials have the rigidity to span the space left between the boards. Either 1×4s or 1×3s are nailed perpendicular to the rafters. They are spaced so that their "on center" distance equals the weather exposure of the roof shingles to be used. Common low-quality softwoods are usually used. The sheathing is quick and easy to apply. It cannot be used, however, if it is to be exposed to the view from below, in which case, you would see a not too appealing collage of slats, shingles and tar paper. In garages or utility or storage spaces you may want to consider exposing it to view.

SQUARE EDGE BOARDS: (Photo 14-3.) Before the advent of plywood, common square edge boards were used as sheathing. These are usually nominal 1×6s or 1×8s. Their end splices need to meet over a rafter and each board has to span at least 3 rafters. Boards that extend over the edges of the roof to the rake rafters have to span at least 4 rafters. End splices also need to be staggered by at least 2 rafters. Usually it is best to use stock that has a 12% moisture content or less so as to minimize gaps. These boards are slower to apply than plywood and not as strong, so I would suggest using plywood, unless you have a very inexpensive source of square edge boards.

NEW PRODUCTS: (Photos 14-4, 14-5.) There are several new products available in roof sheathing material. One type is a solid board bonded together by layers of Kraft paper. The boards come in sizes up to 2×16 feet. Another product is an insulate board that uses a composite material with some insulating properties. It usually comes in 2-×-8-foot panels, 2 inches thick, and has tongue and groove edges. Both of these products have various types of finished surfaces, and can be used as an exposed beam ceiling.

Another type of sheathing I have seen effectively used at the Heartwood Owner Builder School in Massachusetts is a thicker sheathing that has a layer of drywall for the interior facing, a pressboard for the exterior and a center core of 3 inches or so of foam insulation. The advantage of this type of sheathing is that it provides the sheathing, insulation and interior finish in one application. Check with your local suppliers for more info on these and other new types of sheathing.

Now, decide which sheathing is best for you. The rest of this chapter is in three parts: installing plywood sheathing, installing tongue and groove 2-inch decking, and installing skip or space sheathing. Proceed to the appropriate section.

Installing Plywood Sheathing

What You'll Need

TIME 4 to 8 person-hours per 320 square feet (ten 4-×-8 panels).

PEOPLE 2 Minimum (1 semi-skilled, 1 unskilled); 3 Optimum (1 semi-skilled, 2 unskilled); 6 Maximum (2 teams of 3).

TOOLS framing hammer, power saw, hand saw, metal tape, chalkline, framing square, pencil, nail belt, knee pads, ladders, combination square, safety goggles, nail-pulling tools, saw blades, extension cords, terminal plug boxes, staple gun or hammer tacker, staples.

RENTAL ITEMS: Pneumatic nailer, scaffolding, safety harness.

MATERIALS You will be using a ⅜-inch, ½-inch, ⅝-inch or ¾-inch-thick plywood. Usually an exterior glue plywood is used in cases where it may rain before it is covered. If a plywood is used that does not contain an exterior glue, be sure that you seal any edges that will be exposed so that it does not delaminate. Unless you plan to expose the interior surface, a CD grade will do. Usually a straight edge plywood is used with metal clips (discussed later), though some builders use T&G boards with no clips.

Figure 14-1. A typical stamp on a piece of plywood. "C-D" refers to the grade of veneer of the panel faces. "Interior" designates the type of plywood. "Exterior glue" refers to the type of glue used.

ESTIMATING MATERIALS NEEDED

PLYWOOD: Divide the number of square feet of roof surface by 32 square feet (4-×-8 panel), and add 15% for waste.

NAILS: Calculate the number of pounds per square feet needed and multiply times the number of square feet to be covered.

TAR PAPER: Enough to cover the surface of the roof in square feet.

INFORMATION For the most part, this section will give you all the information needed to apply typical plywood roof sheathing.

PEOPLE TO CONTACT Contact your roofer (if you are using one) and your roofing supplier to let them know you will be needing them soon. Contact a sheet metal person if you are using one to provide any flashing on the roof. Check with the plumber to be sure all the proper plumbing vents are through the roof before you begin the application of roofing materials (the sheathing can be placed before).

INSPECTIONS NEEDED Before the roof sheathing is covered with roofing paper, the inspector may want to inspect the sheathing for proper nailing. Check your local codes.

Reading the Plans

Usually the plans will indicate the type and thickness of the roof sheathing to be used. Plans should also show details of any special situations, such as slats nailed to plywood sheathing or 2-×-6 decking. You may want to reconsider any decisions made by the designer; be sure you agree with their choice of materials and thicknesses.

Safety and Awareness

SAFETY: Be very cautious when working on the roof; it is very dangerous. A fall from the roof, especially through the rafters, can cause severe injury. Workman's compensation insurance is almost 50% higher for roofers than for carpenters; this gives you a sense of the dangers involved in working up high. Do not lift panels to the wind—they will act as a sail.

AWARENESS: Keep the panels perpendicular to the rafters, stagger the joints, and be sure you do adequate nailing.

Overview of the Procedure

Step 1: Temporarily nail on the first (eave) course
Step 2: Check and permanently nail on the first course
Step 3: Nail on the remaining courses
Step 4: Do sheathing at ridges, hips and valleys
Step 5: Apply the tar paper

Step 1
Temporarily Nail on the First (Eave) Course

Margin of Error: Perpendicular to rafter—*exact.*

Most Common Mistakes: Falling off the roof; aligning course with edge of roof rather than perpendicular to rafters; plywood wrong side up; nailing intermediate rafter that becomes the next course's edge rafter.

Diagram: Figure 14-2.

Begin applying the sheets from the eaves (bottom) of the roof and work your way up to the peak. The last course at the peak may need to be ripped if the roof length is not in 4-foot intervals. If the overhangs are going to be exposed to view from below, with no soffit, you may want to consider using plywood with a finished surface and exterior glue where it will be exposed at the eaves and overhangs.

The main thing to watch for here is to see that the eave line is indeed exactly perpendicular to the rafters. Often it is best to only temporarily nail this course, until you have checked it out. If the eave line is not exactly perpendicular to the rafters, be sure to adjust the edges of the plywood until they are. It is more important that the edges be perpendicular than that they be flush with the edge of the roof at the eaves. A tapered piece can be cut to fill in if needed.

Check the rafter ends (or tails) also, to be sure they are all on a straight line. Often they are not. You may need to pop a straight line and recut them, as explained in Chapter 13, *Roof Framing,* "Step 7." If there will be no soffit to hide any discrepancy, it is important that these rafters be cut straight before the sheathing is applied.

Don't forget to leave some overhang at the eaves if a fascia board is to be added on later, unless your plans call to cover the edge of the plywood with the fascia. Face the better surface of the plywood towards the sky. In areas where rain is a threat during construction, you may want to leave expansion gaps of ⅛ inch at the edges, ¹⁄₁₆ inch at the ends. Some builders double these spaces in very wet or humid areas. You will occasionally have to cut a panel in order to make up for these gaps as you go along.

Step 2
Check and Permanently Nail on the First Course

Margin of Error: Same as for "Step 1."

Most Common Mistake: Same as for "Step 1."

After the first course is up and temporarily nailed, check it out to be sure that the sheets are running perpendicular to

Figure 14-2. Note that a tapered piece has been used at the eaves. This is done to keep the inside edge of the plywood on the center of the rafter.

Figure 14-3. Use half sheets of plywood for alternating courses to be sure that joints are not aligned.

the rafters and their ends are falling on the centers. Make any needed adjustments. Once they are in line, nail them, using 8d CC Sinkers or annular groove nails, 6 inches along the edges and 12 inches in the intermediate rafters. As you nail, do not nail the field rafter that will become the next course's end rafter (see Chapter 10, *Subflooring*, "Step 3" for further explanation). This allows you to move the rafter around a little if you need to. As in subflooring and wall sheathing, pop chalklines across the sheets to locate the centers of the rafters as you nail.

Step 3
Nail on the Remaining Courses

Margin of Error: Nail end of panel within ¼ inch of the center of the rafter.

Most Common Mistakes: Falling off roof; no gaps.

Diagrams: Figures 14-3, 14-4.

After the first course is properly set, you can begin nailing the remaining courses. They are applied as the first one, with a few things to remember. First, stagger your joints. You can do this by cutting panels in half and using a half sheet to start every other course. Then, remember to leave the gaps as you go along, if they are needed. Some areas require the use of metal plywood clips to support the panels along their edges between the rafters. You can avoid this either by using a

Figure 14-4. Metal plywood clips.

⅛-inch-thicker plywood than required, by using tongue and groove panels, or by blocking under the panel, i.e., nailing blocks between the rafters. Continue to work your way carefully up the roof, checking for alignment and end support as you go.

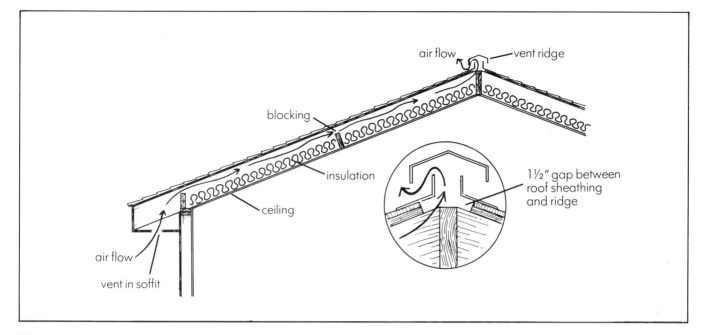

Figure 14-5. Example of how to allow ventilation through the roof panel. Note how smaller-sized blocking allows the air to pass from the soffit to the ridge.

Step 4
Do Sheathing at Ridges, Hips and Valleys

Margin of Error: ¼ inch.

Most Common Mistake: Falling off the roof.

Diagram: Figure 14-5.

Photograph: Photo 14-6.

Where the panels meet at the hips, ridges and valleys, no special beveled or angled cuts are needed, unless the sheathing will be exposed from underneath. Otherwise the sheathing needs to be nailed down flat and tight and the sheets should touch, but no special treatment is needed.

If you are using a ridge vent to ventilate the roof panel, leave a 1½-inch gap on both sides at the ridge to allow a continuous flow of air.

Step 5
Apply the Tar Paper

In order to make the house weather tight as well as protect the sheathing from the weather and possible expansion and buckling, it is advisable to apply the tar paper (roofing felt) as soon as possible after the sheathing is on. The roofing felt, also called underlayment, provides additional weather protection for the roof, and places a barrier between the shingles and the wood.

Usually the material used is a 15-pound (15 pounds per 100 square feet) roofing felt. This is a breathable material. You do not want to use a non-breathing material, which will act as a vapor barrier and trap moisture below—it can possibly rot the sheathing. Follow instructions for felting in accordance with the type of roofing to be used.

Many builders and roofers apply a metal drip edge if they are using asphalt shingles. These are applied both at the eaves and along the slope. Drip edges are usually ready-made and are of 26 gauge galvanized steel with a top flange of 3 to 4 inches. At the eaves, the paper is placed *over* the drip edge; at the edge of the slope, the paper is placed *under* the drip edge.

Photo 14-6. A plywood roof sheathing being applied. Note how all the joints are staggered.

Installing Tongue and Groove 2-Inch Decking

What You'll Need

TIME   15 to 25 person-hours per 500 square feet.

PEOPLE   2 Minimum (1 skilled, 1 unskilled); 3 Optimum (1 skilled, 2 unskilled); 6 Maximum (2 teams of 3 working on 2 sections of the roof).

TOOLS   Framing hammer, framing square, combination square, power saw, hand saw, metal tape, pencil, nail belt, knee pads, ladders, safety goggles, sledge, nail-pulling tools, saw blades, extension cords, terminal plug boxes, staple gun or hammer tacker, staples.

RENTAL ITEMS: Scaffolding, ladders, safety harness.

MATERIALS   Usually this sheathing is called select dry decking (Figure 14-6). It's done with fir or pine or the more expensive redwood or cedar. Use the type of wood that is "V" grooved on one surface, or all your gaps will be highlighted. Be sure that the material is dry, or it will shrink. Since in most applications, it will also serve as the interior ceiling, it is important that the material look good on the "V" groove side, showing no discoloration, yard marks or scratches. Usually 2×6s or 2×8s are used (occasionally thicker stock is used). I recommend the 2×8s; the boards are likely to be straighter and therefore easier to apply than

2×6s. Do not use anything wider than 8 inches; it will tend to cup.

When you order, take into account a waste factor of 10 to 15%. As you estimate the materials, remember the boards are 5½ inches, not 6 inches, wide. Order the longest stock possible. Check the stock for quality while it is in the yard or on the delivery truck, *before* they dump it on your site.

ESTIMATING MATERIALS NEEDED

DECKING: Each board foot will cover one square foot. Add 15% for waste.

NAILS: Estimate the number of pounds per square foot.

TAR PAPER: Estimate the number of feet that will cover the roof surface.

INFORMATION   This chapter should give you everything you need in the way of information to apply this type of sheathing.

PEOPLE TO CONTACT   Contact your roofer (if you are using one) and the roofing supplier to let them know you will be needing them soon. Contact a sheet metal worker if you are using one to provide any flashing for your roof.

You may also need to call your plumber back (unless you are doing your own plumbing). All plumbing vents, as well as electrical weatherheads, must be run through the roof before the roofing is applied.

INSPECTIONS NEEDED Before you cover the roof decking with tar paper, the inspector may need to inspect the nailing pattern of your sheathing. Check your local codes.

Reading the Plans

The plans will simply state that you are using tongue and groove decking. Actually, there is little else you need to know before you install it. You may want to change the overhang areas, as mentioned in "Step 2," if you are going to enclose these with soffits.

Safety and Awareness

SAFETY: Be very cautious in doing any work on the roof; it is very dangerous. A fall from the roof, especially through the rafters, can cause severe injury. Workman's compensation insurance is almost 50% higher for roofers than it is for carpenters, which should give you a sense of the dangers involved in working up high.

AWARENESS: Because the decking will be your finished ceiling, inspect the boards well before you apply them. Be care-

Figure 14-6. Tongue and groove dry decking.

Figure 14-7. Checking rafters with a framing square to be sure they are perpendicular to the wall.

ful of dings and dirt. Do not step on them before they are applied; a footprint on the ceiling looks rather strange. Be sure the boards are running in a good straight line—parallel with the walls. Hopefully this will make them exactly perpendicular to the rafters as well.

Overview of the Procedure

Step 1: Check rafter alignment
Step 2: Apply the first course
Step 3: Apply the remaining courses
Step 4: Make cut for the ridge
Step 5: Apply the tar paper

Step 1
Check Rafter Alignment

Margin of Error: Rafters ¼ inch off proper alignment.

Most Common Mistake: Allowing too great a margin of error.

Diagram: Figure 14-7.

Before beginning your application, check the rafters. Walk around the building to see if they are all running parallel to each other. Very often one was installed on the wrong side of the layout mark. Check to see if the rafters are running at true right angles to the walls they are resting on. If they are not, either they were installed improperly or the walls are not running parallel to each other. Try to determine what has gone wrong. If it is not easy to correct or if the discrepancy is not too great, you can let it go and learn to live with it. Chances are you will never notice it unless you are lying on the living room carpet, staring up at the ceiling.

If the rafters are not running perpendicular to the walls they are resting on, and you install the decking boards perpendicular to the rafters, the decking will not be running parallel to the walls. I think it is more important that the decking runs true parallel to the walls than it is for the decking to run true perpendicular to the rafters. The mistake will be less noticeable.

Check to be sure the rafter ends at the overhang are all on a straight line. Often they are not. You may need to pop a straight line and recut them, as explained in Chapter 13, *Roof Framing*, "Step 7." If there will be no soffit to hide any discrepancy, it is important that these rafters be cut straight before the sheathing is applied.

If the rafter ends are running in a straight line and this line is parallel to the wall the rafters are resting on, you can apply the first course of deck boards, which will be aligned with the edge of the rafters. If this is not the case, you will have to pop a line on the top of the rafters to mark where the first course will go.

If you plan to enclose the overhang areas with a soffit, you do not need to use the expensive T&G in these areas of the roof. Since this area will not be seen from below, you can use the less expensive plywood sheathing. The top of the plywood will have to be shimmed to make it flush with the top of the thicker decking.

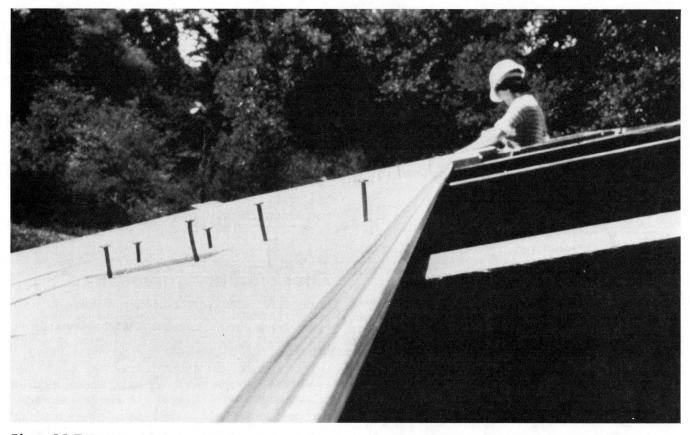

Photo 14-7. Do not nail the butt end of 2 boards down where they meet over a rafter until the course above it is installed.

Step 2
Apply the First Course

Margin of Error: ¼ inch off proper alignment.

Most Common Mistakes: Course not running parallel with wall; installing boards upside down with "V" groove facing the sky (see "Types of Roof Sheathing: 2-Inch Tongue and Groove Boards" in the beginning of this chapter); not pointing the tongue downroof.

Photograph: Photo 14-7.

You are now ready to apply the first course. Choose good straight pieces for this course because all the other courses will be laid against this one. The rafters should be marked where the course will be laid (unless you are using the ends of the rafters as marks). Place the boards on the rafters with their "V" grooves facing down, not up. See that the tongues are facing downhill of the slope, and the grooves are facing uphill of the slope; you will be banging against the uphill sides of the boards and it is better to be banging against the grooves, which are not so easily damaged, than the tongues.

Nail the first course on with 16d nails, 2 at every rafter. Apply pressure, where needed, to bring the board in a straight line. You may not want to nail in the uphill nail at each rafter until after the next course is installed. Nailing it here can bring the decking so tight against the rafter that it will be difficult to bring the tongue of the next course into the groove. You may not want to nail in any of the nails at the

ends of the boards where the 2 pieces of stock come together. This allows you to move these ends, making sure their grooves line up, so the tongue of the next course can be easily inserted.

Usually the T&G is cut flush with the outside edge of the rake or overhang rafters. Then a trim or fascia board is applied to cover this raw, exposed edge. Before you apply your sheathing, be sure you understand how you plan to finish out the edges of the roof. If you do not know, leave some overhang that can be cut later, when you decide.

Step 3
Apply the Remaining Courses

Margin of Error: ¼ inch off alignment; ⅛ inch crack between boards.

Most Common Mistakes: Boards not fitted tightly enough; boards upside down; dirt or dings on underneath (exposed) side.

Photographs: Photos 14-8, 14-9.

Continue applying each course up to the top of the roof. As with the first course, avoid nailing the upper edges or ends until the adjacent course has been installed. Every now and then go below to see if you are looking good—the boards are still running parallel to the wall.

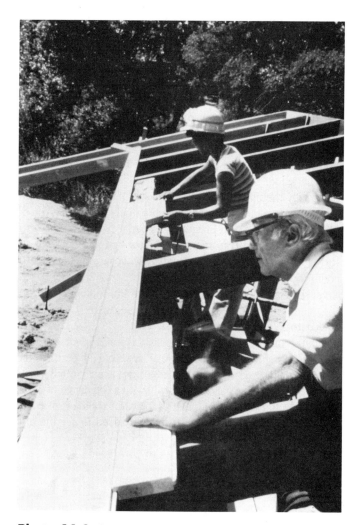

Photo 14-8. Be sure to use a "beater block" so as not to damage the tongue or groove of the decking during installation.

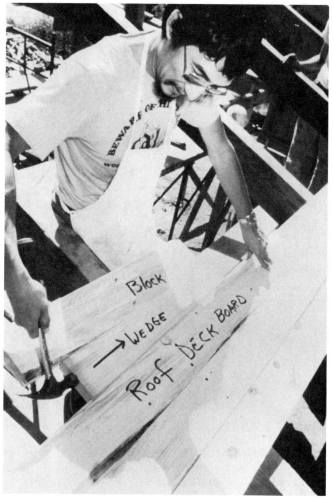

Photo 14-9. Using a temporarily nailed block and a wedge to force a bowed roof deck board tight against the lower one.

One of the hardest things about applying this type of sheathing is getting the pieces to fit tightly along the edges. Because almost all boards have a bow, if the pieces are not fit tightly together, you will see the cracks from below. Usually a sledge is used to pound these boards into place. A scrap piece of T&G is used so you will not be hitting against the groove of the piece you are installing. This works to some degree, but bowed boards still keep popping out after they are knocked home with the sledge.

One of our teachers taught me a great way to bring the boards together. Temporarily nail a block of wood to the rafter 2 to 3 inches above the unnailed board. Insert a precut wedge block between the T&G stock and the block you just nailed. Using your framing hammer (or sledge for difficult pieces), tap the wedge until it pushes the unnailed piece of decking tightly to the lower nailed piece. It works, even for badly bowed pieces.

In most cases, with an exposed beam ceiling, the rafter or beams will have no blocking between them. Because of this, any warps or twists will prevent them from running straight and parallel to each other. If you do not straighten them, if you nail the decking on and trap them crooked, it will be very noticeable from below. As you apply the decking, you may want to straighten the rafters and nail a temporary brace to the rafters to hold them straight until the decking is applied.

Step 4
Make Cut for the Ridge

Margin of Error: ⅛-inch gap between ridge pieces.

Most Common Mistake: Too great a gap.

Photograph: Photo 14-10.

At the ridge, you may need to make a special cut on the decking so that the ridge pieces fit together well. If there is a large ridge beam and the interior decking will not be exposed from below at the ridge, this will not be needed. But if the decking at the ridge is visible, you will want it to fit tightly together. To do this, you will need to bevel cut the upper edge of the last course of stock on both sides. If there are metal ridge straps running from rafter to rafter on the top edge (as in earthquake areas), you will have to drill through these metal straps to nail on the last few courses of decking.

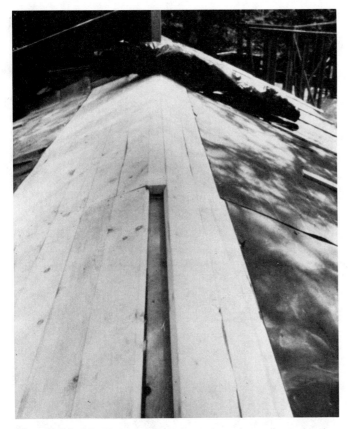

Photo 14-10. The final boards at the ridge will need to be beveled.

Step 5
Apply the Tar Paper

In order to make the house weather tight as well as protect the sheathing from the weather and possible expansion and buckling, it is advisable to apply the tar paper (roofing felt) as soon as possible after the sheathing is on. The roofing felt, also called underlayment, provides additional weather protection for the roof, and places a barrier between the shingles and the wood.

Usually the material used is a 15-pound (15 pounds per 100 square feet) roofing felt. This is a breathable material. You do not want to use a non-breathing material, which will act as a vapor barrier and trap moisture below—it can possibly rot the sheathing. Apply the tar paper according to the type of roofing you are using. Secure the paper well with staples to be sure that it does not blow off before the roofing is applied. Top sheets should overlap the sheets below by 4 to 6 inches to create a shingle effect.

Many builders and roofers apply a metal drip edge if they are using asphalt shingles. These are applied both at the eaves and along the slope. Drip edges are usually ready-made and are of 26 gauge galvanized steel with a top flange of 3 to 4 inches. At the eaves, the paper is placed *over* the drip edge; at the edge of the slope, the paper is placed *under* the drip edge.

Installing Skip (Slat) Sheathing
What You'll Need

TIME   16 to 25 person-hours per 1500 square feet of roof area.

PEOPLE   1 Minimum (skilled); 2 Optimum (1 skilled, 1 unskilled); 4 Maximum (2 teams of 2).

TOOLS   Framing hammer, combination square, power saw, saw blades, hand saw, metal tape, pencil, nail belt, ladders, safety goggles, nail-pulling tools, extension cords, terminal plug boxes.

RENTAL ITEMS: Scaffolding, ladders, safety harness.

MATERIALS   Usually the least expensive grade of 1×4 is used. If you have access to used 1-inch material, this may be a good place to use it, even if it is wider than 4 inches and has to be ripped down. Try to buy pieces that are as long as possible (14 feet, 16 feet, 18 feet) so less cutting is required.

ESTIMATING MATERIALS NEEDED

In order to estimate the materials needed, you will have to know the weather exposure of your roofing shingles (see "Step 3"). Knowing this, you can then figure your on center distance of the slats, and from that you can calculate the number of courses you will need and the amount of material you will need.

INFORMATION   You may want to check with your roofing supplier as to the on center distance between slats they recommend. Otherwise this chapter tells you all you need to know.

PEOPLE TO CONTACT   Contact your roofer, if you are using one, and the roofing supplier to let them know you will be needing them soon. Contact a sheet metal worker, if you are using one to apply the flashing on your roof and the solar panel installer, if you're using solar panels.

Unless you are doing your own plumbing, call the plumber. All plumbing vents, as well as electrical weatherheads, must run through the roof before the roofing is applied.

INSPECTIONS NEEDED   None.

Reading the Plans

Most plans should simply indicate the use of slat or skip sheathing. If your plans call for wood shakes or shingles, you will probably be using skip sheathing (in some cases solid sheathing can be used).

If skip sheathing is being used on top of plywood or 2-inch T&G sheathing, the plans may even show it in detail. Many builders add skip sheathing on top of solid sheathing when using wood roofs (shakes or shingles), to ensure greater ventilation and thereby reduce the possibility of rot.

If you are using other types of rigid roofing, e.g., tile, metal, etc., you will probably be using skip sheathing; it is cheaper and easier to apply.

Safety and Awareness

SAFETY: This is a very dangerous procedure. As with all roof work, the height is a dangerous element, but unlike the solid types of sheathing, with skip sheathing you can step between the slats or step on the slat between the rafters and break through. *Always step directly on top of the rafters, or very close to one. Never step on a slat between the rafters.* Be careful also while cutting on the roof. Be sure both you and the board you are cutting are stable before proceeding.

AWARENESS: Be sure the slats stay at the proper spacing, by checking with a tape every 8 to 10 courses. Other than that, there is little to watch for.

Overview of the Procedure

Step 1: Check rafter alignment
Step 2: Apply the first course
Step 3: Apply the remaining courses
Step 4: Apply the ridge course

Step 1
Check Rafter Alignment

Margin of Error: Rafter ¼ inch off proper alignment.

Most Common Mistake: Allowing too great a margin of error.

Before beginning your application, check the rafters. Walk around the building to see if they are all running parallel. Very often they are installed on the wrong side of the layout mark. Check to see if they are running perpendicular to the walls they are resting on.

Applying skip sheathing is not an exacting procedure. The sheathing will not be exposed to the inside (as in the case of T&G) and the slats can be cut to any length; therefore, the locations of the rafter centers are not as vital as with the plywood sheathing. There is one situation to watch for, though. If you are planning to apply sheetrock panels or other fixed-length ceiling panels directly to the bottom side of the rafters, it is important that there be a rafter at all the right places to receive the splice in the ceiling panels. If this is the case for you, check this out with your tape as you apply the slats, and move the rafters around as needed. At times this may involve knocking out blocking in the rafter system and replacing it with different size blocking.

Unless the above situation applies, fix any major discrepancies, but otherwise don't worry too much about rafter alignment.

Step 2
Apply the First Course

Margin of Error: ¼ to ½ inch off proper placement.

Most Common Mistake: Falling off the roof.

Diagram: Figure 14-8.

Photograph: Photo 14-11.

After you have checked the rafter placement, you can begin to apply the skip sheathing. If you do not plan to use a soffit, which would enclose the underside area of the rafters where they hang over beyond the walls, you will want to deal with the overhang areas in a way that you will not look up and see the slats. That can be done by using solid slats or an attractive ¾-inch plywood (the same thickness as the slats) such as plywood siding. If a soffit is planned, it will hide these areas from view, so just your common slats can be used.

Apply the first course of slats so that the outside edge is flush with the outside edge of the band rafter. At the end of the roof, apply the outside end of the slat flush with the outside edge of the rake rafter. If you are using no soffit and using solid sheathing at the eaves and overhangs, apply the solid sheathing in the same manner. Be sure that all splices between slats occur in the center of a rafter.

Use two 8d nails where the slats cross each rafter. Avoid placing any cracks or large knotholes between the rafter spans. This creates weak spots.

Usually I bring a power saw up on the roof with me and make the few cuts I need up there. You can allow the slats to hang over the edges of the roof and then cut them all at once when you are finished applying the slats.

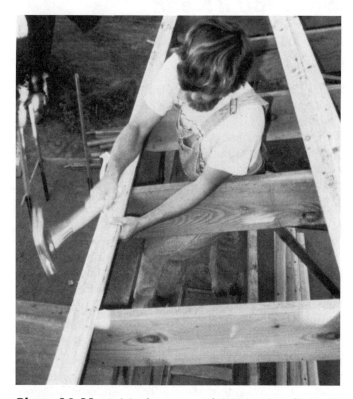

Photo 14-11. Nail the first course of skip sheathing flush with the edge of the band rafter. Be sure it is applied in a straight line.

skip sheathing

solid sheathing

solid sheathing

Figure 14-8. Solid sheathing is being used on the eaves where it will be exposed from below.

Photo 14-12. After every few rows of skip sheathing, check your courses to be sure you are still on line.

Photo 14-13. Applying skip sheathing. The board in the middle is a spacer board and will be removed.

Photo 14-14. Skip sheathing as it is being applied to the roof. Note how the builder is stepping close to a rafter.

Step 3
Apply the Remaining Courses

Margin of Error: ¼ to ½ inch off alignment.

Most Common Mistakes: Getting off line; falling off the roof; sticking your foot through a weak spot.

Photographs: Photos 14-12, 14-13, 14-14.

Using the on center distances for the slats in relation to the weather exposure of the roofing, continue applying the remaining courses on the roof. If, for example, you are using a wood shake roof with a 10-inch weather exposure, the on center distance between slats would be 10 inches. The gap between two 3½-inch-wide boards would be 6½ inches. In some wood shingle applications, where there is a small weather exposure (3 to 5 inches), this formula does not apply. In this case the on center distance of the slats would make the slats butt together, thereby forming a solid sheathed roof with no ventilation for the shingles. Consult the suppliers in your area if you are using a wood shingle roof with a small weather exposure. If you are using a metal roof, consult the manufacturer's instructions on how to space.

Every 8 to 10 courses, take your tape out and measure from the bottom of the roofline to see if you are running true.

If not, make whatever adjustments are needed in the courses you have yet to apply. You do not need to tear up the courses you have nailed to correct discrepancies; exactness is just not that important.

Step 4
Apply the Ridge Course

Margin of Error: ¼ to ½ inch.

Most Common Mistake: None.

Photograph: Photo 14-15.

Be sure that there is a course at the top of the ridge. This course will be needed to provide a nailing surface for the last course of shakes or shingles that are to be applied to the roof. If you are using a ridge vent to ventilate the roof panel, leave a 1½-inch gap at the ridge, on both sides, to allow a continuous flow of air.

You may or may not have to apply an underlayment layer of tar paper. Wood shingles use no tar paper (roofing felt) at all. Wood shakes use shake paper applied in a very definite manner (see Chapter 15, *Roofing,* "Wood Shakes," Step 1, p. 355). Other rigid roofings may or may not use a tar paper underlayment; ask your supplier.

Photo 14-15. Skip sheathing completed on the roof.

Worksheet
Plywood Sheathing

ESTIMATED TIME

_____

_____

_____

_____

CREW

Skilled or Semi-Skilled

_____ Phone _____

_____ Phone _____

_____ Phone _____

Unskilled

_____ Phone _____

_____ Phone _____

_____ Phone _____

_____ Phone _____

_____ Phone _____

MATERIALS NEEDED

Plywood, nails, sealing glue, tar paper, staples, metal clips.

ESTIMATING MATERIALS

PLYWOOD

No. of sq. ft. of roof surface _____

divided by 32 sq. ft. (4-×-8 panel) + 15% waste =

_____ sheets

TAR PAPER

_____ sq. ft. roof surface = _____ rolls.

NAILS:

_____ lbs. cover _____ sq. ft.

Total no. of lbs. needed _____.

COST COMPARISON

_____ Store:

Cost per sheet _____ total $ _____

_____ Store:

Cost per sheet _____ total $ _____

_____ Store:

Cost per sheet _____ total $ _____

_____ Store:

Cost per sheet _____ total $ _____

PEOPLE TO CONTACT

Roofer _____

Phone _____ Work Date _____

Roofing materials supplier _____

Phone _____ Work Date _____

Sheet metal person _____

Phone _____ Work Date _____

Plumber _____

Phone _____ Work Date _____

Solar panel installer _____

Phone _____ Work Date _____

Daily Checklist

CREW:

_____ Phone _____

_____ Phone_____

_____ Phone _____

_____ Phone_____

_____ Phone_____

_____ Phone _____

TOOLS:

☐ framing hammer

☐ power saw

☐ hand saw

☐ metal tape

☐ chalkline

☐ framing square

☐ pencil

☐ nail belt

☐ knee pads

☐ ladders

☐ combination square

☐ safety goggles

☐ nail-pulling tools

☐ saw blades

☐ extension cords

☐ terminal plug boxes

☐ staple gun/hammer tacker

☐ staples

RENTAL ITEMS:

☐ pneumatic nailer

☐ ladders

☐ scaffolding

☐ safety harness

MATERIALS:

_____ sheets of PLYWOOD

_____ lbs. of NAILS

_____ rolls of TAR PAPER

_____ SEALING GLUE

_____ boxes of STAPLES

DESIGN REVIEW: Re-evaluate any skylight locations.

INSPECTIONS NEEDED:

☐ YES   ☐ NO

Inspector _____ Phone _

Time of inspection _____

WEATHER FORECAST:

For week _____

For day _____

If heavy rain is expected, try to cover the plywood sheathing after each day's work. Do not apply sheathing on windy days.

Worksheet
Tongue and Groove
2-inch Decking

ESTIMATED TIME

_____

_____

_____

_____

CREW

Skilled or Semi-Skilled

_____ Phone _____

_____ Phone _____

_____ Phone _____

Unskilled

_____ Phone _____

_____ Phone _____

_____ Phone _____

_____ Phone _____

MATERIALS NEEDED

T&G stock, tar paper, nails, staples.

ESTIMATING MATERIALS

DECKING:

_____ sq. ft. of roof surface + 15% waste = _____

NAILS:

16d CC Sinkers _____ lbs. per _____ sq. ft.

TAR PAPER:

_____ sq. ft. roof surface = _____ rolls.

COST COMPARISON

_____ Store:

Cost per bd. ft. _____ total $ _____

_____ Store:

Cost per bd. ft. _____ total $ _____

_____ Store:

Cost per bd. ft. _____ total $ _____

_____ Store:

Cost per bd. ft. _____ total $ _____

PEOPLE TO CONTACT

Roofer _____

Phone _____ Work Date _____

Roofing materials supplier

Phone _____ Work Date _____

Sheet metal person _____

Phone _____ Work Date _____

Plumber _____

Phone _____ Work Date _____

Solar panel installer _____

Phone _____ Work Date _____

Daily Checklist

CREW:

_____ Phone _____

_____ Phone _____

_____ Phone _____

_____ Phone _____

_____ Phone _____

_____ Phone _____

TOOLS:

- ☐ framing hammer
- ☐ framing square
- ☐ combination square
- ☐ power saw
- ☐ hand saw
- ☐ metal tape
- ☐ nail belt
- ☐ knee pads
- ☐ ladders
- ☐ safety goggles
- ☐ sledge
- ☐ nail-pulling tools
- ☐ saw blades
- ☐ extension cords
- ☐ terminal plug boxes
- ☐ staple gun/hammer tacker
- ☐ staples

RENTAL ITEMS:

- ☐ scaffolding
- ☐ ladders
- ☐ safety harness

MATERIALS:

_____ linear feet of T&G STOCK

_____ lbs. 16D CC SINKERS

_____ rolls of TAR PAPER

_____ boxes of STAPLES

DESIGN REVIEW: You may want to re-evaluate any skylight locations.

INSPECTIONS NEEDED:

☐ YES   ☐ NO

Inspector _____ Phone _____

Time of inspection _____

WEATHER FORECAST:

For week _____

For day _____

Beware of rain before decking is covered with tar paper. If the decking is applied and then gets wet, it will strain and buckle due to expansion. Do not apply on windy days.

Worksheet
Skip Slat Sheathing

ESTIMATED TIME

_____

_____

_____

_____

CREW

Skilled or Semi-Skilled

_____ Phone _____

_____ Phone _____

_____ Phone _____

Unskilled

_____ Phone _____

_____ Phone _____

_____ Phone _____

_____ Phone _____

_____ Phone _____

MATERIALS NEEDED

1×4s and nails.

ESTIMATING MATERIALS

SLATS:

_____ No. of courses _____ ft. long (for each course)

= _____ total linear feet + 20% waste.

NAILS:

_____ lbs. of 8d CC Sinkers.

COST COMPARISON

_____ Store:

Cost per bd. ft. _____ total $ _____

_____ Store:

Cost per bd. ft. _____ total $ _____

_____ Store:

Cost per bd. ft. _____ total $ _____

_____ Store:

Cost per bd. ft. _____ total $ _____

PEOPLE TO CONTACT

Roofer _____

Phone _____ Work Date _____

Roofing materials supplier _____

Phone _____ Work Date _____

Sheet metal person _____

Phone _____ Work Date _____

Plumber _____

Phone _____ Work Date _____

Solar panel installer _____

Phone _____ Work Date _____

Daily Checklist

CREW:

_____ Phone _____

_____ Phone _____

_____ Phone _____

_____ Phone _____

_____ Phone _____

_____ Phone _____

TOOLS:

☐ framing hammer

☐ combination square

☐ power saw

☐ saw blades

☐ hand saw

☐ metal tape

☐ pencil

☐ nail belt

☐ ladders

☐ safety goggles

☐ nail-pulling tools

☐ extension cords

☐ terminal plug boxes

RENTAL ITEMS:

☐ scaffolding

☐ ladders

☐ safety harness

MATERIALS:

_____ linear feet 1×4S

_____ lbs. 8D CC SINKERS

DESIGN REVIEW: You may want to re-evaluate any skylight locations.

WEATHER FORECAST:

For week _____

For day _____

Roofing

Photo 15-1. Roofing material has been delivered to the top of the roof and is stacked near the ridge.

What You'll Be Doing, What to Expect

APPLYING YOUR ROOFING (Photo 15-1) consists of installing a waterproof covering over your roof sheathing to protect the house from the weather. This covering is not only the roofing material itself but can also involve underlayment (roofing felt); flashing; ridge caps; vents; or flashing for plumbing vents, wood stoves and skylights.

There is a lot to consider before you choose any one type of roofing. Your choice will affect not only the appearance of your house, but your pocketbook and work schedule as well. In this chapter the different types of roofing and their advantages and disadvantages will be discussed in detail. We will also describe, in detail, how to apply two of the most common types of roofing: wood shakes and asphalt shingles. Each will be presented in separate sections.

For the most part, roofing is a rather simple procedure. There are a few key areas that are a little tricky; it is important that you understand how to roof these areas properly or you will have leaks. These areas include: valleys, hips, ridges, vent pipes, skylights and vertical walls intersecting

sloping roofs. Other than these areas, roofing is straightforward and simple. Laying shakes or shingles on the broad uninterrupted areas of the roof is simple, and monotonous, and can cause back strain from all the bending. Being up off the ground with a good view, on the other hand, can often get you into a rhythmic, almost meditative, flow of installing the shakes or shingles; the work becomes enjoyable and almost effortless.

More than in almost any other area of housebuilding, you want to constantly strive for an efficient system in roofing that allows you to install the greatest number of roofing materials with the least amount of effort in the least amount of time. Go watch a few professionals at work. Note the way they sit, where the materials are in relation to where they are working, what their assistants do, what tools they have and what tricks they use. Often observing a professional for half an hour can save you many hours on your own roof. Speed and efficiency of energy use are essential here.

Be sure in whatever you do with the roofing: you do not want a leak! A leak can turn a cozy, rainy evening into a nightmare, and have you kicking your behind from here to Toledo for not doing it right the first time.

Jargon

BUNDLE. Term used for wood shakes or shingles, describing a stack of material banded together. Usually there are 4 or 5 bundles in a square.

BUTT END. The bottom end (lower end) of the shake or shingle.

EAVES. The lower edges of the roof.

FLASHING. A metal or composition material used on a roof around skylights, chimneys, vents, intersecting vertical walls, etc., or on a wall above doors and windows. The flashing is placed in such a way that it will shed rain water.

GABLE ROOF. A roof sloping on 2 sides, named for the triangular wall section, the gable, created by the slopes of each end wall.

HIP. The external roof angle formed by 2 inclined sides of a roof.

PLY. Layer.

PREFELT. To apply the roofing felt before the roofing material goes on.

RAKES. Sloping edges of roof that frame the gable.

RIDGE. The horizontal line at the top of the roof formed by the intersection of sloping roof surfaces.

RISE. The vertical distance covered by a rafter or roof.

RUN. The horizontal distance covered by a rafter or roof.

SLOPE. The angle of the roof.

SQUARE. Materials needed to cover 100 square feet of roofing.

STARTER COURSE. A layer of shingles that is installed directly below the first course on the roof, at the eaves.

VALLEY. The internal roof angle formed by 2 inclined sides of a roof.

WEATHER EXPOSURE. The section of any roofing material, shake or shingle, that is exposed to the weather (outside).

Purpose of the Roofing

To provide a weather tight covering over the house (as if you didn't know), protecting it from rain, wind, ice, snow, dust and sunlight.

Design Decisions

Selecting your roofing material is a rather important decision, involving a large amount of money, a lot of application time and a heavy impact on the looks of the home. You can better grasp the scope of the decision when you realize that during the life span of a normal roof, it will withstand 1,000,000 gallons of water weighing 5,000 tons; 50,000 hours of direct sunlight; 2 million miles of wind and ½ million degrees of temperature changes. Your choice affects other parts of the construction process also, e.g., a tile roof will need heavier rafters and sheathing material to hold the weight of the tiles. Read the following section and consider your choice well.

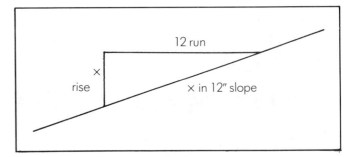

Figure 15-1. Roof slope represented in a triangle.

Factors to Consider in Selecting a Roofing Material

SLOPE: (Figure 15-1.) The slope of the roof refers to the angle or pitch of the roof. It is always written in relationship with the number of inches a roof rises over 12 inches (1 foot) of horizontal run. Therefore, a roof with a 4 in 12 slope rises 4 inches for each 12 inches of horizontal run. Your plans will indicate the roof slope by using a triangular symbol; 12 will be on the horizontal bottom side of the triangle with a variable number on the vertical side of the triangle representing the rise over 12 inches of run in number of inches.

The greater the slope, the steeper the roof. The steeper the roof, the easier it will be for water to run off the roof and, therefore, the less likely it will be to leak. Some roofing materials must have at least a minimum slope angle in order for them to work effectively. If the roof has too shallow a slope, rain can be blown under the roofing and it will leak. Other roofing materials (wood shakes and shingles, for instance) will vary in their weather exposure for different slopes, i.e., the amount of exposure used depends on the length of the shake or shingle and the angle of the slope. The following chart shows the minimum slope you can have for the various roofing materials.

ROOFING MATERIAL	MINIMUM ALLOWABLE SLOPE (in inches)
Hot tar built-up roofing	0 in 12 (flat)
Roll roofing (single coverage)	0 in 12
	(3 in 12 maximum)
Roll roofing (double coverage)	1 in 12
Metal	2 in 12
Composite shingles (wind resistant)	2 or 3 in 12
Composite shingles (standard)	4 in 12
Wood shingles	3 in 12
Wood shakes	4 in 12
	(7 in 12 in some rainy climates)
Slate	4 in 12
Tile	4 in 12

DURABILITY: Different roofing materials have different life spans. These life spans are not fixed; they can vary from area to area or even in the same areas, depending on whether they are in the shade or sun, etc. The greater the life span, the greater the cost. The cheapest roofing, single coverage roll roofing, has a life span of 5 to 8 years. The most expensive roofing, terne metal, has an indefinite life span. You pay for what you get. You will have to consider this within the framework of your overall budget. We would all like the best of everything, but can you afford it? If the roof with a longer life is $1500 more than what you planned, what are you giving up? Looking at it another way, if you use, say, a 20-year roof instead of the more expensive 30-year roof, and place the savings in a savings account, it may be that in 20 years you would have enough to buy 5 new roofs. If you can get 20 years out of your roof, that seems adequate.

COST: As mentioned above, cost is related to durability, for the most part. Galvanized metal roofs are an exception. They last a long time, but are relatively inexpensive. Costs for roofing can run into many thousands of dollars; shop well for the materials—this is an area where big discounts and savings can be found, especially if you are buying with cash or check.

Another consideration is the resale value of the house in relationship to the roof. Some very good roofs, e.g., galvanized metal or double coverage roll roofing, have a negative effect on the resale value. Others, terne metal and wood shakes or shingles, have a positive effect.

If you are paying for labor, you must consider labor cost in the choice of the material you plan to use. Metal roofs are very quick and easy to apply and therefore less costly, whereas wood shingles and shakes are more costly. Roll roofing is easy and composition shingles are somewhere in the middle.

Slope may also affect materials and application costs. If the roof has a steep pitch and is difficult to work on, the labor price may go up. On the other hand, shallower slopes may require greater quantities of materials, as in the case of cedar shingles. On a 4 in 12 slope, a 16-inch-long shingle can have 5 inches exposed to the weather; on a 3 in 12 slope, only 3¾ inches can be. You do not get as much coverage from the same shingle in this shallower slope, so you need more shingles (25% more). Because there are more materials to apply, the roofing workers will charge you more to do the shallower slope roof.

COMBUSTIBILITY: In making a choice of roofing material, combustibility of materials must be taken into consideration (e.g., wood shakes and shingles are highly combustible, while composite shingles, tiles, slate and metal are not). If you live in an area where there is a history of brush fires or you are building close to another home, this should definitely be a consideration. Your roof, and consequently your home, could ignite from an outside fire. Fire insurance premiums may be higher if you choose a material that's more combustible. In some areas, where brush fires have been a problem, wood roofs are not allowed. In some places it is required that roofs be treated with a liquid fire retardant. This is of limited value however, as it usually washes off in a few years.

NUMBER OF LAYERS: In applying most roofs, several layers of material, overlapping each other, are used in order to waterproof the roof. Water cannot flow up the back of a shingle or shake that overlaps the one beneath it. Lateral overlap, with staggered joints between the shingles or shakes, prevent sideway leakage. This overlapping process creates layers of roofing material at any one point on the roof. This is called coverage. Roofs can have double or triple coverage depending on the length of the shingle or shake exposed to the weather. When about ½ of the length of the shingle or shake is exposed, there is a double coverage (2-ply) roof; if about ⅓ of the length is exposed, there is a triple coverage (3-ply) roof.

APPLICATION: Some roofs are much easier to install than others. Some materials, such as terne metal or hot tar, need to be applied by professionals and can be quite costly. Consider the application differences when you choose your roof (this is discussed in more detail in the next section). Consider how the differences of application will affect your budget, time, pace, energy, etc.

APPEARANCE: Like siding, the roofing material you choose, in regards to both the type and the color, will have a major impact on the looks of your house. It can enhance it, have a neutral effect or detract from it. Look around your neighborhood at the different roofing materials and envision them on your house. Your choice in this matter can have almost as great an effect on the house as the design itself. After you have considered it well, your final decision should be a definite "yes," not a definite "maybe."

Types of Roofing

HOT TAR BUILT-UP ROOFING: (Photos 15-2, 15-3.) This type of roofing is most common on flat roofs and shallow slope roofs (1 or 2 in 12). It is used very often on stores and commercial buildings which use the flat roofs to support their mechanical equipment for heating, cooling, and sprinkler systems, etc. The roof consists of layers of roofing felt bonded together with hot tar or pitch. The first layer of 30-pound (30 pounds per 100 square feet) felt is applied directly to the solid sheathing and fastened with large-headed nails. This first layer, applied dry, keeps the melted tar from penetrating the joints in the sheathing. Between each layer of felt (3 to 6, depending on the quality of the roof) melted tar is mopped or sprayed on. On top of the last ply of felt, the tar is applied, and finally a layer of gravel, crushed stone or marble chips is placed. This allows you some choice in color and texture. At the edges of the roof, gravel stops are installed. Where a hot tar roof intersects a vertical wall, it is flashed.

Advantages: The greatest advantage of this type of roofing is its ability to provide a watertight membrane on a flat or low slope roof. Its life span is from 10 to 25 years depending on the site specifics, the local weather, the quality of the materials and the number of layers or plies used. It is moderately expensive. (Melted coal tar is better than asphalt. Find out which one your roofer plans to use.)

Disadvantages: The greatest disadvantage in hot tar roofing is that it is relatively expensive, since it usually needs to be applied by a professional. To do it yourself, you would need to use large equipment to melt the tar that would be

Photo 15-2. Hot tar is being pumped to the rooftop for application. The cord operates the on-off switch for the pump.

Photo 15-3. A hot tar roof after the final layer of gravel has been applied. Note how tar is being used to flash the vent pipes.

hard to locate at rental yards. Even if you could locate it, I would recommend against applying this type of roofing yourself. It is an incredibly messy job, and information on how to apply it is hard to find. It also has little fire resistance and leaks are hard to locate.

There are several alternative types of materials now available for flat or low sloped roofs. These include liquid rubbers you paint on, sealants you spray on and fiberglass roofs applied in the same way as hot tar roofs. There are even cold tar applications that require no melting of the tar. As with all products, their manufacturers tell you it is the best thing since sliced bread. Before you use any of them, talk to the people who apply them and the people who live in houses where they have been used for many years to see if there are problems.

ROLL ROOFING: (Photo 15-4.) Roll roofing is made from the same materials as asphalt shingles, only put together in a different size and form. It is made of long rolls of asphalt impregnated paper with an exterior coating of different colored mineral granules to help resist the elements. This material is also called mineral surfaced asphalt, SIS and salvage roofing. Because of its appearance, which is considered to detract from the structure, it is most often seen in rural areas or on out buildings. If this is not a problem for you, you may want to seriously consider it for your house because of its low cost and ease of application. It can be used for awhile and then covered over with a better material when your ravaged pocketbook has recovered.

This material comes in two different types: single coverage and double coverage. Both come in 36-foot rolls, 3 feet wide. The weight is from 55 to 90 pounds per square (100 square feet). In the single coverage type, the mineral granules cover all but the top 3 to 4 inches of the roll and it is applied with a 3- to 4-inch top overlap. This creates a single coverage which is good for 5 to 8 years. It weighs about 90 pounds per square. It is good on a 2 to 3 in 12 slope.

The double coverage roll roofing only has about ½ the width of the roll covered with mineral granules. This requires that you use a 19-inch overlap, creating a double coverage. This roof is good for 12 to 20 years.

Advantages: The advantages to this type of roofing are its low cost and ease and speed of application. It is also easy to maintain.

Disadvantages: It does not have the durability of some of the other roofings, which can affect the resale value of the home. It has poor fire retardant properties as well.

Warning: With either type of roll roofing, unroll the material a day before you plan to install it so it will expand and

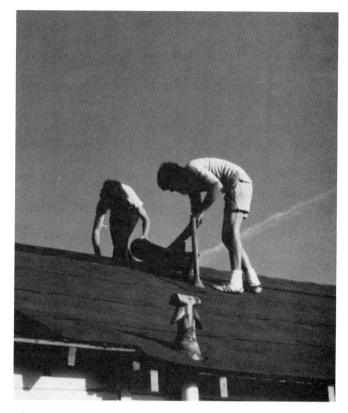

Photo 15-4. Roll roofing being applied to the roof. Installation is quick and easy.

lie flat. Otherwise, it will buckle, even if you have installed it flat. Also do not use this material on a steep slope as its heavy weight can cause it to pull away from the nails.

METAL ROOFING— ALUMINUM AND GALVANIZED: (Photo 15-5, Figure 15-2.) Metal roofing comes in many forms and materials. In the old days you could buy small metal shingles and they were installed very much like wood shingles. Today, most metal roofs come in long sheets, 2 feet wide and up to 18 feet long. These long sheets make metal roofing one of the quickest and easiest types to install. Most panels have 2 crimps on either edge and a center crimp. The edge crimps are water guards, since water running down the roof will not work its way over both interlocking crimps. The center crimp, as well as the edge crimps, are for nailing. Metal roofing is one of the few types of roofing that has its nails exposed. Because of this, all nailing is done through the peak of the crimps, not on the flat areas where it would be more prone to leak. Because the metal expands and contracts,

Figure 15-2. The crimps in metal roofing interlock with adjacent pieces and make them weather tight.

Photo 15-5. Metal roofing on an owner built home.

Photo 15-6. A terne metal roof being installed. The cost of this roof makes it prohibitive for most residential construction.

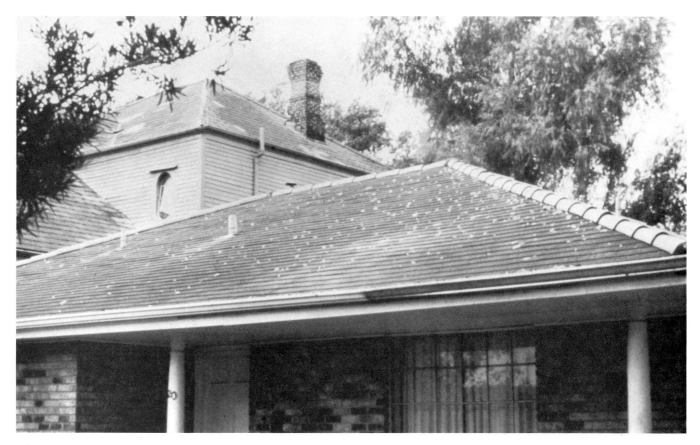

Photo 15-7. A composite shingle roof with tile ridges and hips for accent.

threaded nails are used to prevent the nails from eventually working themselves loose. The nails have either a lead head that spreads out over the nail hole or a neoprene washer underneath the head that seals the hole.

The most common metal roofs are either galvanized or aluminum. Unless other factors are involved, I would go with the galvanized. It has been around longer (the old "tin roofs"). Certain tree saps falling on aluminum roofs can cause them to corrode. In the South where I was raised, tin roofs were very common. I have seen some 60 years old or older still in good shape.

A good quality galvanized roof will have at least 2 ounces of zinc per square foot. Be sure if you use a galvanized roof that you use galvanized nails and flashing. *Never allow galvanized metal to touch aluminum; they will cause each other to corrode.* Use at least one roofing nail per square foot. If more than one sheet is needed to cover the slope of the roof, overlap the sheets 8 inches if the slope is less than 3 in 12, and overlap 4 inches if it is more.

Advantages: The advantages of this type of roofing are its ease and speed of application. It goes on in a day or two. The materials cost approximately the same as composite shingle roofing. It also has a very long life span, 30 to 60 years. The sheets now come in various colors and patterns and with insulation in the roof panel; they are not noisy in a rainstorm. It is fire resistant.

Disadvantages: The disadvantages are that these roofs can affect resale value, since they are considered shoddy (mis-takenly so), and sometimes they do not sit as flat nor trim out as well as you would like. Every few years you will need to crawl on the roof and drive the nails back in that have worked themselves out. It is also subject to damage by wind or falling objects.

METAL ROOFS—TERNE AND COPPER: (Photo 15-6.) These two types of metal roofs are much more expensive than their cousins, galvanized and aluminum. They are perhaps the most expensive of all roofs. (Terne costs six times as much as galvanized roofing or asphalt shingles, twice the cost of cedar shakes. Copper is $795 a square. Someone may steal your roof one day.) Terne metal is a copper-bearing steel. Both of these roofs will probably outlast the house. The terne metal roof on Thomas Jefferson's home in Virginia, the Monticello, is still the original one installed in the 1790s. Today only major commercial or institutional buildings use these types; only banks or governments have that kind of money to waste. Sometimes these roofs have to be put on with a special machine and professional labor since their application, using folded or soldered seams, is complex.

COMPOSITE (ASPHALT) SHINGLES: (Photos 15-7, 15-8.) This is the most common roofing used. Like roll roofing it is composed of asphalt impregnated paper and mineral granules, which line the exposed area. There are many different colors, qualities and styles on the market. They even make one that looks very much like wood shakes. The quality differs according to the weight per square (100 square feet).

Photo 15-8. A composite shingle roof on an owner built passive solar home.

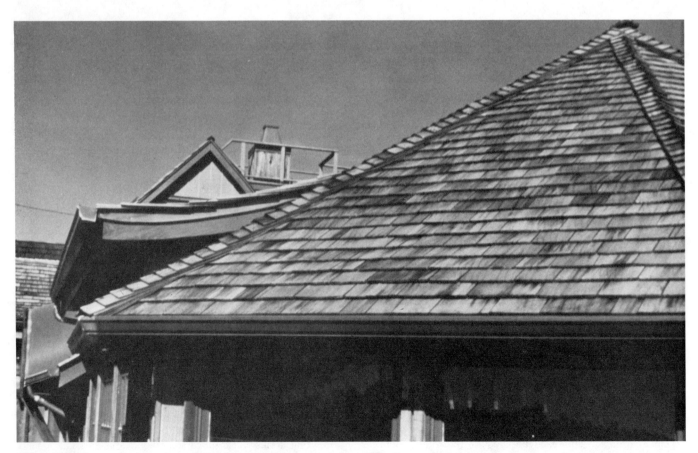

Photo 15-9. A cedar shingle roof. Shingles lie flat, for a smooth, even finish.

Anything at 235 pounds or more is pretty good, and should last 15 to 25 years. Standard types are used with a slope of 4 in 12.

Wind resistant or wind sealed shingles have a dab of roofing cement under each shingle, along the bottom edge. When the sun hits these shingles after they are installed on the roof, the cement melts and sticks the shingle to the one below it. This type of shingle can be used on shallower slopes (3 in 12) since there is less likelihood that the wind can blow the water underneath the shingles. I would advise using them no matter what the slope; they cost only a little more.

The shingles are usually 3 feet long with 3 tabs per shingle. At the bottom of the shingles, there is either a butt cut or another decorative cut. There are many manufacturers to choose from. Stick with one of the larger, better known brands to avoid problems.

Advantages: This roofing is easy to install and comes in a large selection of styles and colors. It requires little maintenance and is easy to repair.

Disadvantages: It has little fire resistance.

WOOD SHINGLES: (Photo 15-9.) There is a difference between wood shingles and wood shakes. Wood shingles are machine sawn from cypress, redwood or, most commonly, cedar logs. They are uniform in length (16 inches, 18 inches, or 24 inches), tapered from ½ inch to about 1/16 inch and have random widths. They are very uniform and lie flat and smooth on the roof. Wood shakes, on the other hand, are rougher, thicker and more irregular. They are hand or machine "split" from logs, much like the shakes made by the pioneering immigrants of this country. They are from 24 to 36 inches long and taper from ¾ inch to about ¼ inch. The various kinds of shakes will be dealt with in the next section.

Wood shingles are most often made of cedar. Cedar has a low expansion rate, a high impermeability level and an even grain that allows the water to flow off easily. The rougher shakes require at least a 4 in 12 slope. Because of their uniformity, which allows them to lie flat, shingles can be used with a 3 in 12 slope. No tar paper or roofing felt is used in shingle application, because ventilating is more important.

Wood shingles come in different grades for roofs, walls, and starter courses of the roof. Many code areas require that shingles be approved shingles; they must have an approval label attached to each bundle. The weather exposure of shingles varies according to the length of the shingle and the slope of the roof. The table shows some common exposure lengths in relation to pitch and length, but check these with your local codes or suppliers before you use them.

ROOF PITCH		SHINGLE LENGTH (in inches)	EXPOSURE (in inches)
4 in 12		16	5
or	{	18	5½
Steeper		24	7½
Less than		16	3¾
3 in 12 to	{	18	4¼
4 in 12		24	5¾

If you will note, almost always ⅓ or less of the shingle is exposed to the weather. This creates a triple coverage, which is what is recommended for this type of roofing (an exception to this is a 4 in 12 or more slope, using a 24-inch shingle).

Advantages: The value in the wood shingle is its beauty and uniformity as well as its prestige and resale value. It is also easy to install and has some insulating properties.

Disadvantages: This type of roofing is expensive, and for the money, does not really give you a long life span. It costs almost twice as much as composite shingles, with about the same life span (20 to 30 years), and almost as much as wood shakes, which have a longer life span (30 to 45 years). Installing this type of shingle is time-consuming and can be expensive if you are paying for labor. It is combustible and can be a fire hazard; in some areas it is prohibited for this reason.

WOOD SHAKES: (Photo 15-10.) As described in the section on wood shingles, wood shakes are split from cedar or red-wood rounds. There are several different types of shakes. Taper split shakes are split at a taper and are irregular on both sides. Straight split shakes are straight with no taper. When these are sawn in two, they are called resawn shakes. Resawn shakes have one irregular side and one smooth side, allowing them to sit flatter on the roof than taper split or straight split shakes.

All of these shakes are split, not sawn, from logs. Splitting cleanly separates the wood fibers and leaves the cell walls

Photo 15-10. A shake roof is being applied. Shakes, being rougher than shingles, lend a handcrafted touch. Note the large flashing where the upstairs deck joists intersect the veranda roof.

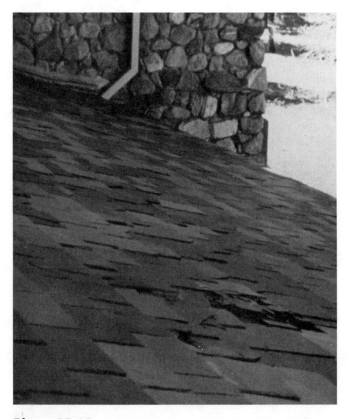

Photo 15-11. A slate roof. Note the broken slate shingles— this is a major problem with these roofs.

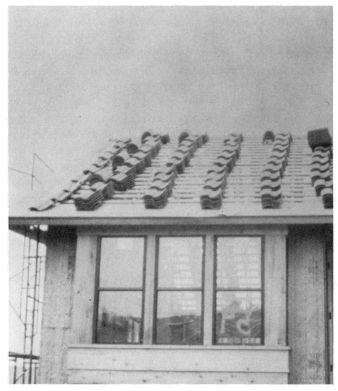

Photo 15-12. A ceramic tile roof is being applied. The wave pattern in the tiles will allow them to interlock. Note that skip sheathing is used here.

intact. The wood consequently absorbs little of the runoff water. Most shakes are from heartwood, with little or no sapwood. The shakes come in random widths and the lengths are 24 or 36 inches. On the roof they have a hand-hewn irregular look which is desired by many people. It is often called the aristocrat of roofs because of its beauty and long life. This chapter includes a section on installing this type of roofing.

Advantages: The value in using wood shakes is their beauty and durability (30 to 45 years and sometimes longer). Shakes have a very high resale value and are considered prestigious. Because of the thickness of the wood, shakes do offer a small amount of insulating value. They are also easy to install.

Disadvantages: The disadvantages of shakes are their combustibility and relatively high cost. Cost-wise they are twice as much as composite roofing and, with installation, can run even more.

SLATE SHINGLES: (Photo 15-11.) Slate shingles have been used in many homes, especially in the New England areas where the quarries are located. Because of the cost, they are seldom used on new homes. If you can afford them, however, or know of a good supply of used slate, you may want to consider them. They are flat pieces of slate, usually black in color, that are uniform in length, width and thickness. They can weigh up to 850 pounds per square. There are 2 holes drilled in each tile and the shingles are attached with nails or wires. Usually the slate is $^3/_{16}$ inch thick and 18 or 24 inches long. They need at least a 4 in 12 slope and often require additional roof support to handle their added weight.

Advantages: It is a permanent roof that should outlast the house. Aesthetically it is appealing and has a great resale value.

Disadvantages: It is a very expensive roof, especially if you live very far away from the quarries. It is also a very time-consuming roof to install, because you have to be very careful. The slate shingles are prone to crack and break should a branch or something fall on them. Due to their dark color, they retain a lot of heat in the summer months.

TILE ROOFS: (Photos 15-12, 15-13, Figure 15-3.) There are now several types of tiles on the market. There is the old type of clay tile, the cement tile, the fiberglass tile and there are probably a few I have not heard of yet. Clay tile can weigh from 800 to 1600 pounds per square and costs more than concrete tile. Concrete tiles can weigh from 700 to 1000 pounds. The old type of clay tile is rather time-consuming to apply; it is brittle and you have to use a tile cement or mastic at the ridges and the eaves. The newer tiles have done away with that, but they still take more time to install than composite shingles or metal. For most tiles, some sort of interlocking or overlapping structure is used to prevent leaks.

Like slate, tiles may require additional roof support to carry their extra weight. Some of the newer cement-based tiles, however, require no additional support. This type of roofing comes in many different styles and colors and can be quite attractive and durable, lasting many years longer than composite shingles. The life spans differ according to the type you are using, but 30 to 60 years is the range.

Photo 15-13. A ceramic tile roof after installation. Tile is durable and the price is within reason.

Advantages: Tile is both beautiful and durable, and it adds to the resale value of the house. It comes in a wide choice of colors and styles and can be applied by the owner builder. Because of its fireproof quality, it is good in fire prone areas.

Disadvantages: Like any long-life roofing material, it is expensive. Prices vary according to what type you get, so check with your local suppliers. Tile is a labor-intensive product in regards to application. It is also brittle and can break should anything fall on it.

NEW MATERIALS: (Photos 15-14, 15-15, 15-16.) Aside from the common materials mentioned, there are many new materials on the market. Three are new types of composite shingles, new types of rigid shingles, new waterproof membranes for flat roofs, wood shakes joined together to make a panel, etc. All of these products have their advantages and disadvantages. Be careful, the sales people will only tell you their advantages and are often trained to give the proper response when asked about their disadvantages (it's called in sales language "overcoming objections"). Evaluate each product carefully and try to talk to a professional roofer, as well as someone who has been using the roof for several years, before deciding.

Figure 15-3. Different styles of tile roofing.

Photo 15-14. Sod roofs are becoming popular for earth-sheltered homes. You can grow your garden on your roof, which might be needed on small lots.

Photo 15-15. A thatched roof. Beautiful, but probably would not get by the local codes.

Photo 15-16. Your guess is as good as mine!

Applying Wood Shakes

What You'll Need

TIME   The time varies according to the complexity of the roof. A roof with skylights, intersecting vertical walls, or a lot of hips or valleys will take longer than a simple straightforward roof with few special situations. It is also important to have your materials delivered to the rooftop. If they are set on the ground, more time will be required to carry the bundles up to the roof. Also your ability to get an even flow of work going is a big factor in how long it will take. Keep stepping back to see if there are ways to streamline your operations.

For a straightforward roof: 40 to 60 person-hours per 1000 square feet (10 squares).

PEOPLE   1 Minimum (semi-skilled); 3 Optimum (1 semi-skilled, 2 unskilled); 6 Maximum (2 teams, one on each side of the roof).

TOOLS   Rubber soled shoes, knee pads, chalkline, power saw, tape, tin snips, ladders, extension cord, utility knife, staple gun or hammer tacker, staples.

Aside from these common tools, there are a few special tools that you will need to make the work go easier.

NAIL STRIPPER: (Photo 15-17.) A nail stripper is a small metal box filled with roofing nails that hangs from your neck

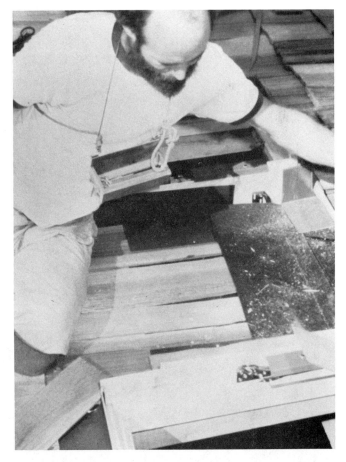

Photo 15-17. A nail stripper. These come in both right- and left-handed versions. They are good for applying siding as well.

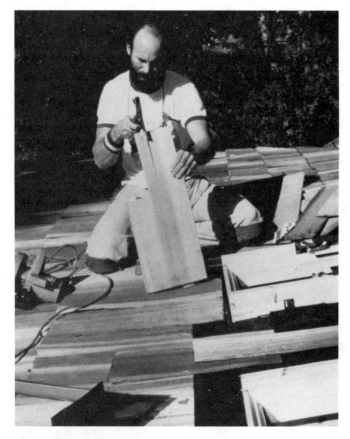

Photo 15-18. The roofing hatchet comes with a wrist strap so it will not fall off the roof.

Photo 15-19. A compressed air gun makes roofing a lot quicker, if one is available to you. Note the use of ear phones.

Photo 15-20. A safety harness. A good idea for steep slopes or high roofs.

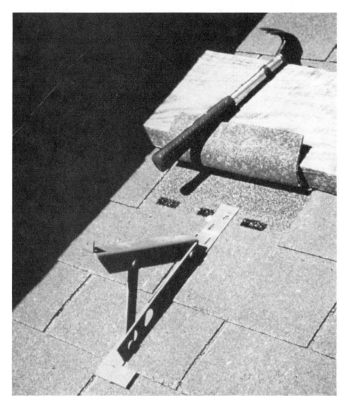

Photo 15-21. A roof jack to support the foot. Note how a support nail is driven under the butt line of a shingle.

Photo 15-22. A toe board. This is used like the roof jack, to provide support on a sloped roof.

with a strap around your back supporting it. The stripper causes the nails to all hang point down and in line, so you can reach across and pull several nails out at once, all with their heads up. Do not overload the stripper; put in a handful at a time and jiggle the stripper so the nails will settle. Strap the stripper tightly to your chest, so you can pull on it to get the nails. You can lubricate the nails or the discharge doors of the stripper with mineral oil for easier use. Wear a nail bag to hold extra nails to supply the stripper. Strippers come in both right-handed and left-handed models, for both composite shingle nail sizes and nails for wood roofs. Usually a roofing supplier or a good lumberyard will stock them. If not, they can be ordered from:

Roofmaster Products Company
P. O. Box 63167
Los Angeles, CA 90063
or
South Coast Shingle Company
2220 East South Street
Long Beach, CA 90805

ROOFING HATCHET: (Photo 15-18.) A roofing hatchet is used in applying wood roofs. There is a hatchet end that can be used to split the shakes or shingles to any needed width. It has a non-skid, waffle-surfaced head to grip the rough-surfaced galvanized nails. The roofing hatchet also comes with an adjustable pin, and notches on the handle, to easily measure the proper weather exposure for wood shingles or shakes during application. Keep the hatchet very sharp; dull cutting tools are very dangerous.

COMPRESSED AIR NAILER AND EAR MUFFS (Optional): (Photo 15-19.) Like sheathing and subflooring, roofing is an area where you may want to consider using a compressed air nailer. Many professionals do, and even if you have to rent one, it may be well worth your while. Get one with a rubber air hose for mobility. Be sure that the nails you use are right for your roofing and sheathing situation.

SAFETY HARNESS: (Photo 15-20.) On steep roofs, you may want to consider a safety harness for added protection. This can be fastened to something on the other side of the ridge from where you are working; should you start to fall, it will catch you. Attach it to a tree or stationary object. A friend of mine attached it to the bumper of his truck, and his wife came out and got into the truck to drive away. Fortunately she felt the tug before going very far, but can you imagine the way he felt when he heard the truck start!

ROOF JACK: (Photo 15-21.) An apparatus nailed to the roof to support your foot while working on the roof.

TOE-BOARD: (Photo 15-22.) A board attached to the roof to provide support to a person who is working on a steep slope.

LADDER JACK: These jacks allow you to support planks (2×10s, up to 9 feet long) from the rings of 2 ladders, up to 20 feet above the ground. The ladders rest against the house so that they are 2½ feet from the house, where you will be standing. Bracket arms holding the planks are levelled by adjustable braces. The planks should extend 1 foot past the arms. This can be used for working on the lower areas of the roof.

	SHAKE WEATHER EXPOSURE (in inches)					
Pitch	**No. 2 Blue Label** Length of shakes in inches			**No. 3 Red Label** Length of shakes in inches		
	16	18	24	16	18	24
3 in 12 to 4 in 12	3½	4	5½	3	3½	5
4 in 12 or steeper	4	4½	6½	3½	4	5½

ADJUSTABLE SCAFFOLDING: This is a type of portable scaffolding that has jacks to pump the platform up and down wooden uprights. Pumped up to 30 feet off the ground, they can be used to stand on as well as to transport materials up to the roof. Follow the manufacturer's directions for use.

LADDER HOOKS: These are used to hang a ladder from the ridge so that it can be used as a toe-hole while applying the roofing. They may be needed for steep roofs.

MATERIALS Shakes are graded according to their thickness. There are two basic grades: heavy and medium heavy (there are lesser grades also). The various types of cuts include taper split, straight split and resawn, as mentioned earlier under "Types of Roofing." Most builders are using a medium grade shake, which is thinner, of lower quality and has a shorter life span than the heavy shake that used to be the standard in the industry. In the past, 80% of the shakes produced were heavy shakes, and 20% were medium heavy. Today those numbers are reversed.

If you decide to order the heavy shakes to get a better roof, you may find that the heavy shakes delivered are also of low quality, come with many knots, are not very wide and have waves and irregularities. This is because most shake mills today are milling mostly medium-heavy shakes. Those pieces that are too irregular to cut into the thinner medium-quality shakes are thrown aside and used as heavy shakes, since they are thicker and may survive the milling process. If you are planning to use heavy shakes, which I advise because of their durability, try to locate a mill that is still milling a lot of heavy shakes, or at least look closely at the shakes before you buy them. Check to see if there are a fair number of wide shakes (12 to 18 inches), if there are too many knotholes, or if the shakes are straight and without a lot of splits.

Watch the newspaper (the classified ads) if you live in an area of the country where shakes are still milled (wherever cedar grows). Often there are small one- or two-person mills that sell shakes directly to the public at a greatly reduced cost. Some owner builders even buy the redwood or cedar rounds and cut their own shakes. A week's work doing this could save you several thousand dollars.

Shakes are usually graded according to their quality. Some areas require that only graded shakes be used. Number 1 Blue Label shakes are the best. Number 2 Red Label or number 3 Black Label shakes can sometimes be used with less weather exposure or on walls.

When you order your shakes, be sure the delivery is made to the rooftop, not to the ground. Find out if there is an extra cost per square for this service; argue against it, if there is. A supplier can deliver the materials to the roof via a scissors truck (Photo 15-23), conveyor belt or forklift. It saves you a lot of effort to have it placed on the roof for you. You can rent an electric ladder hoist (Photo 15-24) if your supplier doesn't have the equipment to deliver materials to the roof.

Aside from the shakes, you will need various types of flashing, nails and roofing felt. Flashing is used where vent pipes or chimneys penetrate the roof, around skylights, in the valleys and where vertical walls for dormers or other parts of the house intersect the sloping roof. These will be described in detail later in the chapter. The nails used are rust-resistant hot-dipped galvanized 6d or 7d nails. They are 13 gauge with $7/32$-inch-wide heads and are 2 inches long. Be sure you use galvanized nails to secure galvanized flashing, and aluminum nails to secure aluminum flashing. *Never mix the two; they will corrode.* The type of roofing felt you will need is 36-inch and 18-inch-wide, 30-pound roofing felt. You can buy shake felt already cut 18 inches wide or buy standardized 36-inch-wide rolls and cut them yourself.

ESTIMATING MATERIALS NEEDED

In estimating the materials needed to do your roofing job, you will need to estimate not only how much roofing material you will need, but also the roofing felt, metal flashing and nails, as well as any hip and ridge shakes. (See Photo 15-25.)

In order to estimate the number of squares (shakes that will cover 100 square feet of roof surface), you first must determine the square footage of the roof. Simple roofs can be easily estimated by multiplying their dimensions. More complex roofs are somewhat more difficult. A simple method is to determine the square footage of the house at ground level, then multiply this times a factor, the roofing coverage factor, related to the slope of the roof. If there are overhangs and eaves, you will have to account for these in your square foot measurements. The factors are as follows:

Slope	Roofing Coverage Factor
2 in 12	1.02
3 in 12	1.03
4 in 12	1.06
5 in 12	1.08
6 in 12	1.12
7 in 12	1.16
8 in 12	1.20

Add on 10% for wastage.

Once you know the number of square feet of the roof surface, you must relate this figure to the exposure of the

Photo 15-23. A scissors truck. Ask your supplier if one is available, and if the price includes rooftop delivery.

Photo 15-24. An electric ladder hoist. You may want to consider renting one if carrying roofing materials to the roof by hand is the only alternative.

Photo 15-25. Shakes and shake felt (18 inches wide) ready to be applied.

shake, in order to know what to order. (Note that for every 100 feet of valley, allow 2 extra squares of shakes.) A roof with a 10-inch exposure will need fewer shakes than a roof with a 7½-inch exposure. Your supplier will have conversion tables and can help you figure your needs once the roof surface in square feet is known.

In ordering shake felt, order enough to cover the square footage of the roof. You will need 1 or 2 rolls of 36-inch-wide felt for the first course, and the rest will be 18-inch-wide shake felt. You will need about 2 rolls of 18-inch-wide felt for each 120 square feet of roof surface.

To estimate the number of hip and ridge shingles you will need, measure the length of all the hips and ridges, convert that number to inches, and divide by the exposure of the shakes. One bundle will cover 16⅔ linear feet of ridge or hip. You can either build these yourself from common shakes or order special hip and ridge shingles.

Measure for all your flashing needs: center crimped valley flashing, flashing where a vertical wall intersects a sloping roof, step flashing for skylights, bottom and top flashing for skylights, flashing for the different sized vent pipes, chimney flashings and flashings for mounts for solar panels.

In nails, you will need about 2 pounds, per square of shakes, of hot-dipped galvanized or galvanized 6d or 7d nails of 13 inch gauge with 7/32-inch-wide heads, that are 2 inches long. Plus, you will need 2 to 4 pounds of 8d nails for starter courses, hips and ridges.

INFORMATION Shake application is rather routine and simple. The information given in this chapter should get you through the process with no trouble. If you have any unique situations that are not covered here or any other doubts, talk to your supplier before proceeding. Be clear in whatever you do; re-doing a roofing section is a hassle. For more information, write to:

> Red Cedar Shingle and Handsplit Shake Bureau
> 5510 White Building
> Seattle, Washington 98101

Be aware of the code requirements for roofing in your area. Most codes require that the starter course be doubled, that there be a 1½-inch overhang, that a ½-inch gap is left between the shakes, that joints be staggered (1½ inches between), that all protrusions through the roof, and all intersections, be properly flashed, and some areas require that you use inspected and marked shakes only.

PEOPLE TO CONTACT You may want to check with your plumbers and electricians (unless they are you), to be sure all plumbing vents and electrical weatherheads are in place. Check with the solar panel installer to be sure mounts are in place. Contact your insulation installer at this time to let them know that the house will soon be watertight and the insulation can be installed. Often it is cheaper to pay an insulation contractor to install the insulation than it is for you to just buy the materials. They buy the stuff by the train car loads. Check it out; it may save you from a lot of itching.

INSPECTIONS NEEDED Before the roofing is applied, usually an inspector will need to look at the way you nailed your roof sheathing, to be sure it meets code.

Reading the Plans

Most plans will simply indicate the type of roofing to be used; e.g., composite, wood shake, cement tile, etc. Seldom will the plan tell you the type or quality, unless the plans are well detailed. Some plans will say nothing about the type of roofing to be used but will simply leave this to the owner's discretion. Usually there is nothing indicated on the plans about the application procedure, unless there is a unique problem that the designer has detailed. Otherwise, it is assumed that the roofing installer has all the information needed to install the roof.

Safety and Awareness

SAFETY: As in roof sheathing or any work up high, applying the roof is very dangerous. Be extremely careful; accidents can happen before you even realize it. Do not step on the slats between the rafters, keep good balance and do not lean over the sides of the roof too far.

When using a ladder, lean it against the wall so that the bottom is placed at a distance from the wall equal to ¼ the height of the wall. Rest scaffolding and ladders on level, solid ground, or on a secure foot on one side. One person on a ladder at a time; someone should hold on to the ladder as you climb; and avoid overhead electrical wires. Stay off scaffolding or ladders in high winds or rain.

AWARENESS: Water, water, water! Everything you are doing is to stop water from leaking into the house. As a contractor, the worst call back I could ever have was for a leak (fortunately, there were few). Where was the leak coming from? How do I locate it? Do I have to strip off large portions of the roof to repair it?

Be sure you understand what you are doing before proceeding. It is all simple, but don't trust your common sense, and make no assumptions. You want to welcome that first rainstorm.

Also with long sections of repetitious work the system you use is very important in order to finish the job with the least amount of effort and time. Constantly be seeking quicker and easier ways to apply the shakes. One hour watching professionals and adopting some of their tricks may save you many hours on the roof.

Overview of the Procedure

Step 1: Prefelt the roof
Step 2: Apply the valley flashing
Step 3: Apply the starter course

Figure 15-4. Prefelting using 36-inch felt for the first course and 18-inch rolls for all the successive courses. The first spacing is 20 inches and all the rest are 10 inches (assuming a 10-inch weather exposure).

Step 4: Apply shakes
Step 5: Flash for plumbing vents and chimneys
Step 6: Apply hips and ridges
Step 7: Flash for skylights
Step 8: Flash where vertical walls intersect the roof

Step 1
Prefelt the Roof

Margin of Error: Within 1 to 2 inches of prescribed distances and overlaps.

Most Common Mistakes: Not using 36-inch-wide starter piece; not spacing felt sheets at proper intervals.

Diagram: Figure 15-4.

Photographs: Photos 15-26, 15-27, 15-28.

Unlike wood shingles, which require no felt underlay because they lie flat and are therefore less prone to leak, the rougher shake roofs must have a felt underlay or they will leak. Usually a section of the roof is pre-felted before the roofing is applied and the shakes are inserted underneath the laid felt as you go along. Lay the felt in sections, as much as you can roof at a time, because the felt can be affected by the wind or sun if left uncovered for too long.

Use a 30-pound felt in both 36-inch-wide and 18-inch-wide rolls. The 36-inch-wide rolls are used only at the eaves and the 18-inch for the rest of the roof. Buy precut 18-inch-wide rolls of shake roofing felt. It is especially made for this application and is much easier than buying the 36-inch-wide rolls and cutting them yourself.

There is a certain system of prefelting, explained here, that must be followed to ensure that the roof will not leak. It allows for the upper 4 inches of each shake to be inserted under a piece of felt interlay. This will prevent water, should any run below the shakes, from penetrating the felt; the water will simply be carried back to the top of the shakes and then over the roof and into the gutters.

Begin at the lowest point of the roof (eaves) and apply a 36-inch-wide piece of felt so that it hangs over the roof ⅜ inch. This overhang will ensure that the water is delivered into the gutters. Apply this sheet smoothly, stapling it with a hammer tacker or a staple gun every 12 inches. Be careful not to rip the felt. Overlap all side laps 12 inches. At these overlaps, double back the ends of the felt 12 inches for added protection against water moving sideways under the shakes. Do this also around any openings, such as skylights, etc. Overlap in any valleys or over any hips by 6 inches.

After the first 36-inch piece is in place, you will be using 18-inch pieces of felt the rest of the way up the roof. The second piece of felt (the first piece of 18-inch-wide felt) begins 2 times the weather exposure above the bottom edge of the first course. If your weather exposure is 7½ inches,

Photo 15-26. Note how all the materials are stacked from the ridge down. This is because you will be starting from the eaves and working towards the ridge.

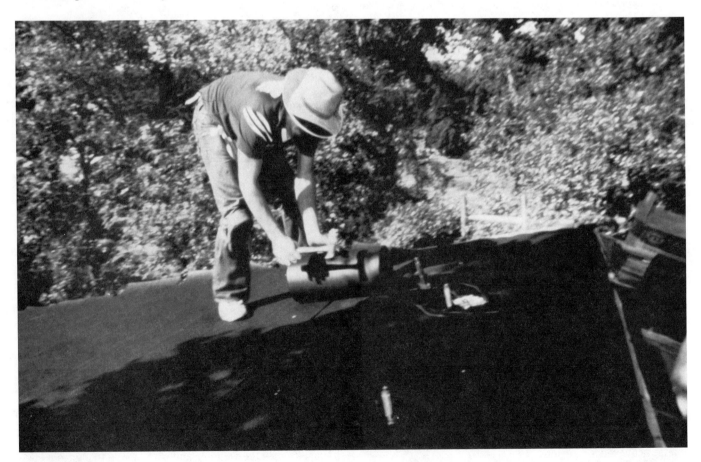

Photo 15-27. Prefelting the roof is the first step.

Photo 15-28. Roofing felt is overlapped at the hips, valleys and ridges.

then begin this second (18-inch-wide) course 15 inches above the bottom edge of the first course (36-inch-wide course). If the weather exposure is 10 inches, use 20 inches as the measurement.

Continue applying 18-inch-wide courses up the roof so that they begin the distance of the weather exposure above the bottom of the course below. For 7½-inch exposure, the courses are spaced 7½ inches; for a 10-inch exposure, the felt courses are spaced 10 inches. At the ridge, apply a sheet so that it overlaps both sides of the ridge.

Be careful working around the felt, especially if it is being installed over slats. Do not step on a slat between 2 rafters; step near the rafters. Cover about as much area as you plan to shake in a day. Measure up from the ridge every now and then to be sure you are going straight. If the roof intersects any vertical walls, run the felt 10 inches up the wall for added protection. Some builders use a drip edge at the sides of the roof to divert the water back to the center.

In snow-free areas, no felt interlay or underlay is required for straight split or taper split shakes if the weather exposure is less than ⅓ the total shake length (3-ply roof). In snow areas, you may want to use an extra 18-inch strip at the bottom so that it is about 8 inches up from the eave for 10-inch exposure, 6 inches up for 7½-inch exposure. This allows more of the first course of shakes to be inserted under the felt and allows you to cover the holes in the starter course.

Step 2
Apply the Valley Flashing

Margin of Error: 1 to 2 inches off proper location.

Most Common Mistakes: Using valley flashing with no center crimp; nailing aluminum flashing with galvanized nails or vice versa; placing nails in exposed section of flashing.

Diagrams: Figures 15-5, 15-6.

Photographs: Photos 15-29, 15-30, 15-31, 15-32.

If you have any valleys in your roof, you will need to apply the valley flashing before the shakes are applied, but after the underlay felt has been applied. Valley flashing is usually 20 inches wide, 28-gauge galvanized metal with a center crimp or ridge. This ridge prevents water running down one side of the roof, from running across the valley and under the shakes on the other side. The flashing usually comes in long sheets; you may need 2 or more pieces to run the entire length of the valley. Be sure the upper piece overlaps the lower piece (by about 8 to 12 inches), and not the other way around. I advise wearing gloves when handling this material, because it has very sharp edges.

Before applying the valley flashing, run a 36-inch-wide piece of roofing felt down the valley on top of the pre-felting, pressing it tight against the deck and stapling or nailing its edges. This is for added water protection. After this is done,

Figure 15-5. Valley flashing is applied on top of the felt layer.

Figure 15-6. This shows how the shakes are cut at an angle to match the center crimp (the felt is omitted for clarity).

Photo 15-29. Valley flashing has been applied to this roof. Usually felt is applied first below the flashing. Note how the upper flashing overlaps the lower flashing.

apply the flashing, the lowest piece first. Nail with 1¼-inch galvanized nails (aluminum nails, if using aluminum flashing) about every 12 inches, an inch or so from the edges. Never nail in the exposed area of the flashing; this will cause a leak.

After the flashing is nailed in place, you need to pop a line with a chalkline where the shakes will fall on the flashing. The shakes taper in such a way that the exposed trough gets wider and wider as you go down the trough. At the peak, pop the line 3 inches from the center crimp on each side; and at the bottom, at a point so that the exposed flashing area expands at a rate of ⅛ inch per foot on each side.

Your shakes should be cut in such a way that their edges will line up along this line. Use wider shakes in the valleys. Lay them into the valley, scribe lines where to cut them and then cut and nail them in place. Always nail each shake 1 to 2 inches above the butt line of the shake to be applied on top of it. Be sure no nails are exposed. There should remain, at minimum, a 3-inch trough of exposed flashing on both sides of the center crimp.

If 2 valleys intersect at a ridge, fit the valley ends of the flashing snugly over the ridge and each other by making small cuts and bands along the edge. Cover with shakes.

You can paint the valley flashing, as well as any other flashing, to closer match it to the color of the shakes. First clean the metal with a solvent, and then apply a zinc-based primer coat. Spray on 2 coats (not one heavy coat) of rust-resistant metal paint.

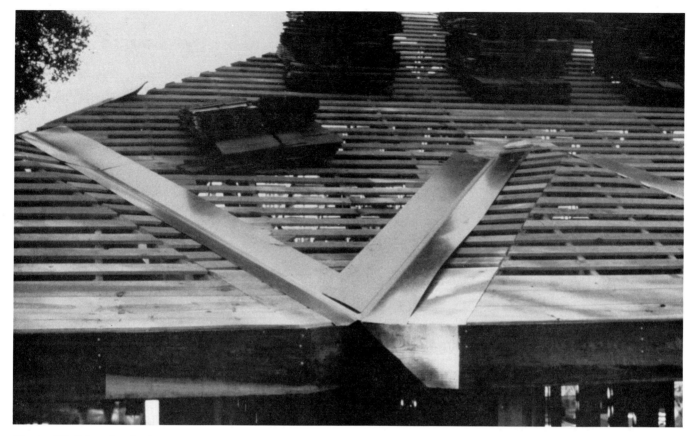

Photo 15-30. Valley flashing is intersecting at the eaves on this roof.

Photo 15-31. Valley flashing with shakes laid 4 inches from the center crimp and cut at an angle, parallel to the crimp.

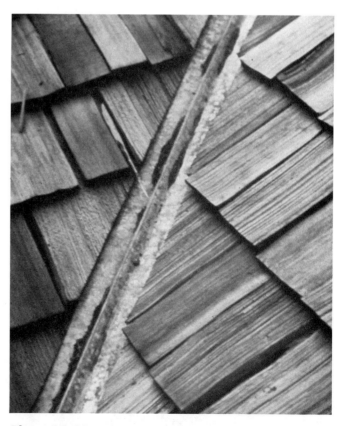

Photo 15-32. A finished valley flashing. The center crimp is to prevent water running down one slope from going under the shakes on the other slope.

Figure 15-7. In applying shakes, note that the first 18-inch-wide felt begins 20 inches above the eave line. All other 18-inch-wide felt layers are 10 inches above the course below it.

Photo 15-33. Starter shingles are being applied with a 1½- to 2-inch (2 finger digits) overhang. Note how shingles are tucked under the shake felt.

Step 3
Apply the Starter Course

Margin of Error: ¼ to ½ inch off proper location.

Most Common Mistakes: Using rough shakes for starter course; not overhanging starter course 1½ inches; not leaving gap between shakes.

Diagram: Figure 15-7.

Photograph: Photo 15-33.

After you have prefelted a section of the roof and applied any needed valley flashing, you are ready to begin applying the shakes. The first course in shake application is different from the rest of the courses because it must be doubled to prevent water from running through the cracks of the first course (this is a code requirement). To accomplish this, the first course is a double layer with the joints staggered (at least 1½ inches in between), so that water will not penetrate the felt.

The lower course is made up of starter (thin) shingles, not shakes. These starter shingles are 15 inches long and lower in quality than most shingles. Place nails ¾ to 1 inch from the side edge and 1 to 2 inches above the butt line (bottom edge of the shake that will be on top). This ensures that no nails will be exposed, because they will be covered by the shake above. Be sure that you drive the nail just so it is flush with the shake; if you try to drive it deeper than this, you may break the shake. Use only 2 nails per shake. You will want to use the longer 8d nails for the second layer of the starter course, since they need to penetrate the lower layer. Leave a ½-inch gap between each shake or starter shingle to allow for expansion and remember to offset the joints in each succeeding course by at least 1½ inches (code requirements). Overhang the eaves 1 to 1½ inches, so that water drips into the gutters. Overhang the rakes about 1 inch.

The last 4 inches of the shakes (if you are using 24-inch-long shakes) will be tucked under the second course of roofing felt. Be sure in all your shake courses that the upper portion of the shake is tucked underneath the felt. This provides the necessary waterproofing. Work along the eaves and nail in both layers of the starter course. After this is done you are ready to start laying the remaining shakes.

Step 4
Apply Shakes

Margin of Error: Within ½ to 1 inch of proper location.

Most Common Mistakes: Using poor quality shakes; having improper weather exposure; not leaving a sufficient gap between shingles; not inserting top of the shake under the felt; not nailing above the butt line.

Diagram: Figure 15-8.

Photographs: Photos 15-34, 15-35.

After the starter course has been applied, you are ready to start laying the rest of the shakes up the roof. With standard shakes, the tapered end is up and the thicker end is down,

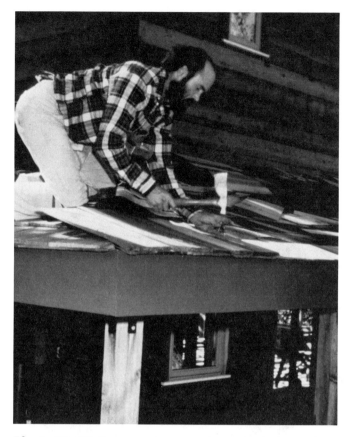

Photo 15-34. The second course is being applied. Note how the shakes overlap at the hip. These will be cut flush later.

Photo 15-35. The second course of shakes being applied. Note how the upper 4 inches of the shakes are tucked under the felt. The weather exposure here is 10 inches.

the rough side is always exposed and the smoother side is down. Work your way across the roof, applying shakes in an area that is comfortable for you without straining, and then move. The more efficient your system for applying shakes is, the quicker the job will go. Observe some professionals, before you begin, to see where they place the shakes, how they sit, how they hold the nails, how big an area they cover at once, etc. Having a system can make a great deal of difference in how much you get done, in how long a period of time, with how much effort.

As mentioned earlier, use two 6d nails for each shake, ¾ to 1 inch in from the side, 1 to 2 inches above the butt line (the bottom edge of the course above). Do not go higher or further in than this or the shakes might curl. Remember not to drive the nail too deeply into the wood, or the shake may crack. Use the head or handle of the shake hatchet as a guide for your weather exposure. An 18-inch-long shake usually uses a 7½-inch exposure; for one 24 inches long, use a 10-inch exposure. A superior 3-ply roof can be created by using a 7½-inch exposure with a 24-inch shake. There will be a slight increase in cost.

Be sure to leave approximately a ½-inch gap between shakes and offset the joints of succeeding courses by at least 1½ inches. Tuck the last 4 inches of the shake underneath the felt for waterproofing. Also save your wider shakes to be used at the edges and in the valleys. At the rakes, overhang the edge about 1 inch and nail as close to the edge as possible to prevent curling. Should a shake split while nailing, treat it

as 2 shakes, unless this disturbs the 1½-inch offset of joints, in which case, it will have to be removed.

Work your way up the roof. Should you encounter hips, ridges, valleys, skylights, plumbing vents, chimneys, etc., do these as you go, as explained in this chapter. You can measure the exact distance to the ridge and adjust the weather exposure to finish out evenly at the ridge. On steep roofs, you may want to build a toe-board out of a long 2×4 and shakes at 3-foot intervals. Be careful and work smoothly and without strain. Pace yourself well and enjoy the view.

Figure 15-8. Note that 4 inches of each 24-inch shake are under the roofing paper.

Photo 15-36. The finished application of vent pipe flashing. Note how the flashing overlaps the lower shakes and is overlapped by side and upper shakes.

Photo 15-37. Pre-made vent pipe flashings with rubber gaskets.

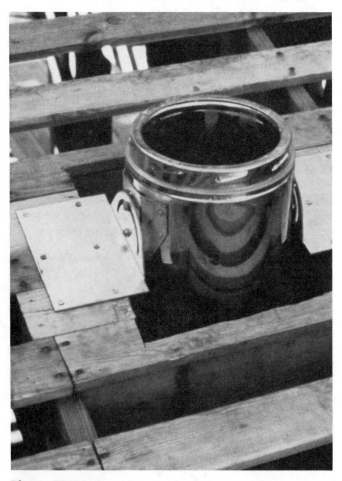

Photo 15-38. To roof around fireplace or wood stove chimneys, first apply insulated pipe assembly. Adjustable "wings" on the roof mount adjust for any slope.

Photo 15-39. After the roof mount is installed, continue to apply the felt. Install the chimney flashing, tucking the upper edge under the felt.

Figure 15-9. Note that the step flashing is placed against the vertical projection (chimney, skylight, etc.) and under the shake or shingle. It lies on top of the shake or shingle in the course below. (Counter flashing, embedded in the brick mortar, has been omitted for clarity.)

Photo 15-40. Continue to apply shakes, cutting the shakes that are directly below the chimney, as shown. Note that the flashing overlaps the lower shakes.

Step 5
Flash for Plumbing Vents and Chimneys

Margin of Error: ½ to 1 inch off proper location.

Most Common Mistakes: Placing upper shakes underneath the flashing; placing lower shakes on top of the flashing; not leaving a 1½-inch gap between shakes and the neck of the flashing; nailing in exposed parts of the flashing.

Diagram: Figure 15-9.

Photographs: Photos 15-36–15-42.

Most builders use pre-made plumbing vent flashing, though it can be made at the site. I highly recommend the pre-made units with neoprene gaskets, where the pipe pokes through the flashing. It ensures that no water will run between the vent pipe and the flashing into the house. They are made of galvanized metal and come in the common vent pipe sizes, 1½ inches, 2 inches, and 3 inches. Another model, made of lead, simply bends at the neck, into the opening of the pipe, to stop water from getting between the pipe and flashing.

There is a certain manner in which the flashing is installed that allows it to be interwoven with the roof in such a way that the roof will not leak. This procedure is the same for plumbing vents or chimneys. The sequence is as follows:

First, lay the shakes up against the protruding vent pipe. You may need to notch the shake to fit around the pipe. (Note that the pipe has been poked through the roofing felt.) Never apply the course of shakes above a pipe vent until after you have installed the flashing.

Photo 15-41. After the lower shakes are applied, install the shakes above and on the sides of the chimney. These shakes will overlap the flashing, as shown.

Photo 15-42. The finished application of the shakes around the chimney. Unlike the photo, it is best to leave at least 2 inches between the shakes and the edge of the flashing.

After the shakes are properly laid against the pipe, slip the flashing over the pipe so it overlaps the lower shakes. If possible, tuck the top part of the flashing under the building felt. If the bottom of the felt is too far above the top of the flashing for you to slip the flashing under it, cut a piece of felt 3 feet wide and slip one edge underneath the felt and the other over the flashing. Press the flashing against the deck and nail it to the deck along the sides and top where shakes will cover over the nails. Use flat-headed galvanized roofing nails (or aluminum if using aluminum flashing).

Now, continue laying shakes on both sides of the pipe. Leave a 1½-inch gap between the shake and the flashing neck to ensure drainage and to prevent debris from damming up.

Finally, lay the course of shakes immediately above the pipe. You will probably need to cut the shake right above the pipe so it fits. These upper shakes overlap the flashing. Leave a 1½-inch gap between the bottom of this shake and the top of the flashing neck.

You can now continue along the roof, applying shakes until you are finished or come to another flashing situation.

Wood stove chimney flashings

Wood stove chimneys protruding from the roof are flashed in a similar way, only on a larger scale. Special flashing and the insulated pipe that goes through the roof section are available for all different sized pipes. Often your stove manufacturer can provide these or will recommend a certain model. These are applied exactly like the plumbing vent pipes, unless the flashing manufacturer directs otherwise. Before making this final, be sure that your wood stove will be the required distance away from any interior wall. Don't forget to tuck the upper part of the flashing under the felt.

Step 6
Apply Hips and Ridges

Margin of Error: ½ to 1 inch off proper location.

Most Common Mistakes: Applying line of shakes crooked; not beginning with double starter course; using wrong weather exposure.

Photographs: Photos 15-43–15-52.

You can buy special hip and ridge shakes by the bundle. These are shakes approximately 5 inches wide that are

Photo 15-43. Pre-assembled ridge and hip shakes, as opposed to site-built ones, are advised.

Photo 15-44. Hip shakes being cut flush at the hip.

Photo 15-45. Shakes are cut flush at the hip and are ready for the hip/ridge shakes.

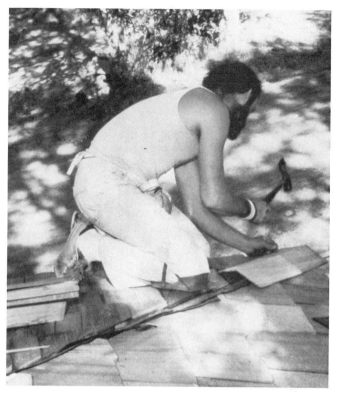

Photo 15-46. Applying hip/ridge shakes at a hip. Use the same weather exposure and a double layer for the first course. Pop a line 5 inches from the hip line as a guide to align the hip shakes.

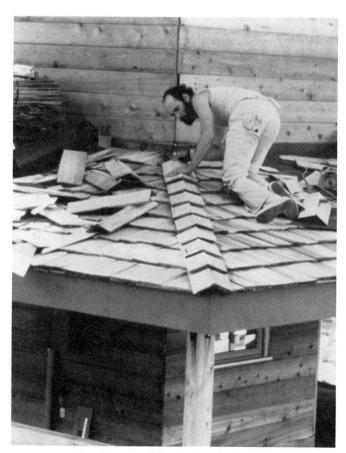

Photo 15-47. A hip almost completed.

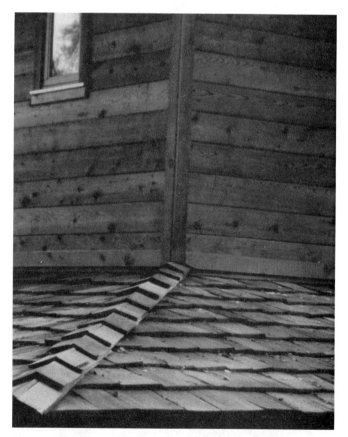

Photo 15-48. A hip completed. Note how straight the hip shakes have been applied.

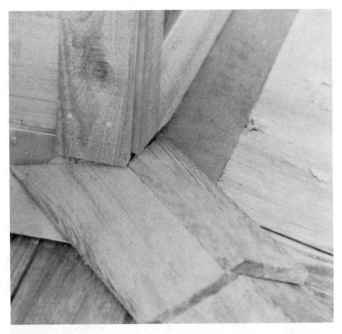

Photo 15-49. Flashing where a hip and a corner of a second-floor section of the house intersect.

stapled together to form a peak or a ridge. If you don't want to buy these pre-made, you can make them yourself by cutting 5-inch-wide shakes and assembling them at the job site. For the added money, I recommend buying them pre-made, unless every dollar is important to you.

Hips

Before finishing off hips, remember to overlap the felt paper at the hips, about 6 inches. As the shakes are applied up both sides of the hip, they are scored and cut at the proper hip angle. Shakes that intersect the hip (as well as those at the overhangs and the valleys) should be wider shakes, since you will be cutting them. Score them with your hatchet and carry a power saw to the roof to cut them. After the shakes are cut back at the ridge, cut a 6-inch-wide piece of felt and run it the length of the hip for added protection. You are now ready to apply the hip shakes.

Applying hip shakes is the same as applying standard shakes. Use the same weather exposure and apply a double course at the eave. Alternate the joints where the 2 shakes meet in the assemblies, one on your left, the next on the right. It is best to pop a line 5 inches from the ridge on one

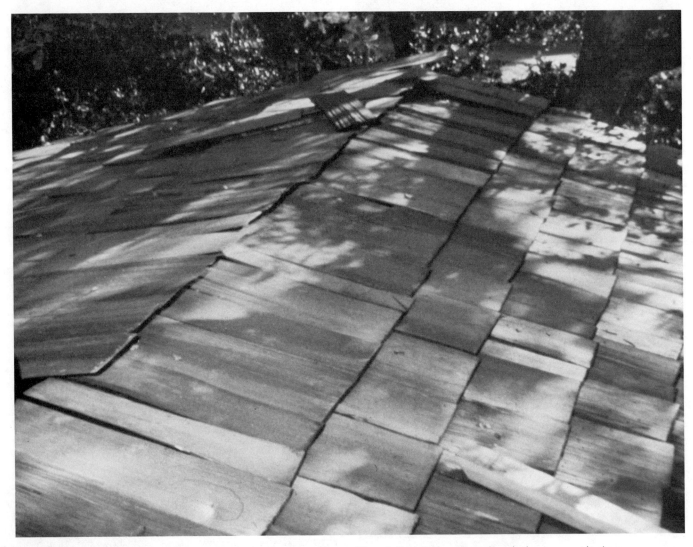

Photo 15-50. The shakes have been applied to the ridge. They will be cut flush before the ridge shakes are applied.

Photo 15-51. A ridge vent has been used, instead of ridge shakes, to ventilate this roof section.

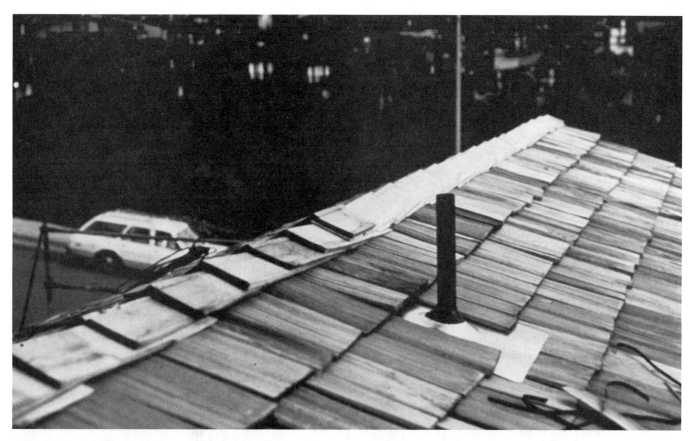

Photo 15-52. Ridge shakes have been applied from both directions and a "saddle" has been placed where they intersect in the middle.

side, to use as a guideline, to be sure the line of hip shakes is running straight. Any waver or irregularities can be easily spotted. Some roofers cut back the lower shakes of the starter course so that they don't underlap the second row of shakes. This will allow a smoother hip. You will need to use your longer, 8d nails for hips and ridges since you need to penetrate more shakes. At the top of the hip they are cut to follow the roof line or a wall they may be intersecting.

Ridges

Ridges can be done in several ways, mostly depending on whether you plan to use a ridge vent or not. Many builders are now using a ridge vent (see Chapter 14, *Roof Sheathing*—Plywood Sheathing, "Step 4") in order to rid the roof panel of any possible moisture build-up. It is especially recommended in colder climates, though I would check with local, open-minded builders for their opinions. When in doubt, put one in (unless you have an exposed beam ceiling with no real roof panel); it couldn't hurt.

RIDGE VENTS: If you are planning a ridge vent, you will have to leave a 1½-inch vent space in the sheathing and the shakes to allow the air to flow. After you have done this, purchase a ridge vent in your desired color, either in plastic or metal, and nail it over the ridge. See if there are any special manufacturer's instructions as to its installation.

RIDGE SHAKES: If you are planning to use a common ridge with no ridge vent, apply your pre-made or job-site built ridge shake assemblies. It is best to begin the ridge shake application from the side opposite the prevailing winds, so that no water will be blown under the shakes. If the winds do not come from a consistent direction during the rainy season, you can start from both ends and meet in the center, covering the joint with a ridge shake to form a "saddle." As with hip shakes, begin your shakes with a double starter course. If the ridge line will be noticeable (and even if it won't), pop a guideline to keep it straight. Alternate the joints on the assemblies; one on your left, the next on your right. If you are using no vent space, cover the ridge with a 6-inch-wide piece of roofing felt, applied along the ridge and beneath the shakes (use 30-pound felt).

Step 7
Flash for Skylights

Margin of Error: ¼ to ½ inch off proper locations.

Most Common Mistakes: Not using step flashing; not overlapping step flashing onto bottom skylight flashing; not overlapping top skylight flashing onto step flashing; not using shop-made bottom and top flashing.

Photographs: Photos 15-53, 15-54, 15-55, 15-56.

Installing the skylights and their flashing properly is essential if they are not to leak. Most skylights are put on over a curb, or a box-like wooden protrusion coming from the roof, that is somewhat smaller than the lip of the skylight frame. The frame is inserted over this curb to stop leaks. Most curbs are built to specification (usually ½ to ¾ inch less than the width and height of the skylight frame) at the job site from 2×6s. Some skylights are provided with their own curbs and flashing, but this is not common.

Most curbs for skylights are built directly over the rafters, which are on 16-inch, 24-inch or 48-inch centers. The roof will need to be framed in such a way that there is a rafter directly underneath each side of the curb in the area you want the skylight (see p. 318, "Skylights" in Chapter 13, *Roof Framing*). After the decking is applied to the rafters, build the curb and nail it to the decking directly above, and in line with, the rough opening you have left in the rafter framing. Check this opening, once again, to be sure it is the proper size. Then begin applying the felt and shingles. When the felt reaches the curb, run it up the sides of the curb, at the bottom and top and along the sides.

I advise that you get the bottom and top flashing made at a sheet metal shop. The flashing in these areas is very important, and soldering the corners is an added protection against leaks. It's wrapped around the curb a certain distance and comes up on the sides of the curb at both the top and the bottom. Many sheet metal shops have experience in making this type of flashing, and some places may even have it ready-made. If you cannot find it ready-made, give the metal shop the details on the slope of your roof, the type of roofing you plan to use and the width and height of the curb (outside edge to outside edge), and for a reasonable price ($10 to $25) they will make your flashing. You may want to order the step flashing at this time, too, rather than bending it at the job site.

Bring the shakes up to the bottom of the curb. You may need to cut some of the shakes directly below the curb for them to fit. After these shakes are applied, install the bottom flashing. This flashing must overlap the shakes below it in order to keep the water moving down the roof. Nail this curb with galvanized nails (aluminum nails, if you are using aluminum flashing). Place all nails into the curb or along the areas of the flashing that will be covered by shakes. Never nail in an exposed area.

You are now ready to begin laying shakes again. This is done as you have been doing the rest of the house, with one important difference: the use of step flashing. Step flashing is a separate piece of flashing, the same length as the shake or shingle, that is bent in an L-shape to extend up the sides of a protrusion on the roof, to lie flush with the bottom of the shake on the roof. It is used whenever a sloping roof with shakes or shingles intersects a vertical plane, such as a skylight curb, a brick chimney, a dormer, a vertical wall, etc.

Step flashing, cut the same length as the shakes, is inserted directly below each shake so that its bottom is flush with the bottom of the shake and its upper end is tucked under the roofing felt along with the shake. The flashing should extend 6 inches onto the roof, under the shake, and be within an inch or so of the top of the curb. It is nailed into the curb, using small rust-resistant nails, and nailed to the roof, with the nails that hold the shakes to the roof decking. Work your way up both sides of the roof, using the flashing interlaid

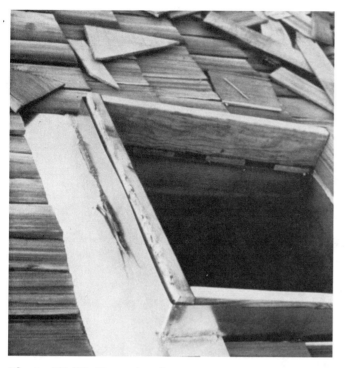

Photo 15-53. This curb is flashed and ready to receive the skylight. Note how the upper shakes overlap the top flashing and the top flashing overlaps the side step flashing.

Photo 15-54. Applying the lower section of the flashing for a skylight installation. This flashing was supplied by a manufacturer. Note the soldered corners.

Photo 15-55. A close-up of skylight flashing. Step flashing is being used. Note how the flashing always overlaps the piece below.

Photo 15-56. The finished installation of a skylight. Note the upper and lower flashing sections and the side step flashing.

with the shakes, until you reach the top of the curb. Always leave a 1½-inch gap between the curb and the shake for drainage.

At the top of the curb, insert the top flashing in such a way that the very top of the step flashing will be inserted *underneath the top flashing,* and the shakes above that will overlap onto the top flashing. Your concern is, once again, delivering the water from layer to lower layer until it is off the roof. Leave a 1½-inch drainage gap between the shakes at the top and the curb. After the shakes are applied at the top of the curb, begin your normal pattern of applying the shakes. You may have to cut some of the shakes so they will fit around the top of the curb.

Step 8
Flash Where Vertical Walls Intersect the Roof (optional)

Margin of Error: Flashing ¼ to ½ inch off proper location.

Most Common Mistake: Not flashing properly.

Photographs: Photos 15-57–15-63.

Flashing in this area is very similar to skylight flashing. I advise you to have the corner flashing made at your local sheet metal shop also. Step flashing is applied along the sides in the same manner as described in "Step 7." The siding and its under layer of tar paper are applied after the roofing,

overlapping the step flashing and the roofing felt that has been continued 6 inches up the side of the wall. As always, leave a 1½-inch gap between the shake and the wall and a 1½-inch gap between the bottom of the siding and the roof.

Photo 15-57. Pre-made soldered corner flashing can be bought at local sheet metal shops. These are recommended to ensure against leaks.

Photo 15-58. Step flashing always overlaps the flashing below it, to provide proper drainage.

Photo 15-59. Applying step flashing where a sloping roof intersects with a vertical wall. Note how the step flashing lies directly below a shake and is tucked under the felt.

Photo 15-60. Shakes are applied directly on top of the step flashing and are tucked under the felt.

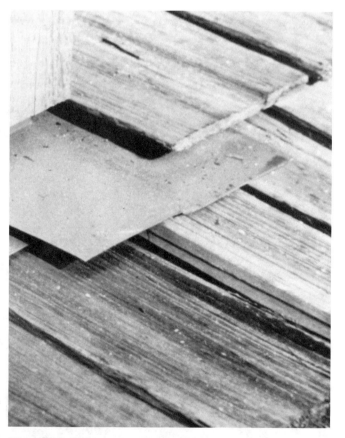

Photo 15-61. Pre-made corner flashing is in place here. Note how the flashing overlaps the shakes.

Photo 15-62. The roofing is almost completed.

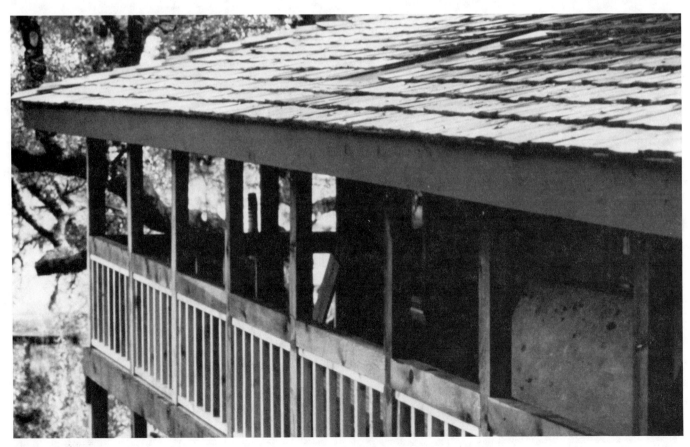

Photo 15-63. Shakes as viewed after application.

Applying Asphalt Shingles
What You'll Need

TIME   25 to 40 person-hours per 1000 square feet of roof.

PEOPLE   1 Minimum (semi-skilled); 3 Optimum (1 semi-skilled, 2 unskilled); 6 Maximum (2 teams, 1 on each side of the roof).

TOOLS   Rubber soled shoes, knee pads, chalkline, power saw, tape, tin snips, ladders, extension cord, utility knife, staple gun or hammer tacker, staples, framing hammer, nail stripper (Photo 15-17).

RENTAL ITEMS: Pneumatic nailer (Photo 15-19), safety harness (Photo 15-20), ladder jack, adjustable scaffolding and ladder hooks.

(For a description of the last 6 items, see "Tools" under "Applying Wood Shakes," pp. 359–362.)

MATERIALS   Asphalt or composite shingles are made from wood or rag fibers, impregnated with asphalt and coated with gravel. There is also a lighter weight shingle with a fiberglass base, that is usually 3 feet long, 12 inches wide and sectioned into 3 tabs by two 5-inch-deep slots called cutouts. Most shingles have dabs of roofing adhesive on the surface, directly above the cutouts. This adhesive, heated by the sun, adheres to the shingle above it, and holds it in place in the event of high winds or curling due to heat.

Shingle quality is graded by the weight. A 232-pound shingle means that the shingles of this grade used to cover 1 square will weigh 232 pounds. The heavier the shingle, the higher the quality and the longer the life. The exception to this is fiberglass-based shingles, which are light in weight but still high in quality. A 232-pound-standard-shingle roof is considered a good roof.

In making a choice of the type of shingle best suited for your house, select carefully; it will make an immense difference to the appearance of the house. Shingles come in many different styles and colors to choose from. Buy all the shingles at the same time, and be sure they are from the same lot number; colors can vary slightly. Patterns can be formed on the roof through creative application of the shingles. You can, for instance, use 3 layers at every eighth course, with their bottoms flush, to create a ribbon course. This will give emphasis to the horizontal lines of the house. (You can test this effect by taking a picture of the house and then drawing the lines on the photograph). In hot, humid climates, you can buy shingles treated with an agent to help resist fungus and algae. Do not store the materials in the sun or allow them to get wet.

ESTIMATING MATERIALS NEEDED

You will need to estimate shingles, roofing felt, metal flashing and nails. To estimate the number of shingles you need, first determine the square footage of the roof surface and then the number of squares (the number of shingles that will cover 100 square feet of roof surface) needed. The roof surface can be calculated simply, by finding the square footage of the house at ground level and multiplying this times a factor, the roof coverage factor, related to the slope of the roof, given in the chart below. (Include all overhangs and eaves in the measurements.) Add on 10% for wastage.

Slope	Roofing Coverage Factor
2 in 12	1.02
3 in 12	1.03
4 in 12	1.06
5 in 12	1.08
6 in 12	1.12
7 in 12	1.16
8 in 12	1.20

Once you know the number of square feet in the roof surface, this must be used in relation to the shingle exposure you will use. Your supplier will have a conversion table to ascertain the quantity of shingles your roof will need.

Order enough shake felt to cover the square footage of your roof. You will need 36-inch-wide felt for the first courses on each side, and the rest will be 18-inch-wide felt.

You must measure for your flashing needs. Be sure to include all protrusions (vents, chimneys, etc.) through the roof, the center crimp valley flashing and flashing where vertical walls intersect sloping roofs.

In nails, you will need 2 pounds per square of shingles (12-gauge galvanized with ⅜-inch head, 1¼ inches long).

The number of hip and ridge shingles needed is determined by measuring the length of the hips and ridges, converting this measurement to inches and dividing by the exposure of the shingles.

INFORMATION   Asphalt shingle application is one of the easiest procedures in housebuilding. There is little complexity or difficulty. The information given in this chapter should get you through with no trouble. If you have any unique situations that are not covered here or any doubts, talk to your supplier or a professional before proceeding. Be clear in whatever you do; you do not want leaks.

PEOPLE TO CONTACT   People to contact at this time include the plumber and electrician, to be sure the plumbing vents and electrical weatherheads are in place; the solar panel installer, to be sure mounts are in place; and the insulation contractor, to let them know the house will soon be ready for insulation.

INSPECTIONS NEEDED   Usually before the roofing and roofing felt are applied, the inspector will want to inspect your roof sheathing to be sure the nailing pattern meets code.

Reading the Plans

Most plans will simply indicate the type of roofing to be used; e.g., composite, wood shake, cement tile, etc. Seldom will the plan tell you the type or quality, unless the plans are well detailed. Some plans will say nothing about the type of roofing to be used but will simply leave this to the owner's discretion. Usually there is nothing indicated on the plans about the application procedure, unless there is a unique problem that the designer has detailed. Otherwise, it is assumed that the roofing installer has all the information needed to install the roof.

Safety and Awareness

SAFETY: As in roof sheathing or any work up high, applying the roof is very dangerous. Be extremely careful; accidents can happen before you even realize it. Keep good balance and do not lean over the sides of the roof too far.

When using a ladder, lean it against the wall so that the bottom is placed at a distance from the wall equal to ¼ the height of the wall. Rest scaffolding and ladders on level, solid ground, or on a secure foot on one side. One person on a ladder at a time; someone should hold on to the ladder as you climb; and avoid overhead electrical wires. Stay off scaffolding or ladders in high winds or rain.

AWARENESS: Water, water, water! Everything you are doing is to stop water from leaking into the house. As a contractor, the worst call back I could ever have was for a leak (fortunately, there were few). Where was the leak coming from? How do I locate it? Do I have to strip off large portions of the roof to repair it?

Be sure you understand what you are doing before proceeding. It is all simple, but don't trust your common sense, and make no assumptions. You want to welcome that first rainstorm.

Also with long sections of repetitious work the system you use is very important in order to finish the job with the least amount of effort and time. Constantly be seeking quicker and easier ways to apply the shakes. One hour watching professionals and adopting some of their tricks may save you hours on the roof.

Overview of the Procedure

Step 1: Prepare the roof deck: felt, flashing, and drip edge
Step 2: Apply the starter course
Step 3: Apply the first course
Step 4: Apply the remaining courses
Step 5: Apply hips and ridges

Step 1
Prepare the Roof Deck: Felt, Flashing and Drip Edge

Diagrams: Figures 15-10, 15-11, 15-12, 15-13.

Roofing Felt

Before applying the asphalt roofing, inspect the roof deck. Some roofers go so far as to fill any knotholes with filler, but most simply ascertain that the deck is clean and free of debris. Measure the deck itself to see if it is square and the proper dimensions. If it is not square, adjust the course of shingles or the lengths of shingles as they are applied to make any discrepancies less noticeable. Be sure that the deck is dry; if it has rained, allow one or two days' drying time before beginning. Once it is clean and dry, you can begin to apply the roofing felt.

Snap horizontal lines on the decking to align the upper edge of the felt. The first line is popped 35⅝ inches above the eave (the 36-inch-wide felt overlaps the eave ⅜ inch). All horizontal lines after that are popped at 34-inch intervals, since there is a 2-inch overlap between the courses. Begin by applying 15-pound felt at the eaves, overlapping the edge by ⅜ inch to ensure proper drainage into the gutters. The felt should be flush at the rake edges and have 4-inch side laps wherever 2 pieces of felt are joined. There should be 6-inch overlaps over all hips, valleys, and ridges as measured from their center-lines. Be sure the felt lies flat and smooth. Secure the felt with a hammer tacker, staple gun or pneumatic stapler, using enough staples to secure the felt against any possible wind damage.

Drip edges, metal flashing installed along the eaves and rakes, are often used. They extend in from the roof edge about 3 inches and keep draining water free from any cornice construction. In snow areas, eave flashing is also recommended. This is a cut strip of either smooth or mineral-faced roll roofing that is wide enough to extend from the edge of the roof to a point that is 12 inches inside the wall line. It is installed over the drip edge and the underlayment (felt). The lower edge of the strip is placed even with the drip edge.

Flashing

Roofing is basically a very easy operation in the housebuilding process. The only really complicated areas are where intersections occur with other roofs or walls, or where pipes or chimneys protrude through the roof. These areas must be properly dealt with or they will leak, and repair work is frustrating and hard to do. Be sure you clearly understand how to flash all these areas before you begin. Properly done, there will be no leaks; but one small mistake can cause a big hassle.

VALLEY FLASHING: A valley is where 2 sloping roofs meet. Heavy drainage from both roofs occurs at this point and proper flashing must be installed. Usually a heavy roofing felt (90-pound) is used as flashing and installed in a double layer: first an 18-inch-wide layer with the mineral surface down; and

Figure 15-10. Drip edges are often installed before the roofing goes on. Note how the felt overlaps the bottom drip edge, but not the side edge.

Figure 15-11. Note how shingles are cut at an angle to be parallel to the valley center crimp.

second, directly on top of this, a 36-inch-wide layer with the mineral surface pointing up. Overlap pieces about 12 inches and join them with roofing cement. Be sure a good, distinct valley is created.

Once both pieces have been installed, pop a chalkline in the center and 2 more on each side of this centerline. The exterior lines are the boundaries; the shingles will come only as far as these lines, thereby creating a waterway in the center. This waterway will be 6 inches at the ridge (highest point), expanding ⅛ inch per foot as it progresses down the roof. Your shingles will be cut to meet this line to create the valley.

Valleys are sometimes created using the shingles themselves as the valley flashing. These are called woven or closed-cut valleys and are commonly used in re-roofing work. I will not go into this type of valley flashing here, but you may want to ask your roofing supplier about its installation if you are interested.

VENT OR PIPE FLASHING: Where plumbing vent pipes protrude through the roof, the pipes must be properly flashed. Because this is done during the roofing process, all plumbing must be completed before the roofing is started. It is very difficult to install a vent pipe through roofing that has already been installed.

You can buy pre-fabricated vent pipe flanges, made of metal, for different sized pipes. First, lay the shingles up to the pipe itself, cutting the shingle to fit around the pipe. The flange is then installed over the lower shingles, and the remaining courses are applied around it, cutting the shingles slightly to fit near the pipe.

NOTE: For skylight flashing and flashing where the roof meets a wall, see "Step 7" and "Step 8" at the end of the wood shake section in this chapter. Be sure the upper shingles overlap the flashing.

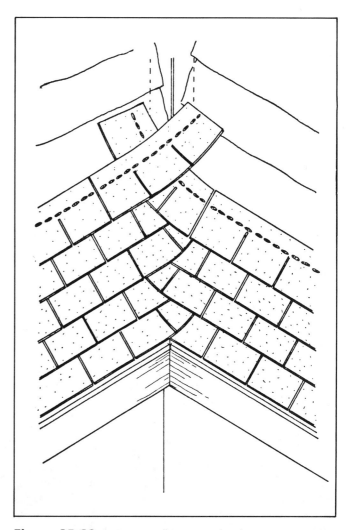

Figure 15-12. A woven valley created with interwoven composite shingles.

Figure 15-13. Parts of a house that require roof flashing.

Step 2
Apply the Starter Course

Margin of Error: ¼ inch off proper alignment with roof edge.

Most Common Mistakes: Leaving out starter strip; not over-hanging roof with starter strip.

Diagram: Figure 15-14.

As with wood shakes, asphalt roofing makes use of a starter course of shingles at the eaves. This course fills in the spaces between the tabs of the first regular course, which is installed directly above it. It also adds extra protection to the roof.

Usually the starter course is a standard row of shingles installed in an inverted position, the tabs facing towards the ridge instead of the eaves. This course is 9 inches wide, and you will need to cut 3 inches off the tab end of the shingles (9-inch strips of roll roofing can also be used). Install these cut shingles (tin snips are used to cut shingles) with the wind seal down and the mineral surface pointing up. Cut 6 inches

off the length of the first shingle to stagger the joints of the tabs of the shingles of the starter course with the first stan-dard course of shingles. For proper drainage, overhang the eaves and rakes by ½ inch and leave a ¹/₁₆ inch space between the shingles. Use 4 nails 3 inches above the eaves, 1 inch and 12 inches in from each end. If you are using a drip edge, be sure the starter course is installed *on top* of the drip edge at the eaves and *underneath* the drip edge at the rakes.

Step 3
Apply the First Course

Margin of Error: ¼ inch off proper alignment and location.

Most Common Mistake: Not overhanging shingles at eaves and rakes.

Diagram: Figure 15-15.

The first course is installed directly on top of the starter course and is made up of full-sized shingles. Repeat the same

Figure 15-14. Shingles used for the starter course have their 3-inch tabs cut off.

Figure 15-15. The first shingle of the first course being installed.

Figure 15-16. The first 3 courses have been applied. Note how an additional ½ tab has been cut from the first shingle of each progressive course in order to stagger the joints between the tabs.

Figure 15-17. The first 6 courses have been applied. After this, begin the process again, using a whole shingle.

overhangs (½ inch) at the eaves and rakes, and space the shingles ¹/₁₆ inch apart. Use 4 nails per shingle, placed 5⅝ inches above the bottom line of the shingle (the butt line) or ⅝ inch above each cutout. Nail the shingles 1 inch and 12 inches from each end. Nails are usually 12-gauge galvanized roofing nails, 1¼ inches long (2 inches for some textured roofing). They usually have a ⅜-inch-diameter head and are nailed flush with the top edge of the shingle. To prevent buckling, start nailing each shingle from the end next to the shingle you just laid.

Step 4
Apply the Remaining Courses

Margin of Error: ¼ inch off proper alignment and location.

Most Common Mistakes: Off alignment; not staggering joints.

Diagrams: Figures 15-16, 15-17.

After the starter and first courses are applied, you are ready to install the rest of the roofing for the remaining courses.

This is monotonous, repetitive work, so always be asking yourself if there is an easier, quicker way to do it. Be careful not to strain your body or endanger yourself by a precarious perch. Relax and enjoy the view.

As in all parts of construction, the joints, in this case, the joints between the tabs, are staggered. You will want the joints (or cutouts, as they are called) to be centered over the tab of the course below. To do this, cut 6 inches off the first shingle of the second course, at the rake. The third course, cut 12 inches off (one full tab), the fourth course, 18 inches (a tab and a half), and continue to reduce the length by 6 inches for each subsequent course. After the sixth course, the sequence is repeated, with the seventh course starting with a full shingle. There are variations on this pattern if you want different visual effects, but the above is the most common.

Many roofers pop chalklines on the felt to make sure that the shingles are aligned, as they are installed, in straight vertical and horizontal lines. For the novice roofer, this is probably a wise thing to do; just to be sure. These lines are popped every 36 inches vertically down the roof and every 10 inches horizontally across the roof, thereby allowing you to align the top and side edges of the shingles along straight lines.

Usually roofers work a number of courses at a time. In the method we have been describing, usually 6 courses are worked at one time, in a fan-like pattern. Remember to allow 1/16 inch between shingles, and to cut an additional 6 inches off the first shingle as each course progresses.

Step 5
Apply Hips and Ridges

Margin of Error: ¼ inch off alignment and location.

Most Common Mistakes: Ridge or hip shingles not in a straight line; installing ridges before hips.

Diagram: Figure 15-18.

After the roofing has been applied in the field areas and around the flashing for pipes and valleys, you are ready to complete the roofing process by applying the hip and ridge shingles. Always apply the hip shingles first, as these are overlapped by the ridge shingles, which are installed next. Hip and ridge shingles are simply one 12-inch tab of a standard shingle. They can also be purchased pre-fabricated, as hip and ridge shingles. If you are making your own, bend them in the middle to conform with the ridge or valley. In cold weather, you may need to warm the material up before bending it.

Now pop lines 6 inches on each side of the centerlines of the hips and ridges. These will be guidelines for the edges of your hip and ridge shingles. For the hips, start at the eaves with a double layer and work towards the ridge with the standard 5-inch exposure. Use 2 nails, 1 inch from each side and 5½ inches above the butt line, in each shingle. To finish hips where they intersect with the ridge, cut 4 inches up the center of a tab and nail this so that the unslit portion is nailed to the ridge and the 4-inch slit portion overlaps and is nailed to the top of the hip, covering the last hip shingles.

For the ridges, start from the ends and work towards the center, nailing a saddle where they meet. Overlap the tab portions where they come together in the middle. Finish off so that the last tab installed on the left leaves a 5-inch exposure of the last tab installed on the right. You will need to cut the left-hand tab to do this. Finally, install a tab, the saddle, over this joint with a nail in all 4 corners. Cover these 4 exposed nails with roofing cement as the final frosting on the cake. Pat yourself on the back, take a long look around (you might not be this way again for awhile), and your roof is completed.

Figure 15-18. As the shingles from both directions meet at the center of the ridge, overlap their top portions. The last tab installed should be cut so that it leaves 5 inches exposed on the tab next to it. Over this place the saddle, the lower half of a cut shingle, and nail it at each corner. Finally, put roofing cement over each nail.

Worksheet
Applying Wood Shakes or Asphalt Shingles

ESTIMATED TIME

_____

_____

_____

CREW

Skilled or Semi-Skilled

_____ Phone _____

_____ Phone _____

Unskilled

_____ Phone _____

_____ Phone _____

_____ Phone _____

MATERIALS NEEDED

Shakes or shingles, felt, flashing, nails.

ESTIMATING MATERIALS

SHAKES OR SHINGLES:

_____ sq. ft. of house at ground level (including

overhangs and eaves) × _____ (the roofing

coverage factor related to the slope of your roof) =

_____ sq. ft. of roof surface. (Add 10% for wastage.)

_____ shake or shingle exposure

_____ no. of squares (as determined by your supplier's conversion table)

_____ + 2 squares for every 100 ft. of valley

_____ + squares for hip and ridge shakes or shingles

_____ = Total no. of squares.

FELT:

_____ sq. ft. of roof surface =

_____ rolls (36 inches wide)

_____ rolls (18 inches wide).

FLASHING:

_____ ft. of standard flashing

_____ no. of pieces of step flashing

_____ no. of pieces of vent pipe flashing, size ___

_____ no. of pieces of top flashing (skylights)

_____ no. of pieces of bottom flashing (skylights)

_____ no. of pieces of chimney flashing, size ___

_____ ft. of center crimped valley flashing

_____ no. of pieces of solar panel mount flashing,

size _____

NAILS:

_____ squares of shingles × 2 = _____ 12-gauge galvanized nails.

_____ squares of shakes × 2 = _____ lbs. 6d or 7d nails.

_____ lbs. 8d nails for starter course, hips and ridges.

COST COMPARISON

_____ Store:

Cost per square _____ total $ _____

_____ Store:

Cost per square _____ total $ _____

_____ Store:

Cost per square _____ total $ _____

Daily Checklist

CREW:

_____ Phone _____

_____ Phone _____

_____ Phone _____

_____ Phone _____

_____ Phone _____

_____ Phone _____

TOOLS:

☐ rubber soled shoes   ☐ nail stripper

☐ knee pads   ☐ roof jack

☐ chalkline   ☐ toe-board

☐ power saw

☐ tape   RENTAL ITEMS:

☐ tin snips   ☐ pneumatic nailer

☐ ladders   ☐ safety harness

☐ extension cord   ☐ ladder jack

☐ utility knife   ☐ adjustable (or

☐ staple gun/hammer tacker   regular) scaffolding

☐ staples   ☐ ladder hooks

☐ roofing hatchet (for shakes)

☐ framing hammer (for shingles)

MATERIALS:

No. of squares _____

No. of hip and ridge shakes or shingles _____

Pounds of nails _____

Rolls of 36-inch-wide roofing felt _____

Rolls of 18-inch-wide roofing felt _____

Linear feet of center crimped valley flashing _____

No. of pieces of step flashing _____

Top flashing for skylights:

No. _____ Size _____ ; No. _____ Size _____

Bottom flashing for skylights:

No. _____ Size _____ ; No. _____ Size _____

Vent pipe flashings:

No. _____ Size _____ ; No. _____ Size _____

Chimney flashing: Size _____

Solar panel mount flashing: No. _____ Size _____

DESIGN REVIEW:

For asphalt shingles, determine:

Color _____ Type _____

Lot no. _____

INSPECTIONS NEEDED:

☐ YES   ☐ NO

Inspector _____ Phone _____

Time and date of inspection _____

WEATHER FORECAST:

For week _____

For day _____

Avoid working on wet roofs; it is even more dangerous.

16 *Siding*

Photo 16-1. Siding, as it progresses up the wall. Note that the deck ledger board has been installed.

What You'll Be Doing, What to Expect

I HAVE ALWAYS loved putting up the siding. Finally, you are starting to look at a finished product. All the rough work you have been doing up till now, with the exception of the foundation, will be covered up. What you put up during the siding stage will be seen forever. Basically the process, applying the siding course by course from the bottom up, is a simple one. There are a few tricky areas, mostly at the beginning, around the doors and windows and at the corners, but they do not offer any real trouble—if you know what you are doing. The work goes easily, though not always quickly; there is little physical strain; and I have always found it to be one of the most satisfying of all the building processes. It is finish work, but not as demanding as trim or cabinets.

Because it is finish work that will be exposed, you need to enter a new mind-set about the work you are doing. There is no great event to mark the transition from rough work to finish work (you may want to create one, however, a small party, a day off, etc.). Because of this, many people take the pace, attitudes and standards of quality into the siding that they used on the framing. Be careful not to do this. Each board must be separated and selected in order to use the most attractive boards in the most visible places (around entrance doors, at eye-level, on the street side, etc.). The less attractive or discolored boards can be used up high or down low, in areas of the house where there is little traffic, below decks, etc. Switch over to your lighter-weight finishing hammer, and be careful not to leave too many hammer marks (though many will disappear after a few rains swell them out, or a steam iron can be used to steam them out). Just keep in mind that what you do at this stage will be seen; it will be a part of your autograph—so keep your standards high and your pace efficient, but not rushed.

For high areas, I highly recommend using scaffolding rather than ladders. Many builders do not want to spend the time or money to rent and set up metal scaffolding. Ladders or benches will work well for one-story houses on relatively level lots, but if you have many high areas, I would recommend setting up scaffolding and doing all the high work at one time, e.g., fascias, siding, trim, paint, window installation, etc.

Keep in mind that the siding is a final protective skin of the house, as is the roof. You need to always be thinking about any possible water or air penetration. The weather tightness of the wall panels will depend on the quality of the siding application, trim and caulking. Flashing is also very important. It is often overlooked, done incorrectly or left out, or caulking is used instead. Apply a tight, unbroken flat underskin of felt paper; flash and caulk properly; trim well; and your walls and house will be well protected.

Jargon

BEVEL CUT. To cut a board at an angle.

FINISH HAMMER. A lightweight (14- to 16-ounce smooth faced hammer used for finishing work.

FLASHING. A plastic or metal material used in wall and roof construction that prevents water from entering at the joints.

HOT DIPPED GALVANIZED NAILS (HDG). Rust-proof nails with a zinc coating.

SHIPLAPPED. Boards whose edges have been rabbeted to form a lap joint between adjacent pieces.

TONGUE AND GROOVE. Boards that are cut in such a manner that their sides (edges), and sometimes their ends, have a tongue or protruding strip on one side and a corresponding groove or continuous indentation on the other.

TRIM. The finish materials of a house, including the mouldings around openings (door and window trim), at the outside corners, around floors and ceilings, etc.

Purposes of the Siding

1) Cosmetic covering
2) Protection from weather
3) Adds shear and rigidity to the walls

Design Decisions

Your decision as to the type of siding (Photo 16-1) you plan to use is a crucial one. It will have a profound effect on the final exterior appearance of the home and can have even a more profound effect on your money and energy budgets. Many people make their decision without all the necessary data or thought. Decisions made in this way can often have devastating effects (as you may already know). Check your conclu-

sions carefully—be sure you feel good about your choice or don't act on it.

In making your decision, keep in mind the overall trend of housebuilding in this country. Most materials and techniques developed have been worked out for large volume builders, who build several thousand houses per year, or for small contractors, whose annual income often depends on the number of houses (not number of hours worked) they build per year. For the large builder, small changes or "improved" building techniques, that may save only a few dollars per home, can be used in several thousand houses and save many thousands of dollars. These changes often lower the quality of the home and are simply not worth the effort when building one house.

For the small contractor who is building several houses per year and needs to complete them all in order to get his 20% profit, time is of the essence. For these contractors, higher quality methods or materials may not be more expensive, but simply take more time and therefore slow up the building process. So they may opt for a quick method and lower quality. This may not be the wisest decision for someone building their own home.

When choosing your siding, you will find that some types of siding, such as plywood, aluminum, stucco, etc., can be installed very quickly. Other types, such as board and batten, vertical or horizontal wood, shakes or shingles, take more time to install, but add a certain quality or handcrafted appearance to the home (along with a week or two of extra building time). As you consider your decision about siding, evaluate each type and consider the following:

☐ Price
☐ Resale value
☐ Appearance
☐ Sound insulation
☐ Installation labor
☐ Repair
☐ Maintenance
☐ Combustibility
☐ Resistance to scratching and impact

The following is a discussion of various types of siding materials. The remaining part of the chapter will show in detail how to install horizontal board siding. I have chosen this type because it is one of the more difficult ones to apply. Actually stucco is perhaps the most difficult, but this is usually applied by professionals, and only used in areas where there is little or no freezing. Other sidings, such as plywood and aluminum, are very easy to install by simply reading the manufacturer's instructions.

Types of Siding

PLYWOOD SIDING: (Photos 16-2, 16-3; Figure 16-1.) I have begun with this type of siding, not because it is my favorite, but because it is becoming one of the most common. The reason for this is that it has one great asset: it goes up

Photo 16-2. A smooth-surfaced plywood siding.

Photo 16-3. Trimming out plywood siding is easy and can hide even large mistakes. The horizontal trim should be flashed so it won't trap water behind it.

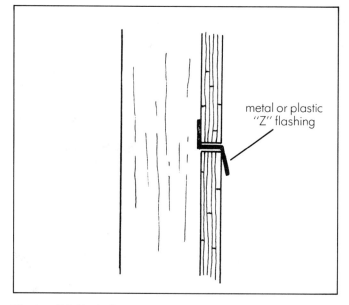

Figure 16-1. Flashing used with a plywood siding.

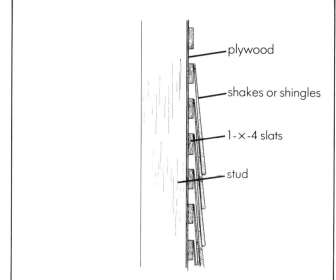

Figure 16-2. Here 1-×-4 slats are used over plywood sheathing. The shakes or shingles are then nailed to these.

quicker than any other type of siding, and as I mentioned in my introduction, this can be quite an inducement for many builders. It may be the best decision for you as well, especially if your time is very limited (though, in 20 years, you may wonder what difference a few weeks would have made).

Exterior plywood, often known as Texture 1-11 (Texture, one eleven) is an exterior grade panel made from thin sheets (plies) glued (laminated) together under pressure with waterproof glues. The interior plies are of mixed woods, but the final exposed exterior ply is Douglas fir, western red cedar, southern pine or redwood. The redwood and cedar plies are more expensive than the others and can run so high as to be the most expensive types of siding to use per square foot. The cheaper boards often have up to 12 plugs per panel (plugging for exposed knotholes), and can be used only if they are painted.

The panels come in a large range of textures and designs. They can come with grooves, to appear as different individual boards; rough or smooth; or straight, with no grooves. They are 4 feet wide and 8 to 10 feet long. Usually they are installed vertically. Horizontal application is sometimes used, but there is the danger of water getting between the plies into the joints. They also come as lap boards, 6 to 12 inches wide and up to 16 feet long. Thicknesses vary from ⅜ to ⅝ inch and are priced accordingly. They also come with various types of treatments: painted, primed, stained, untreated or treated with a water repellent.

The types of plywood siding also vary according to their use. Medium-density overlaid (MDO) is recommended for paint. The exterior surface is a resin-treated sheet, hot bonded to the panel to make a smooth surface for painting. 303 is for stain. It comes in many textures and patterns, often with tight knots or holes that must be filled with synthetic filler. It has a questionable look with the knotholes, but the clear stock is more expensive. Texture 1-11 has shiplapped edges and parallel grooves, and is a higher quality material.

All panels are applied with rust-resistant nails that penetrate at least 1 inch into the studs. Horizontal joints between sheets should be flashed with pre-fabricated "Z" flashing. Trim above doors and windows and other horizontal trim should also be flashed. Often for horizontal joints, a nailing surface between the studs needs to be provided.

Perhaps the greatest drawback of this product is that the boards can delaminate over time, especially if they are not properly maintained or sealed every 2 to 5 years. This siding can give a certain flatness or dullness to the appearance of the house, while the more attractive panels can be very expensive. It is not fire resistant.

Cost: Moderate to expensive.

Lifetime: 20 years to life of building.

Maintenance: Treated every 2 to 5 years.

Installation: Quick and easy; requires 2 people.

WOOD SHAKES AND WOOD SHINGLES: (Photos 16-4–16-8; Figure 16-2.) Wooden shakes and shingles are perhaps the most attractive and, correspondingly, the most time-consuming to install of all the sidings. Since each piece covers only a few square inches (compared to 32 square feet, with 4-×-8-foot plywood panels), application can take a *very* long time. One of our students, who covered his 3200-square-foot home with shakes, said towards the end that he bordered on insanity and/or enlightenment. Shakes or shingles can give a home anywhere from a classy look to a funky look. Be sure you have the patience, if you are working by yourself; or the money, if you are hiring the labor.

Most of the shakes or shingles are made from cedar or redwood, and occasionally from oak or sugar pine. Shingles are cut and shakes are split (see discussion in Chapter 15, *Roofing,* p. 355, "Types of Roofing"). Shingles come in various grades, Number 1 Blue Label, Number 2 Red Label, and other utility grades. The blue label shingles are considered the best. Red label shingles are often used on walls or as underlayment when double coursing in roofs. The weather

Photo 16-4. Shake siding is rougher than wood shingles. It is also more costly and time-consuming to apply, but lends a real handcrafted feeling.

Photo 16-5. Shingle siding is beautiful, but costly and time-consuming.

Photo 16-6. Cedar shingle siding can be bought in 8-foot strips for quicker application.

Photo 16-7. If you are willing to take the time, the siding can tremendously affect the looks of the house.

Photo 16-8. An adjustable jig for applying shakes or shingles. The horizontal bar is supported with 2 vertical pieces.

exposure for shingle siding varies, but it is greater than that of roofs, since weather protection is not as critical on a vertical surface. Shingles are usually 12 to 16 inches long with random widths, and are about ¼ inch thick at the thick end. They are sometimes cut with fancy, rounded or pointed or patterned ends for more decorative applications.

Shakes are thicker, rougher pieces split from the wood. They are usually 18 and 24 inches long and up to ½ to ¾ inches thick at the thick end. Sometimes shakes can be bought pre-bonded to 8-foot panels for quick application. Shakes can be installed over either solid or spaced sheathing.

Both shakes and shingles can be very expensive, especially if you are paying for labor. Be sure you compare prices of installing shakes or shingles with other types of siding before you decide. Wooden shakes and shingles are rather fire prone and are not suited to all areas. Termites can also be a problem. They are, however, beautiful, easy to work with, easy to repair and replace and can add to the resale value of your home.

Cost: Moderate to expensive.

Lifetime: 30 years to the life of the building.

Maintenance: In humid climates a fungicide is recommended; in other areas, oil every 5 years to preserve resiliency.

Installation: Easy, but very slow; can be done by one person.

Photo 16-9. Horizontal lap siding offers beauty and durability.

metal corner pieces

2-×-2 strip

Figure 16-3. Two different ways of trimming corners when applying horizontal siding.

WOOD BOARDS: (Photos 16-9, 16-10, 16-11; Figure 16-3.) Natural wood boards, milled from pine, fir, cypress, redwood, or cedar, are often used as siding. I personally favor this type of siding; it has the beauty and durability of natural wood, and a moderate impact on time and money budgets. Though its application is much slower than plywood, it goes on much quicker than shakes or shingles, and it can easily be applied by a novice. It adds beauty to the design and a high-quality look to the home.

The boards are usually ¾ inch thick, 4 to 12 inches wide and up to 20 feet long. They are applied horizontally, vertically or diagonally, depending on the type. They can be butt-cut, shiplapped, clapboard, beveled or tongue and groove. The price for this type of siding can vary from very inexpensive to very expensive. It all depends on 3 main factors: the type of wood, the quality of the wood and the number of milling processes required.

If redwood or cedar is used for the boards, the price will be high. Many people think these woods are used because they are resistant to rot. All woods will wear well if they can thoroughly dry after periodic wettings, and this is the case with siding. It is only when a wood gets wet and stays wet, as when it is near or in the ground, that a rot-resistant wood such as cedar or redwood is needed. Cedar and redwood are used for siding many times because they have fewer knotholes and have straight, smooth grains. If good pine or fir is available, either one will be adequate for siding, provided it has a chance to dry after a rain. You may want to consider using one of these and save some money.

The quality of the wood you use will also affect the price. Clear lumber, boards with no knotholes, will be more expensive than lumber with knotholes. (Knotholes are often attractive on walls.) In some types of woods, the knots will fall out in time; in others they will remain in for the life of the house. Two kinds of redwoods are available: all-heart (all red), or

redwood containing some sapwood (white areas). The all-heart clear redwood siding is very expensive. You can also find dry or wet lumber for siding. Dry lumber is more expensive, but it will not shrink and leave unsightly cracks. Usually a relatively dry siding is recommended, unless you are using a clapboard or board and batten siding, where the boards overlap sufficiently to dry without showing cracks. Be on the lookout for good deals: lower quality boards that are still attractive.

The number of milling operations that a board must pass through before the final product will also affect the price. Trees in the forest are the cheapest lumber you can buy; for comparison sake, say $50 per 1000 board feet. Once it is cut into logs and trucked to a mill, it runs $80 per 1000 board feet. After it's rough cut in the mill, it's about $180. When it's finished and planed in the mill, it's $280; dried in the kiln, $360; picked for clear (no knots), $800; and finally, run through a special process to shiplap or tongue and groove the edges, it is $1500 per 1000 board feet. So if you are planning to use a high-grade redwood or cedar dry lumber siding, you will pay a lot for the materials. If you are paying for installation, it will cost a good bit more.

The way to use wood boards, if you are on a tight budget, is to use wet rough-cut lumber (in a board and batten or clapboard style), or the lower grades with knots, or some sapwood (redwood), and apply it yourself. Application is simple for a novice; it will be thoroughly explained later in this chapter.

The boards can be run horizontally, vertically or diagonally. The main consideration is the looks of the house. Running the boards vertically will give the house a greater sense of height; running them horizontally will tie the house more into the ground plane. Most styles of board siding can be used in any of the three positions, except the butt-cut boards, which must be used vertically in a board and batten style, and the

Photo 16-10. Board and batten siding is inexpensive and offers a handcrafted look.

Photo 16-11. Individual shiplapped boards have been applied diagonally. This application adds shear strength to the wall.

Photo 16-12. Aluminum siding.

Photo 16-13. Aluminum siding being applied.

beveled boards, which are most often used in a horizontal position. The shiplapped and tongue and groove boards can be used in any of the three directions (if using tongue and groove horizontally, be sure to point the tongue, *not the groove,* up or the groove will trap water).

Cost: Inexpensive to expensive.

Lifetime: 30 years to the life of the house.

Maintenance: Often no maintenance is needed; with redwood, seal it immediately after application to prevent darkening; other types of wood may require an occasional treatment to keep resiliency.

Installation: Moderately time-consuming, but easily mastered by the careful novice.

HARDBOARD SIDING: Hardboard is manufactured from wood chip pulp, which is compressed and bonded under heat and pressure. It is often made to appear like real wood boards or even stucco. It comes in many styles and textures and costs less than the expensive real wood sidings, but not particularly less than the inexpensive ones. It comes in panels like plywood or individual boards and is often primed or painted, and sometimes stained. It takes paint well and has no knotholes. It needs to be kept out of any direct contact with the ground because it rots easily. It is available in tongue and groove or shiplapped.

This siding does allow you the appearance of wood without the cost of the expensive real wood siding. If you can locate a moderately priced real wood siding, however, I would advise that over hardboard; it looks better, and I am more trustful of nature-made materials than manufactured materials for siding. Hardboard can delaminate and buckle over the years.

Cost: Moderate.

Lifetime: 20 years to lifetime of building, depending on the maintenance; finishes are guaranteed for 5 years.

Maintenance: Edges must be sealed upon installation and all siding painted shortly after; repaint every 3 to 6 years.

Installation: Rather quick and easy and well within the scope of the novice builder.

ALUMINUM, VINYL AND STEEL: (Photos 16-12, 16-13.) Metal and vinyl types of siding have become rather popular in many areas of the country. They are often used over an existing siding. Like many things nowadays, they seldom stand up to the manufacturer's claims (whereas with real *wood* siding, the Manufacturer never lets us down). These types of siding are usually molded or extruded panels that simulate lap siding (and sometimes shakes or shingles). Vertical panels are made 8 inches wide with battens, to simulate board and batten siding. The standard length is 12 feet 6 inches with other styles available.

Except for vinyl, these types of siding are fireproof; something to consider, if fires are a problem in your area. Usually

Photo 16-14. Stucco is often used in Florida, California and the Southwest, where freezing is not a problem.

Photo 16-15. Wire mesh is stretched across the house before the stucco is applied. In this case, the felt paper and wire mesh are fastened together at the factory.

Photo 16-16. Applying a brick veneer. Laying bricks is a challenge to the novice.

they won't rust, peel or blister or, needless to say, rot. The siding does dent and scratch easily though, and the aluminum can corrode near salt water. The biggest problem, however, is that the pre-finished surfaces can get chalky after a few years and start to buckle, and this is hard to repair or repaint.

Cost: Inexpensive to moderate.

Lifetime: 40 years to lifetime of home.

Maintenance: Vinyl—none; aluminum and steel—hose off every year and repaint according to manufacturer's instructions; paint all scratches on steel siding to prevent rust.

Installation: Easy and quick.

STUCCO: (Photos 16-14, 16-15.) Stucco is a cement or mortar-type material made from three parts fine sand, one part Portland cement and water. The stucco is prepared at the site and then applied wet over wire laths in 2 or 3 coats. It can be finished smooth or rough, or in various textures and patterns. Pigment can be added directly to the mixture, or the stucco can be painted after drying. This type of siding is found mostly in moderate or temperate climates (Florida and California), because in areas where there is freezing weather, any water in the wall will freeze and cause the stucco to crack.

Stucco can be an attractive, durable siding. Its main drawback for owner builders is that it is difficult to master its application the first time around. Because of this, it is most often done by professionals, which can be costly (though still within reason). You may want to try applying some on a mock-up or outbuilding first, to see if you can learn to do it yourself. It provides a seamless, even surface that is easy to repair. It is fireproof and durable, and surprisingly, has good

shear strength. It can easily be molded to rounded or curved surfaces. Its greatest drawbacks are the cracking, due to either freezing or the house settling, and the fact that it may require a professional to install.

Cost: Moderate.

Lifetime: Life of the building.

Maintenance: None, except for repainting every few years.

Installation: Difficult and time-consuming for the novice.

BRICK: (Photos 16-16–16-19.) Brick siding is still commonplace in many areas of the East. You seldom see it in the West, and almost never in the earthquake areas of California (for apparent reasons). Brick is a veneer that covers and is attached to either a wood frame or concrete block walls. It is expensive and difficult to apply, but it gives a permanent veneer that is both attractive and maintenance-free. If you have a knack for this type of work and the patience, you may want to try to do it yourself, otherwise it is best left to professionals.

Many people think the brick veneer is one of the structural components of the house. Actually, the bricks are not structural and bear no load; they simply are a veneer. In the past they have been considered a mark of quality, and in many cases this is still true. If you plan to use this type of siding, you must adapt the foundation so it can support not only the house but the brick veneer as well. This is often done by using a 12-inch-wide concrete block with 4 inches of it extending to the outside of the wall line to support the 4-inch-wide bricks. Consider the expense and labor before deciding on this high-quality siding.

Photo 16-17. A brick veneer being applied.

Photo 16-18. Brick veneers are often used only on the side of the house facing the street.

Photo 16-19. This is not a real stone house, it's only a stone veneer over a frame house.

Cost: Expensive.
Lifetime: The life of the house.
Maintenance: None.
Installation: Difficult and time-consuming; usually done by professionals.

Horizontal Siding
What You'll Need

TIME   16 to 32 person-hours per 30-foot wall, 8 feet high.

PEOPLE   2 Minimum (1 skilled, 1 unskilled); 3 Optimum (2 skilled, 1 unskilled—2 nailers, 1 cutter); 6 Maximum (2 teams of 3 each).

TOOLS   Finishing hammer, ladders, utility knife, staple gun or hammer tacker, staples, measuring tape, hand saw (fine toothed), power saw with finishing blades, extension cords, pencil, nail belt, level, caulk gun, combination square, chalkline, sabre saw (if needed), bevel square for odd angles, copycat (if needed), nail punch.

RENTAL ITEMS: Scaffolding (Photo 16-20), transit.

MATERIALS   In this chapter, we will be doing horizontal, shiplapped wood board siding. You will need enough 15-pound felt to cover the entire building, enough siding materials (include a 10 to 15% waste factor; more if using a poor-quality stock), flashing materials, trim materials, caulking and hot-dipped galvanized nails. (See the Design Decisions section of this chapter, "Wood Boards," for a discussion of the different types of lumber and their quality.)

Clear, shiplapped redwood or cedar siding can be very expensive ($1100 to $1500 per 1000 board feet). I have often located a lower grade cedar siding with tight knots, that seldom fall out, for about $600 per 1000 board feet. Shop well, because the siding for a home can run to several thousand dollars. You need to shop prices before deciding. Be sure that the supplier you buy from will continue milling your type of siding, in case you did not order enough. You don't want to be looking for a match for your siding when you are 90% finished.

Store and protect the siding boards very well; you don't want to lose any to the elements. Siding is much more expensive than framing lumber, and therefore should have few, if any, unusable pieces. Check the stock as it is unloaded and do not accept any pieces that have been damaged or marred, such as from strapping, marking crayons, greying or weathering. You are paying for boards that will be exposed—they should be in good shape. Unload the truck by hand if there is any danger that the boards could be damaged by dumping.

Trim boards should be 1×4s that are of dry, knot-free stock. Use cedar, if the trim will be left unpainted, and fir or pine if you are going to paint the trim.

Always buy hot-dipped galvanized siding nails. Siding nails

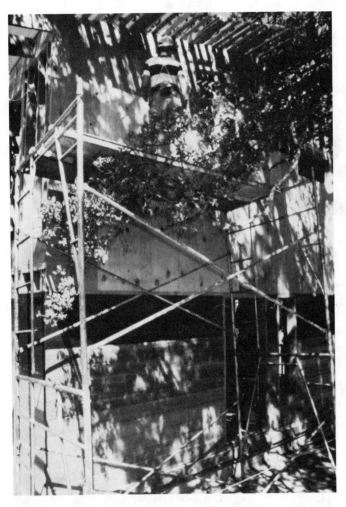

Photo 16-20. Though it takes a little time and money to set up, scaffolding makes all exterior work on second floors easier and quicker.

have smaller heads so they are not so visible. There are a few other types of non-rusting nails, but hot-dipped galvanized nails are recommended. Electro-plated galvanized nails often rust, and aluminum nails bend easily.

ESTIMATING MATERIALS NEEDED

SIDING BOARDS: To calculate the amount of siding boards you will need, you must first figure out how many square feet of walls need to be covered. Deduct for door and window openings and add 10 to 15% for waste. Order the longest boards you can get, or try to calculate the number of boards for each length you will need. If you have a 12-foot wall and a 16-foot wall, order 12- and 16-footers, etc. Take your time and work out a figure that comes close to your needs; the material is expensive.

TRIM: Trim boards are often dry, high-quality stock and therefore expensive. Try to estimate the exact amount of trim you will need and order the pieces in the proper lengths, to keep waste to a minimum. Include inside and outside corners, door and window trim, gable trim, etc. Also remember that many doors and windows come with their own trim, and you do not need to order trim for these.

NAILS: Figure 2 pounds of nails per sheet (4×8).

INFORMATION This chapter should provide you with all the info you need to complete the siding. For unique trim situations, consult an expert or use your problem-solving abilities.

PEOPLE TO CONTACT If you have opted to do the siding before the roofing, this is a good time to contact your roofer or roofing supplier. A plumber and electrician and sheet metal people, for ductwork, may need to be contacted also.

INSPECTIONS NEEDED If you are installing a plywood sheathing below the actual board siding (this is recommended, especially in earthquake, hurricane or tornado areas), you must get the nailing pattern of the sheathing inspected before covering the sheathing with felt and siding boards.

Reading the Plans

The plans will usually indicate what type of siding is to be used. Also they may indicate the type of trim. If a certain window manufacturer's model numbers are listed, you can check to see if the windows are pre-trimmed or have been ordered that way. Complex trim situations are sometimes detailed on the plans also. The plans should indicate any sheathing and may indicate the felt underlayment. (See Chapter 17, *Windows*, p. 421, "Materials: Trim," for trim applied before siding.) Other than this, everything else about siding is worked out at the job site.

Safety and Awareness

SAFETY: Unless you are dealing with heights, there is little danger involved in handling this type of siding, other than the common hazards at any construction site.

AWARENESS: Appearance should be of utmost importance as you apply the siding. Remember, this is finishing work you are doing and will be seen in the final product. As you apply, be aware of the following:

1. Horizontal lines must meet at the corners where 2 walls come together;
2. The best looking boards should be placed in visible areas;
3. The color matches in adjoining areas;
4. Hot-dipped galvanized siding nails are used;
5. Flashing is applied above all horizontal trim pieces where water will be running down the wall;
6. There is a felt underlayment;
7. Your siding is always level and aligned, especially on either side of an opening;
8. No dents, scratches or marks have been inflicted on the wood.

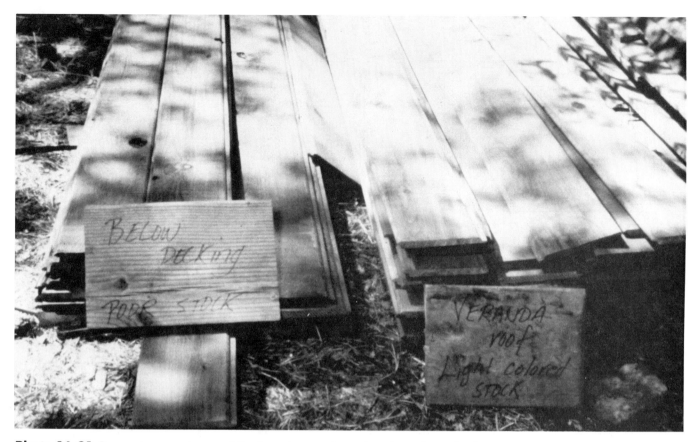

Photo 16-21. Be sure to separate your siding boards according to length, quality and color.

Overview of the Procedure

Step 1: Inspect and select the stock
Step 2: Pop a straight line to align the first board
Step 3: Apply the felt paper and locate and mark studs
Step 4: Apply the first course
Step 5: Apply successive courses
Step 6: Side and flash around openings
Step 7: Apply the trim

Step 1
Inspect and Select the Stock

Most Common Mistakes: Mixing colors; using poor-quality stock in highly visible areas.

Photograph: Photo 16-21.

Once the siding stock has been delivered to the site, spend some time selecting the good pieces and if necessary, separating the boards into different color shades. I have seen in one shipment of cedar siding colors vary from red to brown to white, and we had to separate the colors for various walls (often the difference in color diminishes with weathering). Separate out badly bowed pieces or pieces with flaws that are too extreme. Often, in the process of placing the siding, you will nail up a piece before noticing the bad knothole or ding in

it. The unacceptable pieces can be cut up and used where shorter pieces are needed, to cut down on waste. Put these in a separate pile and stack the good full-length pieces according to color and quality.

Select some of the straightest pieces to use for the first course, which needs to be really straight. Be on the lookout for especially beautiful pieces, ones with unique grain patterns or coloring, and use these around the main entrance doors at eye-level.

Step 2
Pop a Straight Line to Align the First Board

Margin of Error: Exactly level and in the exact location.

Most Common Mistake: Sloppy work.

Diagram: Figure 16-4.

Photograph: Photo 16-22.

Before applying the tar paper, it is best to snap a chalkline on the foundation to use to align the bottom of the first board. This line is usually about one inch below the top of the foundation. Bringing the felt paper and the siding down to this mark ensures that no water can run behind the bottom of the siding onto the top of the foundation and wet the sill plate. If the top

Figure 16-4. Pop a line for the first course about 1 inch below the top of the lowest level of the foundation, or ¼ inch below plywood sheathing at that level.

Photo 16-22. Scribing a level line on the foundation wall to serve as a guide for the first course.

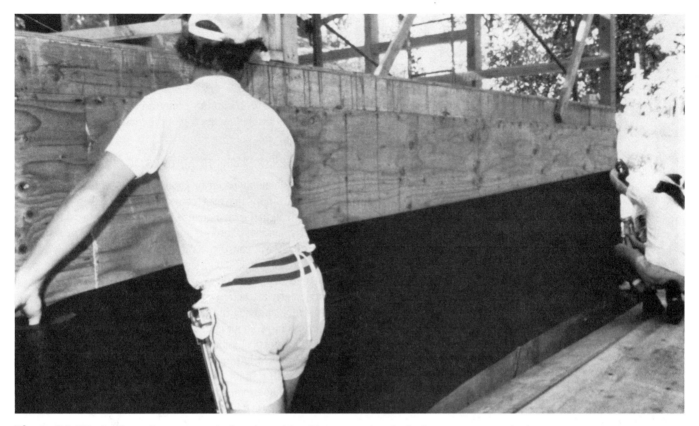

Photo 16-23. Applying the tar paper before the siding. Always overlap the higher courses onto the lower ones.

of the foundation is exactly level (and it seldom is), you could simply measure down one inch at either end of the foundation and snap a line between these 2 points. Most likely the foundation will be somewhat off level, so I would recommend using a transit (as described in Chapter 4, *Layout,* p. 77) to locate exactly level points. Be *very* exact; off-level boards are highly visible on the side of a building.

If you have a single-level foundation, where the top of the entire foundation wall is the same level, you can simply snap level lines around the entire foundation, one inch below the top. If, however, you have a stepped foundation, where the top of the foundation is at several different levels, start at the lowest section of the foundation wall and pop a level line one inch below the top of this section. Then, as the boards are applied, you will have to cut the pieces that break at a step. Do the same at each level.

Step 3
Apply Felt Paper and Locate and Mark Studs

Margin of Error: Apply felt smooth and approximately level; mark studs within ¼ inch of its center.

Most Common Mistakes: Not providing adequate overlaps at side or edges of felt; eliminating felt entirely; not overlapping felt courses so that the top overlaps the bottom.

Photographs: Photos 16-23, 16-24.

You are now ready to apply the felt. Usually 15-pound asphalt or rosin paper is used. Sometimes a brown paper called building paper is used. Whatever is used, it must breathe, in order to allow any water vapor that has built up inside the wall cavity to escape to the outside. Therefore, this paper should be water resistant, but not waterproof. Do not use a non-breathing surface such as polyethylene sheets or other types of plastic.

Do a good job as you apply this moisture barrier. Avoid punching holes or tearing the paper. Apply it flat and smooth. Begin at the bottom with the bottom edge ¼ inch above the line you popped, so the line is still visible when you apply the first course of boards. Apply the first (lower) course of paper and then overlap subsequent courses so that the one above overlaps the ones below.

Remember to get the nailing pattern of the sheathing inspected before you cover it with paper. In some areas the paper may be omitted. Inquire about the local building practices. Use a staple gun to affix the paper to the studs, using enough staples to keep it smooth and prevent any possible wind damage. Overlap the edges about 4 inches and where the ends of 2 sheets meet, overlap them 6 inches. Wrap one of the pieces about 6 inches around the inside and outside corners. Work up as high as you can and, after the ladders or scaffolding is erected, you can continue up higher.

After the paper is up on a section that you plan to side, locate and mark the centers of the studs, so you will know where to nail. This is done by simply snapping a chalkline down the centerline of the stud on top of the felt paper.

Photo 16-24. Before installing the siding, locate the center-line of studs on the felt with a chalkline.

Photo 16-25. Be very careful, when applying the first course, to use the straightest boards and check closely for level.

Step 4
Apply the First Course

Margin of Error: Exactly level.

Most Common Mistakes: Using a bowed board; not starting the first board below the top of the foundation.

Diagram: Figure 16-5.

Photographs: Photos 16-25, 16-26, 16-27, 16-28.

With the building paper or asphalt paper in place, you are now ready to apply the first course. These boards should be of very straight stock because the next course will be nailed directly against them. If there is a bad bow in these first boards, it will cause the other boards to bow. This is really true of the whole siding application process, and you should not use badly bowed boards at all, though they need not be particularly attractive boards unless they will be easily seen.

Before applying the first board, there are a few things you need to know about installing any wood board siding.

1. All vertical joints, where 2 boards meet at their ends, must be beveled and the joint must occur over a stud for solidity. Butt cuts will not work—they show cracks very easily. These joints are crucial to the quality of the job, because if they are badly cut or fitted, there will be a large crack showing. Using a jig and setting the saw blade at a true 45° angle is the best way to ensure good cuts. Shown here is a jig you can build at the job site. Bevel cuts are hard to make, but with a good straight jig and an accurate blade angle of 45°, it can be done. If a radial arm saw or table saw is available, it can be used to get an even better cut.

2. The vertical joints should be staggered on the wall so that joints in successive courses are offset by 4 to 8 feet; joints in alternating courses will line up. Keep this in mind when you order your board lengths to eliminate waste.

3. Use 3 hot-dipped galvanized siding nails at each stud if the boards are 6 inches wide or more. You may want to place these 3 nails in a straight line for appearance sake.

With all this in mind, nail on your first course. Be sure the bottom edge is flush with the line popped on the foundation wall. Place a level on the board to be sure the board is level before you permanently nail it on.

Figure 16-5. A jig used to cut siding.

Photo 16-26. Bevel cut the ends of the boards and be sure they meet over a stud. Be careful to avoid irregularities, like those shown here, in highly visible areas.

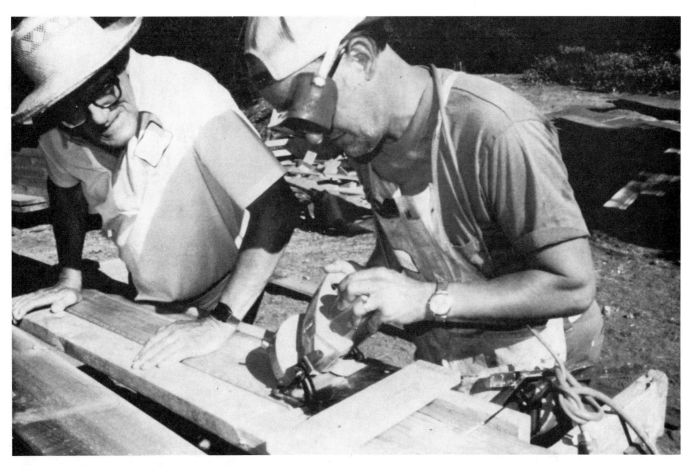

Photo 16-27. Using a site-built jig and a power saw at a 45° angle to bevel-cut the ends of the siding boards.

Photo 16-28. To bevel cut siding boards without a jig takes a steady hand.

Photo 16-29. Siding being applied. Note how the boards, on both sides of the openings, are level with each other.

Step 5
Apply Successive Courses

Margin of Error: Within ⅛ inch of level.

Most Common Mistakes: Not pushing new top board all the way down on to the top of the lower board; pushing top board too far down, causing it to buckle outwards; nailing boards from both ends towards the middle, thereby trapping a bow; board off level.

Diagram: Figure 16-6.

Photograph: Photo 16-29.

You can now start to apply the successive courses. This is a rather simple process as long as you are careful not to make any of the common mistakes, and you follow the guidelines set forth in "Step 4." Just continue working your way up the wall. If you find you are starting to get off level, adjust your next few boards to return to level (the transit comes in handy here). Check your level every second or third course to see how you are doing. Remember to choose each board for its visual effect and work on getting "grade A" joints where 2 boards meet at their ends.

Some builders use a story pole to be sure the boards are staying aligned and level. This is a straight 1×4 or 1×6 marked very accurately at intervals equal to the width of the boards. This marked pole can then be held at each end of the wall with the bottom of the pole aligned with the level marks, and the top of each board is aligned with an interval mark. Where 2 walls meet at an inside or outside corner, be sure the horizontal joints of the boards on each wall line up, or it will look very strange.

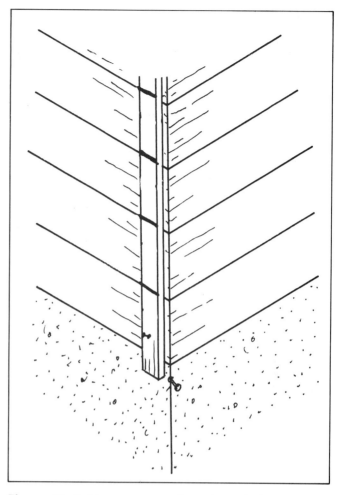

Figure 16-6. Using a story pole, with marked intervals, to keep individual boards level.

Figure 16-7. Using a scab piece to stop air infiltration through the openings left by the grooves.

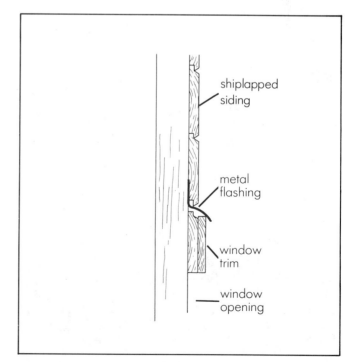

Figure 16-8. How flashing is applied to horizontal trim when using shiplapped siding.

Step 6
Side and Flash Around Openings

Margin of Error: ⅛ inch off alignment and level.

Most Common Mistakes: Omitted or improperly installed flashing; boards on either side of the opening getting off line.

Diagrams: Figures 16-7, 16-8.

Photographs: Photos 16-30, 16-31.

The only really challenging part of siding is around the door and window openings. These areas must be sided so that the boards in the same course on opposite sides of the opening are aligned with each other. If these boards get off line, the first full piece installed above the opening will not fit properly. There may be some fancy cutting needed wherever a full-size piece is notched to fit around the top or bottom of an opening. To be sure the pieces on opposite sides are level, simply make level marks on each side of the opening, using a level to represent the top of each board.

One-inch-wide strips, that run from the top to the bottom of the opening on the vertical sides only, are used as wind stops. These scab pieces prevent air from penetrating the small V-shaped grooves created where the shiplapped boards meet along their edges. They will be covered, in turn, by the wider exterior trim. Many builders eliminate this step and use pre-made plugs or caulking. I prefer the strips.

Flashing must also be installed above all door and window openings where water will be running down the wall. If the openings are well under the overhangs of the roof and no water will get above them, the flashing can be eliminated. This was the case with the opening in the photos.

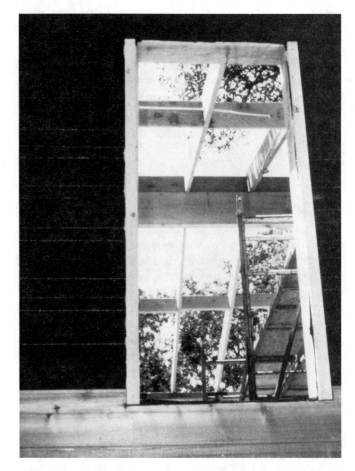

Photo 16-30. Note how the horizontal siding below the window is notched to fit around the opening. The strips on the sides of the window are to stop air infiltration through the grooves in the siding.

Photo 16-31. Be sure to continually check the level on the boards applied to each side of the openings. They must stay aligned.

Photo 16-32. The corners can be left rough until the trim is applied. Be sure that the horizontal lines of the grooves are aligned where the 2 walls meet.

Where any roofs are joined to the wall, flashing is necessary. The flashing here will be exposed above the trim, but it is unavoidable if you want good weather protection. Usually an aluminum or galvanized flashing cut from rolls of standard 12-inch-wide flashing is used. This can be painted with a bituminous paint for longer life and a more attractive appearance. Terne metal, a copper-bearing steel, can also be used. This is not only attractive, but will last the lifetime of the house as well (it is expensive).

Step 7
Apply the Trim

Margin of Error: ⅛ inch.

Most Common Mistakes: Sloppy work; no flashing on exposed horizontal pieces.

Photographs: Photos 16-32, 16-33, 16-34.

The siding is now finished and you are ready to apply the trim at the corners, around the openings and at the gables. Check to see if your doors and windows are coming pre-trimmed (most windows are pre-trimmed). If they are, you might want to coordinate the rest of the exterior trim with the trim provided by the manufacturer.

Use high-quality dry stock for the trim and be sure all the trim pieces around any one opening are color-matched. Be sure the trim is applied level or plumb and has tight-fitting joints. These joints can be either mitred or butt-cut.

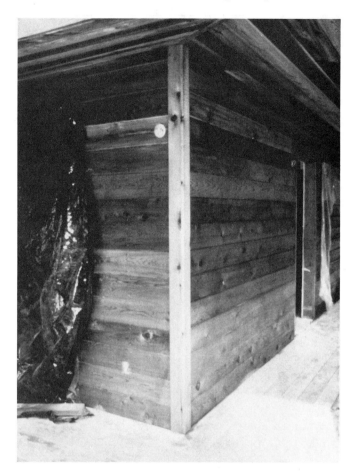

Photo 16-33. This corner has been finished with 1-×-4 trim.

Photo 16-34. The house after the siding has been applied and the deck added.

Worksheet

ESTIMATED TIME

_____

_____

_____

CREW

Skilled or Semi-Skilled

_____ Phone _____

_____ Phone _____

_____ Phone _____

Unskilled

_____ Phone _____

_____ Phone _____

_____ Phone _____

_____ Phone _____

MATERIALS NEEDED

Siding, felt, flashing, trim, caulking, nails.

ESTIMATING MATERIALS

SIDING BOARDS:

No. of sq. ft. of walls _____

+ 15% _____ = total _____ sq. ft.

No. _____ 8-foot boards (No. of sq. ft. _____)

No. _____ 10-foot boards (No. of sq. ft. _____)

No. _____ 12-foot boards (No. of sq. ft. _____)

No. _____ 14-foot boards (No. of sq. ft. _____)

No. _____ 16-foot boards (No. of sq. ft. _____)

No. _____ 18-foot boards (No. of sq. ft. _____)

No. _____ 20-foot boards (No. of sq. ft. _____)

FELT: _____ sq. ft. of wall surface = _____ rolls

FLASHING:

_____ linear ft. of flashing above doors

_____ linear ft. of flashing above windows

_____ linear ft. of flashing for wall-roof joints

_____ total linear ft. of flashing

TRIM:

Corners:

_____ No. of boards _____ ft. long

_____ No. of boards _____ ft. long

Gables:

_____ No. of boards _____ ft. long

_____ No. of boards _____ ft. long

Doors:

_____ No. of boards _____ ft. long

_____ No. of boards _____ ft. long

_____ No. of boards _____ ft. long

_____ No. of boards _____ ft. long

Windows:

_____ No. of boards _____ ft. long

_____ No. of boards _____ ft. long

_____ No. of boards _____ ft. long

_____ No. of boards _____ ft. long

NAILS: _____ lbs. of nails.

COST COMPARISON

_____ Store:

Cost per board _____ total $ _____

_____ Store:

Cost per board _____ total $ _____

_____ Store:

Cost per board _____ total $ _____

Daily Checklist

CREW:

_____ Phone _____

_____ Phone_____

_____ Phone _____

_____ Phone_____

_____ Phone_____

_____ Phone _____

TOOLS:

☐ finishing hammer ☐ pencil

☐ ladders ☐ nail belt

☐ utility knife ☐ level

☐ staple gun/hammer tacker ☐ caulk gun

☐ staples ☐ combination square

☐ measuring tape ☐ chalkline

☐ hand saw (fine toothed) ☐ sabre saw (if needed)

☐ power saw ☐ bevel square

☐ finishing blades (for saw) ☐ copycat

☐ extension cords ☐ nail punch

RENTAL ITEMS:

☐ scaffolding

☐ transit

MATERIALS:

_____ No. of boards _____ ft. long

_____ No. of boards _____ ft. long

_____ No. of boards _____ ft. long

_____ No. of boards _____ ft. long

_____ No. of boards _____ ft. long

_____ rolls of felt

_____ linear ft. of flashing

TRIM:

_____ No. of boards _____ ft. long

_____ No. of boards _____ ft. long

_____ No. of boards _____ ft. long

_____ No. of boards _____ ft. long

_____ No. of boards _____ ft. long

_____ lbs. of nails

DESIGN REVIEW: Make decision on trim design.

INSPECTIONS NEEDED: ☐ YES ☐ NO

Inspector _____

Phone _____

Time and date of inspection _____

WEATHER FORECAST:

For week _____

For day _____

Do not put boards up wet; they may shrink and crack, or leave gaps.

17 Windows

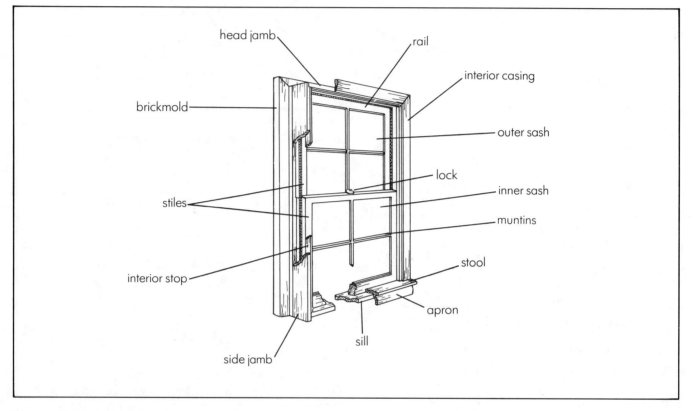

head jamb

rail

interior casing

brickmold

outer sash

lock

inner sash

stiles

muntins

interior stop

stool

apron

sill

side jamb

Figure 17-1. Parts of a window.

What You'll Be Doing, What to Expect

WINDOW INSTALLATION is easy, enjoyable and exciting. The exterior appearance of the house will go through final changes as large gaping openings are filled with attractive windows and trimmed. It is one of my favorite days at the job site. In regard to appearance, the home leaps way ahead. It is a job to enjoy, even relish. The only real problems come in two areas: if you ordered the wrong window or if you provided the wrong size opening. This can cause frustration and gnashing of teeth.

Basically, you are placing the window in the opening and levelling it; nailing it in place, and then doing the trim. If the window is pre-trimmed, even the trimming step is eliminated. If you are cutting and installing the exterior trim, precision is required; this will be finished work. Go slow and be careful; dropping a window can be dangerous, and expensive. Use caution installing the windows on high walls, especially on windy days.

Jargon

(Figure 17-1)

APRON. The interior trim piece below the sill.

BRICKMOLD. The exterior trim around a door or window.

CASING. The interior and exterior trim around the top and sides of a window or door.

FINISH FRAME. The stationary pieces surrounding the movable window (side jamb, head jamb, sill, etc.).

JAMB. The tops and sides of a door or window frame that are in contact with the door or sash; referred to as side jamb and head jamb (top).

LIGHT. A window, a section of a divided window, or a pane set in a window.

MULLION. A slender vertical bar (usually wood) separating adjoining windows.

MUNTIN. A narrow vertical or horizontal strip separating panes of a window.

RAIL. The horizontal top or bottom piece of a door or window sash.

SASH. The movable part of a window or the frame that holds the glass.

SILL. The horizontal member at the bottom of the window frame. It is often slanted towards the exterior to shed water.

STILE. A vertical side piece of a door or window sash.

STOOL. A molded, horizontal interior trim piece at the bottom of the frame, resting on the sill and protruding into the interior of the home.

STOP. The narrow strip of trim along the face of a door or window jamb. It prevents the door or window from swinging too far out and retards air flow. It also creates the channels in double hung windows.

Purposes of a Window

1) To provide light
2) To provide view
3) To provide ventilation
4) In solar application, to allow the sun to hit the thermal mass
5) In some instances, to provide an emergency exit

Design Decisions

Design decisions on windows, their size, style, placement, etc., could fill a book or several courses at architecture schools. The decisions you make here are key to creating the proper feeling in each room—the feeling that you really want. Often I have felt that a room simply did not work or fall together properly, due to the window decisions. These decisions are vital to the success of the design and are, all too often, just made at random.

Visualize each decision you are making. If visualizing is difficult for you, visit a room that has a similar window set-up to the one you are contemplating. Then close your eyes and imagine doing what you will be doing in that room and see how it feels. Does the window decision support the activity of the room or does it fight it? If it doesn't support it, then change a few things: the location, the size, the height. Go back into your visualization of the activity in the room and see if this changes the way you feel about the room, better or worse. Your ability to visualize the decisions before you physically enact them, and your ability to honestly get in touch with your innermost feelings about these decisions and their impact (whether they support the activities in the room or not), are keys to successful decisions in this and all areas of the home.

I remember visiting a friend in Florida, who proudly showed me his home, that had just been completed. The livingroom sitting area, an area meant to make people feel relaxed and communicative, was a 20-×-20-foot platform raised 12 inches off the ground that faced a floor-to-ceiling window wall, that looked out onto a ship canal. The couches were arranged in a U-shape with the open section of the "U"

being the window wall. As we sat and talked, a yacht passed through the canal, only 200 feet from the livingroom, people on deck waving and laughing. Our attention, needless to say, was drawn towards the canal, away from our "intimate" conversation. Only after the boat passed could the conversation continue, only to be followed by another boat pulling a couple of skiers, drawing everyone's attention back to the canal again. It was impossible to have a real group interchange in the one area that had been designed just for that purpose. The design was sabotaging the activity.

Before choosing the window design for your house, be aware of what is available. In the following section, the different types of windows are discussed.

Types of Windows

Windows affect the view, privacy, air flow, temperature, safety and security, solar gain, and most important, the feel of a home. The type of window, its size, location, style, and manufacturer all need to be carefully considered. We would all like to put the best windows in our home, but few of us can afford it. Windows for the same house can range from $8,000 to $12,000 for the top of the line, to $3,000 to $4,000 for the same sized windows of a lower quality brand. You have to consider what you will have to give up to put in the more expensive brands (better carpeting or cabinets, a hot tub, the garage, etc.). I usually recommend getting a medium-priced brand, between the best and the cheapest, unless you can afford the best. Avoid, however, installing anything of questionable quality in the home. It is permanent and if it gives you poor service it's very difficult to replace.

Usually you need to have made these decisions about windows by the plan drawing stage, and no later than the wall framing stage, when you need to be providing the proper rough opening sizes specified by the manufacturer (for more on this see "Sizes of Doors and Windows and Rough Openings," p. 227, in Chapter 11, *Wall Framing*). If in your house you are implementing a passive solar energy plan (an essential, unless you live in a very moderate climate—and it is even recommended there), your window size and placement must be co-ordinated with your passive solar design to allow the sun in at the proper times. For these reasons the design decision for your windows would have been made long before the window installation stage discussed in this chapter.

PREHUNG WINDOWS: Most windows today come "prehung." This means that the window, its casing (trim), moulding, sill, weatherstripping, hardware, etc. is assembled at the factory and is installed as one unit. Because of the simplicity and speed of installing "prehung" windows, they come highly recommended. Often old windows, just the window without the frame, can be purchased very cheaply. You can also find classy, decorative windows that add to the appearance of the house. These will take much longer to install. A prehung will take about 1 hour to hang and trim, an old window about 3 to 5 hours. Multiply this times the number of windows you plan to use and it adds up. If you are paying for finish carpenters to install the old window, it might even end up costing you more than a high-quality prehung window.

WOOD OR ALUMINUM: Wood and aluminum are the standard materials used in making windows. Wood windows, usually made from kiln-dried high-quality ponderosa pine, have some real advantages. They are better insulators (wood as opposed to metal), they have a nice appearance and they do not condense water as metal frames do. They may, however, be more expensive and they do require paint periodically.

Aluminum windows, which are often less expensive than their wood counterparts, do not need painting and are more scratch-resistant. They also make use of a smaller frame because of the added strength of metal, thereby allowing more window glass. They do, however, transfer more heat and are not as energy-efficient, and tend to "sweat" in certain climates.

New developments in both wood and metal windows have overcome some of their disadvantages. There is now an aluminum clad wooden window that incorporates an aluminum cladding or covering on the exterior so you do not need to paint it. (Aluminum clad windows are very good in solar greenhouses where moisture content is high.) Aluminum windows are now constructed to have insulation breaks built into the frame so they are more energy-efficient. Both these improvements will cost you more money, but may be worth considering.

The quality of all these windows can vary greatly. The National Woodwork Manufacturer's Association sets minimal standards, but quality varies greatly beyond these. Usually the better brands are known by their reputation. Your local lumberyards will usually carry several different brands to allow the customer a choice in prices and style. If you order the windows with your lumber order, you will get a better price on everything, since the total bill is large.

Styles

Basically there are three different styles of windows: sliding, swinging and fixed. Within these basic styles there are many possibilities. Your choice should not be random, but well thought out, as it will subtly, but profoundly, affect the house. Windows that open out (casement, awning, etc.) allow the full window area to vent and can redirect cooling breezes into the building. However, if they open on to a walkway or porch, they can be dangerous. Fixed windows are inexpensive and adaptable but offer no ventilation. Read this section and choose well. (Be sure to read the Information section in this chapter for the code requirements).

CASEMENT: Casement windows are hinged on the side and open outwards. They are opened by a cranking mechanism or push bar. Because of this opening procedure they are a good choice above sinks or cabinets where the windows are hard to reach. These windows allow 100% opening for ventilation and are weather tight when clasped shut. They can act as a wind scoop to catch the summer breeze. To do this properly, be sure you know the prevailing wind pattern and therefore on which side to hinge the window to redirect these winds into the home. Be careful if they open out into a walkway or porch (especially if children are to live in the home) as they can be dangerous.

AWNING: Awning windows usually have one or more sashes that are hinged at the top and swing at the bottom (usually outwards). Like the casements, they use a push bar or cranking mechanisms. They have the same advantages and disadvantages as the casement windows, but unlike the casement window, they cannot be used as an emergency exit. If the window is hinged at the bottom and opens inward at the top, it is called a "hopper" window. Usually this is just the awning window upside down.

DOUBLE HUNG: Double hung windows are windows with 2 sashes that slide up and down by friction, balancing devices or springs. They are very common and usually very economical. They provide adequate ventilation if opened partially from the top and partially from the bottom, and can be used as an emergency exit. This type of window was one of the first real improvements in windows and it goes back over 100 years. The old, hard-to-repair balancing weights used to open and close the windows have been replaced by springs.

HORIZONTAL SLIDERS: These windows are made up of 2 or more sashes that slide horizontally in a track by pushing on the window. Some are spring assisted. They offer adequate ventilation and can be used as an emergency exit. Though they are not a particularly common type of window, such as their up-and-down sliding double hung cousin, they are available from most window manufacturers.

FIXED: Fixed windows are simply sheets of glass permanently fixed in their frames. Oftentimes these are used in combination with other opening windows to create a certain effect with a series of windows without having to pay the added expense to have all the windows in the series open. They offer the view and lighting qualities of opening windows but offer no ventilation and cannot be used as an exit. A fixed window is generally used in the south wall of a passive solar home where a lot of sunlight, but not as much ventilation, is needed.

These windows can be bought from manufacturers in different sizes, already set in a frame. They can also be built at the job site by ordering the proper size glass and building your own frame. This can be more economical, especially if you are doing the work yourself. Oftentimes you can find double-glazed glass panels very cheap. As seconds used in sliding glass doors, they can run as cheap as 30% of their usual cost (you can then design your openings to fit these panels).

Other than these, there are a few other kinds of windows, but these are the most common. There are jalousies, which are horizontal glass slats in metal frames that operate like venetian blinds. These are used in warm climates or in porches in cold climates, as they are not weather tight. There are multiple use windows that incorporate an outward swinging sash that can be installed either horizontally or vertically. These are usually simple windows with no complicated hardware.

SINGLE, DOUBLE AND TRIPLE PANES: Double or triple paned windows have been around for a long time. At Thomas Jefferson's Monticello, I was surprised to see he had used double paned windows on the entire north side. With energy a great consideration in homes today, double and triple paned windows are becoming increasingly popular. In some states they are even required by code. The reason for the popularity of multiple paned windows is obvious. Glass by itself is a very poor insulator. The R factor (insulation property) of a standard wall is about 14. A single pane window is about .75. If you add another pane of glass with an air space between the two, you have increased the R factor to 2.0. The claim is then made that double paned glass cuts the heat loss through windows by 50%, which is true. But still even a double paned glass has only $\frac{1}{7}$ the insulating property of the wall (insulated).

Fortunately, most heat loss occurs through the roof areas, since the hot air is rising, and through cracks and small openings. Around 10 to 20% of your total heat loss occurs through the windows. Double and triple paned windows also reduce heat loss through radiation to a colder surface (the window) and act somewhat as a noise barrier.

If you are working on a limited budget and are very concerned about heat loss, you may want to use window quilts instead. These are thick (1-inch) insulated window drapes that pull down and fit with velcroe around the edges. They raise the R factor up to 5 or 6, 3 times that of double paned windows. If you can afford it, using both double (or triple) paned windows and window quilts would be good. Check to see the difference in cost between the same windows with double, triple or single panes. Check the prices of window quilts. Evaluate the possible savings in energy in your area with your fuel bills (you may want to consult a professional solar designer to help), and decide which is the best way to go.

What You'll Need

TIME

FOR PREHUNG WINDOWS: About 1 person-hour per window, unless there are problems with the window or openings.

FOR FIXED WINDOWS: About 2 to 4 person-hours per window.

PEOPLE   2 Minimum (1 skilled, 1 unskilled); 2 Optimum (1 skilled, 1 unskilled); 4 Maximum (2 teams).

TOOLS   Finish hammer, nail set, utility knife, caulking gun, tape measure, framing square, power saw, hand saw, shim material, pencil, nail belt, chisel, level, safety goggles, nail-pulling tools, saw horses, extension cord.

MATERIALS   You will need windows, trim materials (if the windows aren't pre-trimmed), caulking, felt paper and hot-dipped, galvanized finishing nails (16d).

ORDERING WINDOWS: Ordering windows is no simple matter. Aside from choosing the proper size, type and model number, there are several things that must be stated in ordering each window. There always seem to be a lot of mistakes and misunderstandings in this area. Below is a list of some of the things that must be included when ordering each window:

1) The model number (this tells size, style, etc.).
2) Whether it opens out and if it hinges on the left or the right (usually, facing the window from the outside).
3) What type of exterior trim do you want? What type of interior trim do you want?
4) Can it be used as an exit window in the bedroom if one is required?
5) Do you want blinds or screens?
6) Do you want it painted, stained or primed?
7) Do you want aluminum clad or all wood?
8) Are different types of sills available?
9) Do you want it with mullions, and if so, are there different styles?
10) Do you want single, double or triple glazed?
11) If there are fixed and opening units in a series, which units are fixed, which are open?

THICKNESS OF JAMBS: Depending on the combined thickness of the entire wall panel, special jamb extenders may be needed or the window will have to be ordered with wider jambs. If you are using a 2-×-4 wall, with drywall for the interior surface and plywood for the exterior, your wall will only be about 4⅝ inches thick (stud, 3½ inches; drywall, ½ inch; and plywood siding, ⅝ inch). If you were using, for example, a 2-×-6 wall with ⅝-inch interior drywall surface, ½-inch plywood sheathing outside plus ¾-inch vertical siding on top of that, the wall would be 7⅜ inches thick (stud, 5½ inches; drywall, ⅝ inch; plywood sheathing, ½ inch; and siding, ¾ inch). To accommodate the wider wall, many manufacturers use either wider jamb boards or jamb extenders. Either of these run into an extra cost of $20 to $60 per window. You will need to *tell your manufacturer the wall thickness, from the inside edge of the interior wall to the outside edge of the exterior wall,* so they can order or build your window accordingly.

TRIM: Each manufacturer will have several different types of interior and exterior trim to choose from. Or the window can be ordered with no trim and you can provide this yourself (in this case, some windows will come with an exterior nailing flange). The exterior trim is usually assembled as part of the window, and the interior trim will come precut in a bundle to be installed after the window is in.

Usually the trim is installed around the openings after the siding is in place and the window is installed. A few sidings, such as clapboard, which has a layered rather than a flush surface, may require that the trim be installed *before the siding*. If the trim was installed after the siding and was attached on top of it, gaps would be created between the siding and the trim, since the siding is at different levels. Check before you begin siding to see if the trim should be installed first.

ESTIMATING MATERIALS NEEDED

NAILS: ½ pound per window.
CAULK: ½ tube of caulk per window.
FLASHING: Measure feet of flashing needed.

Figure 17-2. Check the level and plumb of the rough opening before installing the window. Use shims to correct it, if needed.

INFORMATION This chapter plus any manufacturer's installation instructions should be all you need, unless you are framing windows in unique shapes or windows that are non-rectangular. In this case, consult a professional or see the Time/Life book on doors and windows.

Be aware of the building codes in your area concerning windows. Most codes require that you have at least one window in each bedroom that fully opens and with its sill not more than 44 inches from the floor. Some codes also require that any windows within 12 to 18 inches of a door or the floor be made of tempered glass.

PEOPLE TO CONTACT Now is the time to contact the insulation contractor, the drywall contractor, and the painter, if you haven't already done so.

INSPECTIONS NEEDED None.

Reading the Plans

As mentioned in the plan reading section of the *Wall Framing* chapter, every window opening will be marked with an identifying number that corresponds, in the window schedule, to a certain manufacturer's model number. The model number will then indicate the exact rough opening that needs to be provided. However, there still may be many decisions to make in regard to that particular window (see "Ordering Windows" under "Materials" in this chapter).

Safety and Awareness

SAFETY: Be very careful working around glass. One clumsy move can cause a serious injury or can break a window worth several hundred dollars.

AWARENESS: Remember, this is all finishing work, so be very particular. Have windows properly flashed and caulked and be sure they are level.

Overview of the Procedure

Step 1: Check opening and window
Step 2: Caulk, set into opening and level the window
Step 3: Nail the window in place

Step 1
Check Opening and Window

Margin of Error: Whatever it takes to get the window into the opening.

Most Common Mistakes: Window will not fit opening; damaged window; improperly ordered window.

Diagram: Figure 17-2.

Photographs: Photos 17-1, 17-2, 17-3, 17-4.

Before the actual installation of the window, uncrate the window and check for the following:
1) For any shipping damage
2) The manufacturer's installation instructions
3) If it is square
4) If it is the correct window
5) If it opens properly
6) If all pieces are there

If you plan to paint the window and it is not primed, you may want to paint it with primer before installing it (be careful not to paint weatherstripping or channels). If diagonal braces are attached to the window to keep it square, leave these on until the window is installed. You can climatize your window to local humidity by leaving it inside the house for a few days before installing it. Manufacturers advise that you wear clean, dry cotton gloves to handle windows. Be careful; frames are made from soft wood.

Be sure to check the thickness of the jambs to see that they were properly constructed to fit your wall panel (see "Thickness of Jambs" under "Materials" in this chapter). If any jamb extenders or interior trim pieces are provided with the windows, be sure they are all there and are the proper length and thickness. (Note: With some windows the sills and side jambs need to be cut flush with the frame before installing the window.)

Check the opening to be sure it is square and the proper dimensions. If there is any siding or sheathing protruding into the opening (thereby reducing the size of your opening), cut this out with a hand saw or power saw, or chisel it out. Some builders wrap the rough frame with felt paper or building paper. The best time to do this, however, is when you install the building paper under the sheathing or siding. Check to be sure the flashing has been included, or that you have flashing at the site for windows that will get wet from water running down the walls above them (see "Step 6" in Chapter 16, *Siding*).

If a window opening is too big or too small for the window, use your best problem-solving abilities to remedy the situation.

Photo 17-1. A rough opening before installation.

Photo 17-2. Check the measurements of the rough opening before installing the window.

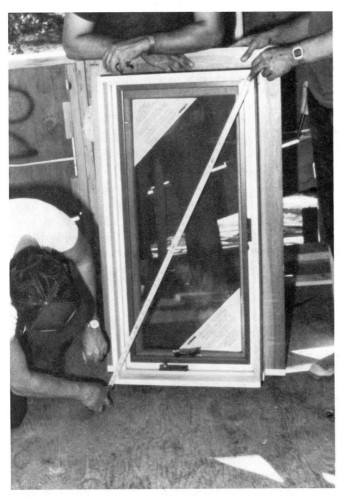

Photo 17-3. Check the measurements and squareness of pre-hung windows.

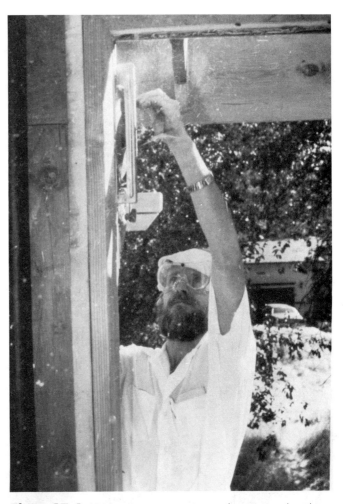

Photo 17-4. Using a power saw to cut the excess sheathing out of the rough opening.

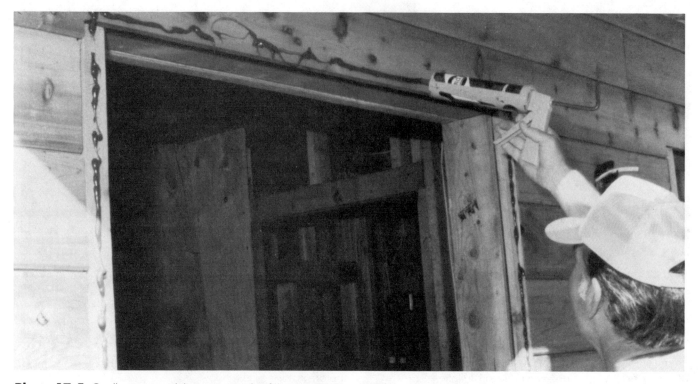

Photo 17-5. Caulking around the exterior side of the rough opening before installing the window.

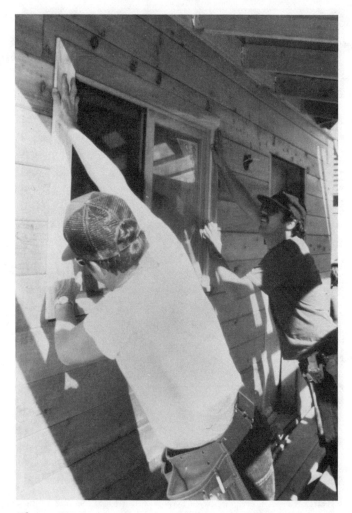

Photo 17-6. Press the window flush against the siding.

Step 2
Caulk, Set into Opening and Level the Window

Margin of Error: None.

Most Common Mistakes: Eliminating caulking or flashing; putting window in upside down.

Photographs: Photos 17-5, 17-6, 17-7, 17-8.

Hopefully everything is working fine and the window fits the opening. It will mostly depend on how careful you were back at the wall framing stage. Prepare the window to be installed by running a bead of silicone caulk on the backside of the exterior trim (if the window is pre-trimmed). This adds an extra protection against possible water or air infiltration. If you want, you can caulk the siding where the trim will be, as shown in the photo.

Before installing the window, place some cedar shims every 16 inches on the horizontal rough sill. These will be used in the final levelling of the window. Now lift the window into place and, trying not to disturb the shim stock, set it in the opening. Most windows are installed from the outside, but some can be installed from either direction, especially if they are untrimmed. Installing untrimmed windows from the inside may be the way to go on high walls.

Now, before you nail the window, be sure of four things: (1) that the window is level, (2) that the window is plumb, (3) that the trim is flat against the exterior siding, and (4) that the jamb is the proper thickness for the wall. Check to be sure that the flashing properly overlaps the top of the horizontal trim piece.

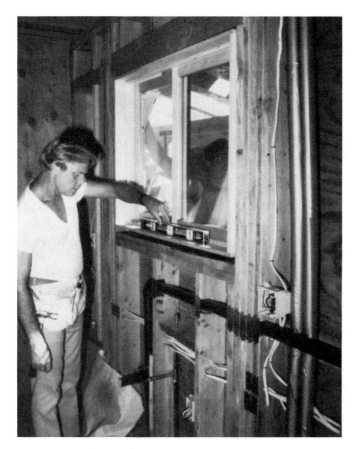

Photo 17-7. Check the level of the window after installation.

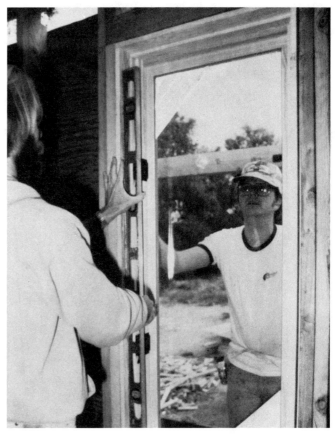

Photo 17-8. Check the plumb of the window after installation.

Photo 17-9. Nailing through shims. Place shims every 16 inches or so.

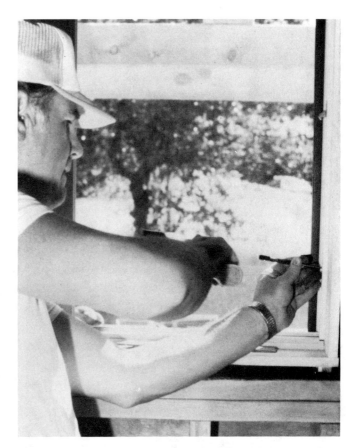

Photo 17-10. Toenailing finishing nails into the casing.

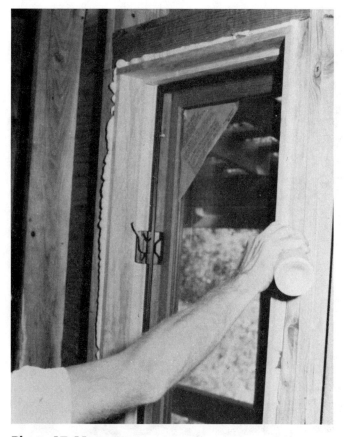

Photo 17-11. Applying insulating foam in the cracks between the windows and the trimmer studs of the rough opening.

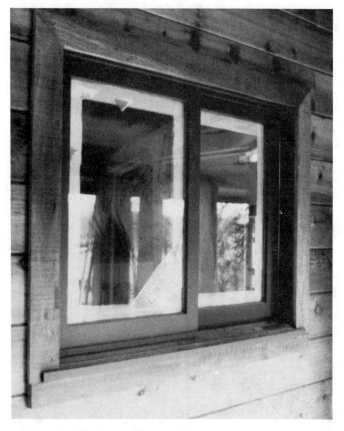

Photo 17-12. The window installed.

Step 3
Nail the Window in Place

Margin of Error: ⅛ inch off level.

Most Common Mistakes: Trim not flat against siding; no caulking; improper flashing; off level; jamb not wide enough.

Photographs: Photos 17-9, 17-10, 17-11, 17-12.

Once the window is properly positioned, you are ready to nail it in place. Have someone press against the trim (with pre-trimmed windows) as you nail, to be sure it is flat against the siding. Use shims every 16 inches around the window and nail through the jamb into the shims. Be sure there are no bows or waves in the jamb. Use 12d or 16d hot-dipped galvanized finishing nails and countersink them with a nail punch. After you have nailed every 16 inches around the jamb, nail the exterior trim, using the same nails. You may want to insulate around the window with foam or insulation at this time.

Special Situations

FIXED GLASS WINDOWS: Most houses involve some fixed glass as well as the regular opening windows. There are two approaches to fixed glass windows: you can buy windows pre-framed from manufacturers, or frame them yourself at the job site. I highly recommend framing them yourself at the job site; the savings are considerable and it's not very difficult or time-consuming.

You can order the glass from a local glass company. It is wise to have *them* measure the frame openings and install the glass. Then if a piece doesn't fit or gets scratched or broken, they pay the price, not you. Usually the glass is double plated and sometimes it is tempered. Tempered glass is hardened glass that will not break easily. It is twice the price of regular glass, and is used in all opening windows and doors with glass panels. It is not necessary to use in fixed glass areas unless the code requires it. Usually it is required when the fixed glass is within 18 inches of a door. It may also be required if the glass comes within 18 inches of the ground, but even then a railing will satisfy the requirement. If glass panels need to be tempered, see if you can buy seconds, e.g., patio door panels. These are often available at a third the usual cost and come in several sizes.

Some builders build the frame and install it without the glass. Other builders build the frame directly into the opening. I think both processes are about equal. Usually the frame is made of a clear, dry wood such as pine, fir or redwood. Make the frame ½ inch larger, in height and width, than the glass panels. Either 1-inch or 2-inch material can be used (I often use 1-inch for the side and head jamb, with a 2-inch-thick sill). The jambs must be wide enough to extend from the inside edge of the interior wall to the outside edge of the exterior wall. As with prehung windows, be sure the opening is square and has true dimensions; slope the sill outwards to shed water.

After the frame has been nailed level and plumb in the opening, cut the interior stops to go around the entire frame.

Photo 17-13. A bow window after installation.

Spread a small bead of caulk on the underside of the stops, between the stops and the jambs, for added protection.

Once the stops are in, spread a generous bed of silicone caulk on the back stop. Do not use putty.

Next snap pre-made neoprene setting blocks every 12 to 16 inches on the bottom of the glass and spacer strips along the edges and the top. Set the bottom edge in position on the sill. Press the glass in until the spacer strips and setting blocks are flat against the back stop. Nail in the face stop (exterior), again caulking between the face stop and the glass and jambs with silicone caulk. Do not toenail, since you may hit the glass. And there you have it.

BAY AND BOW WINDOWS: (Photo 17-13.) Aside from the windows mentioned, many people use bay or bow windows in their homes. These windows create an appealing interior nook and give the room a larger feeling. Bow and bay windows can be bought pre-made from most manufacturers and are usually made up of several standard casement or double hung windows, along with some fixed glass windows. You can frame these areas yourself at the job site and then install prehung windows into your openings.

Worksheet

ESTIMATED TIME

_____

_____

_____

_____

CREW

Skilled or Semi-Skilled

_____ Phone _____

_____ Phone _____

_____ Phone _____

Unskilled

_____ Phone _____

_____ Phone _____

_____ Phone _____

_____ Phone _____

_____ Phone _____

MATERIALS NEEDED

Windows, flashing, trim, caulking and nails.

ESTIMATING MATERIALS

WINDOWS:

_____ No. of windows _____ size

_____ No. of windows _____ size

_____ No. of windows _____ size

_____ No. of windows _____ size

FLASHING:

_____ ft. of flashing

TRIM:

_____ ft. of trim

CAULKING:

½ tube (per window) × _____ no. of windows

= _____ tubes

NAILS:

1½ lbs. of nails (per window) × _____ no. of windows

= _____ lbs. of nails

COST COMPARISON

_____ Store:

Cost per window _____ total $ _____

_____ Store:

Cost per window _____ total $ _____

_____ Store:

Cost per window _____ total $ _____

_____ Store:

Cost per window _____ total $ _____

PEOPLE TO CONTACT

Insulation contractor _____

Phone _____ Work Date _____

Drywall contractor _____

Phone _____ Work Date _____

Painter _____

Phone _____ Work Date _____

Daily Checklist

CREW:

_____ Phone _____

_____ Phone _____

_____ Phone _____

_____ Phone _____

_____ Phone _____

_____ Phone _____

TOOLS:

☐ finish hammer

☐ nail set

☐ utility knife

☐ caulking gun

☐ tape measure

☐ framing square

☐ power saw

☐ hand saw

☐ shim stock

☐ pencil

☐ nail belt

☐ chisel

☐ level

☐ safety goggles

☐ nail-pulling tools

☐ saw horses

☐ extension cord

MATERIALS:

_____ No. of windows _____ size

_____ No. of windows _____ size

_____ No. of windows _____ size

_____ No. of windows _____ size

_____ ft. of trim

_____ ft. of flashing material

_____ tubes of caulking

_____ lbs. of nails

DESIGN REVIEW: At this point it's a little late to change anything, but if you really don't feel right about some of the window decisions, consider changing them now. Once you move in, you may wish you had.

WEATHER FORECAST:

For week _____

For day _____

Index

The Owner Builder Center

THE OWNER BUILDER CENTER is a non-profit, self-funded educational organization located in Berkeley, California. We are dedicated to providing high quality information to the public on housebuilding, remodeling, energy efficiency, and solar energy. Founded in 1978, we have taught over 8,000 people in our classes and seminars and assisted many others in our consulting and design services. We have a highly qualified and dedicated teaching staff of thirty part-time teachers and five full-time employees who do the work of ten and still smile. Our classes are both local and national in scope.

Local Classes and Services

Locally, we teach classes in six San Francisco Bay area cities in the following: housebuilding, remodeling, design, plan drawing, cabinet making and solar hot water system installation. We also offer a series of seminars four times each year and sponsor local hands-on workshops. Our services are rounded out by financing packages, realtor and contractor referrals, and an in-house line of kit homes. We maintain a bookstore, reference library, and consultation service to assist people with individual needs.

Summer Residence Program

Of interest to people outside our immediate area, we offer summer residence housebuilding programs in Grass Valley, California in the foothills of the Sierra Nevada Mountains. These two- and three-week courses run between May and September, and include both hands-on and classroom instruction. During each summer we build several structures, usually including at least one passive solar home. The structures are begun at various times during the summer to allow for a great variety of jobsite work during each semester. Evenings are free for social time, a guest speaker or additional classes. On weekends are raft trips, swimming, hiking or exploring the Mother Lode country. Students are housed and fed at a local Quaker high school with a beautiful three hundred acre campus. Both cabins and campsites are available.

Consulting Service

The Owner Builder Center operates a full-service consulting business specializing in the needs of owner-builders and passive solar and energy-efficient design. The service operates on an hourly fee basis and consultation can be done by mail or by phone for those out of the area. Plans, photographs of the site, topographic maps, etc., can be sent to us with the questions you would like to be advised on and we will send you back either written replies or cassette tapes with our recommendations. You can, for instance, send us a copy of your plans and we can assist you with the estimate, do a materials take off, evaluate the plan for solar and energy efficiency, evaluate its complexity for a novice builder, or just do a general critique from a design perspective. We can do a feasibility study on the project as well, to assist you in determining whether the money, time and energy you have allocated to the project are sufficient. We can also assist you in designing your own house, and our draftspeople can draw up your plans. This is somewhat more difficult to do by phone or mail and it is advised that you visit in our Berkeley office if at all possible.

Bookstore

We have three in-house publications of interest to owner builders. The *Plan Book* contains floor plans, perspectives and descriptions of 25 energy efficient (mostly solar) houses appropriate for the owner builder. The *Owner as Contractor* kit contains a workbook and cassette tape for those intending to manage the construction of their homes, while the *Estimating* kit shows owner builders how to estimate the cost of their project from the plans, again with workbook and tape.

Training for New Centers

The Owner Builder Center is interested in assisting other individuals and groups in opening centers similar to ours or teaching housebuilding or remodeling classes in their local areas. At present we have trained twenty groups around the country (see list below). Our training programs last three to five days and take place in our Berkeley office. The program includes training in advertising, graphics, renting classrooms, media and public relations, enrollment procedures and hiring and training teachers. Also included is a full set of 3,600 slides on housebuilding, and 2,800 slides on remodeling, with which these classes are taught. A franchise program will be available late in 1984.

Organizations Trained by The Owner Builder Center

Building Resources
Community Housing Investment Fund
121 Tremont
Hartford, Connecticut 06105
(203) 233-5165

Chico Housing Improvement Program
539 Fume Street
Chico, California 95926
(916) 342-0012

Colorado Owner Builder Center
P O Box 12061
Boulder, Colorado 80302
(303) 449-6126

Denver Owner Builder Center
5835 West 6th Avenue, Unit 4D
Lakewood, Colorado 80214
(303) 232-8571

Durango Owner Builder Center
P O Box 3447
Durango, Colorado 81301
(303) 247-2417

Fine Homes Unlimited
512 Mystic Way
Laguna Beach, California 92651
(714) 494-6411

Hanford Adult School
120 East Grangeville Road
Hanford, California 93231
(209) 582-4401

Matsu Community College
University of Alaska
P O Box 899
Palmer, Alaska 99645
(907) 745-4255

Michigan Owner Builder Center
1505 East Eleven Mile Road
Royal Oak, Michigan 48067
(313) 545-7033

Minnesota Owner Builder Center
2608 Bloomington South
Minneapolis, Minnesota 55407
(612) 721-8887

Northwest Owner Builder Center
1139 34th Avenue
Seattle, Washington 98122
(206) 324-9559

Owner Builder Center of Fairfield and Westchester
335 Post Road West
Westport, Connecticut 06880
(203) 226-7095

Owner Builder Center at Miami-Dade Community College
Environmental Demonstration Center
11011 South West 104th Street
Miami, Florida 33176
(305) 596-1017

Owner Builder Center of New York
160 West 34th Street
New York, New York 10001
(212) 736-4909

Owner Builder Center of Sacramento
P O Box 739
Fair Oaks, California 95629
(916) 961-2453

Owner Builder Center of Southern California
361 East Magnolia
Burbank, California 91502
(213) 841-1942

Pacific Owner Builder Center
4562 Aukai Avenue
Honolulu, Hawaii 96816
(808) 523-8056

Tasmania Owner Builder Center
4 Dallas
Taroona, Tasmania
AUSTRALIA

Yestermorrow
P O Box 344
Warren, Vermont 05674
(802) 495-3437

Mail to: **THE OWNER BUILDER CENTER**
1516 Fifth Street
Berkeley, California 94710
Call: (415) 526-9222

Name _____

Address _____

_____ Zip _____

Phone (____)_____

Store where book was purchased:

_____

City and State: _____

☐ Please send a copy of the *Owner Builder* quarterly including information about the summer residence program

☐ Please send me information about your consulting service

☐ Please contact me about starting classes or a center

☐ Please send a free copy of the *Owner Builder* quarterly to my friend:

Name _____

Address _____

_____ Zip _____

To order additional copies of this book, send $17.95 per copy plus $1.00 for handling (and 50¢ for each additional copy) to **The Owner Builder Center,** address above (California residents add 6% sales tax; Bay Area residents add 6½%). Inquire about quantity discounts.